INTRODUCTION TO OPERATING SYSTEMS

Behind the desktop

INTRODUCTION TO OPERATING SYSTEMS

Behind the desktop

John English

First published 2005 by
PALGRAVE MACMILLAN
Houndmills, Basingstoke, Hampshire RG21 6XS and
175 Fifth Avenue, New York, N. Y. 10010
Companies and representatives throughout the world

PALGRAVE MACMILLAN is the global academic imprint of the Palgrave Macmillan division of St. Martin's Press LLC and of Palgrave Macmillan Ltd. Macmillan® is a registered trademark in the United States, United Kingdom and other countries. Palgrave is a registered trademark in the European Union and other countries.

ISBN 0–333–99012–9

This book is printed on paper suitable for recycling and made from fully managed and sustained forest sources.

A catalogue record for this book is available from the British Library.

10   9   8   7   6   5   4   3   2   1
14   13   12   11   10   09   08   07   06   05

Printed and bound in China

CONTENTS

To my father, John Robson English, who provided me with so many opportunities

PREFACE

Anyone who uses a computer uses an operating system every day, and yet very few people appreciate what an operating system is or what it does. For most people, the most visible part of an operating system is the graphical user interface, which allows programs to be executed and files to be manipulated. Programmers use operating system facilities to create windows, open and close files, establish network connections and so on, but most programmers use high-level languages like Java which provide the ability to do all this without having to be aware of the operating system's role in providing these facilities. Most of what an operating system does is completely invisible.

However, operating systems are undoubtedly the largest and most complex software systems ever devised. They comprise millions of lines of code and they are used daily on millions of machines. Bugs in those millions of lines of code will affect millions of people; either machines will crash of their own accord or security loopholes will allow someone else to crash them if they want to. Because of the issues involved in designing and implementing reliable software on this scale, a knowledge of operating system design should be an essential part of any serious software engineer's education.

WHO SHOULD READ THIS BOOK?

This book is aimed primarily at undergraduate-level operating systems courses. It assumes that the reader has some knowledge of programming, preferably in an object-oriented language such as Java or C++, and a basic appreciation of how programs are executed on a real computer (that is, the role of processors, memory and I/O devices). It also assumes that the reader has used an operating system like Microsoft Windows or Unix and has a machine available that runs at least one (preferably both) of these operating systems. I use Windows and Unix (particularly Linux) as a source of examples and exercises throughout this book because of their wide availability. Microsoft Windows is more or less universally available on all IBM-compatible PCs, and versions of Linux for most hardware platforms can be freely downloaded from the Internet. It is possible to install Windows and Linux side-by-side on a single PC, but some distributions of Linux (e.g. Knoppix) will run from CD-ROM without the need to install anything on disk.

The book contains occasional examples of program code, although I have tried to avoid being too system-specific. I have tried to use Java (or Java-like pseudocode) whenever possible for such examples, as I assume that many readers will be familiar with Java. Java is also very similar in appearance to C and C++, which are the languages most commonly used for writing operating systems and related programs. However, it is occasionally necessary to resort to using other languages. The code examples I use are described in the text, so it should be possible to understand them without a knowledge of any specific language.

WHY THIS BOOK IS DIFFERENT

There are already many excellent books on operating systems. However, the approach that they generally take is a 'bottom-up' approach, beginning with hardware issues, the implementation of processes and memory management, and so on. Changes to computing curricula mean that many students have never done any assembly-level programming and have little knowledge of the low-level issues of computer system design. Many of these books can therefore prove difficult for undergraduates, as they deal with the underlying nuts and bolts before dealing with any of the aspects of operating systems that the readers are most familiar with, namely a system with a graphical user interface programmed in a high-level language such as Java.

This book is written as an antidote to this approach. I have adopted a top-down approach to operating system design which begins with the most visible and familiar aspects of a typical modern operating system and which only examines the internal 'nuts and bolts' implementation issues once the behavioural aspects of the systems being discussed have been dealt with. I have concentrated primarily on the operating systems and hardware that readers are most likely to be familiar with, namely Windows and Unix running on Pentium-based machines, and I use these as a source of detailed examples to deepen the broad coverage of the field that this book provides. I have also avoided detailed mathematical analyses and discussions of issues which are now only of historical interest. The result is a medium-sized book which nevertheless covers a wide range of operating system design and implementation issues with specific detailed examples taken from real systems in common use today.

HOW THE BOOK IS ORGANISED

The book revolves around the 'desktop', which most people see as the most visible part of any modern operating system, and it is divided into three parts entitled 'Behind the desktop', 'Beneath the desktop' and 'Beyond the desktop'.

BEHIND THE DESKTOP

The first part of the book concentrates on the features of an operating system that are visible to the user and to the programmer. It describes shells, both graphical and text-based, and the use of system calls to access operating system facilities. It also covers filesystems, since the filesystem is one of the most visible features of any operating system. It introduces the concept of a virtual machine and uses emulated virtual machines as an analogy for processes, where each process appears to have its own separate processor, memory and I/O devices, with graphical windows as virtual screens. The virtual processor accessible to a process is described as a version of the physical processor with some instructions removed (privileged instructions) and others added (system calls). The concept of multithreading is also introduced, with examples from high-level languages such as Java which support multithreading, and also synchronization issues. If a process is a virtual computer, multiple threads correspond to multiple virtual processors within this virtual computer. Synchronization issues are also discussed at this point, and the concepts of mutual exclusion, critical sections, deadlock, livelock and starvation are examined.

BENEATH THE DESKTOP

The second part of the book looks at how the features from the first part are actually implemented. This begins by looking at memory management, which is central to the way that processes are kept separate from each other. It deals almost entirely with virtual memory systems; other, older methods of memory management that are rarely if ever used in modern systems are only mentioned briefly. A chapter on hardware issues describes the salient features of a typical modern processor and its interaction with the rest of the system. This includes features such as privileged instructions, system calls and exception handling, the memory management unit and cache, interrupt controllers, and power management systems. I concentrate on the Intel Pentium processor, as the majority of people use IBM-compatible PCs based around Pentium-family processors. The next two chapters look at the kernel itself and device drivers. These chapters take an essentially object-oriented view of the matters being discussed, as this is the programming paradigm that most readers can be expected to be familiar with. The description of the kernel includes a look at how the kernel uses hardware facilities and virtual memory to construct the environment of a process, as well as issues such as scheduling. The chapter on device drivers discusses issues such as interrupt handling and the way that the kernel interacts with device drivers.

BEYOND THE DESKTOP

The final part of the book deals with multiprocessor systems and distributed systems. This is motivated by the fact that most modern computers are not the isolated uniprocessor systems that were common in the recent past. It discusses multiprocessor machines, networking and distributed systems, as well as the design problems (such as cache coherence, distributed mutual exclusion and distributed deadlock detection) that occur in such systems. It provides a review of the networking technologies in common use today, primarily Ethernet and the TCP/IP protocol suite, and describes some of the higher-level technologies which build on these to provide the means of constructing distributed systems (e.g. RPC and Java RMI, CORBA, Jini, COM and DCOM) as well as distributed filesystems (NFS and CIFS). It also deals with some commonly available distributed systems (Beowulf and Windows Cluster Server) and examples of distributed operating systems (Amoeba and Chorus). It concludes with a discussion of security issues, many of which are particularly important on networked systems. This includes coverage of such aspects as guarding against hardware failures, user authentication issues, network security, cryptography, and viruses and other malicious programs.

KEY FEATURES

- Instead of providing end-of-chapter exercises, I have chosen to sprinkle **exercises throughout the chapters**. Each chapter contains about a dozen exercises of various kinds. By placing them in the chapter at the points where the relevant topics are being discussed, I hope they will stimulate the reader into thinking more deeply about the issues under discussion and into reading some of the references that I have provided in search of answers. If this book is being used as a class text, the exercises can be used to encourage wider research and tutorial discussions of the issues that they raise. They are categorised as *questions*, which are intended to promote review of or reflection on the material presented; *exercises*, which are of a more practical nature; and *projects*, which are typically lengthier practical exercises.

- Each chapter concludes with a **list of additional resources**, a **glossary** and a **list of references**. I have tried to avoid embedding references in the main body of the chapters, and instead I have used the 'additional resources' section to relate the topics discussed in the chapter to the references at the end and to give guidance for further reading. I also point to online resources from time to time, including useful software. To make it easier to get copies of papers that I have referenced, I have also provided links to online copies where I have been able to find these. For the sake of convenience there is also a **glossary and bibliography** at the end of the book.

- There is also a **web site** for this book at `http://www.palgrave.com/science/computing/` which provides solutions to exercises, a set of lecturer's slides and various other resources.

ACKNOWLEDGEMENTS

I would like to thank David Hatter and the staff at Palgrave for their help in making this book possible (particularly David for making sure I kept my nose to the grindstone); the various reviewers who looked at this book, especially Bob Eager; my colleagues at the University of Brighton and also those students who have had to put up with my courses on operating systems over the years; and especially Jan and Vivian for being so understanding when I spent more time with my computer than with them.

PART 1

BEHIND THE DESKTOP

OVERVIEW: BEHIND THE DESKTOP

Everyone who uses a computer uses an operating system. Most modern operating systems provide a graphical user interface that uses a 'desktop' metaphor as a way of interacting with the system, and the chapters in this section look at the visible features that operating systems normally provide. These features are all able to be implemented by normal programs with no special privileges, so this section also looks at the programmer's view of the features that an operating system provides as well as the end user's view.

Chapter 1 inevitably begins by posing the question 'What is an operating system?'. This chapter provides an overview of the issues that will be developed further in the rest of the book. Chapter 2 describes an operating system from the point of view of a user or programmer, discussing how programs are able to use operating system facilities and how the user is given the ability to create processes to execute programs and to combine these in various ways. This includes a look at user interfaces and how they are implemented.

The filesystem is one of the most visible parts of any operating system, so Chapter 3 discusses how filesystems are organised and implemented so that information can be catalogued and accessed in a transparent user-friendly way. Another major visible feature is that most systems allow multiple programs to be executed as concurrent processes, as well as allowing individual programs to be composed of several concurrent threads of execution. Chapter 4 therefore examines the issues involved when processes and threads interact with each other, the problems that arise and how they can be resolved.

BEHIND THE DESKTOP

Let's begin by looking at what an operating system does. For most people, what they see is a graphical desktop which lets them run programs, organise information in files, categorise files into directories or folders, copy files from one place to another, and so on. Many people are misled into thinking that the graphical desktop is the operating system itself, whereas in fact it's just the tip of a largely invisible iceberg.

1.1 ☐ WHAT IS AN OPERATING SYSTEM?

I'm sitting here writing this book on a computer which is running a popular operating system from Microsoft called Windows 2000, which like most modern systems has a **graphical user interface** (GUI) which I use to control it. The **desktop** it provides on the screen is fairly distinctive in appearance, so much so that many people identify the operating system with the desktop. There are a number of **icons** representing programs and documents on the left of the screen, and several **windows** corresponding to programs that I'm running. At the bottom of the screen there is a **taskbar** containing buttons which can be used to control the programs that are running. This is shown in Figure 1.1.

Of the windows displayed on the screen, the foremost one is used by the word processing package I'm using to write this chapter. It appears in front of the other windows on the screen, some of which are partly covered up by it. In one of these windows, an MP3 player is entertaining me with music as I write; I can see some of it, but not all, as the MP3 player's window is partially covered by my word processor's window. Several other programs are also active at the same time. Each of these programs is completely independent of all the others, and each one behaves as if it

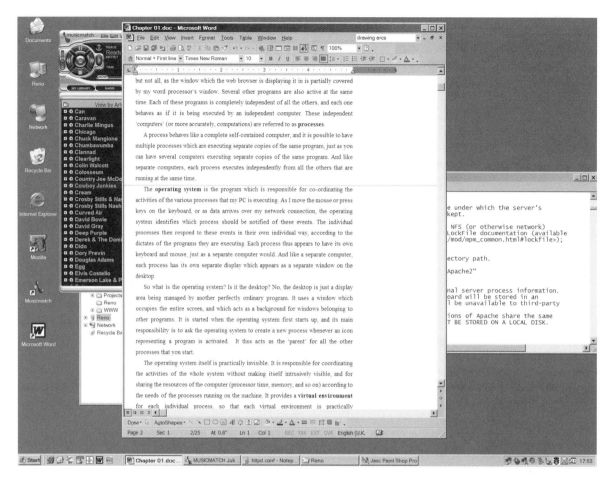

Figure 1.1 A Windows 2000 desktop.

is being executed by an independent computer. These independent 'computers' (or more accurately, computations) are referred to as **processes**.

A process behaves like a complete self-contained computer, and it is possible to have multiple processes which are executing separate copies of the same program, just as you can have several computers executing separate copies of the same program. And like separate computers, each process executes independently of all the others that are running at the same time.

Question 1.1   What is the relationship between a process, a program and a processor?

The **operating system** is the program which is responsible for coordinating the activities of the various processes that my PC is executing. As I move the mouse or press keys on the keyboard, or as data arrives over my network connection, the operating system identifies the process to be notified of these events. The individual processes then respond to these events in their own individual ways, according to the dictates of the programs they are executing. I use the mouse and keyboard to interact with the process associated with the foremost window (the **active window**), or to bring another window to the front so that I can interact with it. The active window handles all the mouse events that occur while the mouse is within its boundaries, and all keyboard events except a few special key combinations are also handled by the active window. From the point of view of each process it appears that the process has its own keyboard and mouse, just as a separate computer would. And like a separate computer, each process has its own separate display which appears as a separate window on the desktop.

So what is the operating system? Is it the desktop? No, the desktop is just a display area being managed by another perfectly ordinary program. It uses a window which occupies the entire screen, and which acts as a background for windows belonging to other programs. It is started when the operating system first starts up, and its main responsibility is to ask the operating system to create a new process whenever an icon representing a program is activated. It thus acts as the 'parent' for all the other processes that I start.

The operating system itself is practically invisible. It is responsible for coordinating the activities of the whole system without making itself intrusively visible, and for sharing the resources of the computer (processor time, memory, and so on) according to the needs of the processes running on the machine. It provides a **virtual environment** for each individual process, so that each virtual environment is practically indistinguishable from a real computer. It also provides facilities such as the ability to create new processes.

1.2 ☐ EMULATION

Once upon a time I used to own an Apple II, a well-known machine of the 1980s which supported a large number of popular games, but it broke down several years ago. Several of these games are no longer available except for the Apple II, and no-one makes these machines any more. So what should I do? Throw away all those games and resign myself to never playing them again?

Of course not! One of the programs I'm running in Figure 1.2 is an **emulator** for an Apple II which runs on Windows 2000. Anything you can do in hardware can be mimicked exactly in software, and this is what my emulator does. My emulator is a piece of software which implements a **virtual machine** which behaves in exactly the same way as a real Apple II would have done.

Question 1.2   What does the term 'virtual' mean in phrases like 'virtual machine'?

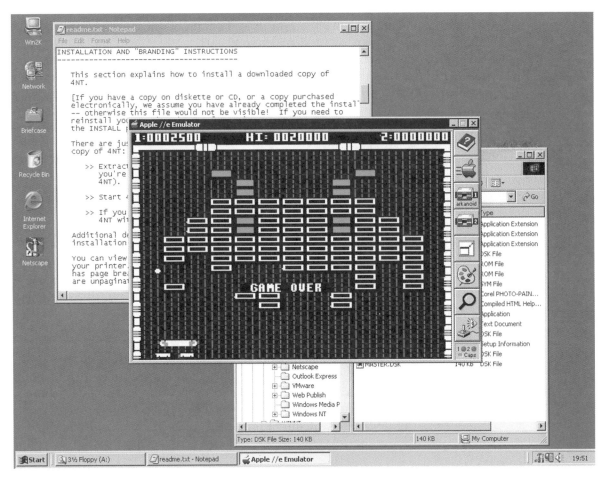

Figure 1.2 An Apple II emulator running on Windows 2000.

The original Apple II had a maximum of 64 KB (KB = kilobyte) of memory. My emulator uses an array of 64 KB to **emulate** (that is, to mimic) the Apple II's physical memory. The original Apple II was based on a popular processor of the time (the Mostek 6502). My emulator has no problems with this. What the 6502 processor did was to repeatedly fetch instructions from memory and execute them, at a rate of a few hundred thousand instructions per second. The processor also used a handful of internal **registers** to provide the few bytes of working storage it needed to keep track as it did this. What my emulator does is to read instruction codes from the array which mimics the Apple II's memory, decode them to identify what the 6502 processor would have done with them, and then perform the corresponding action, as shown in Figure 1.3. It uses a few extra bytes of memory to emulate the processor registers. Because modern hardware is so much faster than older hardware, the emulator can actually do this a lot faster than the original Apple II hardware would have done, and it is necessary to introduce artificial delays to mimic the original timing to stop games running at impossibly fast

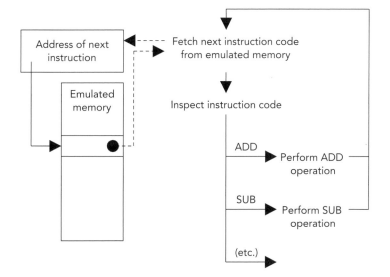

Figure 1.3 Emulator operation.

speeds! I can also run other applications as well as Apple II emulators; the screenshot shows that I'm also running a couple of other programs at the same time, each of which has its own window which is partially covered by the window for the emulator.

Since I have so much memory and processor power available, it's no effort to emulate the memory of dozens of Apple II systems within the confines of a single machine. All the emulator has to do is to have (say) a dozen blocks of memory each comprising 64 KB of main memory plus a few bytes for the processor registers, and to fetch and execute a single instruction from each block of memory in turn. That is, my emulator is fetching and executing an instruction from each of a dozen emulated Apple IIs in turn, then fetching and executing the next instruction for each, and so on. This is illustrated in Figure 1.4. There is enough processor power available that the emulator can process an instruction for each of the emulated machines in the time it would have taken for a real Apple II to execute a single instruction. This effectively gives me a dozen Apple IIs executing at full speed, apparently simultaneously, within a single physical machine. (Whether I can cope with playing a dozen simultaneous action games is another matter, of course!)

Emulating a dozen Apple IIs simultaneously raises a lot of other issues. Each Apple II had its own display screen measuring 40 characters wide by 25 lines deep. Each Apple II had its own keyboard as well, and possibly other things too (separate disks, separate modems, separate mouse).

What modern operating systems do is to represent each such screen in a separate window. A 40×25 screen fits into a fairly small window. The windows can be arranged so that they overlap one another. I only have one mouse and keyboard, so I can only interact with one virtual machine at a time; the convention used to deal with this is to have only one active window at any given moment. Most desktop displays give the active window a recognisably different title bar; for example, the

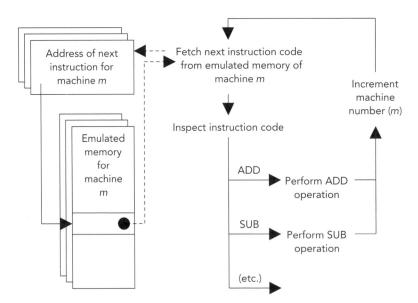

Figure 1.4 Emulating multiple machines.

classic Windows colour scheme gives the active window a blue title bar while all the others have grey title bars. The active window is the one that gets notified when a key is pressed or when the mouse is used inside its boundaries. The mouse and keyboard can also be used to select a different window to be activated.

However, this is not the full story. There is no reason why a Pentium processor can't equally well mimic another Pentium processor rather than a Mostek 6502.

Figure 1.5 shows the real truth: the version of Windows that my Apple II emulator is running on is also running on an emulator. I'm actually running another operating system (Linux) on my Pentium hardware, and one of the processes that Linux is controlling is an emulated Pentium machine running Windows 2000, and this emulated Pentium machine is running a process which is emulating an Apple II. The emulator is inside a window on the Linux desktop, and there is also another Linux application running in a separate window at the bottom right of the Linux desktop which is partially covered by the emulator window. Of course, you'll just have to take my word for it that I am really running Linux on my Pentium hardware, and that it's not actually inside yet another layer of software emulation!

Question 1.3   What are the similarities and differences between an emulator and an operating system?

Each process, including the ones executing within the Windows 2000 emulator, provides the illusion of a complete Pentium-based computer to the program that it

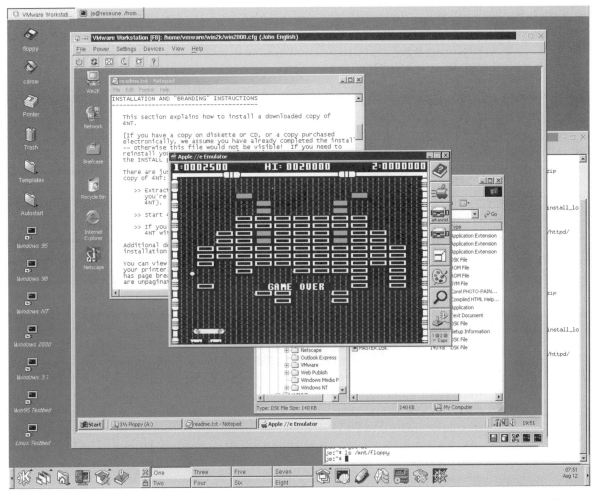

Figure 1.5 An Apple II emulator running on Windows 2000, which is running in an emulator on Linux.

is executing. A Pentium processor uses 32-bit addresses to access memory, so it has an **address space** (the range of memory addresses it can reference) of 2^{32} bytes, or 4 GB. One of the processes in the Windows 2000 emulator is running a copy of a standard Windows text editor called Notepad. Within its address space there is a copy of the Notepad program, a copy of the operating system, the data that Notepad is processing, and the data which is used by the copy of the operating system. It behaves as if it is running on a separate Pentium-based computer of its very own. The processor for this computer is a subset of the real thing; certain instructions do not behave as they would on the real thing, and there are extra instructions to access extra capabilities provided by the operating system. For example, the Pentium has a 'halt' instruction which would halt the processor and prevent it from executing any more instructions. If my process tried to execute this instruction, the operating system would be notified and it would then display an error message and terminate the process. On the other hand, the operating system provides a mechanism by which a program can suspend the process which is executing it for a specified period of time, which is accessed by a particular **system call** instruction. There is no standard 'sleep for 100 milliseconds' instruction on a Pentium processor, but the system call instruction which asks the operating system to do this will appear to be just another perfectly normal instruction which happens to take 100 milliseconds to execute. Also, during the time that the process is sleeping, the operating system is of course free to deal with the demands of other processes in the system. System call instructions effectively allow the operating system to extend the normal instruction set that the hardware provides.

Question 1.4	What is the distinction between the terms 'memory' and 'address space'?

Emulation is a widely used technique. Emulators are used to test designs for new processor hardware before the designs are committed to silicon (which is where the design process starts to get expensive, especially if there are bugs in the design which you've managed to miss). The Java programming language runs on the Java Virtual Machine (JVM), a software emulation of some imaginary hardware that was designed specifically with Java in mind. The JVM is implemented inside most web browsers so that Java applets can be executed by the browser. Although the JVM is normally implemented using an emulator, Sun Microsystems (the developers of Java and the JVM) have also produced hardware implementations of the JVM (picoJava, microJava and UltraJava; the names are of course case-sensitive!) for use in consumer devices such as telephones and personal organisers. The idea behind the JVM is not new. Some Pascal implementations were based on a virtual machine which executed an instruction set known as PCODE, which was also implemented in hardware at one point. BCPL had OCODE, Algol 68 had ZCODE, and so on. The idea dates back to the notion of UNCOL (the Universal Compiler-Oriented Language) in the early 1960s, which would be the emulated machine that all compilers would generate code for. UNCOL never made it off the drawing board (if that far), but its successors are alive and well.

1.3 ❑ WHAT AN OPERATING SYSTEM DOES

An operating system like Windows does something similar to my Apple II emulator. It provides me with as many virtual machines as I want on a single physical machine. However, it is implemented quite differently. An emulator is constructed entirely out of software, and this will make it run perhaps a hundred times slower than real hardware would run. For old hardware, like an Apple II, this is not a problem; a modern PC is so much faster than the original Apple II hardware that it more than makes up for the performance cost of emulation. However, if you're trying to use Windows to run software designed for Windows, that sort of performance penalty is unacceptable; most people would choose to run one program at a time at full speed on real hardware rather than two or three simultaneously on a software emulation at a hundredth of the speed.

Although emulation is not acceptable as an implementation technique for an operating system, it's a useful mental model. What we refer to as a **process** when we are talking about operating systems can be pictured as an emulation of a complete computer system, with its own processor, memory and peripheral devices.

The primary difference between an emulator and an operating system is that the processes that an operating system controls run on the same hardware as the operating system itself does. While a process is executing, the operating system is not. An emulator is in control at all times; it can do extra work in between emulating the execution of individual instructions. While a process is executing under the control of an operating system, it's using the same processor that the operating system would need to use to do anything. This means that the process runs at full speed, but the operating system is no longer completely in control in the way that an emulator would be. The operating system hands over complete control of the processor whenever it lets a process run. To make this work, some specialised hardware support is needed that can **interrupt** a running process to let the operating system regain control from time to time. The mechanisms that make this possible are described in Part 2 of this book.

The core of the operating system (usually referred to as the **kernel**) has an intimate relationship with the underlying hardware. The kernel is where all the clever tricks are performed that manage the 'emulations' that the rest of the system depends on. To make this work, the hardware provides a number of special features which are expressly designed to allow the kernel to perform these clever tricks. Experience has taught hardware designers what features operating systems need, so all modern processors incorporate these features as a matter of course.

Other parts of the system may be responsible for managing particular hardware resources. These are known as **device drivers**. For example, a **disk driver** will need to deal with the disk controller hardware to transfer information backwards and forwards between disks and memory. However, its relationship with the hardware is much more specific than that of the kernel, and it does not need to achieve the same privileged level of intimacy with any hardware except for the devices that it manages. The operating system kernel is responsible for ensuring that the disk driver, along with everything else in the system, is given access to the resources it needs to do its job. These may include specialist resources that are not generally accessible to other parts of the system. The operating system can therefore be thought of as a **resource manager** which allocates resources such as memory, processing time and access to hardware devices to the processes that it is supervising.

Exercise 1.1   What resources does your computer provide?

By contrast, the desktop is the visible manifestation of a program generally referred to as a **shell**, a name which continues the 'nutty' terminology already introduced. The shell is a 'wrapper' around the kernel which provides a convenient user interface to some of the basic system functionality: loading and running programs, manipulating files, and so on. It doesn't need any special access to the hardware or the kernel to do these things; the operations it uses are all available as system calls that any program can use.

In general, any part of the system which requires special 'supervisor' privileges can be regarded as being part of the operating system; programs which only require normal 'user' privileges are not. From this point of view, the shell is *not* part of the operating system itself. A shell is always supplied with any operating system to provide some sort of user interface, but there are usually alternative shells which can be used equally well instead. For example, the 'Program Manager' desktop which was the standard shell supplied with older versions of Windows can still be used as an alternative to the standard shell. (In my opinion, you shouldn't try this unless you are feeling nostalgic or masochistic.)

Question 1.5   Why do books on operating systems deal with shells if they are not really part of the operating system?

1.3.1 PROCESSOR MANAGEMENT

The primary resource that the kernel needs to manage is, of course, the processor itself. Modern processors are extremely fast, and most programs are unlikely to need to make use of more than a fraction of the power available. It is also convenient for users to be able to run several programs at the same time and transfer information between them, rather than having to end one program before another one can be started. For example, you may want to store a spreadsheet on a removable disk, but the disk needs to be erased before you can do this. Just leave the spreadsheet for a moment, run another program to erase the disk, then go back to the spreadsheet and carry on saving it as if nothing had happened. Having to close the spreadsheet so that the disk could be erased would be much less convenient.

It therefore makes sense to design the operating system in such a way that it can share out the available processor time between the various processes that need it. The kernel needs to know what processes are executing and share out the time between them. Ideally it should do this with a minimum of overhead; the kernel should not use a significant proportion of the processor time. Because of the sheer speed of the processor (which normally performs tens or hundreds of millions of operations every second) it can allocate a program a **timeslice** of, say, 20 milliseconds, which will be enough for the process to carry out several tens of thousands of instructions. A timeslice of 20 ms means that there are 50 timeslices every second, so up to 50 processes can be given a timeslice every second (or five processes can be

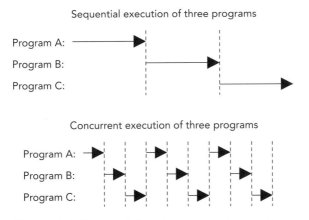

Figure 1.6 Sequential and concurrent execution.

given 10 timeslices each every second). To the human eye, this is usually enough to make all the processes appear to execute simultaneously, with no perceptible delay. Figure 1.6 illustrates the difference between the sequential execution of three programs and the concurrent (timesliced) execution of the same three programs. Smaller timeslices would increase the illusion of simultaneity, but the percentage of the available processor time used by the operating system to switch between processes would be a larger proportion of the whole. Similarly, increasing the length of the timeslices would make process execution appear jerky, although the operating system would use a smaller percentage of the total processor time. The choice of timeslice length depends on how responsive the system needs to be, and if this only needs to be enough to fool a human operator, a value of 20 ms is normally adequate.

1.3.2   MEMORY MANAGEMENT

Each process has access to its own personal memory space which appears to be separate from the memory space of any other process. In fact, all processes share a common memory space provided by the hardware of the underlying machine, so one of the things that the operating system has to do is to divide the available memory among the various processes (Figure 1.7). Each process has the illusion that it has a range of available memory addresses that it can access from address 0 up to some maximum address. In fact, what a process sees as address 0 might be located at some completely different address in the physical memory of the machine. Address translation is performed by some additional specialised hardware, and the operating system is responsible for managing how this hardware translates the addresses used by processes into the corresponding physical addresses before they are used to access physical memory.

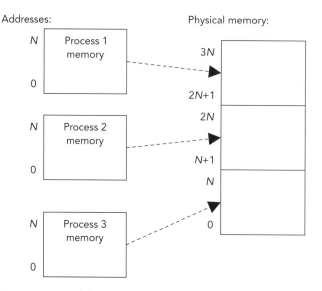

Figure 1.7 Address translation.

1.3.3 NAME MANAGEMENT

One of the most useful things that an operating system does is to allow names to be given to files stored on disk, to devices such as modems, and to computers elsewhere on a network (and to files stored on those computers). Because the operating system keeps track of the names and their corresponding meanings, you can stop worrying about where information is stored and just use the appropriate name to refer to it when you need it. This also gives the operating system the freedom to arrange where information is stored so that it can be accessed quickly and efficiently. It also means that you can treat information uniformly; you don't have to write a program differently depending on whether the data it is dealing with is coming from a keyboard, a modem, a file on disk, or a file on a different machine somewhere else in the world. The program stays the same; only the name of the data source has to change. It can access the data in exactly the same way, no matter where the data is really coming from.

Exercise 1.2   List the types of object that your operating system allows you to refer to by name.

1.4 ☐ EVENT-DRIVEN SYSTEMS

Programs for a modern operating system with a graphical user interface (GUI) are necessarily **event-driven** in nature. Users interact with programs in an unpredictable way, and programs need to be written to wait for events such as keypresses and mouse events, and then respond in an appropriate way, as shown in Figure 1.8. They do this by calling an operating system function to fetch the next event. Of course, if there are no events pending at the time, the operating system can take advantage of this to suspend the current process and activate another process which *does* have some pending events to process.

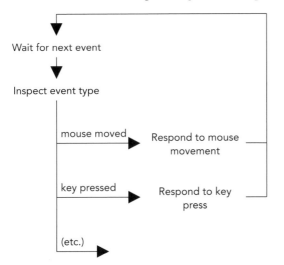

Wait for next event

Inspect event type

mouse moved → Respond to mouse movement

key pressed → Respond to key press

(etc.)

Figure 1.8 Structure of an event-driven program.

Pressing a key might insert a character into a document on a word processor, or it might activate a button or menu item. Similarly, clicking a mouse button might reposition the text cursor or display a pull-down menu. At the lowest level, these events are generated by the system hardware. The mouse generates events when it is moved or when its buttons are pressed or released, and the keyboard generates events when keys are pressed or released.

At the lowest level, it is the processor hardware that responds to hardware-generated events, known as **interrupts** because they interrupt the normal processor sequence of fetching and executing instructions. The state of the processor at the moment of interrupt is saved so that the interrupted process can be resumed later, and the operating system kernel then routes the interrupt to an **interrupt service routine** in the appropriate **device driver**, a software module which is responsible for handling interactions with the specific device. For example, moving the mouse generates an interrupt which the kernel routes to the mouse device driver, which translates the information from the mouse into a 'mouse move' event which incorporates the new position for the mouse cursor on the screen. The mouse cursor will also be moved to the corresponding position on the screen as part of this sequence of events.

The operating system kernel is now able to take the 'mouse move' event and route it to its ultimate destination. It can identify which window the mouse position is within, and from this it can identify the process which is responsible for responding to the event. The event is then added to a queue of pending events for that process.

At this point, the operating system must decide which of the available processes should be given the use of the processor next. This may or may not be the one that the event which was just handled was routed to; this depends on the **scheduling policy** that the operating system uses. One of the goals of modern operating system designs is to separate **mechanisms** from **policies**; the **mechanism** determines how the operating system is able to switch between processes, whereas the **policy** determines how the choice is made between the available processes it can switch to. Whichever process it chooses, it must now restore the state of the processor to the state it was in at the time the chosen process was interrupted. So the kernel gives the use of the processor back to the chosen process.

The process that was given the 'mouse move' event may want to deal with it in a specific way, or it might want to deal with it in the standard way. The standard way involves changing the shape of the mouse cursor to the cursor shape associated with the window it is within (for example, an arrow, an hourglass, a cross or a little animated dinosaur).

Translate this into what you see when you use your computer. You move the mouse around; the mouse cursor moves as well, and as it enters different regions of an application's main window, it changes shape. On the word processor I'm using, it is an I-shaped bar when it's within the main text input area of the window, an arrow when it's over the toolbar buttons or menu items at the top of the window, and a double-ended 'resize' arrow when it's over any of the main window's borders. When the application does something that may take a long time to complete (for example, while it's saving the current document to disk), it normally signals that it's busy by changing the default mouse cursor shape for the window to an hourglass.

It is when programs **crash** (that is, fail) that this mechanism becomes most evident. Each program is responsible for handling 'paint' events which tell it that the windows that it owns need to be redisplayed; for example, if you click on a window that's partially hidden by another window, the process for the hidden window is sent an 'activate' event. The standard response to an 'activate' event is to change the colour of the window title bar to show that it is now the active window and to send a 'paint' event to the process which owns the window so that the program can redraw it in the correct colours on top of all the other windows on the screen. The exact response to a 'paint' event is program-specific, since only the program being executed is in a position to know what the content of the window should look like at any given moment. When a program crashes (perhaps because it has got stuck in a loop waiting for something that will never happen), it will not be able to process any events, so 'paint' events will not be dealt with and the screen area occupied by its window will not be redrawn. If you partially hide it with another window and then minimise that window, the window for the crashed program will continue to show a portion of the other window as the program will not be able to erase and redraw its own window. And you might not be able to minimise it or move it or interact with it in any way, because none of these things can happen unless the program processes the events that are pending in its event queue.

Question 1.6   On more recent versions of Windows you can still resize and drag windows even when the program has crashed. How is this possible?

1.5 ❑ PROTECTION MECHANISMS

In a system where multiple processes are being executed at the same time, the operating system is responsible for ensuring that they don't interfere with each other. An error in the program being executed by one process which causes it to crash should not affect any other process that is executing at the same time. A related concern is the issue of security in **multi-user** systems, where multiple users may be running programs on a single system; a process belonging to one user should not be able to snoop on a process belonging to another user, as this might be used to obtain confidential information such as credit card numbers or passwords.

The system hardware has to cater for this by providing mechanisms which ensure that processes are not able to interfere with one another in any way. In particular, a process should only be able to access memory that has been allocated to it; it should not be possible to access any memory that belongs to another process. The hardware must provide **memory management** mechanisms that will restrict processes so that they can only access memory which has been allocated to them. Each process will therefore have its own **address space** (the set of addresses which it can access), which is disjoint from the address space allocated to every other process in the system.

Processes certainly should not be able to disrupt the operating system either. The operating system kernel itself is, after all, just another set of programs being executed by the processor. It is not something external which controls the processor from outside; it relies on being allocated processor time and other resources to do its work, just like any other process. The operating system requires some special privileges, but these are relatively limited. It will occasionally need to be able to access the entire system memory rather than just a restricted region, but this is only for tasks like allocating memory for a new process when a new instance of a program is launched.

The processor hardware needs to provide at least two separate modes of execution to separate normal 'user' processes from the special 'supervisor' privileges that the operating system will sometimes require. There are certain

privileged instructions that the processor provides which should only ever be executed by the system kernel. These include the 'halt' instruction mentioned earlier, instructions for enabling and disabling interrupts and memory management functions, and of course switching between 'user' and 'supervisor' modes. Clearly, if user processes could execute any of these instructions they could disrupt the activity of the whole system. Disabling interrupts would prevent hardware devices from notifying the operating system of events that need to be dealt with; disabling memory management would allow the memory allocated to other processes to be interfered with; and entering supervisor mode would allow any process to execute any other privileged instruction and then be able to do whatever it liked.

Exercise 1.3   Can you think of any other operations that need to be privileged apart from the ones mentioned here?

1.6 ☐ VIRTUAL RESOURCES

To a large extent, the role of the operating system is to manage system resources. A good way to do this is to **virtualise** resources; this is, to provide a simplified, 'ideal-ised' representation of the resource which is easier to use than the real thing. For example, when I decide to open a file (sometimes referred to as a **document**) to edit with my word processor, a dialog appears which allows me to choose the file from a list of existing files. Some of these files will be on a local hard disk, some will be on CD, and some will be accessed across the network. What's really happening here?

One of the major components of an operating system is the file management system. This provides the ability to deal with files irrespective of their location or their physical representation. It provides a useful abstraction, the idea of a 'file' as an entity which is divorced from its physical implementation. The names of the files are arbitrary names that I gave them when I first created them. When I want to open a file, all I need to do is to identify it by name. The operating system's file management system uses that name to discover the location of the file (and hence the device driver responsible for the device that it is stored on) and creates a **file descriptor** which encapsulates information such as the current position within the file and the device driver which is responsible for reading and writing information to the file. This is illustrated in Figure 1.9.

When I want to read information from the file, I refer to the file using the descriptor I've been given. The system then invokes the 'read' method identified by the file descriptor to read some data starting at the current position. This in turn might invoke the device driver for the local disk to read one or more blocks from the disk and return some of the data from them, or it might invoke a network driver to send a 'read' request across the network and wait for a reply. I don't care how it

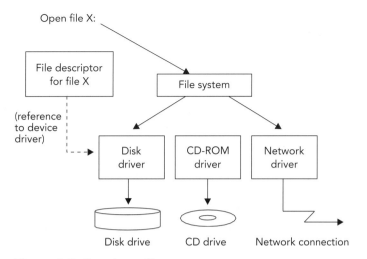

Figure 1.9 Opening a file.

happens as long as I end up receiving the data I've requested. A file is simply a high-level abstraction built on top of low-level concepts like disk blocks or network connections.

With this abstraction, someone writing a program which accesses a file no longer needs to worry about where it is physically located or how it is organised internally; the only thing needed to access it is its name. The name might refer to a file on a local disk, or it might be a communications link to another process, or it might be a device like a printer, or it might be a network link to a machine on the other side of the world. The way in which the operating system internally implements a filesystem operation such as 'read the next line from this file' will vary according to what kind of device the name actually represents.

Sharing a printer between several processes is another good illustration of the way in which an operating system can virtualise system resources. If two processes want to use the same printer at the same time, one is going to have to wait for the other to finish. In the case of a disk, it's perfectly feasible to let the processes access the disk alternately: the first one writes something to its allocated area on the disk, then the other writes something to a different area, then the first writes something else to the original area, and so on. This works because the disk is a **direct access** device, so that operations on different parts of the disk can be interleaved without any ill effect, whereas a printer is a **sequential** device. It isn't sensible to let one process print a page on a printer and then let the other process print a page, because then the output of the two processes will be interleaved and will have to be separated later, probably by hand. A disk is a **shareable** resource because of its direct accessibility, but the printer isn't because of its sequential nature. Making one process wait for access to the printer until the other one has finished using it is not a solution, as this will lose all the benefits of being able to run more than one process at a time.

Exercise 1.4   What unshareable resources does your system provide?

The solution is to provide a 'virtual printer' as shown in Figure 1.10. The operating system tricks each process into thinking it's writing to a printer when in fact the output is being stored in a file, a trick known as **spooling**. (The term 'spool' originated as an acronym, Simultaneous Peripheral Operation Off-Line, but hardly anyone remembers that now; it's become a word in its own right.) The operating system maintains a list of spooled **print jobs** waiting to be printed and prints them one by one, possibly some time after the programs that generated them have finished executing. A virtual printer behaves exactly like a physical printer except that it is always ready for use: you never have to wait for the paper to be changed and it can't be left offline by accident. A virtual printer is an emulation of an idealised printer.

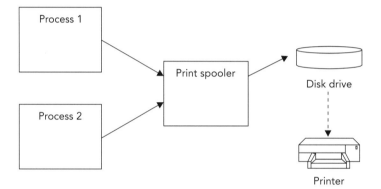

Figure 1.10 Virtualising a printer.

Virtualising resources is a powerful trick. An operating system will generally manage the physical resources of a machine by hiding them behind successive layers of virtual resources, turning ugly hardware into clean, simple and friendly abstractions.

1.7 ☐ THE EVOLUTION OF OPERATING SYSTEM DESIGNS

Originally, operating systems were designed as monolithic units. The entire system was just a collection of procedures that implemented the various operations that were required, and any procedure might call any other procedure. This approach leads to maintenance problems. Since any procedure can be called by any other, keeping track of where each procedure is called from is extremely difficult, as is keeping track of what expectations the caller has for the behaviour of the procedure being called. As the system evolves, the problem becomes worse. Operating systems are perhaps the worst case of software maintenance. As with other software systems, users and developers are continually requesting new features, and these demands are hard to resist if they are sensible and viable. And as with other software systems, they have bugs which must be fixed. They are usually subtle bugs, but thanks to the Internet they can be exploited by malicious individuals on millions of machines within hours. However, they also need to be able to run on machines whose underlying hardware is different. Different machines will have different disk controllers, different video controllers, different network adapters and so on. A single monolithic operating system will have difficulty dealing with this sort of variation.

Problems like this affect all software development projects. By the late 1960s, many of these problems had been recognised and new programming paradigms were being developed to cope with ever-increasing software complexity. As operating systems are among the largest software systems in existence, they were among the first to be subjected to the new paradigms. The 'structured programming' movement of the late 1960s and early 1970s is reflected in the design of many modern operating systems. A typical operating system can be visualised as being made up of a number of layers, with the innermost layer of software (the kernel) being the only one which has access to the full hardware resources of the underlying machine. Device drivers are implemented as separate 'plug-in' modules which provide a standard interface to particular pieces of hardware. Each layer's services are implemented in terms of a restricted set of hardware operations in combination with the services provided by the more privileged layers below. This is illustrated in outline in Figure 1.11, and is sometimes referred to as the 'onion skin' design approach.

More recent programming paradigms are also reflected in operating system designs. Some systems (notably Mach) are based around a 'microkernel' which adopts a **client–server** design approach. In a microkernel operating system, a small

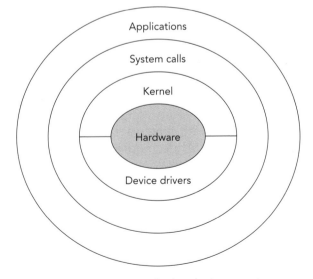

Figure 1.11 Structure of a layered operating system.

kernel provides basic scheduling, memory management and communications services. All other services are provided by **server** processes which have no special privileges. Any other process can act as a **client** by sending a message requesting a particular service from a server; for example, a message asking a **filesystem server** to open a particular file. The filesystem server sends back a reply indicating the outcome of the operation, including a file descriptor if the file was opened successfully. The filesystem server can be designed in such a way that it requires no special privileges. In particular, the disk subsystem on which the filesystem is implemented will be managed by another server process and the filesystem server will access the disk server by sending it messages in exactly the same way as any other process would, as shown in Figure 1.12. This obviously requires some further restrictions to prevent programs accessing low-level disk services whenever they feel like bypassing the filesystem to read someone else's confidential files.

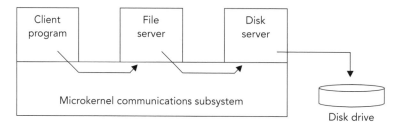

Figure 1.12 Accessing a disk in a microkernel operating system.

The microkernel viewpoint makes it easier to justify talking about shells in this book. In a microkernel system, the only true 'operating system' components are those in the kernel, and other subsystems such as the filesystem server are just application programs, with no more privileges than a word processing package (or a shell). A book on operating systems which avoided talking about filesystems would be considered to be incomplete, and avoiding any discussion of shells would arouse the same objections.

One of the latest trends in programming is the object-oriented paradigm, and several recent systems based on the object-oriented paradigm have been produced. Windows NT and its successors (Windows 2000 and Windows XP) adopt a largely object-oriented approach in their designs. An object-oriented design structures the operating system as a collection of interacting objects, each of which belongs to some specific class which defines some specific behaviour. New classes can be derived from existing classes which can provide additional behaviour or specialised implementations of existing behaviour. For example, all classes of object that are derived from a base 'file' class will provide a filesystem-compatible set of operations such as *open*, *read* and *close*. Each derived class will provide this same interface but will implement it differently. This means that the connection to a local disk appears the same as the connection to a remote disk on another machine, despite the underlying differences in implementation. In the case of filesystems, existing operating systems (which are not necessarily designed in an object-oriented manner) do this anyway, but object-oriented operating system designs generalise the idea to other areas than the filesystem and make it a more explicit part of the design.

1.8 ☐ WHAT MAKES A GOOD OPERATING SYSTEM?

From the point of view of a user, there are several obvious characteristics that any good operating system should have:

- **Efficiency.** The purpose of a computer is to perform tasks for you, the user. The more time and space the operating system uses, the less there is left over for you to use productively.

- **Reliability.** You want to be able to guarantee that the operating system will not fail unexpectedly. If the operating system crashes and you have to restart your machine, you might find that you have lost some of your recent work and have to redo it.

- **Ease of use.** You want to be able to use the operating system's facilities to do your work in a way that you find natural. Exactly what this means varies from person to person, so ideally you want to be able to configure your system to make it easy for you to do the things you consider important.

- **Security.** You do not want outsiders to read your confidential files or infect your system with viruses. You also do not want the system to lose or corrupt your valuable data.

There are also some characteristics that are less obvious but which nevertheless have an impact on the way the operating system can respond to changes:

- **Maintainability.** Now that computers are part of the consumer electronics market rather than the province of a specialist 'priesthood', hardware and software upgrades are common requirements. The operating system must have the ability to cope with new types of hardware device; it must also make it possible to install new software (including patches to fix errors in the operating system itself, or a completely new version of the operating system) or remove software that is no longer needed. This requires a **modular** design, where individual modules can be added and replaced as necessary.

- **Flexibility.** Many things to do with operating systems involve trade-off decisions, between for example the amount of time it takes to do something and the amount of disk or memory space involved. It should be possible to 'tune' a system to provide what you would consider optimal behaviour, for example by adjusting how time reductions are traded off against increases in memory requirements. Once again this involves separating **mechanisms** from **policies**. A mechanism is basically an algorithm, and a policy is a set of parameters which control how the mechanism behaves in practice. For example, the operating system might provide a mechanism for prioritising processes so that high-priority processes take precedence over low-priority processes. A corresponding policy decision would then be needed as to which processes are given a high priority.

There is, alas, no such thing as the perfect operating system. The ideal operating system would use no memory or disk space and take no time to do anything. It would be perfectly secure, never crash, and be infinitely upgradeable. In reality, systems do crash from time to time; they are insecure, so that they can be infected by viruses; and they sometimes have inconvenient features, such as needing to be restarted when a new hardware device is attached, when a new software package is installed or when a network address is changed. Recently I installed a new software package and I had to shut down the entire machine and restart it before I could use the package. This sort of behaviour does not endear operating systems to their users.

1.9 ❑ EXAMPLES OF OPERATING SYSTEMS

In this book I'm going to concentrate on a couple of example operating systems rather than trying to cover the entire spectrum. These systems account for the vast majority of the operating systems in use today. I'm not going to say very much about older systems that have fallen into disuse, except when then have a novel insight to offer, and neither am I going to say much about some of the 'cutting edge' systems that may or may not make it into the mainstream in the future. I'm going to try to concentrate on the systems that are likely to be most familiar and accessible to my readers, and these are Unix and Microsoft Windows.

1.9.1   UNIX

Unix is an operating system which was originally developed by Thompson and Ritchie for internal use at Bell Laboratories (part of AT&T) in the early 1970s. Its name is a pun on Multics, a large and extremely complex operating system that provided much of the inspiration for Unix. Some of the inspiration was negative; unlike Multics, Unix is a small, simple and extremely efficient system. It also introduced a number of significant innovations which have been widely adopted by other operating systems. It was originally implemented in 1969 on a DEC PDP-7 system, and was later rewritten in a high-level language (C, a descendant of BCPL, designed by Kernighan and Ritchie at Bell Labs) to enable it to be ported to a PDP-11 system.

AT&T was not allowed to compete in computing-related markets due to its dominant position in the US telecommunications market, so it could not release Unix as a commercial product. Instead, Unix was released outside Bell Laboratories for academic use in the early 1970s and was developed further at a number of academic institutions. The University of California at Berkeley was one of the major development sites as a result of Department of Defense funding for research into networking, and the Berkeley Standard Distribution (BSD) soon became the most common version of Unix in academic installations. As a result of its openness, with source code available to all and with no shroud of commercial secrecy, Unix became established as one of the most popular operating systems in the world.

Because the source code was available, and because it was mostly written in the high-level language C rather than in assembly language (as many operating systems were at that time), it was relatively easy to build versions for a wide variety of hardware platforms. As a result there are versions of Unix available for most machines. However, these versions are not identical to each other, although they are generally very similar, and it is more correct to regard Unix as a family of closely related operating systems than as a single system. Most hardware manufacturers provide their own version of Unix — Apple's A/UX and OS/X, IBM's AIX, SGI's IRIX, Sun's SunOS and Solaris, to name but a few. On the IBM PC, available Unix-based operating systems include Xenix, SCO Unix, Solaris, Linux, and FreeBSD. Of these, Linux and FreeBSD are both 'free software' products which are available via the Internet, as is their source code. The word 'free' in this context means 'liberated' rather than 'without cost' (compare 'free speech' with 'free beer'); in other words, they are open systems with no proprietary secrets involved. Interestingly enough, these free systems are among the most reliable and stable operating systems available. Bugs are fixed by a worldwide community of developers, and support for new hardware is developed and released very quickly, and then refined by others around the world. This sort of responsiveness is not possible where the operating system is a commercial product with only a (relatively) small team of in-house developers to do all the work. Also, where the operating system is a commercial product, customers will have already paid for the product before they discover any bugs in it, and there is perhaps less incentive to fix problems in a product which has already been paid for.

FreeBSD is, as the name suggests, derived from BSD Unix. Linux was developed as a collaborative effort which was initiated in 1991 by Linus Torvalds, a Finnish undergraduate. It has been contributed to by thousands of developers worldwide, but Torvalds has overseen and guided the whole project since its inception. Most successful software projects are the result of one or two people with a clear vision of what it is they want to accomplish. The original development of Unix definitely falls into this category, as does Linux.

The difficulty with open source software, where anyone can modify it at will, is that it tends to diversify into a number of mutually incompatible versions. POSIX is an attempt to curb the diversity of the different flavours of Unix and develop a set of open standards (IEEE 1003.1 and related specifications) which will ensure the future cohesion of different Unix implementations. As a result of US government agencies requiring POSIX as a procurement standard for government contracts, most Unix implementations are rapidly being made POSIX-compliant. Other operating systems such as Microsoft Windows have also been forced to provide POSIX-compliant environments for the same reason.

Because of the basic similarity of different versions of Unix, I will use the term 'Unix' as a generic term which applies equally well to any specific flavour, such as Linux or Solaris. When I want to discuss implementation details, I will use Linux as a specific example because it is widely used, is well documented, and its source code is freely available.

1.9.2   MICROSOFT WINDOWS

Windows is a commercial operating system from the Microsoft Corporation. It originated in 1983 as a graphical user interface for MS-DOS, but has gradually evolved into a complete operating system in its own right as a result of the Windows NT (New Technology) project which was headed by David Cutler, one of the designers of the VMS operating system used on the Digital Equipment Corporation's hugely successful VAX series of machines. Windows NT was first released in 1993. Conspiracy theorists have noted that moving the letters in VMS one place further on in the alphabet yields WNT, just as HAL (the name of the rogue computer in the Stanley Kubrick movie '2001: A Space Odyssey') yields IBM when each of the letters is moved one letter further on. However, these may just be happy coincidences.

Since the origin of Windows NT, there have been several different versions of Windows which are all based on a common internal architecture referred to as **Win32**; that is, Windows for 32-bit processors such as the Intel 386 and its successors. These versions include Windows 95, Windows 98, Windows NT, Windows ME, Windows 2000 and Windows XP. These have generally been aimed at IBM-compatible PCs based on the Intel 386 processor and its successors (the 486 and Pentium series). Microsoft has also implemented Windows NT on DEC Alpha systems and MIPS R4000 systems as well as IBM PCs. However, in recent years the declining market share of these systems has meant that support for them in more recent versions of Windows has been downgraded or dropped entirely.

Unlike Unix, Windows is a purely commercial product. There are at present no freely available implementations, nor does Microsoft make the source code available. The commercial secrecy behind it makes it less useful as a source of examples than Unix systems, but it is now in such widespread use that it cannot be ignored; an estimated 90% of computers worldwide run some version of Windows. This includes a number of handheld devices which use a version called Windows CE, which is designed explicitly with the consumer electronics market in mind.

Although they are very similar to each other, the different versions of Windows are not completely compatible. Windows 95 and 98 were developed based on the earlier MS-DOS operating system for the sake of compatibility, so they do not implement certain features of the Win32 architecture, notably most of the security-related features. On the other hand they can still run many old MS-DOS applications. Windows 2000 is the direct successor to Windows NT and for the first time fused the separate development strands of Windows 95/98 and Windows NT, However, some applications which will work on Windows NT systems will not work on Windows 2000 systems, apparently as the result of changes made to the operating system kernel, and this process has continued with the release of Windows XP. Rather than attempting to describe this diversity of implementations, I will use the term 'Windows' as a generic term for the various different versions of Microsoft Windows which implement the Win32 architecture (primarily NT, 2000 and XP), and I will only refer to specific versions where there is a need to do so.

Question 1.7   What are the advantages and disadvantages of developing an operating system as an open source product and as a commercial product?

1.10 ❑ SUMMARY

An operating system is basically responsible for managing the resources of a computer system in order to make it more convenient to use. It provides users with a simplified abstraction of the underlying hardware which hides much of the complexity inherent in raw hardware. In particular, it provides support for executing multiple processes concurrently, where each process behaves as if it is an emulation of a complete independent computer in its own right.

Operating systems are probably the most complex software systems ever produced. They are used by anyone who uses a computer, so they must be efficient, reliable, easy to use, secure, flexible and maintainable. The extent to which they achieve these goals is somewhat variable. However, the pursuit of these ideals has resulted in an evolutionary development in the design of operating systems, where each new generation of operating systems builds on the successes of previous generations and adopts the latest techniques in program design to improve on its predecessors. This book illustrates the result of this progression using examples drawn from two of the major families of operating systems which are currently in widespread use, namely Unix and Microsoft Windows.

Operating systems can also be viewed in a similar way to emulators, where each process that is managed by the operating system appears to operate in an environment which is comparable to that provide by an emulation of an idealised computer system. Although the analogy has its limitations, it is a useful mental model and so it is one which is developed further throughout this book.

1.11 ❑ ADDITIONAL RESOURCES

Information about Linux is fairly easy to come by, most of it online at The Linux Documentation Project (http://www.tldp.org/). Welsh *et al.* [12] gives a general introduction to installing, using and administering a Linux system; Greenfield [4] provides a general guide to using Unix, and Frampton [3] explains how to administer and configure Linux. The POSIX standard is also available online [5]. If you prefer printed matter, Cornes [1] covers installing, using, administering and programming Linux, as well as some information about system internals.

Linux software is available from a wide variety of sources, including Red Hat (http://www.redhat.com/) and Mandrake (http://www.mandrake.com/). A list of available Linux distributions can be found at http://www.distrowatch.com/. Users who want to experiment with Linux without going through the process of installing it can try a distribution like Knoppix (http://www.knoppix.com/) which boots and runs directly from CD, with no installation necessary.

Windows, being a commercial system, is much less open. However, there are many books on using and programming Windows, including an excellent book by Petzold [8]. Also, Solomon and Russinovich [11] provide a comprehensive guide to the internal implementation details of Windows.

The emulators that I used to generate the examples in this chapter are Applewin (http://www.jantzer-schmidt.de/applewin/), a free Apple II emulator for Windows which also includes full source code, and VMware (http://www.vmware.com/), a commercial product for Windows or Linux which emulates a Pentium-based PC capable of running Windows, Linux or a variety of other operating systems for the PC platform (and which is well worth the price they charge for it, in my humble opinion). However, the idea behind VMware is far from new; Creasy [2] describes the VM/370 environment introduced by IBM in the late 1960s. This used essentially the same techniques as VMware uses to allow multiple operating systems to be run concurrently on a single machine in separate virtual machines. Parmake *et al.* [7] is an earlier paper on this subject.

As a sideline, a contrast between the open-source and commercial development models is given by Raymond [9], an essay which has now been expanded into a book [10], and the so-called 'Halloween documents' originating from Microsoft [6] provide an interesting insight into Microsoft's attitude to the potential threat to their business posed by open-source software like Linux.

1.12 ❑ GLOSSARY

active window   in a graphical user interface, the window which is currently in active use and which will respond to the mouse and keyboard.

address space   the set of memory addresses that a program can reference.

client–server system   a system arranged as one or more client programs which request services provided by one or more server programs.

desktop   the background of a graphical user interface, which models a set of documents arranged on the surface of a desk.

device driver   a program associated with the operating system which manages a particular type of hardware device.

direct access device   a storage device which allows any stored item of information to be accessed in essentially the same amount of time as any other.

emulator   a program which mimics the operation of a hardware system.

event-driven system   a program which responds to events (such as mouse clicks and keypresses) in whatever order they may occur.

GUI (graphical user interface)   a method of communicating with a computer using a pointing device to interact with graphical objects such as windows and icons.

icon   a small picture representing an object such as a file or program in a graphical user interface.

interrupt   a signal to the processor from an external hardware device indicating that something important has happened.

interrupt service routine   the part of a device driver that responds to an interrupt from the hardware device it is responsible for.

kernel   the core of an operating system.

microkernel system   an operating system with a minimal kernel.

multi-user system   a system which can be used by several users at the same time.

operating system   a program which controls the resources of a computer system.

print spooling   a technique for allowing several users to share a printer by storing the documents to be printed on a disk.

privileged instruction   a machine instruction intended for use by the operating system which cannot be executed directly by a normal process.

process   the environment for the execution of a program provided by an operating system, which behaves like a completely independent computer.

scheduling policy   the policy by which the operating system chooses which process it should allocate processor time to.

sequential device   a storage device which only allows information to be accessed sequentially.

shareable device   a device which can be shared by several users rather than having to be dedicated to use by a single user.

shell   the program which allows a user to interact with a computer system.

system call   a mechanism by which a program can request the operating system to perform some action on its behalf.

timeslice   the amount of processor time allocated to an individual process before the use of the processor will be transferred to another process.

virtual machine   an abstraction of a computer system implemented in software.

window   an area of the display screen used to display the output of an individual program.

1.13   ❑   REFERENCES

[1]   Cornes, P. *The Linux A–Z*. Prentice Hall (1997)

[2]   Creasy, R. J. The origin of the VM/370 time-sharing system. *IBM Journal of Research and Development*, **25**(5) (Sep 1981), 483–490

[3]   Frampton, S. *Linux System Administration Made Easy*. The Linux Documentation Project (Nov 1999). Available online at http://www.tldp.org/LDP/lame/LAME/linux-admin-made-easy/

[4]   Greenfield, L. *The Linux User's Guide*. The Linux Documentation Project (Dec 1996). Available online at http://www.ibiblio.org/pub/Linux/docs/linux-doc-project/users-guide/

[5] IEEE. *Standard 1003.1-2001: POSIX* (2001). Available online at
     `http://www.opengroup.org/onlinepubs/007904975/toc.htm`

[6] Microsoft Corporation. *Open Source Software: A (New?) Development Methodology.* (Nov
     98). Available online at `http://www.opensource.org/halloween/`

[7] Parmake, R. P., Peterson, T. I., Tillman, C. C. and Hatfield, D. J. Virtual storage and virtual
     machine concepts. *IBM Systems Journal*, **11** (1972), 99–130

[8] Petzold, C. *Programming Windows.* Microsoft Press (1998)

[9] Raymond, E. S. *The Cathedral and the Bazaar* (1998). Available online at
     `http://www.openresources.com/documents/cathedral-bazaar/`

[10] Raymond, E. S. *The Cathedral and the Bazaar.* O'Reilly & Associates (2001)

[11] Solomon, D. A. and Russinovich, M. E. *Inside Microsoft Windows 2000.* Microsoft Press
     (2000)

[12] Welsh, M., Hughes, P., Bandel, D., Beletsky, B., Dreilinger, S., Kiesling, R., Liebovitch, E.
     and Pierce, H. *Linux Installation and Getting Started Guide.* The Linux Documentation
     Project (Mar 1998). Available online at `http://www.tldp.org/LDP/gs/`

2

USING AN OPERATING SYSTEM

This chapter describes the view of an operating system as it appears to a programmer who is writing programs to be run under the control of the operating system. As mentioned in the previous chapter, programs are written so that they run on what is in effect an emulation of an idealised version of the real hardware, so the main thrust of this chapter is to explore the structure of this idealised machine.

The most visible part of any operating system is its user interface (its **shell**) which provides a way of interacting with the system in order to do things like run programs and organise information stored in files. Files and how they are organised are dealt with in the next chapter, but the shell itself is just another program as far as the operating system is concerned. This chapter therefore looks at how shells work and at how different shells provide different ways to interact with the system.

2.1 ☐ THE PROGRAMMER'S VIEW

When you write a program to run on an operating system like Windows or Linux, what you write will be executed by a process which is in effect an emulation of a complete computer system. You don't have to worry about what else might be running at the same time, or do anything special to let the operating system switch between processes. You just write your program with the assumption that it will have the resources of an entire computer at its disposal. This is not quite true; there are some things you will be prevented from doing. For example, a Pentium processor has a 'halt' instruction which will stop the processor, and this is not something a process should be allowed to do. However, since compilers for high-level languages never generate instructions like this, only assembly language programmers will notice this as a restriction.

Any high-level language will also provide a **standard library** of useful functions that your programs can use. Such a library is often referred to as an **API**, an 'application programming interface'. The functions that it provides let you perform common operations like opening and closing files, reading input, and writing output. The library will differ from one language to another, but it will ultimately be based on the operating system's own API. The various different versions of Windows support an API called Win32, and the POSIX standard defines a standard API for Unix systems. There will be a way in just about any programming language to call the functions provided by the operating system's API if necessary.

Ultimately, most API functions are implemented in terms of **system calls** which are instructions which request the operating system to interact with the real hardware on your behalf. It is as if your program in running on an emulated processor which provides extra instructions to do things like open and close files (and where certain instructions like the 'halt' instruction have been removed).

2.1.1   TEXT-BASED PROGRAMS

In the days before graphical user interfaces, programs used a text-based sequential model of interaction. Characters were read in sequence from an input source, such as the keyboard, and then processed, which produced a sequence of characters which were written to an output stream, typically a terminal screen (or a window which emulates a terminal screen). It's still the easiest way to write simple programs; in Windows, programs like this are referred to as **console applications** (a 'console' being another name for a text-based terminal). Even to this day, many programming textbooks still begin with the traditional text-based program to display the message 'Hello world'.

A text-based program has a number of **input/output (I/O) streams** available to it which are used to interact with the user. These are mechanisms which allow sequences of characters to be sent to the program from an input device or from the program to an output device. There is a **standard input stream** which is normally associated with the keyboard and a **standard output stream** which is normally associated with the terminal screen. These are normally used to interact with the user of the program. The operating system sets these up when the process is created to run the program, so you can just use them straight away without any fuss. The operating system can also associate them with files on disk rather than with a keyboard and screen, so that your program can take its input from a file rather than the keyboard and write its output to a file rather than the screen. The program itself is normally completely unaware of this; it just reads characters from the standard input and writes characters to the standard output, without caring where the characters are actually coming from or going to.

Because the program's output may be disappearing into a file, there is also a **standard error stream** which can be used to report errors to the user. This is also normally associated with the terminal screen, so that even if the standard output is redirected into a file, error messages will still be displayed on the screen. Of course, you can also redirect the standard error stream into a file if you really want to, so you can capture a copy of any error messages that the program generates.

Text-based programs need to use facilities provided by the operating system's API (application programming interface) to be able to read their input stream and write to their output stream, and many programs will also want to do things like open and read additional files, establish network connections, and create new processes.

Each process also has a set of **environment variables** which the program can access to get additional information about the context in which it is running. Standard API functions can be used to get and set the value of any environment variable as a string. Typical examples of environment variables on Unix systems include:

- USER: the name of the user executing the program
- HOME: the name of the user's 'home directory', a place where the user's personal files should be stored
- PATH: a list of directories used to store command files (described in more detail below)

Windows provides a similar set of standard environment variables, although their names are sometimes different (e.g. USERNAME rather than USER).

Exercise 2.1   Both Windows and Unix support a command called 'set' which will display the names and values of all the environment variables defined at the time. To try this, open a terminal window (what Windows calls a 'command prompt' or 'MS-DOS prompt' window), type 'set' and press Enter.

One of the features that the operating system's API provides is an operation to create a new process. For example, an integrated program development environment lets you edit, compile and run programs, and to do this it has to be able to create new processes to run the compiler and to run the compiled program. When a process creates a new process, the new process inherits a copy of the environment variables from the original process, as well as the input and output streams from the original process. Each new process can create new environment variables, alter existing ones, or close its I/O streams and open new ones without affecting the original process or any other process.

Programs often require parameter information such as the names of any files to be processed, or options to control their behaviour. For example, a compiler needs to be supplied with a list of filenames to be compiled, together with information about options such as the level of optimisation to be used. This could be done using environment variables or via the standard input stream. Using the standard input stream would, however, make it difficult to use it as a normal source of input. Instead, a program can be supplied with a list of text strings known as 'command line arguments' which the program can interpret as it pleases. In C and C++, the main function of a program is declared like this:

```
int main (int argc, char* argv[]) { ... }
```

The parameter argc is the number of command line arguments, and argv is an array of strings which is filled in with the values of the command line arguments, including the program name as the first element. The Java equivalent looks like this:

```
public static void main (String args[]) { ... }
```

where args is an array of strings. Unlike C and C++, no separate argc parameter is used, since Java arrays encapsulate information about their length. Also, the program name is not included in the array in Java.

Most Unix commands treat any strings starting with a hyphen as options which affect the program's behaviour and any others as the names of files to be processed. For example, the gcc compiler interprets a parameter '-g' as a request to include debugging information in the compiled output.

A process also produces an integer **exit code** when it terminates. This can be used to indicate to the process that created it whether the program it was executing completed successfully or not. For example, a compiler can use this to indicate to a program development environment whether or not a program compiled success-fully. Conventionally, an exit code of 0 indicates successful completion; any other value is an application-specific error code. The main function in C and C++ returns a result of type int (integer) which is the value of the program's exit code. The Java equivalent returns no result (signified by void) and by default produces an exit code of 0. To produce a different exit code it is necessary to terminate the program by calling the standard method System.exit(n), where n is the desired exit code. On Unix systems, a special environment variable called $? always holds the exit code from the last program executed.

Exercise 2.2   Find out how you can access the exit code produced by a program on a Windows system.

2.2 ❑ EVENT-DRIVEN PROGRAMMING

Graphical user interfaces have caused a major change in the way programs for modern systems are written. With a text-based interface, interaction is essentially sequential in nature. Graphical user interfaces require a completely different style, because there is no longer a single input stream. User interaction uses both the keyboard and the mouse, and the next event might come from either source. This approach to interaction is fundamentally two-dimensional since the focus of attention can be moved anywhere around a two-dimensional screen, whereas text-based interaction uses a one-dimensional sequence of characters. Programs need to be written in a way that can cope with an unpredictable sequence of events from several sources, and this approach is generally referred to as **event-driven** programming.

Consider a simple example: a program to add two numbers together. In the traditional sequential approach, the program might have looked like this when it was running, with the input typed by the user in *italics*:

```
Enter the first number: 123
Enter the second number: 456
The result is 579
```

The prompts are displayed sequentially. If you realise that you've made a mistake in the first number while you're typing the second one, it's too late. The program has already read what you've typed, and you have no way to tell it that you want to change it. Compare this with the GUI approach shown in Figure 2.1. Here there are two text entry fields for the numbers, and an 'Add' button. You can enter the numbers in any order; you can go back and make changes to what you've already typed. The program responds to mouse events which select one or the other input field; it responds to keyboard events by entering what you type in the selected field. It responds to the 'Add' button by performing the calculation on the current values of the text fields.

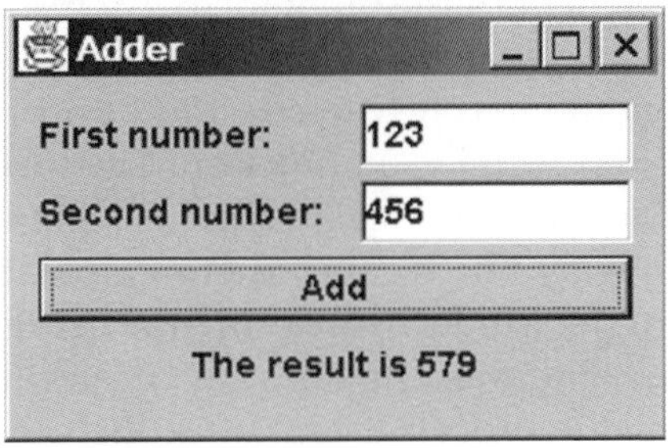

Figure 2.1 A graphical user interface.

The difference is that the program is no longer a sequence of actions (display a prompt, read a number, display another prompt, read another number, display the result), but is instead based around an **event loop** which repeatedly waits for an event and then processes it, whatever it may be. The sequence of events is unpredictable, and the event loop must be able to deal with this.

The example in Figure 2.1 is composed of a number of different standard types of window. There is a **frame** which encloses everything else, with a **title bar** allowing the frame and its contents to be dragged around the screen and **borders** which allow it to be resized. Inside the frame are some **labels** which are non-interactive windows containing some text, used to label the two **text fields** that are used to get the input values and also to display the result when the **button** is pressed. Frames, labels, text fields and buttons are all standard types of window provided by the API. The code which implements these knows how to respond to most events, such as dragging the frame or typing into a text field. All the program's event loop has to do is to respond to the event generated when the button is pressed by reading the contents of the two text fields and setting the text of the result label to their sum. All other events can be processed in the standard way, which in Windows is done by passing the event to another API function.

Question 2.1   What other standard types of window can you think of?

2.2.1   GUIS IN WINDOWS

The Win32 API contains a rich set of functions for creating and interacting with GUI objects. All GUI objects are windows of some sort, and they are all created using one of the variants of the CreateWindow function. The behaviour of each window is determined by the **class** that the window belongs to. A button responds to a mouse click by performing a specific action. A checkbox responds to a mouse click by changing state from checked to unchecked or vice versa. A text field responds to a mouse click by grabbing the 'input focus' (that is, all keyboard events will be processed by the text field until the input focus is transferred to some other window).

The class that a window belongs to is registered with the operating system using one of the variants of the RegisterClass API function. The window class specifies the appearance and behaviour of a particular type of window, including such details as the icon to be used when the window is minimised, the cursor shape to use when the mouse is within the window's area, and the background colour to be used when repainting the window. Most importantly, it specifies the address of a 'window procedure' to be used to process events affecting windows of that class. Because the window is redrawn in response to a 'paint' event, the window procedure is also the ultimate determiner of a window's appearance. There are several standard classes for standard types of windows like buttons and text fields, and these have standard window procedures that know how to handle any events that may occur.

At the heart of every Windows program is a **message loop** which is used to get **messages** (event notifications) and dispatch them to the appropriate window procedure. However, in many modern programming languages you do not have to write the event loop yourself, or even the window procedure; you just have to supply a set of event handlers which will be called from a standard message loop and window procedure provided by the language implementation. It is only when relatively simple languages like C are used that you have to write the whole thing yourself.

The general structure of a Windows event loop is shown in Figure 2.2. Events are generated when a key is pressed or released, when the mouse is moved, when a window receives or loses the input focus, when a window is resized, and so on. Events may give rise to more events; for example, pressing and releasing the mouse button generates 'mouse down' and 'mouse up' events. Doing this over a button generates an 'action' event which is sent to the window containing the button; that is, the window procedure for a button responds to a 'mouse down' followed by a 'mouse up' event by sending a new 'action' event to the enclosing window using the PostMessage API function. The window's response to the 'action' event may cause a 'paint' event to be sent to another window to force it to be redrawn. And so on.

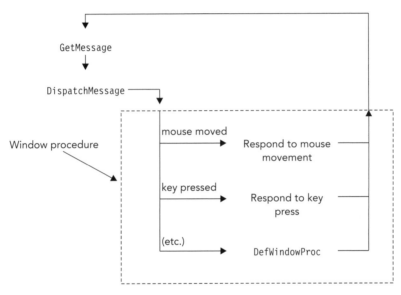

Figure 2.2 A Windows message loop.

The GetMessage function waits for a message to arrive which is directed to a window that was created by the same process (more accurately, the same 'thread', but I'll continue to say 'process' for now until I talk about threads in Chapter 4). This is an example of a **blocking** operation, where execution can't continue until the operation has completed. While it is waiting, the operating system can use the time productively by executing a different process. When a message arrives, the application can pre-process it in various ways before passing it to the DispatchMessage function, which will locate the window procedure for the corresponding window class and call it, providing it with a 'handle' identifying the window to which the message has been sent and the message itself. The message contains a value which identifies what type of message it is (mouse move, key press, action, resize and so on) and additional information such as the mouse position in the case of mouse messages or the code for the key that was pressed in the case of a 'keypress' message. The window procedure can choose to deal with the message itself, or it can pass it to a function called DefWindowProc, which performs default processing for all messages (usually by ignoring the message, but not always).

Consider what happens when you press a button in a GUI. As you click the mouse, the button appears to press 'inwards'; when you release the mouse, the button pops back out again and some action takes place. In more detail, this is what really happens:

- Pressing the mouse button sends a 'mouse down' message to the button's window procedure. The button's window procedure sets the internal button state to 'down' and sends the button a 'paint' message. It also 'captures' the mouse so that any subsequent mouse messages will also be sent to the button even if the mouse is moved away from the button.

- The button's window procedure responds to the 'paint' message by redrawing the button in the appropriate style. In this case, the button is in the 'down' state, so the button is drawn as a 'pressed' button.

- When the mouse is released, a 'mouse up' message is sent to the button's window procedure. The button's window procedure releases the mouse capture, sets the internal button state to 'up' and sends another 'paint' message to the button. Since it was previously in the 'down' state, it also sends an 'action' message to the containing window, which includes a value identifying the button that generated the message.

- The button's window procedure responds to the 'paint' message by redrawing the button in its original 'unpressed' state.

- The containing window's window procedure responds to the 'action' event by doing whatever it needs to do in response to that particular button being pressed.

All but the last step is done by the window procedure for the 'button' window class, which is a standard part of the GUI system. All you have to do as a programmer is to handle any 'action' messages as they occur. In the case of the program shown above that adds two numbers together, a window procedure must be provided for the frame which responds to 'action' messages by reading the two text fields and setting the text of the result label to show the result. Setting the text of the label will automatically cause a 'paint' event to be sent to the label, which will then erase itself before displaying the new text. All other messages sent to the frame (for example, messages to drag or resize it) are dealt with in the standard way by calling DefWindowProc, which will just pass these messages to the system-defined window procedure for handling events relating to frames.

Other more complicated interactions are also possible. For example, if the mouse is moved away from the button while the mouse button is down, the button is sent a 'deactivate' message which causes the button to be redrawn in the 'up' state (via a 'paint' message, of course). If it is then moved back over the button, an 'activate' message is sent to the button which then redraws itself in the 'down' position. This is illustrated in Figure 2.3. Keyboard shortcut keys can also be used to activate the button, generating the same 'action' message as if the button was pressed using the mouse.

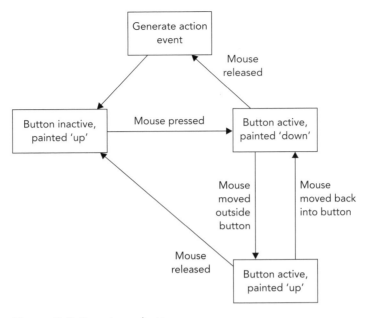

Figure 2.3 Pressing a button.

Exercise 2.3

Describe the different events that the program shown in Figure 2.1 deals with, and explain the ways in which it does so.

2.2.2   GUIS IN UNIX SYSTEMS

The standard GUI system used in Unix systems is known as the **X Window System**, or just plain 'X' for short. Unlike Windows, Unix was originally developed as a multi-user system where each user had a terminal connected to a central machine. In the early days, these terminals were **teletypes** (a combination of a keyboard and a printer) and the central machine routed the input and output stream for each user to their individual teletypes, running processes for each user in parallel with all the other users of the system. However, when graphical workstations became available, it was necessary to develop a window management system which could run processes on a central machine but display the associated windows on a remote workstation. The model used is therefore very different from that used for Windows, which assumes that the computer has a screen, keyboard and mouse attached, rather than lots of remote workstations each with their own separate screen, keyboard and mouse.

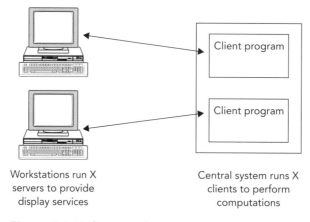

Workstations run X
servers to provide
display services

Central system runs X
clients to perform
computations

Figure 2.4 X clients and servers.

On a Unix system, the users of the system are connected to it by a communications link such as an Ethernet-based local area network. It would be impractical to keep the responsibility for drawing windows or for waiting for mouse movements and other events on the central system; the amount of information being dealt with would swamp the capacity of any communications medium as well as the capacity of the central system to keep up with the mouse movements on dozens of workstations.

The X approach is a **client–server** approach, where a workstation communicates with the central machine in the same way as a web browser connects to a web server. However, whereas a web browser on a user's machine is considered to be a client connecting to a remote server on a central machine, X looks at it the other way round. In X, the user's workstation is the server, and it provides display and interaction services to client programs running on the central machine, as shown in Figure 2.4. This works equally well when there is only one machine involved; in this case, the machine can run both an X server and one or more client applications (as separate processes, naturally). The clients can communicate with the server on the local machine in exactly the same way as they would if the server was on a separate machine.

Some interactions (for example, moving or resizing a window) can be dealt with locally; interactions like these are generally of no interest to the client programs being controlled by the user interface. Changes like this are just concerned with the surface appearance of the interface to accommodate a particular user's tastes, and normally make no difference at all to the behaviour of the program. This means that the client programs do not have the sort of fine control over the appearance of their user interface that programs do on systems like Windows. Instead, the details of the look-and-feel of an application running on an X server are determined by the personal preferences of the user. An X server uses a **window manager** to handle look-and-feel issues, and there are a number of window managers to choose from which provide different look-and-feel styles. Some of these mimic the look-and-feel of systems such as Windows or the Apple Macintosh. Many Windows programs can also be customised by adding 'skins' which change their surface appearance, and the display settings item on the Windows control panel can also be used to make system-wide changes to the surface appearance, although to a more limited extent than is possible by changing to a different X window manager.

On the other hand, pressing a button on a user interface is usually a significant event, and as such the event needs to be communicated to the client program. What events are considered significant will vary from one program to another. Client programs for X therefore need to tell the server which events they are interested in, and the server will then report those events as they occur. All the other events are handled locally by the X server itself. The client expresses its interest in a particular type of event by registering a **callback function** for the event with the X API. As part of the registration process, the client notifies the server that it should be notified of that particular event. When the server notifies the client that the event has occurred, the client calls the registered callback function to deal with it.

Question 2.2   If the program in Figure 2.1 was written as an X application, which events would be handled by the client and which would be handled by the server?

Programs also have to be able to deal with **exceptions**, which are unexpected events that arise as a program is executing. For example, division be zero normally results in an exception. Most modern programming languages provide some sort of exception-handling mechanism. For example, in Java you can write code like this to deal with an arithmetic exception like division by zero:

```
try {
    a = b / c;        // will fail if c == 0
}
catch (ArithmeticException e) {
    a = 0;            // take corrective action
}
```

When an exception occurs, the operating system is notified. API functions are available to let programs register **exception handlers** for particular exceptions, in a similar way to registering X callback functions to deal with specific events. If an exception occurs in a process that has registered a handler for that exception, the operating system calls the handler within the process, as shown in Figure 2.5. The effect from the point of view of the process is that control suddenly and unexpectedly jumps to another part of the program. If there is no registered handler for an exception, the operating system deals with it instead. In the case of an error like

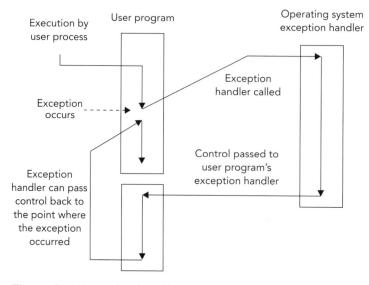

Figure 2.5 Exception handling.

division by zero, it will usually respond by terminating the process abruptly and displaying an error message to let you know what has just happened.

On Unix systems, the *signal* function is used to register an exception handler. This takes two parameters: a number identifying the exception to be caught, and the address of an exception handler function to call when the exception occurs, or the value 0 to deregister an existing exception handler. Programs written in high-level languages like Java with built-in exception handling facilities will use this function internally to allow exceptions to be routed to exception handlers in the program. Programs written in languages with no exception-handling capability (like C) can call *signal* directly to achieve the same effect.

There are many things that can generate an exception; for example, attempting to execute a **privileged instruction** like the 'halt' instruction, or attempting to access an address where no memory has been allocated. Bear in mind that a Pentium processor uses 32-bit addresses, which means that a process has an **address space** of 2^{32} bytes (4 GB); not all of these addresses will correspond to allocated memory, and the operating system will trap any attempts to access an unallocated address. If a process wants to allocate some more memory, it can use an operating system API function to do this; if it just tries to access an address without allocating any memory there, it is treated as an error. A very common programming error is a **null pointer exception**; many programming languages (C and C++, for example) use the value 0 to indicate a **null pointer** which does not 'point to' a valid memory address. If a program actually tries to access this address, it indicates a bug in the program. By making sure that memory is never allocated at address 0, the operating system can detect this common error and report it as an exception.

Not all exceptions are dealt with by terminating the process. External hardware devices generate a type of exception known as an **interrupt** when something of interest happens; for example, the mouse generates an interrupt whenever a button is pressed or released, or whenever the mouse is moved. Similarly, the keyboard generates an interrupt whenever a key is pressed or released. Windows converts these exceptions into event notification messages which are added to the event queue for the corresponding process; X responds by sending messages to the client program which will then cause the appropriate callback functions to be called. After this has been done, the program is allowed to continue from the point where it was interrupted.

The operating system can also use exceptions to extend the processor's instruction set. For example, many older processors needed a separate **floating-point coprocessor** which was separate from the main processor, and this was responsible for processing all floating-point arithmetic instructions. If there was no coprocessor available, floating-point instructions would generate an exception. The operating system could respond to the exception by carrying out the corresponding operation in software. This would be much slower than using a hardware coprocessor, but it would mean that programs that performed floating-point arithmetic would be able to run whether or not a coprocessor was actually present.

2.4 ☐ THE SHELL

Of course, if we want to be able to run a program, we have to have some way of creating a process to run it. This is where the **shell** comes in. The shell is a program that allows users to run programs, manage files, and generally control what the computer does. It is an essential part of the system, as otherwise there is no way to start running any other programs, but it is really just an ordinary program with no special privileges. It uses standard operating system API functions that any other program can use to do things like creating new processes.

The Unix operating system was one of the first to separate the role of the shell from that of the operating system itself. Earlier systems had treated the shell as just another small but inseparable part of the operating system. Unix allows you to specify which program to run as a shell when a user logs in, and different users can have different shells. When the program terminates, you are logged out. Any program can be used as a shell (although for security reasons you may only be allowed to select one of a limited set of programs). One possibility is a program which just terminates immediately, so you can prevent particular users from logging in; if you log in to an account set up with this program as its shell you will just be logged out again immediately. Usually, the standard shell is a text-based program called sh (the 'Bourne shell', named after its creator), which is an interactive interpreter for a **job control language** for Unix. The Bourne shell has spawned a number of descendants, including csh (the 'C shell', with a syntax similar to the C programming language), ash ('another shell'), ksh (the 'Korn shell'), tcsh (a variant of csh) and bash (the 'Bourne-again' shell). All of these are basically very similar, so I will use the Bourne shell as a 'lowest common denominator' to describe generic shell programming features.

2.4.1 UNIX SHELL FEATURES

The Bourne shell is an interpreter which reads a single line of text at a time from an input source, interprets it, and repeats this process until the end of the input source is reached. The input source can be the keyboard, a file, or any other source of characters. This means you can store a list of commands in a file (a **shell script**) and execute them as a single command if you want to, or you can type your commands interactively at the keyboard. When the keyboard is the input source, the shell displays a **prompt** (typically '$') to show when it's ready to read and execute a command. If you type a command and press the return key, the shell executes the command for you and then displays another prompt. If you press control-D (the end-of-file character for keyboard input on Unix systems), the shell terminates and you are logged out.

Each command consists of a sequence of words separated by one or more spaces. The first word is the name of a command to execute, and the remaining words are passed to the command as **command line arguments** which the command can use in whatever way it likes. In some languages (C, C++ and Java, for example) the command line arguments are passed as parameters to the main program. In other languages it may be necessary to call a library function to access them. The command line arguments are typically a list of filenames to be processed by the command. A short example is shown below (with user input shown in *italics*):

```
$ ls
bin        file.c    file.o    private   script.c
$ echo Hello world
Hello world
$ cc file.c
$ wc file.c
   18 65 245 file.c
$ ^D
```

The first command (ls) is the name of a Unix program which will list the contents of the current directory, which in this case contains five files. Unlike Windows, Unix systems are case-sensitive, so the command ls is quite different from LS, while a filename like bin is quite different from Bin.

Exercise 2.4 Try the commands above on a Unix system. You may need to find another file to use instead of file.c in the last two commands.

The second command (echo) is the name of a program which displays a copy of its command line arguments (the two words 'Hello' and 'world'). The third command runs the C compiler (cc), and has a single argument (file.c) which is the name of the file to be compiled. This command doesn't produce any output; like most Unix commands, cc only produces visible output when an error occurs. The fourth command (wc) counts the numbers of lines, words and characters in the file file.c, showing that it contains 18 lines, 65 words and 245 characters. The final line shows control-D being typed (displayed as ^D), which terminates the shell.

When there are a lot of files to be processed, it is possible to use **wildcard** characters to simplify things. Suppose we want to count the number of lines, words and characters in the two files file.c and script.c. The command to do this would be

```
wc file.c script.c
```

A simpler way is to use the character '*' which matches any sequence of characters in a filename. The command

```
wc *.c
```

would have exactly the same effect; before executing wc, the shell would replace the pattern '*.c' with an alphabetical list of matching filenames, so that it would be the same as typing the previous command. Using wildcard characters is only a slight convenience in this particular case, but it is very useful when large numbers of files are involved. Similarly, to count the number of characters in all files beginning with the letter 'f' we could use the following command:

```
wc f*
```

The shell would expand the pattern 'f*' to give the following command:

```
wc file.c file.o
```

The wc program would be unaware of this; expansion of wildcard characters is done by the shell before the program is executed. Command interpreters for Windows provide a similar facility, except that the expansion is not handled by the shell; instead, each program which is required to handle names which might include wildcard characters has to perform the expansion for itself. This gives the programmer more flexibility at the expense of some extra complexity. For example, the Windows rename command can be used to rename a set of files like this:

```
rename *.c *.txt
```

which will rename all files whose names end in '.c' to files with matching names ending in '.txt' (for example, file.c would be renamed file.txt). This won't work for a Unix shell since each of the parameters *.c and *.txt will be expanded into a list of matching filenames before the rename program (called mv on Unix systems) starts running, and mv will probably complain that 'when moving multiple files, the last argument must be the name of a directory'. So in this case the desired effect is much harder to achieve when using a Unix shell.

Exercise 2.5   In a directory containing some files ending in .c, try executing the command 'mv *.c *.txt'. What happens? Try the same thing on a Windows system using the command 'rename *.c *.txt'.

2.4.2 SHELL SCRIPTS

As well as typing commands at the keyboard, you can also store a sequence of commands in a file and execute them as a single operation. Let's assume we've used a text editor to create a file called script which contains these three lines:

```
ls
echo Hello world
cc file.c
```

To execute this sequence of commands, all we have to do is this:

```
$ sh script
bin        file.c    file.o     private    script
Hello world
$
```

The command sh script runs a program called sh (which will be another copy of the shell). The parameter script is the name of a file which the shell will read commands from. The shell reads each line of the file in turn and executes it, just as if the input was being typed at the keyboard; it displays a list of filenames, then the message 'Hello world', then nothing. When the shell reaches the end of the file, it terminates, and the original interactive shell then displays another prompt. Because the shell is just another program, it can be used in exactly the same way as ls or echo or any other command.

     The Unix shell implements a complete programming language in its own right, with conditional commands (if and case) and loop commands (while and for). The condition of an if or while command is a command whose exit code is used to indicate a true or false result (0 means 'true'; anything except 0 means 'false'). You can use variables which are stored in the shell's environment, and you can do arithmetic using a standard utility program called expr. Variable names must be prefixed by a dollar sign ($) to get their values, so for example $PATH gives the value of the PATH environment variable. Special variables ($0, $1, $2 and so on) let you access the command line parameters: $0 is the name of the command, $1 is the first parameter, and so on. Also, $* is the complete set of parameters. The variable $? is the exit code returned by the last command. Altogether this makes a very powerful environment for scripting a sequence of commands, and many common tasks can be achieved with a shell script which runs some of the many standard utility programs that Unix systems always provide.

The following example shows a script which processes a list of filenames and compiles any file whose name ends in .c and ignores all the others:

```
for i in $*
do
  case $i in
  *.c)
    cc $i
    ;;
  *)
    echo Ignoring $i
    ;;
  esac
done
```

The special variable $* is the list of command line arguments which has been passed to the script. The for loop processes the command line parameters given in $*, assigning each one in turn to the environment variable i. The case statement matches the value of the variable i (signified by $i) against two patterns. The first of these patterns (*.c) matches if the value of i is anything ending in .c, and will execute the C compiler (cc) to compile it. The double semicolon (;;) marks the end of the list of actions to take. The second pattern (*) will match anything (that is, anything that wasn't already matched by the first pattern), and displays the message 'Ignoring x' where x is the current value of the variable i.

Project 2.1   On a Unix system, write a shell script which displays its first three command line arguments on separate lines. Display an error message if the script is not supplied with at least three arguments.

Windows also supports shell scripts, which are referred to as **batch files**. The standard Windows command processor (called CMD.EXE, or COMMAND.COM on older versions of Windows) implements a somewhat less powerful language than the various Unix shells, and the numerous utility programs that Unix provides are not available as standard on Windows systems. There is an if statement and a for loop, but these are much less powerful than the Unix shell equivalents. The other main command that is used to control the sequence of events is a goto statement, much like a programming language of the early 1960s. However, versions of the Unix shell and standard utility programs for Windows are available from the Cygwin project; there are also more powerful shells available that can be used instead of CMD.EXE. I use one called 4NT produced by JP Software, which is compatible with CMD.EXE but provides many extra features which I consider essential for serious scripting.

Project 2.2   Write a Windows batch file which displays which displays its first three command line arguments on a separate line. Display an error message if the script is not supplied with at least three arguments.

2.4.3   MORE SHELL FEATURES

In the examples above, the shell waits for each command to finish before it carries on. Consider what happens in the example shell script from the beginning of Section 2.4.2:

```
ls
echo Hello world
cc file.c
```

At the point where the ls command is being executed from the script file, there are three processes running:

- The original interactive shell
- The shell running the script file
- The ls command

The original interactive shell is suspended waiting for the other copy of the shell to finish, and that copy of the shell is also suspended, waiting for the ls command to finish.

You can also run programs without waiting for them to finish; the character '&' at the end of a command is interpreted by the shell as a request to execute the command **asynchronously**, returning to the command prompt immediately rather than suspending and waiting for the command to finish. For example:

```
$ sh script &
$ bin       file.c    file.o    private    script
Hello world
```

Here the command to run the script does not suspend the original shell, so the prompt is displayed immediately, and at the same time, the secondary shell executes the contents of script. The output from script is displayed at the current position on the screen, which is just after the '$' prompt that the interactive shell displayed. The prompt and the output from script will not necessarily be displayed in this order; the interactive shell's prompt could be displayed at any time during execution of the script.

2.4.4   REDIRECTION AND PIPING

Most Unix programs are written so that they will read input from the standard input stream and write output to the standard output stream. For an interactive shell, the standard input is the keyboard and the standard output is the screen. A shell executing a script file uses the script file as its standard input instead of the keyboard. In fact, any source of characters could be used as the standard input stream, and anywhere that characters can be written to could be used in place of the screen as the standard output stream. The shell provides a standard notation to allow the standard input and output streams to be **redirected**: '< source' uses a file called source as the standard input stream, and '> destination' uses a file called destination as the standard output stream, overwriting the original contents of the file if it already exists. You can also use '>> destination' to append the program's output to the file destination if the file already exists rather than overwriting it. The program doesn't know anything about any of this; the shell sets up the standard input and output streams before the program is started. The program just reads from the standard input and writes to the standard output in the normal way. For example:

```
$ ls >x
$ wc -w <x
      6
$ rm x
```

Exercise 2.6   Try this on a Unix system and see what happens.

The output of ls is stored in a file called x instead of being displayed on the screen; the command wc takes its input from this file instead of the keyboard. What wc -w does is to display the number of words in its input, which in this case is 6 (the names of the five files that were there before, plus x itself). The final command (rm, short for 'remove') deletes the temporary file x as soon as it is no longer needed.

A cunning simplification is to connect the standard output of the ls command directly to the standard input of wc. This configuration is known as a **pipe**, and is symbolised by a vertical bar ('|'):

```
$ ls | wc -w
      5
$
```

Exercise 2.7   Try this on a Unix system and see what the difference is between this command and the previous sequence of three commands.

This has two main advantages. The first is that the temporary file x is no longer needed; in fact, the output from ls is only being used as the input to wc, so it doesn't need to be stored permanently at all. As a result, only five files are listed by ls, and the output from wc is 5 rather than 6. Pipes can be implemented by holding the information in memory while it is in transit, which is much faster than writing it to a disk.

Exercise 2.8   Find out what effect each of these commands will have and the differences between them.

- `cat file.c | wc`
- `echo file.c | wc`
- `wc < file.c`

The second advantage is that the shell can start the two commands which make up the pipeline at the same time, and they can run concurrently as two separate processes rather than sequentially. The wc command will wait for the ls command to provide it with some input, in exactly the same way that it would wait for something to be typed in if the standard input was coming from the keyboard, but it doesn't have to wait for the ls command to finish before it can start work.

This remarkably simple mechanism is very powerful; it encourages the development of small, simple programs (like wc) which can be used as 'filters' to perform some relatively minor transformation of their input, rather than building those transformations into other programs (like ls) which might need them. Instead of a special option to tell ls to display the number of files in a directory, just use ls to produce a list of names and then use wc to count them. In fact, ls is an unusual program for Unix; it was one of the first commands provided, and has dozens of options for formatting its output and even sorting it in various different ways. Most commands don't need to provide all these features; if you want to sort the output, it's easier to pipe it to the sort command.

Note that since the shell sets up the input and output streams before the program is executed, doing something like this will not behave as you might expect:

```
sort <file >file
```

Exercise 2.9   Create a file on a Unix system and see what this command actually does.

You might expect this to sort the contents of file, replacing the existing contents with the sorted results. In fact, the shell will deal with the output redirection '> file' before the program starts by creating a new output file of this name, destroying the file's existing contents. By the time the program starts, the file will be empty and the sort command will have no data to sort. Instead, you have to do something like this:

```
sort <file >file2
mv file2 file
```

The mv command moves (renames) file2 to file, replacing the existing contents of file.

Most Unix commands can be given a list of filenames as command line parameters, and will process each of the named files in turn. If no filenames are given, the standard input will be processed instead. This is purely a Unix convention; each program which implements a command conforming to this convention will need to be written so that it will process the filenames given on the command line in the appropriate way. Most Unix commands also allow various options to be specified to control their behaviour, and by convention these begin with a hyphen and precede any filenames on the command line. For example, wc normally counts the number of lines, words and characters in its input, but the -l option makes it count lines only, the -w option makes it count words only, and the -c option makes it count characters only. These can be combined; for example, wc -l -c (or alternatively wc -lc) will count both lines and characters. Windows commands are similar except that they use a slash ('/') rather than a hyphen to indicate an option.

The way that wc deals with its parameters can be seen in its output. If it is processing files whose names are given on the command line, each file is processed separately and the results for each file are listed separately:

```
$ wc *.c
    18    65   245 file.c
    14    83   337 script.c
    32   148   582 total
```

If you just want a grand total, the way to do it is to use the cat ('concatenate') command to copy all the input files to the standard output (thereby combining them into a single file) and then pipe the resulting single file into wc:

```
$ cat *.c | wc
    32   148   582
```

In this case, there are no filenames given on the command line to wc, so it processes its standard input. Since this is not a named file, no name is printed next to the result. Notice that the same happens when you type wc -w <x rather than wc -w x. In the first case there is no filename on the command line, so wc reads its standard input, which has been redirected to come from the file x. In the second case there is a filename on the command line, so the name x will be printed at the end of the output.

Here are some examples of standard Unix tools that can be used as filters to process their standard input:

sort   sort the standard input and write the result to the standard output. Options allow the input to be sorted in numerical (rather than lexicographical) order, and descending rather than ascending order.

wc   count lines, words, and/or characters in the standard input and write the result to the standard output.

tr   copy the standard input to the standard output, translating any character in one set of characters into a corresponding character from another set.

sed   perform one or more editing commands on each line while copying the standard input to the standard output.

uniq   remove duplicate lines from the standard input, leaving only unique lines. An option allows the output line to be preceded by the number of times it occurred in the input.

grep   display all lines from the standard input which match (or which fail to match) a particular pattern.

head   display the first few lines of the standard input (the default is 10) and discard the rest

tail   display the last few lines of the standard input (the default is 10) and discard the rest

To illustrate how these can be combined, here is a sequence which will extract the ten most common words from the standard input:

```
tr 'A-Z' 'a-z' | tr -c -s 'a-z' '\n' | sort | uniq -c | sort -n -r | head
```

This is a pipeline of six commands:

- `tr 'A-Z' 'a-z'` translates all uppercase letters to the equivalent lowercase letter, so 'the' and 'The' will not be counted separately.

- `tr -c -s 'a-z' '\n'` translates all sequences of non-letters to a single newline character, symbolised by '\n'; -c is the 'complement' option which means that a-z specifies all characters *except* a to z, and -s is the 'squeeze' option which squeezes a matching sequence of any length into a single replacement character. The result so far is the standard input, converted to lower case and broken up into one word per line.

- `sort` sorts the input to give a list of words in alphabetical order, so that all occurrences of the same word will be brought together into a single place.

- `uniq -c` removes adjacent duplicate lines, which in this case will be duplicate copies of each word, and the -c ('count') option prefixes each line with a count of the number of occurrences in the original.

- `sort -n -r` sorts the input numerically (-n) so that the list is sorted in order of the number of occurrences of each word. It is arranged in descending order (-r, for 'reverse'), so that the words with the highest number of occurrences are brought to the beginning of the list.

- head displays the first ten lines, which will be the ten commonest words together with their number of occurrences.

Exercise 2.10   Find out what the ten commonest words are in the manual entry for ls, as given by the command man ls. What are the ten least common words?

The individual programs making up this filter are very simple (except for sort, but you'd expect any decent system to provide a sorting utility of some kind). They can easily be implemented in a few lines of code in any high-level programming language. However, this example shows them combined into a pipeline which implements a solution to a problem which would be very difficult to solve in a language like C (the language in which all these filter programs were originally written).

Note that different processes can be running the same program at the same time, in the same way that you can run the same program on separate computers. Here, the programs tr and sort are each used for two different purposes. In the case of tr this is to translate upper-case characters to lower -case, and also to translate non-word characters into line breaks. In the case of sort it is to sort words into ascending alphabetical order and also to sort the results numerically in descending order. While the pipeline shown above is being executed, there will be two separate processes which are each executing the tr program. Similarly, there will be two processes which are both executing the sort program at different stages in the pipeline. Each instance of tr has different parameters and different input and output streams and thus operates on different data, just as it would be if you ran tr at different times. Here the different instances of tr are run at the same time, but they are just as different as if they were run at different times.

Project 2.3   On a Unix system, how can you rename all files ending with '.c' so that the '.c' ending of each file is replaced with '.txt'? Hint: use echo to output the value of a variable containing the filename so that it can be piped to the sed stream editor. Use sed to edit the filename as necessary. Use man sh to get the documentation for the shell and find out how to use backticks (`...`) to treat the output from sed as a command line argument for the mv (rename) command.

2.4.5   HOW A UNIX SHELL WORKS

The various Unix shells are just ordinary programs which use API facilities to create processes and connect them together. The shell has a standard input channel, normally connected to the keyboard, and standard output and standard error channels, normally connected to the display. It reads commands a line at a time from its standard input and uses the first word on each command line as the name of the command to be executed. A handful of commands are built in to the shell, but most commands are not. If the command name is not the name of a built-in command, it is taken to be the name of a file containing the program code; if the name does not specify a directory, the shell uses the PATH environment variable to locate the command. The PATH variable consists of a list of directory names; the shell searches each directory in turn for a file with the correct name, and the first one it finds is the one that gets executed. Once it has located the file, it creates a separate process which loads the program file into memory and executes it. When this process finishes, the prompt is displayed again. However, if the command line ends in '&', the shell does not wait for the new process to finish before displaying the prompt for the next command.

A system call named fork is responsible for creating new processes on a Unix system. What fork does is to create an identical copy of the calling process, so there are now two processes running copies of the same program. Both copies are at the same point in the program to start with (at the point where fork was called). This is illustrated in Figure 2.6. The program can tell whether it is running in the original process or the new one by the result returned by fork, which returns either the value zero if the executing process is the new **child** process, or a process number which can be used to refer to the child process if the executing process is the original **parent** process. If it wants to, the parent process can wait for the child process to complete using the wait system call with the child's process number as a parameter.

When you type a command like ls, the shell calls fork to create a new process, and the parent process calls wait to wait for the child process to complete before it continues. Meanwhile, the child process executes the ls command by using one of the several varieties of the exec system call, which loads a specified program into the memory of the current process to replace the current program and then starts executing it. The shell program in the child process is thus replaced by a copy of the

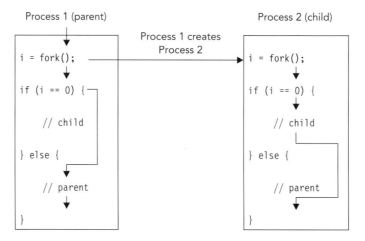

Figure 2.6 Creating a new process using fork.

ls program, which executes from the beginning and then terminates. If instead you type ls &, the parent process does not call wait to wait for the child process; it just carries on reading and executing commands.

The child process inherits the input and output streams that its parent had open at the time of the call to fork, so that a child process will automatically have the same standard input, standard output and standard error streams. To implement redirection using '<' and '>', before the child process calls exec to load the new program it closes the corresponding stream and then opens the specified file in its place. A pipeline of two commands is implemented by creating two child processes and a pipe (which is a combined input and output stream). The standard output of the first command is connected to the pipe's input stream and the pipe's output stream is connected to the second command's standard input.

Exercise 2.11 Find out how you can redirect the standard error stream on Unix systems. How can you do it on Windows systems?

The Windows command processor works similarly but with many differences in detail due to the difference in the architecture of the POSIX and Win32 APIs. For example, on Windows systems, new processes are created using the CreateProcess API call, which effectively combines fork and exec and which can also specify the connections for the standard input, standard output and standard error streams. Although it is possible to construct a Windows command processor with the same range of capabilities as a Unix shell, the standard Windows command processor is much simpler; for example, commands connected in a pipeline run sequentially on many versions of Windows rather than concurrently as they do in Unix. The range of commands that can be used to control the sequence of events is much more limited. Command line interfaces are rarely used in Windows, since the whole system is strongly oriented towards the use of graphical user interfaces.

2.5 ☐ GRAPHICAL SHELLS

Command line interfaces like the Unix shell are very powerful tools, but they have some disadvantages. The main disadvantage is the amount of specialist knowledge needed to use them. To use a Unix shell, you have to remember the names of the commands (which are often short and cryptic) and the options which control their detailed behaviour (like the -n option to make the sort command sort numerically rather than lexicographically). The system manuals are available online and you can use the man command to display the manual page for any command; for example, the command man ls will display the manual page for the ls command which gives details of all the options it provides. On Windows, you can type '/?' after most commands to get a description of the command, so for example DIR /? gives a description of the DIR command (the Windows equivalent of ls). The problem is that this doesn't help at all if you don't know the name of the command to use. The development of personal computers which were intended to be the property of an individual, rather than being controlled by a group of specialists employed by a central corporate computing division, meant that a simpler interface was needed.

A graphical shell like Windows or X is much easier for non-specialists to use, but at the cost of a loss of expressive power. It is much more difficult to say 'delete all the files whose names match this pattern' or 'count how many words there are in all of these files' or 'append this file to that one'. It is even harder to script a sequence of actions: 'move these files to there, but if there's already a file of the same name there, move them to here instead, and at the end tell me how many files there were'. However, most people don't need this level of expressiveness (or maybe they don't realise that such things are possible, so they don't realise they're missing anything!), and for most people the benefits of the graphical user interface outweigh its shortcomings. Other people (like myself) use a graphical user interface but occasionally start a text-based shell running in a window in order to do more complex tasks when necessary. Also, a text-based shell allows you to write shell scripts to automate common operations; scripting actions within a graphical shell is a lot more difficult.

Exercise 2.12 Compare how easy it is to perform the following tasks using a GUI shell as opposed to a text shell:

- Delete all files older than a given date.

- Make backup copies of a set of files where each backup copy has the same name as the original file with a suffix of '.bak' appended.

2.6 ❑ SUMMARY

From the point of view of a programmer, each program has the resources of an entire idealised computer system at its disposal. The facilities of this idealised machine are accessed using the operating system's API via system calls. These allow files to be associated with input and output streams, new processes to be created, and much more. In older systems, text-based programs were the norm, but most modern operating systems support GUI-based programs. These use an event loop to get successive events of interest from the graphical interface, so they use an event-driven programming style which is quite different to the sequential style used for text-based programs.

The operating system provides a program known as a **shell** to allow you to do things like compile and run your own programs. The shell simply creates new processes to run any other programs you want to use. It is really just another application program provided with the operating system, and can be replaced by a different shell if that is what you want. There is normally a graphical shell which manages the system desktop, allowing you to start programs by clicking on the relevant graphical icons, and there is usually a text-mode shell as well which can process commands as you type them in. Commands like this can also be stored in a file as a **shell script** and then executed just like any other program, either by typing the name of the shell script or creating a graphical icon which will run the script when it is activated. Shell scripts allow you to automate many common repetitive tasks which would be hard to perform using a pure graphical interface.

2.7 ❑ ADDITIONAL RESOURCES

Burkett *et al.* [1] provide a guide to programming for Linux systems, while Cooper [2] describes shell scripting using bash, the standard Linux shell. These are both available online. If you want printed material, Kernighan and Pike [4] describe Unix programming in detail and Kochan and Wood [5] cover the use of the Unix shell and shell scripting, while Nye [6] explains how to build GUI applications for X. Petzold [7] is an excellent in-depth introduction to programming for Windows, while Hill [3] describes how to write shell scripts (batch files) for Windows.

The 4NT shell for Windows mentioned in this chapter, as well as 4DOS for earlier versions for Windows, is a shareware product available from JP Software (http://www.jpsoft.com/), while the Cygwin project (http://www.cygwin.org/) provides a free implementation of the bash shell for Windows together with a comprehensive set of standard Unix utilities and development tools.

2.8 ❑ GLOSSARY

API (Application Program Interface)   the interface by which an application program accesses services provided by the operating system and others.

batch file   the name used for **shell scripts** on Windows systems.

blocking operation   an operation which prevents a process from continuing until the operation is complete.

callback function   a function provided by the user which will be called when a specified event occurs, used by the X Window System to notify clients programs when user interface events occur.

child process   a process which inherits characteristics of its execution environment (including environment variables and opened files) from the **parent process** which created it.

command line argument   a string passed to a program as part of the command line used to start the program, often used to supply the names of files to be processed by a program.

console application the name used on Windows systems for non-graphical (text-based) programs.

environment variable a value accessible to a program which provides information about the environment in which it is executing (for example, the name of the user who is executing the program).

event loop in a graphical program, the main loop within the program which waits for a user interface event to occur and then processes it.

exception an indication of an error or other exceptional event which changes the normal flow of program execution.

exception handler a part of a program to which control will be transferred when an exception occurs.

I/O stream a sequential stream of characters which is consumed by or produced by a program.

interrupt an exception generated by an external hardware device.

job control language the language interpreted by a shell which is used to control a sequence of execution of programs being executed as a single job.

null pointer a memory address which refers to an address which is guaranteed to be invalid (usually zero).

pipe a double-ended I/O stream used to connect an output stream generated by one program to an input stream being consumed by another.

privileged instruction a machine instruction which cannot be executed directly by a normal process.

prompt a message displayed by a text-based shell or other program to indicate that it is ready to accept some input.

redirection changing the source of an input stream or the destination of an output stream.

shell a program which is executed when a user first logs in, used to allow the user to run other programs.

shell script a sequence of commands stored in a file which can be executed by a shell as if it were a single command.

standard error stream an output stream provided for writing error messages to, normally connected to the display screen.

standard input stream the primary input stream for a program, normally connected to the keyboard.

standard library a set of functions provided as a standard part of the implementation of a high-level language.

standard output stream the primary output stream for a program, normally connected to the display screen.

system call the mechanism by which a process requests the operating system to perform a service on its behalf.

wildcard character   a special character which is interpreted by the shell as standing for any character or sequence of characters in a filename.

window manager   in the X Window System, the program which defines the 'look and feel' of the graphical user interface presented to the user.

X Window System   the standard graphical user interface used on Unix systems.

2.9 ☐ REFERENCES

[1]   Burkett, B. S., Goldt, S., Harper, J. D., van der Meer, S. and Welsh, M. *The Linux Programmer's Guide*. The Linux Documentation Project (Mar 1996). Available online at http://www.tldp.org/LDP/lpg/

[2]   Cooper, M. *Advanced Bash-Scripting Guide*. The Linux Documentation Project (Dec 1996). Available online at http://www.tldp.org/LDP/abs/

[3]   Hill, T. *Windows NT Shell Scripting*. Que (1998)

[4]   Kernighan, B. W. and Pike, R. *The UNIX Programming Environment*. Prentice Hall (1984)

[5]   Kochan, S. and Wood, P. *Unix Shell Programming*. Sams Publishing (2003)

[6]   Nye, A. *Xlib Programming Manual*. O'Reilly & Associates (1992)

[7]   Petzold, C. *Programming Windows*. Microsoft Press (1998)

CHAPTER 3

FILESYSTEMS

From a user's point of view, one of the most important things an operating system provides is the ability to organise information by storing it in **files**. The **filesystem** is a mechanism which allows a user to organise files into some sort of convenient arrangement so that they can be referred to by a meaningful name. It is often part of a more general facility to allow other resources such as devices and remote computers to be referred to by name.

The filesystem will normally allow related files to be grouped together into **directories** to make it easy to find files when necessary. It also acts to conceal the differences between the various different hardware devices that may be used to store the files. Different operating systems organise their filesystems in different ways, and this chapter examines the facilities that some different filesystems provide and their implementation in terms of the way that files are laid out on disk.

What most programs do is to process information stored in files. A file corresponds to an individual document, or any other collection of data that should be stored as a single unit. Files can be stored on many different types of storage device, including disks, magnetic tapes, optical media (e.g. CD or DVD) and solid state memory (e.g. compact flash cards). Such devices are normally organised as a sequence of fixed-size **blocks**. They can store a large number of blocks of data semi-permanently, and they are generally able to access a particular block of data by using its block number (that is, its position in the sequence of blocks on the storage device) in much the same way that a location in memory can be accessed using an address. For example, a floppy disk for a PC uses blocks of 512 bytes each, whereas a

CD-ROM has a block size of 2 KB. Some devices such as magnetic tape allow variable-sized blocks rather than fixed-size blocks, but I'm going to ignore this here.

Exercise 3.1

Devise an experiment which will show the block size used to store a file on a particular storage device.

One of the jobs of an operating system is to hide the device-dependent details about where a file is physically located. This is similar to the way that when you write a program in a high-level programming language, you don't have to worry about exactly where your program's variables will be stored in memory. The compiler takes care of implementation details like this. You can refer to a particular variable by name in your program and the compiler will generate a reference to the corresponding address in memory.

An operating system does exactly the same thing when it comes to files. Any operating system needs to provide a **filesystem** that lets you give meaningful names to files, and it's up to the operating system to locate the corresponding information whenever you use that name to refer to the file. This will be done in different ways on different types of storage device, but you don't need to be aware of this. All you have to do is use a system call to open a file with a particular name, and the operating system will use that name to locate the corresponding file for you. Another way of looking at this is that a filesystem provides a **namespace**, or in other words a set of unique names that can be used to identify the objects it defines, in much the same way as an address space defines a set of unique addresses.

A device which can store a collection of files is often referred to as a **volume**. A volume is usually a storage device such as a floppy disk or CD-ROM, but it doesn't have to be; a single disk might contain several volumes (for example, a hard disk can normally be divided into a number of separate **partitions**, each of which behaves as if it were a separate disk), or a single volume might span multiple disks. This is illustrated in Figure 3.1.

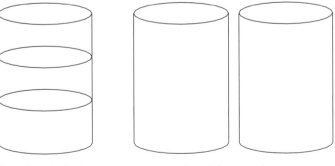

A single disk divided into three volumes

Two disks treated as a single volume

Figure 3.1 Disks and volumes.

Each volume is treated as a numbered sequence of blocks. To access a file by name, the operating system has to keep a list of filenames and their corresponding locations (block numbers) within the volume. The obvious place to keep this list is on the same volume as the files themselves. This list of filenames can also be regarded as a file (it's just data like any other file, after all) and so it can be stored in the same way as the files it describes. It will be a specialised type of file, usually referred to as a **directory** or a **folder**, but it will be still a file with many of the same characteristics as other files stored in the volume.

Ultimately there must be a master directory (the **root directory**) for each volume, from which any file stored in the volume can be located, and this must be stored at a known place within the volume. By treating directories as files, they can be given names which can in turn be recorded in other directories. It is usually convenient to organise groups of related files in their own separate directories. This means that the root directory will contain a mixture of 'normal' files and further (sub)directories, and the subdirectories will then contain normal files and yet more subdirectories, as illustrated in Figure 3.2. This shows a directory containing four entries, one of which is a subdirectory and three of which are normal files, and the subdirectory then contains three entries for three more normal files.

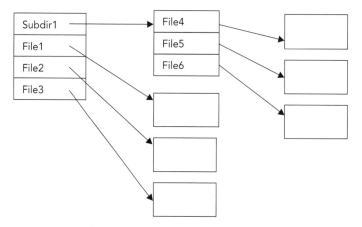

Figure 3.2 A hierarchical file system.

3.2 ❑ PATHNAMES AND FILENAMES

Filesystems where there is a hierarchy of directories and subdirectories are referred to as **hierarchical** filesystems. The name of an individual file is given by a **pathname** which gives the path, starting at the root directory and tracing through successive subdirectories, leading to the file itself. For example, on Unix systems a file whose pathname is '/usr/local/bin/crisp' can be located by looking in the root directory for an entry for a directory called 'usr', then looking in that directory for another directory called 'local', then in the 'local' subdirectory for an entry for 'bin', and finally looking in 'bin' for a file named 'crisp'. This is shown in Figure

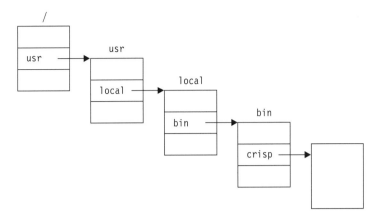

Figure 3.3 Locating /usr/local/bin/crisp.

3.3. The entry for the file crisp will tell you where that file is physically located on the device. Unix uses the character '/' as a **path separator** character to separate the components of the pathname; it also uses '/' by itself as the name of the root directory.

A hierarchical filesystem has the advantage that a volume which holds thousands of files does not need a single directory which lists all those thousands of files. Files can be grouped together and stored in relevant subdirectories, either by topic or by username. For example, I have directories called 'Courses' and 'Projects' which I use to store files related to particular courses that I teach and particular projects that I'm working on. Within the Courses directory there are further directories whose names correspond to the courses that I teach, with names like 'CS236' and 'CS337'. This makes it easy for me to find my way around; it's easy to find all the files related to a particular course that I teach, for example.

Windows and Unix both provide a hierarchical filesystem using similar naming conventions, since the Windows filesystem design imitated much of what was already established on Unix systems. The major visible difference is that Windows uses the character '\' to separate the elements of a pathname, whereas Unix uses '/'. In fact, Windows will also accept pathnames which use '/' as a separator, but Windows also uses '/' as the character to specify options to many commands, so it can occasionally be misinterpreted if it is used in pathnames. Because of the many similarities, the discussion below concentrates on the Unix naming conventions, since they are essentially common to both Unix and Windows.

The screenshot in Figure 3.4 shows a directory hierarchy in Windows. In the left-hand pane of the window, you can see a directory tree where some of the nodes have been expanded by clicking on the '+' icon to the left of their names. The tree is rooted at the local disk (C:); the node 'Documents and Settings' has been expanded to show the directories it contains. Below this, the node 'JE' has been expanded, and under that 'My Documents'. Inside this there is a further subdirectory called 'Courses' which contains a directory called 'CDH01'. This is the name that is highlighted in the left-hand pane, and it also show that it contains further

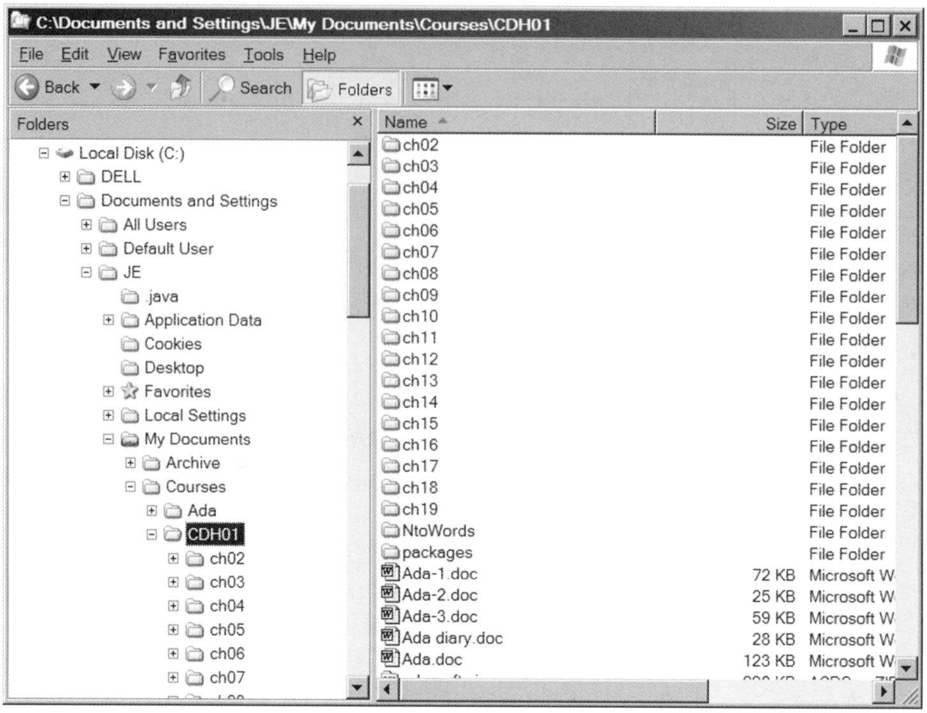

Figure 3.4 A Windows Explorer directory tree.

directories called 'ch02', 'ch03' and so on. In the title bar of the window is the full pathname, 'C:\Documents and Settings\JE\My Documents\Courses\CDH01'. The right-hand pane shows the contents of this directory, including the various subdirectories and also some files, the first of which is called 'Ada-1.doc'. The full pathname for this file would therefore be 'C:\Documents and Settings\JE\My Documents\Courses\CDH01\Ada-1.doc'.

It is quite awkward to have to always use a full pathname to refer to a file, so most operating systems use the notion of a **current directory** to simplify matters, and they provide commands to change the current directory and display its name. If the current directory on a Unix system is /usr/local/bin, the file /usr/local/bin/crisp can be referred to more easily as crisp, meaning 'the file crisp in the current directory'. A pathname like /usr/local/bin/crisp which starts from the root directory '/' is known as an **absolute pathname**, whereas a pathname like crisp which doesn't start with '/' is a **relative pathname**, which is taken to be relative to the current directory.

Question 3.1   When would you use a relative pathname and when would you use an absolute pathname?

As a convenience, the name '.' can be used to refer to the current directory, so that another way to refer to the file crisp is as ./crisp. Also, the name '..' refers to the **parent directory** of the current directory; that is, the directory which contains the current directory (/usr/local in the case of /usr/local/bin). This means that a file called /usr/local/man/crisp.1 could be referred to as ../man/crisp.1, since '..' means the same thing as /usr/local. If the current directory were changed to /home/je/bin, the name ../man/crisp.1 would instead refer to the file /home/je/man/crisp.1. Changing the current directory will change the meaning of a relative filename, but the meaning of an absolute pathname never changes. The first two entries in every directory on a Unix system are always '.' and '..', but you don't normally see them since the ls command will not list files whose names begin with '.' unless the -a ('all') option is used.

Windows is slightly different from Unix in the way that the root directory is treated. All directories on a Unix filesystem contain entries for '.' and '..', including the root directory; in the root directory both '.' and '..' mean the same thing (they both refer to the root directory), since there is no 'parent' directory that '..' can refer to. Windows filesystems do not have entries for '.' or '..' in the root directory, which means that programs using these will not work properly if run with the root directory as the current directory. This is rarely a problem in practice, however.

Exercise 3.2   Assuming the current directory is /usr/local/bin, list five different names which can be used to refer to the file /usr/local/src/ls.

Operating systems which are designed for use by more than one user need a way to keep each user's files separate. This is normally done by providing a separate directory for each user, which is known as the user's **home directory**. When a user logs in on a Unix system, the corresponding home directory is automatically selected to be the current directory, so that the user's own files can be referred to easily. On Windows systems there is usually an icon on the desktop labelled 'My Documents' which will open a window showing the contents of the current user's home directory (although the term 'home directory' isn't used on Windows systems).

3.3 ⬜ MULTIPLE FILESYSTEMS

On Windows, each volume is traditionally viewed as a separate filesystem which is referred to by a single-letter **drive letter** followed by a colon. Up to two floppy disk drives can be present, and if they are present they will be referred to as drives A: and B:; the primary partition on the first hard disk is drive C:, and other volumes are assigned subsequent letters. It is also possible to 'map' a directory on a remote machine across the network to an otherwise unused drive letter on the local machine, in which case the directory on the remote machine can be used as if it were a volume on the local machine. Windows keeps track of the **current drive** which will be assumed if a filename is used which does not begin with a drive letter together with its trailing colon. It also keeps track of the current directory in use on each of the available volumes (which is initially the root directory of each volume), so that a name like `C:file.txt` refers to a file called `file.txt` in the current directory on drive C:, whereas `file.txt` with no preceding drive letter refers to a file in the current directory on the current drive.

The drive letters are assigned automatically for the volumes on the local machine, so that a system with one hard disk drive and one CD-ROM drive would use C: for the disk drive and D: for the CD-ROM drive. The problem with this is that adding new drives or **repartitioning** an existing drive (that is, dividing a single disk into multiple volumes) can change the existing drive letters; for example, a second disk drive might be assigned D: as its drive letter, and the CD-ROM drive would end up as E:. This can cause problems if software is written which expects the CD-ROM drive to be drive D: and the drive letter subsequently changes. Windows allows the drive letters to be specified explicitly to avoid this problem. Personally, I always work backwards from Z: for devices like CD-ROM drives so that I can modify the layout of my hard disks without getting into this sort of mess.

Exercise 3.3   Find out how you can change the drive letter of a CD-ROM drive in your version of Windows.

Another problem with this approach is that it only allows up to 26 drives to be used. This would not normally be a problem except when mapping many different directories from remote machines, but recent versions of Windows (NT and later) introduced a solution called **UNC** (Uniform Naming Convention) filenames, so that a directory called `files` on a machine called `hermes` can be referenced as `\\hermes\files`. However, not all Windows applications support the use of UNC names, so mapping remote directories to drive letters is often still necessary.

Unix filesystems adopt an approach which is similar to UNC, or rather UNC is an approach which is similar to the one that Unix systems have always used. The volume that a Unix system boots from contains the **root directory**, and it defines a single directory tree. Other volumes are **mounted** as subdirectories within this tree, so that the root directory of the volume replaces the contents of the subdirectory that it is being mounted on. Any existing files within the directory will be inaccessible until the mounted volume is unmounted again; to prevent confusion, it is best to mount volumes onto empty directories. On most Unix systems, a special subdirectory called `/mnt` is usually used as a place to keep empty subdirectories where other drives can be mounted. For example, a CD-ROM is usually mounted onto an empty directory called `/mnt/cdrom`. The entire directory tree of the CD-ROM then appears within this directory. Figure 3.5 shows a floppy disk and a CD-ROM which have been mounted on the directories `/mnt/floppy` and `/mnt/cdrom` respectively. A

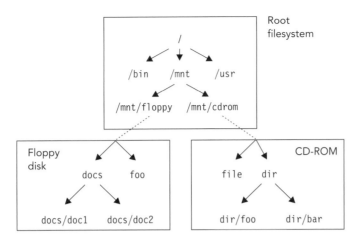

Figure 3.5 Mounting a file system.

file called foo in the top-level directory on the floppy disk would appear as a file called /mnt/floppy/foo. A file called dir/foo on the CD-ROM could be referred to as /mnt/cdrom/dir/foo. Directories on remote machines can also be treated in exactly the same way, so that everything ends up as part of a single directory tree.

Although it is not immediately apparent, modern versions of Windows use the same approach (apart from anything else, they have to do so in order to be POSIX compliant). Drive names like A: on versions of Windows from NT onwards are really just aliases for names in a system folder called \?? which identify the corresponding devices.

Mounting external filesystems in this way leads to some added complications. The root directory is usually a hard disk, which is accessed in a different way from a CD-ROM. Different device drivers within the operating system will need to be used to access the different devices. This is managed by switching from one device driver to another whenever a **mount point** is reached when tracing through the components of a pathname. For example, a search for /mnt/cdrom/dir/foo crosses the mount point /mnt/cdrom, so from this point onwards the filesystem driver specified for the mount point is used to continue the search for the directory dir and then within that directory for the file foo. Linux uses a **virtual filesystem** (VFS) to provide a common interface to whatever filesystem is actually being accessed, so you never need to be aware that you're dealing with what are structurally quite different filesystems at different times. Figure 3.6 illustrates how a system call to open a file on a mounted CD-ROM is routed through the VFS to the correct filesystem for a CD-ROM (the ISO-9660 filesystem) which in turn knows how to talk to the device driver which controls the CD drive to access the required file.

Local disks are usually mounted automatically when the system first starts up, using a file called /etc/fstab to determine what should be mounted where. (The name fstab is short for 'filesystem table'.) Removable devices like floppy disks and CD-ROMs must be mounted before use, and unmounted before they can be removed. The reason why volumes must be unmounted before removal is that the operating system may have 'cached' information due to be written to the volume

open ("/mnt/cdrom/dir/foo", ...)

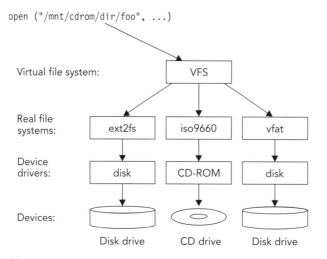

Figure 3.6 Accessing a CD-ROM via the Linux virtual file system.

which it might not actually have got around to writing to the corresponding device yet, so that removing a volume without unmounting it first runs the risk of losing this data. Explicitly unmounting a volume gives the operating system the opportunity to write any cached information onto the volume. A similar thing happens on Windows with removable USB devices and PCMCIA cards that can be unplugged at any time; for safety, you need to 'unmount' the device using the 'Safely Remove Hardware' icon that appears in the taskbar at the bottom of the screen when any such device is connected.

Exercise 3.4   Find out what the Unix command df does.

The Apple Macintosh filesystem uses a slightly different approach. The root directory contains an entry for each mounted volume and is not used for anything else; it is held in memory rather than being stored on a disk. Inserting a removable disk mounts it automatically within the root directory. Ejecting a disk unmounts it automatically before it is physically ejected. Each disk has a **volume label** which acts as a 'filename' for the entire disk. Unix and Windows systems both allow you to read and write volume labels but don't use them to identify disks; they use the name of the corresponding physical drive instead. When you insert a disk into a Macintosh system, an icon appears on the desktop labelled with the name of the corresponding volume. Activating this icon opens a window which lets you browse the contents of the volume.

A Macintosh pathname begins with the volume label, followed by a sequence of pathname components (directory names and filename) separated by colons. For example, the Macintosh equivalent of a Windows file called C:\Temp\File.txt would be System:Temp:File. This assumes that the volume label for drive C: is 'System'.

Also, the Macintosh equivalent of the '.txt' extension (a four-character code indicating the file type) is stored in the file itself rather than being part of the filename. If a name begins with a colon, it is a relative pathname; names which do not begin with a colon are absolute pathnames. There is one exception to this rule: a filename on its own (with no colons to indicate that it is a pathname) is taken to be the relative name of a file in the current directory. There is no equivalent of '.' and '..' in a Macintosh directory, but two or more consecutive colons can be used to go up one or more level in the directory tree, so the Macintosh equivalent of the Unix name ../file would be ::file, and the equivalent of ../../file would be :::file.

3.4 ☐ FILE TYPES

On some older operating systems, different types of files were treated differently. For example, the VMS operating system (one of the ancestors of Windows NT used on the Digital Equipment Corporation's VAX machines) distinguishes between **sequential**, **direct-access** and **indexed** files. Text files are sequential; you can read them as a continuous sequence of characters from beginning to end. Direct-access files are organised as a sequence of fixed-size **records**, but you can go directly to any record by specifying a number giving the position of the record in the file. Indexed files are similar, but they allow you to locate a record using a symbolic **key** rather than a position number; the key is looked up in the file's index and this gives the corresponding position. The filesystem maintains the index automatically as keys are added and deleted; hence the name 'indexed files'.

The problem with this approach is that you can't easily treat one type of file as if it were another. Certain operations (like **seeking** to an arbitrary position within a file) are allowed for certain types of file but not for others. Unix adopts a much simpler approach: a Unix file is simply a sequence of bytes, with no internal structure. Positions within a file are identified by an offset in bytes from the beginning of the file, and you can seek to any position in the file by specifying the byte position as a number of bytes relative to the beginning of the file, the end of the file or the current position. If you want to provide any structure for a file, you have to do it yourself (or use a library of functions that will treat a file as being organised in a particular way). A text file may appear to consist of a number of separate lines, but as far as Unix is concerned it's just a sequence of bytes. If you want to treat the file as consisting of separate lines, you have to use an 'end-of-line' separator character to mark the boundary between one line and the next. If you want to treat the file as a series of fixed-length records, you can calculate the position of a record in the file by multiplying the record number by the record size.

Most modern operating systems now adopt the same approach, with minor variations. For example, Unix systems use the ASCII 'line feed' character as the line separator in a text file; the Apple Macintosh uses the 'carriage return' character for the same purpose, while Windows traditionally uses the two-character sequence 'carriage return, line feed' to do the same thing (although many Windows applications now recognise Unix-style files which just use 'line feed' on its own without a 'carriage return').

Exercise 3.5 Find out how you can use standard Unix commands to translate Windows text files into Unix format and vice versa.

Macintosh files have another unusual feature. Unlike other operating systems, where a file contains a sequence of data items, a Macintosh file is divided into two logically separate parts, a 'data fork' which contains the data content of the file and a 'resource fork' which contains **resources** such as icons, fonts, cursor shapes and executable code. Opening a file in the normal way gives access to the data fork; a separate system call is used to open the resource fork. It is as if every Macintosh file is actually two separate files which are always kept together. A plain text file will typically have an empty resource fork; an executable file will typically have an empty data fork. Word processor documents which use different fonts and images will keep the text of the document in the data fork and the fonts and images in the resource fork. This is quite an interesting idea, but the big disadvantage is that it can make it difficult to transfer files to or from other operating systems which do not subdivide files in this way.

3.4.1 IDENTIFYING FILE TYPES

Although all files are just sequences of bytes, some files are used to hold executable programs while others hold plain text or spreadsheets. There needs to be some way to identify what type of data a file contains. Windows uses an **extension** on the end of a filename to indicate the file type, so for example a text file conventionally ends in '.txt' while an executable program ends in '.exe'. The standard Windows GUI shell allows you to hide the extensions for recognised file types if you want to, since it displays an icon next to the filename for recognised file types. On Apple Macintoshes, a four-character code is used to identify different types of file, but you have to make an effort to get to see this, since icons are normally used to represent the file type visually; for example, text files use the code 'TEXT' while executable programs use the code 'APPL' (short for 'application', not 'Apple'!). On both of these systems, the file type is used to determine which application to use to process the file when its icon is activated using the GUI shell. The operating system maintains a list of file types and the corresponding applications. When you click on a file's icon to activate it, the shell just looks up the file type and starts the corresponding application, passing it the name of the file as a command line argument.

Exercise 3.6 Find out how you can find a list of recognised file types on a Windows system.

On Unix, filenames look much the same as on Windows, but they do not have extensions as such. A file with a name like file.txt is probably a text file, but there is nothing special about the '.txt' suffix; file.txt is just an eight-character name which uses a dot as one of the characters in the name. It is actually just a naming convention rather than a fixed division of the filename into a name and an extension. Multiple 'extensions' are quite common on Unix systems; for example, a file called `file.tar.gz` will normally be a compressed ('gzipped', hence the final '.gz') version of a file called `file.tar`, which in turn will normally be an archive file consisting of a number of files squashed into a single file by a standard utility program called `tar`. There is a standard Unix utility called `file` which will try to identify the type of a file by its name if it can, or by inspecting its contents otherwise.

Unix commands often do different things depending on the name of the file they've been given to process; for example the standard C compiler `cc` (or `gcc`) will compile a file as a C program if it ends in '.c', as an assembly language program if it ends in '.s', or as an object code file to be linked with the other files if it ends in '.o'.

The way in which executable programs are identified varies from system to system. Executable programs on Windows systems have to have one of a number of specific extensions: '.exe', '.com' (a format which is rarely used any more) or '.bat' or '.cmd' (a shell script, or 'batch file'). When you type a command such as `sort`, the shell looks in each of the directories in the current path for files called `sort.com`, `sort.exe`, `sort.bat` and `sort.cmd` (in that order).

Exercise 3.7   Devise an experiment to verify the above assertion. Note that binary executables can use either the '.com' or '.exe' extension, while batch files can use either of '.bat' or '.cmd'.

A Unix program is marked as being executable using one of the **file attributes** (described below) which the system uses to record information about each file. Executable files normally do not have extensions because extensions are not treated specially in Unix filenames; if a program were stored in a file called `sort.exe`, you would have to type in the whole name including the '.exe' part if you wanted to execute it. For this reason, the Unix sorting utility is stored in a file which is just called `sort` but whose directory entry marks it as an executable program. When you try to run a file as a program, the program loader looks at the first few bytes of the file for a 'magic number' which identifies it as a binary image ready to be loaded into memory, or failing that, if the first two bytes are '#!' (pronounced 'shebang' by Unix literati), the loader treats it as a script file and uses the rest of the first line of the file as the pathname of the executable which should be used to process it. For example, a shell script might start with a 'shebang line' like this:

```
#!/bin/sh
```

meaning that the file should be processed by the program /bin/sh, whereas a file containing a Perl script might start like this:

```
#!/usr/bin/perl
```

which means that the file should be processed by the program /usr/bin/perl. This means that a script file can specify the program that should be used to process it, giving the same sort of capabilities as the Windows approach of associating particular file extensions with the program that should be used to process them, but without the need for a particular extension as part of the name of a script.

Exercise 3.8   Find out what happens if you write a shell script which specifies /bin/rm on the shebang line.

3.5 ❑ FILENAMES

There are usually limitations on the names that can be given to files. It's generally safe to stick to alphanumeric characters (A to Z, a to z, 0 to 9) and a handful of 'safe' punctuation characters: underlines ('_'), hyphens ('-') and dots ('.'). Many other characters are not allowed (or best avoided); for example, on Unix systems the path separator character '/' cannot be used, and other characters like '*' should be avoided because they are treated specially by the shell. Unix (and Windows) shells treat '*' as meaning 'all files', and allow file specifications like 'a*' which will be expanded into a list of all files whose names begin with 'a'. If you had a file called '*', the worst thing you could do would be to try to delete it using this command:

```
rm *
```

because the shell would interpret this as meaning 'remove all files', since the pattern '*' would be expanded to a list of all the filenames in the directory. The file called '*' would certainly be deleted, but so would everything else! You can get around this on Unix by putting '*' in quotes:

```
rm '*'
```

Windows avoids this problem by not allowing the use of special characters like '*' in filenames.

Similarly, both Unix and Windows allow spaces within filenames, but this can cause problems since spaces are also used to separate parameters on a command line; if you wanted to sort the contents of a file called 'My file', this would not work:

```
sort My file
```

This would try to sort two separate files called 'My' and 'file', and you'd need to write this instead:

```
sort "My file"
```

Quite a few programs don't handle names with spaces in correctly, so it's generally a bad idea to use spaces in filenames. Interestingly enough, the standard Windows directory for programs is called 'Program files', a name with a space in it, and I've come across quite a few applications that won't work if you try installing them in this directory. This includes offerings from some of the best-known software publishers in the business!

The maximum length of filenames can also be a problem. MS-DOS allowed a maximum of eight characters, plus a three-character extension, and was case-insensitive (lower-case letters were translated into their upper-case equivalents). This made it difficult to give names to files which adequately described their contents. Early Unix systems had a limit of 14 characters, including any 'extension', and this also proved much too restrictive. They were case-sensitive, so 'File' and 'file' would be treated as two completely different names. Most modern Unix systems generally allow names to be up to at least 255 characters long, which allows much more descriptive names. It makes things a bit more difficult if you have to type in the whole of a long name, but usually you either select files using a graphical interface or using the 'file completion' feature of most Unix shells, where you type the first few characters of a filename and then press the 'tab' key to get the shell to display the rest of the name.

Like Unix, Windows also allows much longer names than its predecessor MS-DOS. Windows allows up to 255 characters in a filename, subject to an overall maximum of 260 characters in a complete pathname. Filenames are case-insensitive, but case-preserving (they are stored using their original case); you can create a file called 'File' and it will always be displayed like this, but to reference it you could say 'File' or 'file' or 'FILE'.

Exercise 3.9   Devise an experiment to find the maximum length of a filename on the system you're using, and also which characters you can use without any problems arising.

3.6 ☐ FILE VERSIONS

When you edit a file on some systems, saving the file replaces the original version of the file. A program which edits a file can open the file, read it into memory where it can be edited, and then close it. To save the edited version of the file the program can open the file for writing and write the new version of the file into it, over-writing the previous contents. The big problem with this is that if the system crashes you might lose the new version of the file, and since the original version has been overwritten you would lose that as well. This is obviously not something you would expect to happen very often, but even if it only ever happens to you once you will be seriously annoyed when it does.

A better solution is to rename the original file before saving the new version. For example, a common approach is to append '.bak' (short for 'backup') to the name of the file, so a file called file.txt would be renamed to file.txt.bak. Renaming a file is a very quick operation that either succeeds or fails; it won't leave things in some intermediate inconsistent state, as would be the case if only part of a file was written when the system suddenly crashed. The program can then save the new version of the file using the original name. This also has the advantage that if you discover you've made a mistake and you want to revert to the original version of the file, you just have to delete the new version of the file and rename the backup copy to give it back its original name.

Project 3.1   Write a Unix shell script to make backup copies of all the files in a directory, where the backup copies have '.bak' appended to the name of the original file.

The filesystem used by VMS goes one better than this; it includes a version number in every filename, separated from the rest of the filename by a semicolon (for example, 'file.txt;4' would be version 4 of the file 'file.txt'). When referring to a file you can omit the version number, in which case the most recent version number will be assumed. When a file is opened for writing where a file of the same name already exists but no version number is specified, a new version of the file will be created with a version number one higher than the highest existing version number. This ensures that existing files will never be overwritten, and you can keep as many old versions of a file as you want.

3.7 ❑ LINKS AND SHORTCUTS

It is quite often useful to be able to refer to a file by more than one name. For example, if directories are used to categorise files, a file that belongs in both categories should logically go in both directories. For example, if I have a file that I use on more than one of the courses that I teach (each of which has its own directory) I would want it to appear in each of the corresponding course directories. Copying the file is one solution, but it wastes space, and if one copy of the file is modified it will have no effect on the other copy; I'd have to make sure I copied the new version of the file into all the directories which contained copies of the original version.

Unix filesystems access files using a small data structure called an **inode** ('information node') which is stored on the same volume as the file and the directory entries which refer to the file. A directory entry refers to a particular inode which in turn leads to the data which the file contains. This extra level of indirection means that you can have multiple directory entries (known as **links**) which all refer to the same inode, and hence to the same file.

If a file is modified using one link, all subsequent references to the same file using different links will see the new version of the file after the modifications have been made. The filesystem needs to keep track of how many different links refer to each inode so that when deleting a file, the file itself is only deleted when the last link to it is deleted. This information is stored in the inode itself; in Figure 3.7 the inode records that there are two directory entries which refer to it. Operations like moving a file to a different directory are easy; all you have to do is create a new link to the file in the destination directory and then delete the original link from the source directory.

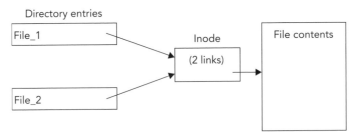

Figure 3.7 Unix directory entries sharing an inode for a file.

Exercise 3.10   Find out how to determine how many links there are to a particular file.

One shortcoming of this system is that links can only be made to files on the same volume as the directory in which the link is to be stored, since each volume has its own inode table, and a directory entry contains an inode number which will be interpreted as an inode on that volume. This means that you can't move a file to a different volume by relinking the inode as described above; the mv (move) command has to copy the file and then delete it.

Most modern versions of Unix also provide **soft links** (or **symbolic links**) which can be used to link to files on different volumes. A soft link is implemented as a file which contains the name of the file being linked to, and a special attribute bit in the inode identifies the file as being a soft link, as shown in Figure 3.8. Opening a soft link results in the file that it links to being opened. However, unlike a normal (**hard**) link, the file being linked to does not keep track of how many links there are. Deleting or renaming the original file will render any soft links to it unusable.

Windows provides a similar facility called a **shortcut**. A shortcut is similar to a Unix soft link, except that a shortcut file contains more than just a filename; it also contains certain file attributes such as the icon to be displayed when the shortcut is displayed. Activating a shortcut, typically by double-clicking on a shortcut icon

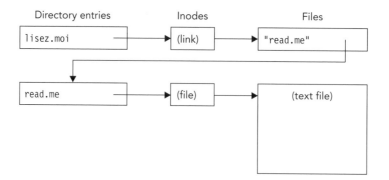

Figure 3.8 A soft (symbolic) link.

displayed on the system desktop or selecting a shortcut from the desktop's 'start' menu, will activate the corresponding application. However, using the name of a shortcut as the name of a file to be opened by an application will not open the file that the shortcut points to, as it would do with a Unix soft link. Instead, it will open the file that contains the shortcut information (a file with a '.lnk' extension). So although there are similarities, shortcuts and soft links are not exact equivalents.

3.8 ☐ FILE LOCKING

It is perfectly possible for more than one process at a time to want to access the same file. If all the processes just want to read the file, there is no problem. However, if any process wants to write to the file, it is generally unsafe to allow any other process to open the file at the same time. On Unix systems, a process can use the flock ('file lock') system call to lock the file against any other processes. If another process attempts to open a locked file, the open system call will just report a 'sharing violation' error. On Windows, the OpenFile system call allows a variety of possible sharing options:

- OF_SHARE_EXCLUSIVE: lock the file so that no other process can open it.
- OF_SHARE_DENY_WRITE: lock the file so that other processes cannot open the file for writing
- OF_SHARE_DENY_READ: lock the file so that other processes cannot open it for reading
- OF_SHARE_COMPAT: do not lock the file.

Apart from read and write access, some systems allow files to be opened for **append access**. This allows the file to be written to, but only by appending to the end of the file. It is possible to allow multiple processes to append information to the same file without conflicts; it is also possible to allow processes to read a file while other processes are appending to it. The Unix tail command displays the last few lines of a file, and it has a -f ('follow') option that will cause it to wait when it reaches the end of the file until something new is appended to it, at which point it will display what has just been added to the file. This can be useful for displaying log files to which new log entries are being added all the time.

Locking an entire file can be wasteful, so some systems support **record locking**, where individual records within the file can be locked, allowing other processes to access the rest of the file. This is usually only possible on systems like VMS where the filesystem treats files as being divided into separate records, rather than just as an amorphous stream of bytes.

3.9 ❑ FILE ATTRIBUTES

Different filesystems differ widely in the information that they store about each file. As a minimum, the directory entry for a file needs to contain the filename and information about its physical location on the disk. The directory entry (or the inode, on a Unix filesystem) can also be used to store a variety of other useful but not strictly essential information about the file. Typical information includes:

- **Timestamps.** This will typically be the date and time when the file was last modified, but it might also include the time of the last access and the date when the file was originally created.

- **Ownership.** Multi-user systems need to record which of the system's multiple users is the owner of the file. On Unix systems there is also a separate 'group ownership'; each user belongs to one or more groups, and each file is associated with one of those groups as well as with the individual user.

- **File size.** The file is unlikely to be an exact number of disk blocks in size, so it is necessary to record the size of the file in bytes so that the filesystem can tell how much of the last disk block is meaningful. Alternatively, you could store the number of blocks together with the number of bytes in the last block, but it would not save much space and would make calculating the file size that much more complicated, so it's actually easier to store the total number of bytes.

- **File type.** Files can usually be categorised as normal files or directories. Unix systems also allow files to be categorised as **soft links**, **character devices** or **block devices**; the VMS operating system also distinguishes between sequential, direct access and indexed files.

- **Access permissions.** On multi-user systems it is necessary to provide a mechanism which allows files to be kept private and to specify how they can be accessed by different users. The permissions that can be granted to an individual user might include permission to read, write, execute, delete or append to the file; which permissions are available varies from one system to another.

Exercise 3.11   Find out what file attributes are supported by the system you are using.

In general, a single file might need different access permissions for different users. On some systems, such as Unix and VMS, users belong to one or more groups such as 'staff' or 'admin'. Each file has an owner and a group, and it also has a separate set of access permissions for its owner, for users in the same group as the file, and for everybody else. On other systems, such as the Windows NTFS filesystem and later versions of the VMS filesystem, the directory entry contains a reference to an **access control list** (ACL) which lists permissions granted to individual users or groups of users, allowing access to be controlled on a per-user basis if necessary.

There are many other possibilities for file attributes. The filesystem might also store a version number as VMS does, or a password which is needed to access the file.

3.10 ❑ DISK STRUCTURE

Most storage devices (including disks and CDs) store information as a set of fixed-size blocks. A filesystem needs to keep track of which blocks are free and which are in use at any time, and to lay out the tree-structured hierarchy of named files onto the physical blocks of storage provided by the device in such a way that files can be accessed efficiently.

On any device, it is generally faster to access the next block in sequence than it is to skip to another block elsewhere in the sequence, so files should be stored sequentially if at all possible for the fastest access. For example, CDs and DVDs are basically sequential devices; the data is recorded as a series of 2K blocks on a continuous spiral which starts at the centre of the disk and spirals out towards the edge. In most cases, they are read-only devices; once the data has been written to the disk it cannot be changed. This makes it easy to arrange files sequentially; each file is written in turn, one after another along the length of the spiral.

Although you can skip to a particular position on the spiral by moving across the spiral rather than along it, this takes a relatively long time to do; you have to calculate an approximate position, moving across the spiral to that position, and then check to see whether you're in the right place. You can then make a better positional calculation and repeat the process, so you will end up 'homing in' on the correct position using a series of smaller and smaller adjustments. This is why music CD players make the noise they do when you skip to a different track; the buzzing noise you hear is the sound of the read head being moved as it searches for the start of the new track.

Disks are generally treated as direct access devices, which means that any block can be accessed directly and can be read or written to individually. This gives much greater freedom in how files are laid out on the disk. There is a slight speed penalty if files are not stored sequentially, but it's generally not too noticeable. For example, a 1.44 MB (MB = megabyte) floppy disk has two sides, each of which has 80 concentric circular **tracks**. Each track is divided into 18 sectors of 512 bytes each, for a grand total of 1440 KB. This is illustrated in Figure 3.9, which shows how each side of a floppy disk is divided into tracks and sectors.

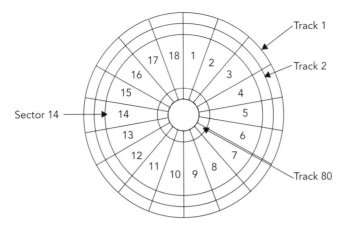

Figure 3.9 Physical structure of one side of a floppy disk.

A floppy disk drive has two **read/write heads** (one on each side of the disk) which move together across the disk surface to the correct track. The time that it takes to do this is known as the **seek time**. The disk rotates at a constant speed, so once you have positioned the head over the correct track, you have to wait for the correct sector to come past as the disk rotates. The time that this takes is known as the **latency**. Floppy disks rotate at 300 rpm, or one revolution every 200 ms, so the average latency will be half this (about 100 ms). The time it takes to read a sector will be the time it takes for the sector to go past the read head, which will be about 11 ms. The same applies to hard disks, except that they are about 15 to 20 times faster than floppy disks, with a typical rotation speed of 5400 rpm or 7200 rpm. They generally consist of multiple platters rotating together on a common spindle, so there are usually more than two surfaces each with its own read/write head. The heads all move together as a single unit since they are all driven by the same motor. A set of corresponding tracks on different surfaces of a hard disk is generally referred to as a **cylinder**.

The average access time to any part of a disk is a combination of seek time and latency. To minimise access time, it makes sense to allocate sectors within a single cylinder where possible (so that the heads don't need to be moved) and then to continue with the next cylinder (which minimises the seek time by moving the heads as little as possible), and so on.

Since you cannot predict where the heads will be when you try to access a disk, you can expect the access time to be roughly average no matter where on the disk you are trying to access. Files do not have to be allocated sequentially, as with a CD. The time taken to access any part of the file will be pretty much constant, being around the average access time. If you are reading a file sequentially it makes sense to try to optimise things by storing the blocks that it uses close together, but even if you can't the penalty is normally not too noticeable since other processes will probably be moving the heads back and forth to access other files in between your accesses, so storing the blocks of a file close together may not make much difference if other processes are using the same disk at the same time. An existing file can be expanded in size by allocating a few more blocks to it, and it doesn't matter very much where those blocks are located.

When files are deleted, the blocks they occupy can be reused by any file that needs them. Depending on the pattern of allocation, this can lead to disks becoming **fragmented** as the data becomes distributed less and less sequentially and more and more randomly, which will eventually lead to noticeable delays in accessing files, even when there are no other processes to interfere. Some filesystems are better than others at avoiding fragmentation due to the way that blocks are allocated for use by files, but where fragmentation becomes a problem you can use a **defragmentation** utility program to rearrange the disk blocks into a more efficient order, as illustrated in Figure 3.10.

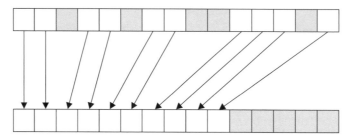

Figure 3.10 Defragmentation.

The filesystem normally treats a volume as a numbered sequence of fixed-size blocks, so that each block can by accessed by specifying its block number. The size of the blocks used by the filesystem may not be the same as the physical blocks on the storage device, and a volume need not correspond exactly to a physical storage device. For example, a disk might be physically divided into 512 byte sectors, and be addressed using a combination of cylinder, head and sector numbers, but the filesystem might regard the same disk as constituting two separate volumes, one of which has a block size of 1 KB and the other of which has a block size of 8 KB, where each volume is a continuous sequence of blocks numbered from zero upwards. When the filesystem wants to access a particular block on a particular volume, the disk driver within the kernel has to translate the volume and block number into a corresponding head, cylinder and sector number. The filesystem itself does not have to worry about this level of detail.

Space is allocated on the volume a block at a time. On average, half of the last block of every file will be wasted, so the block size is generally a compromise between having many small blocks, which waste less space but require more blocks to store large files, and fewer large blocks, which waste more space but require fewer blocks for large files. There is also an overhead involved in keeping track of which blocks are in use and which are free, which is greater where many small blocks are used than when a few large blocks are used.

3.11 ❑ BACKUP SYSTEMS

Because disks are mechanical devices they are one of the most failure-prone parts of any system. If anything does go wrong, having an up-to-date backup copy of all your data will be a lifesaver. One of the difficulties of making backup is the sheer size of modern disks compared with the sizes of removable media which can be used for making backups. For example, hard disks can be upwards of 100 GB (GB = gigabyte) in size; by comparison, CD-ROMs store only 700 MB and DVD-ROMs only 4.7 GB. This means using about 150 CDs or 22 DVDs to make a complete backup of 100 GB of data. Alternatively, another hard disk of similar size, either on the same machine or (preferably) on a remote machine can be used, but this is relatively expensive and makes it difficult to remove the backup for storage. Using magnetic tape is the commonest solution; this is a high-capacity removable medium which is relatively cheap.

The other problem is the amount of time it will take to copy the contents of a 100 GB disk. Of course, a 100 GB disk will not normally be completely full, so the problem is not as bad as it might seem at first sight. Also, many files remain unchanged over long periods of time (application programs, for example) while others are purely temporary files that should not be backed up. Most systems use a specific directory for temporary files (traditionally called '/tmp' on Unix systems), so this entire directory can be excluded when making backups.

To cut the problem down still further, it is possible to perform **incremental backups**, where only the files that have changed since the last complete backup need to be copied. Incremental backups are very much smaller than full backups, and can easily be performed on a daily basis, if not an hourly basis. A backup utility just needs to be given a list of files and directories to exclude from a backup, and it can then trace through the filesystem making backup copies of any files which have been modified since the last backup. This can be done entirely on the local machine, or it can be done remotely across a network by a separate **backup server**.

Incremental backups are not a complete solution. If anything does go wrong, you will have to restore the system from the last full backup, and then restore all the incremental backups made since the full backup was made. It is therefore advisable to make a full backup at weekly or monthly intervals, depending on the needs of the system, with incremental backups in between. Full backups take quite a long time, so most organisations do them late at night at weekends when the system is least busy.

Backups are also subject to failure. If anything does go wrong and you need to restore a backup, the last thing you want to discover is that the tape you used is unreadable. Keeping at least three recent backups is advisable, and it is also advisable to check backup tapes every so often to make sure that they are being written correctly. Ignoring backups until you need them is a bad idea; it's much better to discover that your backup system is going wrong *before* your disk fails, since at least then you can fix it and make a new backup.

3.12 ❑ EXAMPLE FILESYSTEMS

As an illustration of some of the different approaches to filesystem design, this section describes a few of the filesystems in common use. These are:

- **FAT**, the File Allocation Table system used by MS-DOS and extended by Windows, and still commonly used on floppy disks and other removable media such as Zip drives and USB memory devices.
- **Ext2fs**, the Second Extended File System for Linux, which is still the current standard on Linux systems.
- **NTFS**, the NT File System, available on Windows NT and later versions of Windows.

3.12.1 FAT

MS-DOS and early versions of Windows use a filesystem known as FAT (which stands for 'File Allocation Table'), which was originally designed for use with floppy disks. It is still commonly used for floppy disks, and is a 'lowest common denominator' format that most operating systems can cope with.

Directory entries are 32 bytes in length, laid out as shown in Figure 3.11. The first byte of the directory entry is used to indicate whether or not the directory entry is in use. A value of 0 indicates an entry that has never been used; 0xE5 (that is, the hexadecimal value E5, following the convention used in C, C++ and Java of a '0x' prefix to indicate a hexadecimal value) is an entry for a file that has been deleted. Any other value indicates that the entry is in use, in which case the value is the first character of the filename. To delete a file, the first byte of the directory entry is set

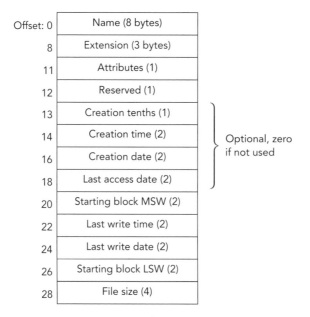

Figure 3.11 Structure of a FAT directory entry.

to 0xE5, but the blocks making up the file are not necessarily released immediately. This means that it is sometimes possible to restore a file which has been deleted accidentally by resetting the first character of the filename in the directory entry, provided that its directory entry has not been reused. To create an entry for a new file, the directory is searched for an entry with a value of either 0 or 0xE5. If the value is 0xE5, the blocks allocated to the file that was deleted are also freed if they have not been freed already.

The file attribute byte contains four bits which specify attributes of the file:

- **Read only:** if set, the file cannot be opened for writing. It also prevents it from being deleted.

- **Archive:** set whenever the file is modified. Backup utilities can use this bit to identify recently modified files, and reset it after a backup copy of the file has been made. This means that you do not need to record the date and time of the last backup.

- **Hidden:** if set, the file is excluded from directory searches (e.g. directory listings).

- **System:** if set, the file is a system file. Like hidden files, system files are ignored when searching the directory.

Two more bits specify whether the entry is for a normal file, a directory, or a 'volume label' (not really a file, just a name for the disk itself). There can only be one volume label per disk, and it can only appear in the root directory.

Dates and times are each held as 16-bit values. A 16-bit value has 65,536 possible values, but there are 86,400 seconds in a day, so times are only accurate to the nearest two seconds. The date requires five bits for the day (1 to 31) and four bits for the month (1 to 12), leaving seven bits for the year. The year is taken relative to 1980, and so will reach its maximum value in 2107. The creation time is optional, and was not supported in FAT versions prior to Windows 95. An extra byte is used to divide the two-second resolution of the creation time to give a value accurate to a tenth of a second. The last access date is also optional. Note that this only gives a date, not a date and time. The only values that are guaranteed to be always used are the date and time when the file was last written to, which is only accurate to the nearest two seconds. This date and time will also be set when the file is created.

As the name suggests, the space on the disk is managed using a File Allocation Table (FAT) which is used to keep track of which blocks on the disk belong to which files, and which blocks are free. There are three different varieties of FAT filesystem, known as FAT12, FAT16 and FAT32. FAT32 was introduced with Windows 95, and is supported by all subsequent versions of Windows except for Windows NT. The numbers refer to the size in bits of the entries in the FAT. The description below is for a FAT32 filesystem, where each FAT entry is 32 bits in size; the other varieties work in exactly the same way, except for the number of bits in the FAT entries.

The number of bits in a FAT entry limits the maximum number of blocks that the disk can hold; FAT12 allows 2^{12} (4,096) blocks, FAT16 allows 2^{16} (65,536) blocks, and FAT32 allows 2^{32} blocks. The number of the first block of the file is held as a 32-bit value; the first 16 bits will always be zero in FAT12 or FAT16 filesystems. FAT12

Table 3.1 Disk block sizes in FAT file systems.

Block size	Maximum disk size	
	FAT16	FAT32
512	32 MB	260 MB
1 kbyte	64 MB	–
2 kbyte	128 MB	–
4 kbyte	256 MB	8 GB
8 kbyte	512 MB	16 GB
16 kbyte	–	32 GB
32 kbyte	–	>32 GB

is only used on floppy disks, and FAT16 is only used for disks less than 512 MB in size. Table 3.1 shows the maximum disk size based on various block sizes from 512 bytes (one disk sector) up to the maximum possible block size of 32 KB. Note that FAT32 does not use block sizes of 1 KB or 2 KB.

FAT was intended for use by MS-DOS, which only allowed filenames of up to eight characters with a three-character extension. Support for 'long filenames' of up to 255 characters was introduced with Windows 95, using 16-bit Unicode characters and allowing additional characters such as spaces in filenames. This is implemented by giving each file a short MS-DOS-compatible filename (eight characters with a three-character extension) which is derived from the long filename. For example, the standard Windows directory 'Program Files' can also be referred to using the short filename 'PROGRA~1' (which is useful to know for working around problems with programs that can't cope with filenames containing spaces!). The command DIR (or DIR /X on more recent versions of Windows) displays the short version of each name in a directory in addition to the long name.

Exercise 3.12   Find out which directories on a FAT filesystem have different long and short names and verify that they can both be used to refer to the same file.

The entry for the short filename is preceded by one or more directory entries which have an invalid set of file attributes declaring them to be read-only hidden system files which are also volume labels and also have an invalid starting block number of zero. The first byte is used as a sequence number and another 26 bytes of the directory entry are used to encode 13 characters of the filename. The entries are stored in reverse order, and the final entry (the first one in the directory, since they appear in reverse order) has the value 0x40 added to its sequence number. The 22-

character name 'Documents and Settings' (another standard Windows directory) will therefore take up three directory entries; one for the short form of the name (DOCUME~1) preceded by two additional entries, the second of which contains the first 13 characters of the long filename and a sequence number of 1 and the first of which contains the remaining nine characters and a sequence number of 0x42. A null character (0x0000) marks the end of the name, and any remaining characters are set to 0xFFFF. This is illustrated in Figure 3.12.

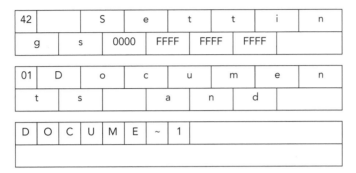

Figure 3.12 FAT directory entries for a long filename.

At the beginning of the disk there is a reserved area which contains a number of important disk parameters, including the number of bytes per sector, the number of sectors per logical block, the size of the FAT, the **bootstrap** (a short program in the very first disk sector that will be executed if the machine is booted from this disk, which will load the operating system if it is a system disk, or which will display an error message if it isn't), and the size of the root directory.

The FAT is a fixed-size area located immediately after the reserved area at the beginning of the disk. There is one entry in the FAT for each block on the disk. If the value of the entry is zero, the block is not in use. Otherwise, with the exception of a few other special values (0xFFFFFFF0 to 0xFFFFFFFF, the hexadecimal equivalents of the signed decimal values –1 to –16), the entry indicates that the corresponding block is part of a file, and the value of the entry is the number of the next block in the same file. The entry for the last block in the file has a value between 0xFFFFFFF8 and 0xFFFFFFFF. The values 0xFFFFFFF0 to 0xFFFFFFF6 are used to indicate a block that has been reserved for some purpose, while 0xFFFFFFF7 indicates a 'bad block' which cannot be read or written reliably.

Figure 3.13 illustrates how this works. A file consists of four blocks, and the directory entry for the file gives block 10 as the first block of the file. The entry corresponding to block 10 in the FAT gives the number of the second block as 12, and entry 12 gives the third block as 15. Entry 15 gives the number of the fourth block as 13, and entry 13 contains the value –1 (0xFFFFFFFF), indicating that this is the last block of the file. The file therefore can be seen to occupy blocks 10, 12, 15 and 13 respectively. When a new block needs to be allocated to expand a file, the FAT is searched for an entry whose value is 0 and the corresponding block is allocated to the file by setting the FAT entry for the last block (13 in the example above) to the number of the newly allocated block.

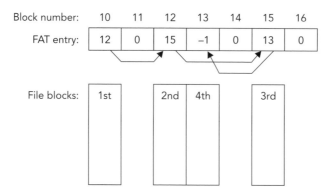

Figure 3.13 How the file allocation table links the blocks in a file.

The root directory follows the FAT. It is slightly different from other directories in that the first two entries in all directories except the root directory are '.' (the current directory) and '..' (the parent directory). This means that you cannot use a name which refers to the current directory when the current directory is the root directory, which is an inconsistency that occasionally causes problems; shell scripts which use '.' to refer to the current directory will work anywhere except the root directory, Also, on FAT12 and FAT16 filesystems the size of the root directory is a fixed value specified in the reserved area at the beginning of the disk, so it cannot grow beyond this size and can therefore only hold a limited number of entries (typically about 64 or 128).

When a new file is created, an unused directory entry is searched for. This is one whose first byte is 00, meaning that it has never been used, or 0xE5, meaning it corresponds to a file which has been deleted. An extra disk block is added to expand the directory if there are no free entries and filled with zeros to initialise the entries it will contain.

At some point after a file has been deleted, the blocks that were allocated to the file are freed. This can happen at any time after the file has been deleted up to the time that the directory entry gets reused. The blocks are freed by tracing through the chain of entries in the FAT, starting from the entry for the first block (specified in the directory entry) and continuing until the entry for the last block is reached (a value between 0xFFFFFFF8 and 0xFFFFFFFF), setting each entry in turn to 0. The contents of the blocks themselves are not altered, so the data making up the file will still be on the disk until the blocks get reused. This means that there will still be a chance to recover a deleted file, at least partially. However, the only way to do this will be to trace through the list of unused blocks (the blocks with a FAT entry of 0) looking for blocks whose contents look like they might be part of the missing file. This is a long shot, but it can yield results when there is no other hope.

One of the major problems with FAT filesystems is that all the information about the layout of the files on the disk is held in the FAT, which only occupies a few sectors at the start of the disk. For the sake of reliability, there can be more than one copy of the FAT on the disk. Whenever the FAT is changed, all copies of the FAT are updated. If one copy gets corrupted, another copy can be used instead. However, only the first copy of the FAT is ever used; if this copy fails, an external utility program must be used to access another copy of the FAT to recover the files from the disk.

Since the FAT filesystem was originally developed for use with floppy disks, it lacks many of the features that more sophisticated filesystems provide. It has no concept of the 'owner' of a file, so there is nothing to prevent anyone accessing any of the files on a disk. For this reason, it is generally unsuitable for use on machines which might be used by more than one person.

Project 3.2

Design a defragmentation utility for a FAT filesystem which will always leave the filesystem in a consistent state even if the system crashes midway through its operation. Assume that writing a disk block will either succeed or will not write any data to the disk (that is, assume that it is impossible to write partial disk blocks where some of the data has been written successfully and the rest of the block is corrupted). In what order do the individual operations on the disk need to be performed?

3.12.2 EXT2FS

The Second Extended File System (ext2fs) is currently the standard filesystem used by most Linux systems. As the name implies, it is based on the original Unix filesystem design. The size of the disk blocks can vary, but are typically 1 KB in size. I will assume that this is the case in the following description.

Like any filesystem, an ext2fs volume begins with a boot sector (since this is a requirement of the hardware to allow an operating system to be loaded from the disk when the machine is first switched on). It is then followed by a number of **block groups**, each of which has the same format. The original Unix filesystem in effect used the whole volume as a single block group; the use of multiple block groups in ext2fs increases efficiency by keeping related data close together and also increases reliability by duplicating critical data in each of the block groups. Wherever possible, entire files and the information about them are allocated space in the same block group.

Unlike most other filesystems, Unix filesystems store most of the information about a file in a structure called an **inode**. The inode contains information about the file type (directory, normal file, soft link and so on), access permissions, date and times of last access and last modification, ownership information and various other details. A directory entry only holds the name of the file and the number of the corresponding inode. Filenames on the ext2fs filesystem can be up to 255 characters long, so for the sake of efficiency a directory consists of a series of variable-length records containing the inode number, the length of the filename and the filename itself.

Each block group begins with a **superblock** containing administrative information for the disk. This includes the number of inodes and data blocks in the block group, the number of free inodes, the disk block size and so on.

The superblock is followed by a **block bitmap** and an **inode bitmap**, which each contain a single bit for each data block or inode to indicate whether or not the corresponding item is in use. This is followed by the **inode table**, which is a series of disk blocks containing the inodes themselves. Each inode is only 128 bytes in size so several inodes can be fitted into a single disk block (8 inodes in each 1 KB block). The remainder of the blocks in the block group are used for file storage. The structure of an ext2fs disk is shown in Figure 3.14.

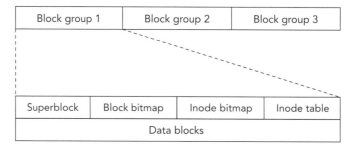

Figure 3.14 Layout of an ext2fs disk.

Since Unix was designed as a multi-user system, where different people would be able to use the same machine, a more elaborate set of access permissions is used than for the FAT filesystem. The entry describing a file specifies the user who owns the file, as well as the name of a 'group' which owns the file. Each user can belong to one or more groups, and there are separate sets of permissions for the user (owner), group and others (anyone who isn't the owner or a member of the file's group). Each set of permissions specifies whether or not the file can be read, written or executed as a program. You can see the access permissions as well as various other file attributes by using the '-l' option for the ls command, as in the following sample:

```
drwxr-xr-x  2 je   wheel      4096 Aug 30 2001 bin
-rw-rw-r--  1 je   wheel    687670 Sep  5 2001 docs.zip
lrwxrwxrwx  1 je   wheel        11 Mar 28 2001 httpd -> /home/httpd/
```

The output consists of a 10-character **permissions field** followed by the number of links to the file, the owner and group names, the file size in bytes, the date of last modification and the filename.

The first column of the permissions field specifies the file type. Most files are either normal files (-), directories (d) or soft links (l); the next three columns give the owner's permissions (rwx means 'read, write and execute access are allowed'; if any character is replaced by a hyphen, this means that the corresponding access is not allowed). The next three give the permissions granted to anyone in the group that owns the file, and the next three give the permissions granted to anyone else.

Thus in the example above, bin is a directory, docs.zip is a normal file and httpd is a soft link to the directory /home/httpd. The file docs.zip can be read and written by the owner (je) or anyone in the group wheel. Everyone else has read-only access.

Exercise 3.13   Find out how to change the permissions for a file on a Unix filesystem, and how to change the default permissions that are used when a new file is created.

The 'execute' permission has a number of different interpretations in Unix systems. For a normal file it means that the file can be executed as a program. If a directory has execute permission for a particular category of users, it means that those users can access files within the directory, but unless they also have read access, they cannot read the directory to discover what files it contains. This means that if you have 'execute' access to a directory but no 'read' access, you can only access files whose names you already know. You also need write access to the directory to change its contents, which means you can't delete a file unless you have write access to the directory which contains its filename as well as write access to the file itself.

Another variation on the execute permission is to specify that an executable file has the 'setuid' or 'setgid' properties. A 'setuid' program can normally be executed by anyone, but while it is executing the effective user identification (the 'uid') is set to be that of the owner of a file. This means that the program can access files that are only accessible to the user who owns the file containing the program. For example, web servers can run programs known as **CGI scripts** on behalf of remote clients; the output from a CGI script is delivered back to the browser that accessed it. These programs are normally executed by a user called 'nobody' who has very limited access to the system for security reasons. The problem is, what if the program needs to write a message to a log file which is not accessible to the user 'nobody'? One approach would be to make all such log files writable by anyone, but this is a potential security risk. The best solution on a Unix system is to make the CGI script a 'setuid' program, so that it runs with the same privileges as its owner would have and can write to files that the program's owner would be able to write to. A 'setgid' program is similar except that only the group identity is altered, so that the program is executed as if by someone belonging to the same group as the group which owns the program file. If a file has the 'setuid' property, the directory listing shows the letter 's' instead of 'x' for the execute permission setting in the owner's permissions. Similarly, a file with the 'setgid' property has 's' instead of 'x' in the group's permissions.

Inodes are also used to hold information about the location of the blocks making up the file. Each inode contains 15 data block numbers; the first 12 of these give the numbers of the first 12 blocks in a file, so small files of up to 12 blocks (12 KB) in size are handled efficiently. The 13th entry is the number of a **single indirect** block containing the numbers of any additional data blocks. This allows for an extra 256 blocks to be identified at the cost of one extra disk access, allowing the file to grow another 256 KB before anything else needs to be done.

To deal with yet larger files, once the single indirect block is full (when the file is just over 256 KB in size) the 14th block number in the inode is used to point to a **double indirect** block. This contains the addresses of up to 256 additional single indirect blocks, each of which can refer to 256 data blocks, so the file can now expand by 256×256 blocks, or another 64 MB. And if this is not enough, the final block number in the inode can be used to point to a **triple indirect** block which can refer to up to 256 further double indirect blocks, each of which can refer to up to 256 additional single indirect blocks, each of which can refer to 256 data blocks. This gives up to 256×256×256 further data blocks, or a further 16 GB. This is illustrated in Figure 3.15, although for clarity the triple indirect blocks are not shown. Using larger block sizes can increase the maximum possible file size still further; a block size of 4 KB allows for files up to 4 Tbyte in size, or 4096 GB. However, the file position is normally represented as a 32-bit number, limiting the maximum practicable file size to 4 GB, although this is likely to change in future versions.

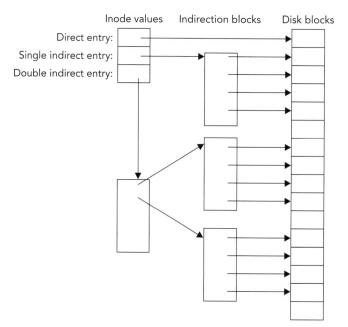

Figure 3.15 How an inode references its data blocks.

Exercise 3.14   Find a way to discover the maximum size of a file on the system you're using.

On Unix systems, devices like disks and modems appear as files whose directory entries are conventionally stored in a directory called /dev. If the file type (the first column of the output from ls -l) is the letter c, this indicates a character-oriented device like a modem, and if it is the letter b it indicates a block-oriented device like a disk. Each such device is identified by a **major device number** and a **minor device number**, which appear in the directory listing in place of the file size. Here are some examples of output from the command ls -l /dev:

```
crw-------    1 root     root      5,  64 May 10  2001 cua0
brw-rw----    1 root     disk      3,   0 May  5  1998 hda
brw-rw----    1 root     disk      3,   1 May  5  1998 hda1
crw-rw-rw-    1 root     root      1,   5 May  5  1998 zero
```

The files cua0 and zero are both character devices; cua0 is only readable and writable by the system administrator (the user root), whereas zero is readable and writable by everyone. The files hda and hda1 are both block devices; hda is the first hard disk, and hda1 is the first partition on the disk. They share the same major device number (3), but the minor device numbers differ (0 and 1 respectively). Both devices are readable and writable by the system administrator (root) or anyone belonging to the disk group.

Exercise 3.15   Describe the internal steps which must be performed to access the 50th data block of a file using each of the FAT and ext2fs filesystems, assuming that there is no information about the file in memory apart from the inode or directory entry.

3.12.3   NTFS

The NT File System (NTFS) was, as its name implies, introduced in Windows NT and is also supported by later versions of Windows (2000 and XP). One of the main design aims for NTFS was reliability, and this includes support for RAID (Redundant Array of Independent Disks), which provides fault tolerance by ensuring that copies of all data written to a file are made on at least two different disks to guard against data loss due to failure of one of the disks. RAID is described in more detail in Chapter 6. To assist in recovering from failures, each update to the filesystem is also recorded in a log file.

In NTFS, everything is treated as a file. This includes things like the bitmap which specifies which disk blocks are free and which ones are in use. The Master File Table (MFT) is at the heart of an NTFS filesystem (Figure 3.16). The MFT is a file which consists of a set of 1 KB records describing each file on the volume, including the MFT itself. Each file is identified by a 64-bit file reference which consists of a 48-bit file number together with a 16-bit sequence number. The file number identifies the entry in the MFT which describes the file, and the sequence number is used for

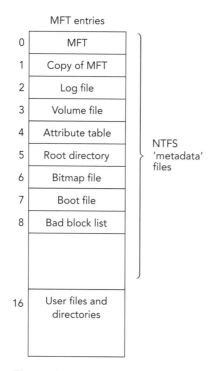

MFT entries

0	MFT
1	Copy of MFT
2	Log file
3	Volume file
4	Attribute table
5	Root directory
6	Bitmap file
7	Boot file
8	Bad block list
16	User files and directories

NTFS 'metadata' files

Figure 3.16 MFT entries.

internal consistency checking; every time an MFT entry is reused, the corresponding sequence number is incremented.

The first 16 MFT entries are used for **metadata files** that describe the overall structure of the filesystem. The first is for the MFT itself, followed by one for a copy of the MFT metadata entries which is held elsewhere on the disk as a backup. The next entry is the **log file** used to record filesystem changes for recovery purposes. The **volume file** records the volume name, filesystem version and a flag which records whether the filesystem was unmounted cleanly the last time it was used. The **bitmap file** records which disk blocks are in use, and contains one bit for each disk block on the volume, and the **bad block list** contains the block numbers of any faulty disk blocks which should not be used.

A file is treated as a set of attributes and their corresponding values, one of which is the data making up the file contents (the **data attribute**). The MFT entry for the file consists of a series of attributes each of which is stored as a header followed by a value (Figure 3.17). The header specifies the length of the header, the length of the value and the name of the attribute. The standard attributes for a file include some standard information (timestamps, read-only and archive bits, and a link count), the filename, a security descriptor giving information on ownership and access rights, and the data for the file. A directory does not have a data attribute; instead it has an **index root** attribute that contains a list of filenames and a corresponding file reference which specifies the MFT entry describing the file. For the sake of backward compatibility with the FAT filesystem, files which do not fit the MS-DOS

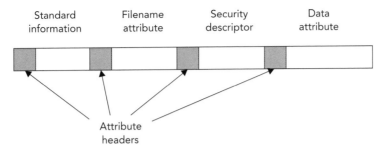

Figure 3.17 Structure of an MFT entry for a small file.

limitations on the format of filenames (eight characters with a three-character extension) are given an MS-DOS compatible 'short filename', which is stored as another attribute in the MFT entry for the file.

The whole of a small file or directory can fit into a single MFT entry. It is possible (although very rare) that there are too many different file attributes to fit into a single MFT entry, in which case an 'attribute list' attribute is used to refer to another MFT entry where the additional attributes are stored. In the more common case that an attribute of a file or a directory is too large to fit into its MFT entry, additional disk blocks known as **runs** (Figure 3.18) or **extents** are used to expand the space available. Such an attribute is known as a **non-resident attribute**, and the attribute value in the MFT is replaced by a set of **mapping entries** which identify the runs that have been allocated to hold the attribute's value. Each mapping entry gives the number of blocks in the run, the block offset relative to the start of the attribute and the disk address for the run. Note that since the MFT itself is a file, it is expanded using runs in exactly the same way, and the MFT entry for the MFT (entry 0) will list the runs used.

Figure 3.18 MFT entry for a large file with two data runs.

In an NTFS directory the data attribute is replaced by an **index root** attribute which contains an alphabetically ordered list of entries for the files in the directory. Each entry contains the filename and the file reference identifying the file's MFT entry, together with duplicate copies of the timestamps and file size information stored in the MFT entry. The duplicated information saves having to access all the MFT entries when displaying a directory listing. Large directories are implemented as a **B-tree** structure as illustrated in Figure 3.19, where each entry also

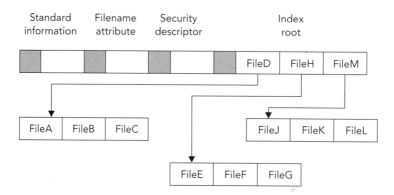

Figure 3.19 MFT entry for a large directory.

points to a 4 KB block containing entries for any files which precede it alphabetically. This produces a wide and shallow tree structure which is fast to search, although the need to keep entries in alphabetical order adds some overhead to the process of creating a new file.

Recovery is handled by using a **transaction-processing** model. The set of disk changes that make up an operation on a file (which might involve updating a directory entry as well as the file itself) are dealt with as a single **transaction** which either completes successfully or fails at some point. The changes made by each successful transaction are stored in a log, and if a transaction fails partway through the changes it has made can be undone so that the transaction can be retried from the beginning. It is worth noting that this recovery only applies to changes made to filesystem structures such as directory entries; data that has been written to a file is not logged, and it can therefore only be recovered by using redundant copies on other disks, as described above.

The individual changes that make up a transaction are always performed in an order which will produce predictable kinds of inconsistencies if they fail, and these can be fixed later. For example, extending a file is done by identifying one or more free disk blocks, marking those blocks as in use, writing the data to the allocated blocks, and only then updating the directory entry to include those blocks. A failure during this sequence of operations will result in some blocks being marked as allocated in the free block bitmap which do not belong to any file.

Records are written to the log which enables operations to be undone or redone later. These must be designed so that the corresponding operations are **idempotent**; that is, they can be repeated without ill effect. For example, setting a bit in a bitmap is an idempotent operation; it can be repeated without making any further change. The operations that are logged include creating or deleting a file, extending or truncating a file, and changing information about the file, such as its name or access permissions.

NTFS updates copies of disk blocks held in memory and these are written to the disk later, so there may be blocks of data in memory that have not been written to the disk. A table in memory is used to record incomplete transactions, and another one to record disk blocks which are waiting to be written to the disk. Update records in the log file refer to changes made to these two structures. Every few seconds these tables are written to the log file, followed by a **checkpoint** record to mark the points in the log where the filesystem is guaranteed to be in a consistent state. A **restart area** at the beginning of the log identifies the most recent checkpoint record.

Recovery after a system crash requires three scans of the log file, starting at the list of incomplete transactions just before the last checkpoint record. The first scan is the **analysis** pass. The transaction list is read into memory and the log file is scanned from this point. Updates in the log file are used to bring the transaction list up to date and to mark blocks which have been modified. Records which show a disk write are used to mark the corresponding memory block as 'clean', and transaction committals remove the corresponding transactions from the transaction list. At the end of the analysis pass, the filesystem has an up-to-date list of incomplete transactions and disk block changes which were not written to the disk.

The second pass is the **redo** pass. Updates which were not written to disk are now carried out in sequence. The final pass is the **undo** pass, which 'rolls back' any uncompleted transactions by reversing the updates that make up each such transaction. At the end of this pass, the filesystem will be in a consistent (though not necessarily complete) state, and any transactions that were undone need to be tried again.

Exercise 3.16   Find out about HFS, the Hierarchical File System used on Apple Macintosh systems. Which of the filesystems in Section 3.11 does it most closely resemble, and what are the significant differences?

3.13 ❑ SUMMARY

A filesystem is one of the most essential services that an operating system provides, and is directly visible to its users. The most important thing that a filesystem does is that it provides a **namespace** framework, or in other words a method for constructing unique names that can be used to identify not only **files** in the normal sense of the word, but also other resources, such as devices, and objects, such as files and printers, which exist elsewhere on a network. One of the things that a filesystem must do if it is to accomplish this is to provide **device independence**; that is, you do not need to know exactly where on a particular device your file is stored, or even what sort of device it is or how it is organised internally. All you need to know is the name, and the filesystem does the rest of the work for you.

There are many different filesystems to choose from, and this chapter has looked at a few of them as examples. They differ not only in their internal organisation, which is largely of no concern to anyone using them, but also in the facilities they provide. Different filesystems have different rules for naming files and for defining what attributes those files can possess. They also differ in crucial aspects such as whether a file is uniquely identified by one name, or whether a single file can have more than one name, as on Unix systems.

3.14 ❑ ADDITIONAL RESOURCES

The FAT32 filesystem specification [5] is available online, but NTFS is less well documented. Solomon and Russinovitch [7] give what is probably one of the most in-depth descriptions of NTFS available. The original Unix filesystem is explained by Ritchie and Thompson [6], while the BSD Unix filesystem from which ext2fs was derived is described by McKusick *et al.* [4]. The ext2fs filesystem itself is described by Card *et al.* [2].

Information on many other filesystems is also available. In particular, Goldstein [3] describes ODS2, the VMS filesystem mentioned in this chapter, while the Macintosh HFS filesystem is described in detail by Apple [1].

3.15 ❑ GLOSSARY

absolute pathname   a pathname identifying a file which starts from the root directory.

access control list   a list of users or groups of users and the permissions they have each been granted for accessing a file

bad block   a disk block which is physically faulty and which should not be used by the filesystem.

block   the smallest unit of storage which can be allocated by the filesystem.

bootstrap   the program loaded from a disk which is then responsible for loading the operating system into memory.

checkpoint   a record of the state of the filesystem which can be used to restore the filesystem if an error occurs.

current directory   the directory currently in use, which relative pathnames are taken to be relative to.

cylinder   a set of corresponding tracks on different disk surfaces on a multi-platter hard disk.

defragmenting   rearranging the layout of files on a disk to increase the efficiency of accessing them.

direct access file   a file where any position within it can be accessed equally easily.

directory   a special type of file which holds information identifying a set of files and directories that it contains.

ext2fs   the Second Extended File System, a standard filesystem on Linux systems

extension   a suffix for a filename generally used to identify the type of the corresponding file.

FAT (File Allocation Table) a simple but universally understood filesystem introduced by MS-DOS which is still used on some Windows systems. It is also a standard format for floppy disks.

filesystem a system for organising the layout of files and directories on a storage device.

folder a near-synonym for 'directory' used on GUI systems (although some folders on Windows systems are not directories).

HFS the Hierarchical File System, a filesystem standard used on Apple Macintosh systems.

hierarchical filesystem a filesystem organised as a hierarchical tree of directories.

home directory on a multi-user system, the directory allocated as the base directory for the files owned by an individual user.

incremental backup a backup system which only copies files which have been modified since the previous backup.

indexed file a file where items stored in a file are located using a corresponding key rather than an absolute position within the file.

inode a data structure which encapsulates information about a file on Unix systems.

latency the delay due to disk rotation before data can be read from or written to a disk.

link on Unix systems, one of several directory entries which refers to a single file via its inode.

mount point on Unix systems, a directory where the root of another filesystem is mounted.

mounting on Unix systems, overlaying a directory in one filesystem with a reference to the root directory of a filesystem on a separate volume, so that the two filesystems are united as a single tree.

namespace a set of unique names.

NTFS the NT File System, introduced by Windows NT and now a standard filesystem on later versions of Windows.

parent directory the directory that contains another directory, which can usually be referred to as '..'.

partition a part of a disk which is treated as a separate volume.

path separator the character used to separate the elements of a pathname, typically '/' or '\'.

pathname a sequence of directory names providing a route through a hierarchical directory tree to a particular file.

relative pathname a pathname which is relative to the current directory (that is, a path from the current directory to a particular file).

root directory the primary directory of a filesystem, which is not contained within any other directory.

sector the smallest accessible unit of physical storage on a disk.

seek time   the time taken to move the heads to the correct track or cylinder on a disk.

sequential file   a file whose contents can only be read or written sequentially.

shortcut   on Windows, a file similar to a Unix soft link which refers to another file elsewhere.

soft link   on Unix systems, a file which contains a reference to another file (which may or may not exist). Accesses to a soft link are automatically redirected to the corresponding file.

superblock   on Unix systems, the block at the start of a volume which defines the layout of the rest of the volume.

track   one of a set of concentric circular sets of sectors on a disk.

UNC (Uniform Naming Convention)   a Windows naming convention that can be used to identify a file on a remote file server.

VFS (Virtual File System)   on Linux systems, a filesystem which provides unified access to files which may be stored on different devices or different machines.

volume   a logical unit which behaves as a single storage device, but which can span several physical disks or can be just part of a physical disk.

3.16 ❑ REFERENCES

[1]   Apple Corporation, *Inside Macintosh: Files*. Addison-Wesley (1992) Available online at http://developer.apple.com/documentation/mac/Files/Files-2.html

[2]   Card, R., Ts'o, T. and Tweedie, S. Design and implementation of the Second Extended File system. *Proceedings of the First Dutch International Symposium on Linux* (1995). Available online at http://www.mit.edu/~tytso/linux./ext2intro.html

[3]   Goldstein, A. C. *VMS file system (ODS2) Files-11 On-Disk Structure Specification* (Jan 1985) Available online at http://vms.tuwien.ac.at/freeware/ODS2/

[4]   McKusick, M. K., Joy, W. N., Leffler, S. J. and Fabry, R. S. A fast file system for Unix. *ACM Transactions on Computer Systems*, **2**(3) (Aug 1984), 181–197

[5]   Microsoft Corporation. *FAT32 File System Specification* (Dec 2000). Available online at http://www.microsoft.com/whdc/hwdev/hardware/fatgen.mspx

[6]   Ritchie, D. M. and Thompson, K. The Unix timesharing system. *Communications of the ACM*, **17**(7) (Jul 1974), 365–375

[7]   Solomon, D. A. and Russinovich, M. E. *Inside Microsoft Windows 2000*. Microsoft Press (2000)

CHAPTER 4

PROCESSES AND THREADS

In previous chapters we've looked at some of the major features of an operating system from the point of view of a user of the system; how a programmer sees the environment provided by the operating system, how the shell works, and how files are organised. Another important feature of an operating system that is visible to its users is its ability to execute several processes concurrently. Many modern operating systems also allow individual processes to contain several parallel 'threads of control', so that a single process can carry out several tasks concurrently. These 'threads' need to be able to communicate in order to synchronise their activity, and indeed the same is often true of separate processes. This chapter looks at the implications of concurrency for the programmer.

4.1 ☐ THE VIEW FROM INSIDE A PROCESS

One of the most important capabilities that an operating system can provide is the ability to execute multiple processes at the same time. As Chapter 2 showed, the ability to string commands together in a pipeline means that complex problems can be solved using combinations of simple tools. The ability to switch between different programs is also a valuable one; for example, you can cut and paste information from a spreadsheet into a document you are preparing on your word processor, and from there into a reply to an email message.

As I've said before, a process can be regarded as an emulation of a complete computer system with its own processor, memory, screen, keyboard and other peripheral devices. From the point of view of a process, the processor is effectively a subset of the real thing. This is necessary to prevent a malfunctioning program interfering with other processes that might be running at the same time. For example, a Pentium processor has a 'halt' instruction which will stop the processor. We don't want to allow processes to use this instruction to halt the entire system, so it must not be available for ordinary processes to use. Also, processes must be prevented from accessing I/O devices directly, since it would otherwise be possible for a process to interfere with the operation of a device that some other process is using. On the other hand, an instruction must be provided to act as a 'system call' instruction to allow processes to request operating system services.

A system call like read may need to wait until the requested data is available before it can return, so it makes sense for the operating system to switch control to another process in the meantime. One of the critical parts of the kernel is the **scheduler** which chooses which process to run next. We will assume for now that the scheduling policy that the kernel uses is fair, so that each process gets a fair share of the available processing power, and that the corresponding mechanism is efficient, so that as little processing power as possible is wasted choosing a new process when rescheduling, but I'll save the details of how this can be achieved for later.

4.2 ❑ THREADS

Processes are like separate computers. Each process is completely separate (or nearly so) from all the other processes in the system. However, it is sometimes useful to have two or more concurrent activities within a single process. For example, the word processor I'm using to write this book keeps track of where each page begins and ends. As I type, the word processor is continually repaginating, moving the position of the page boundaries as the text changes. This could be done by repaginating the entire document after each keystroke, but for very large documents that would lead to irritating delays. An alternative would be to repaginate only when asked to do so, but that would also result in an irritating delay whenever a large document needed to be repaginated. The simplest solution would be to have a separate process handle the repagination, so that spare processor time between keystrokes could be used to adjust the page numbering as the text changed. The problem with this is that processes do not share the same memory, so the repaginating process would have no access to the document being altered by the text management process.

What we need is the ability to emulate the effect of having several processors which share a common memory, which can be used to solve problems which are most easily solved by using multiple processes that have access to a set of shared data structures. In this model, a process still corresponds to the emulation of a single computer, but each single computer can contain several processors. Each processor provides a separate 'thread of control' (or just a **thread**, for short) within a single program in memory. While one thread is executing one part of the program, another thread can be executing a different part, or multiple threads can be executing the same part of the program but using different sets of data. And on computers with more than one physical processor, separate threads can indeed be executed by separate processors to give true parallel execution, rather than an emulation of parallelism. This is illustrated in Figure 4.1.

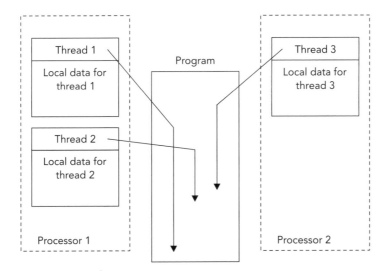

Figure 4.1 Multiple threads executing a program concurrently.

Most modern operating systems support threads. Windows does, as do many flavours of Unix (for example, Solaris). However, others (including Linux) do not, but it is fairly easy to implement threads inside an ordinary process without the operating system needing to know anything about them. How this can be done will be discussed in Chapter 7. A few modern programming languages support multithreading, notably Java and Ada. In these languages, threads are implemented either as native operating system threads if the operating system supports threads or by a function library within the process if it does not.

Exercise 4.1   Find out if the system you are using supports threads. What facilities does it provide to create and use threads if so?

The disadvantage of threads implemented 'by hand' rather than by the operating system itself is that the operating system doesn't know that they exist, so it can't schedule them independently. A **blocking operation** which prevents a process from continuing will block all threads within the process. For example, if one thread tries to read some data from a file, the thread will be unable to continue until the data has been received and the read operation completes. While the thread is **blocked** waiting for the read operation to complete, the operating system can carry on executing something else. If all the operating system knows about is processes, it will have to run a completely different process while the read operation is in progress. On the other hand, if the operating system is aware of threads, only the thread that executed the blocking operation will be blocked, and any other threads within the same process will be free to continue executing. In this case the operating system will treat threads as the basic schedulable unit of execution rather than processes.

From now on I will talk about threads as being the basic schedulable unit of execution (corresponding to a processor within a computer system), and I will use the term 'process' to refer to the environment within which a thread is executed (corresponding to a complete computer system). On systems where processes are the basic schedulable unit you can regard each process as containing a single thread, analogous to a computer system with a single processor.

4.2.1   THREADS IN JAVA

Java provides a standard class called Thread which provides all the basic mechanisms needed to support multithreading. The most important methods of the Thread class are called start and run. To create your own thread, all you have to do is to derive a new class from Thread and override the definition of the run method to implement the desired behaviour. You can then create as many objects of this new class as you wish and start them running by calling the start method. When you do this, the thread will start executing the run method in parallel with the rest of the program, and the thread will terminate when run terminates. A simple example of this is shown below:

```
public class MyThread extends Thread {
  public void run() {
    for (int i = 1; i <= 1000; i++) {
      System.out.println(i);
    }
  }
}
```

This class defines a class of threads that will print all the values from 1 to 1000 in parallel with the rest of the program and will then terminate. You can create and start such a thread like this:

```
MyThread thread = new MyThread();
thread.start();
```

After the call to start, the program continues with the next statement in the normal way, but the code for the run method defined by the class will execute at the same time. The program as a whole only terminates once the last thread has terminated.

Project 4.1   If you have access to a Java compiler, use a class like MyThread above to write a Java program which creates three threads and let them execute. Is the output the same if you run the program again? Is there any predictable pattern in the output?

4.2.2 THREADS IN ADA

Threads in Ada are referred to as **tasks** (a term which, confusingly, is also used by some people as a synonym for 'process'). A task in Ada consists of a specification and a body. Here is an example which is equivalent to the Java example above:

```
with Ada.Text_IO. Ada.Integer_Text_IO;
use Ada.Text_IO. Ada.Integer_Text_IO;
procedure Main is
  task type My_Task;              -- (1)
  task body My_Task is           -- (2)
  begin
    for I in 1..1000 loop
      Put(I); New_Line;
    end loop;
  end My_Task;
  T : My_Task;                    -- (3)
begin                            -- (4)
  -- body of main program goes here
end Main;
```

An Ada task consists of a specification and a body. In this simple example, the specification is given by the single line marked (1), and the body begins at the line marked (2). The line marked (3) creates a task object called T, and this will be started automatically at the beginning of the body of Main, which is the line marked (4). When the end of Main is reached, the thread executing the body of Main will wait until task T has terminated. Note that the thread is started automatically, unlike in Java.

Project 4.2   If you have access to an Ada compiler, write a program like the one above which creates three tasks and lets them execute. Is the output the same if you run the program again?

4.3 ☐ INTERPROCESS COMMUNICATION

Something missing in the description above is a mechanism by which processes and threads can communicate with each other. In the case of text-based interfaces, the input and output streams are an obvious way of transferring data between processes. In a GUI-based environment, data transfer via a **clipboard** can be used to achieve a similar effect, although it is harder to automate than the case where all interaction is via a one-dimensional stream of characters. Other mechanisms are also possible; on Windows the clipboard is an example of a technique known as OLE (Object Linking and Embedding), which in turn is one aspect of a more general mechanism known as COM (the Common Object Model).

Interprocess communication using pipes to connect I/O streams is quite simple; if you imagine each process as an emulation of a separate computer, you can picture a pipe as an output device on one computer which is connected to an input device on another, as shown in Figure 4.2.

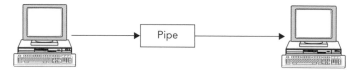

Figure 4.2 A pipe as a device connecting two computers.

What one computer writes as its output, the other reads as its input. More elaborate interprocess communication systems can be implemented; for example, a clipboard can be thought of as an imaginary piece of hardware which is shared between the emulated computers, as in Figure 4.3.

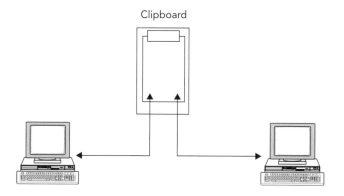

Figure 4.3 A clipboard as a storage device shared by two computers.

More advanced technologies such as COM (the Common Object Model used in Windows to allow interprocess communication) can be pictured as a way of defining the shapes of the connectors that are used to plug such imaginary hardware into the computers, as illustrated in Figure 4.4, so that different hardware can only be plugged in if it has the right shape of connector. We'll come back to considering this in a little more detail in Section 4.7, but for now you can use this description to give you a mental model of what the operating system is doing.

Another way to provide interprocess communication is via shared memory. This is the natural way for threads to communicate, since threads within a single process share a single common memory, but it can also be used for interprocess communication. The emulation of the memory belonging to a particular process can be implemented so that when any one of a specified range of addresses is

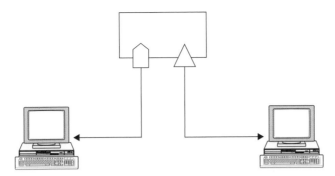

Figure 4.4 A COM object as a device with various types of connectors.

accessed, it refers to an area which is also accessible within the emulated memory of another process, as shown in Figure 4.5. The Windows API function `MapViewOfFile` and the Unix `mmap` system call both allow the same block of physical memory to correspond to a memory area within the 'emulated' memory of more than one process.

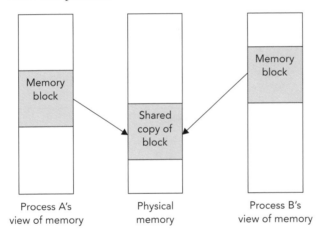

Figure 4.5 Sharing a block of memory between two processes.

This is also a good way to optimise the implementation of processes which share common code; for example, multiple processes which are executing the same word processor program can share the memory areas which contain the program code so that only one copy is ever actually in memory. Other common code such as the GUI system (code to draw buttons, menus and so on) can also be shared, even where different applications are involved; the code used to draw a button is the same no matter which program is doing the drawing. On Unix systems this sort of common code is stored in **shared libraries**; Windows uses the same technique, but refers to the shared libraries as **dynamic link libraries** (**DLLs**). We shall consider this in more detail in Chapter 5 when we look at memory management.

4.4 ☐ SYNCHRONISATION

Interprocess communication generates some problems all of its own. Consider the case where you have two word processors operating on the same document at the same time. Each word processor starts by reading the document into memory for faster access. When you close the first word processor, it updates the original document with the modified version. Unfortunately, any changes you make with the first word processor will be destroyed when the second word processor saves its copy of the document, since it will overwrite the version of the file that the first word processor produced, as illustrated in Figure 4.6. This problem occurs in any situation where more than one process might attempt to update the same item of data as another; if both processes read the data, one process might update it, only to have the update overwritten by another update based on an earlier version of the data.

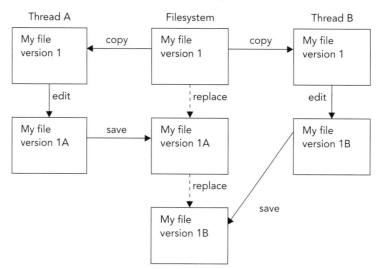

Figure 4.6 A file being updated by two threads.

In the case of disk files, the directory entry for a file will normally record the date and time when the file was created, so a word processor could check the date and time to see if the file has been updated on disk since it was loaded into memory. However, how does that help? If you reload the new version, all the changes you made to the old version will need to be redone for the new version.

Another possibility would be to prevent more than one process from accessing the same file. But if the word processor reads the file into memory and then releases it, another word processor can access it and we are back in the same situation as before. The only way for this to work is if the word processor has exclusive access to the file until it has saved the final version and other processes that might update the file are blocked from accessing it in the meantime. This might be feasible in the case of a word processor, but in other cases it might be unacceptable to block access in this way for an unpredictably long time.

What about if two threads update a shared copy of the file held in the common memory that they share? Unfortunately, updating shared data in memory is no easier than updating shared data on disk. Consider something as simple as incrementing a variable which is accessible to two threads. The increment is usually performed by a sequence of instructions like this:

- Fetch the value of variable v into a processor register
- Increment the processor register
- Store the register contents into v

A problem will arise if a thread fetches the value of v, but doesn't manage to complete the instruction sequence before another thread fetches v as well. Bear in mind that each thread is being executed conceptually, if not in reality, on a separate processor. For example, assuming v = 5:

- Thread A fetches v = 5 into a processor register within processor A
- Thread B fetches v = 5 into a processor register within processor B
- Thread B increments the value in its processor register to 6
- Thread B stores 6 into v
- Thread A increments the value in its processor register to 6
- Thread A stores 6 into v

So A and B have both incremented v, but v has only been incremented once! This is similar to A and B word processing the same document, where only one set of changes gets stored. Any sequence where thread B fetches v before A has had a chance to finish updating it will have exactly the same effect. Situations like this where the result of an operation depends on the precise order of events are known as **race conditions**. They can be very hard to fix, because they can't be reproduced reliably. They're time-dependent, and any slight change in the sequence of events will give a different outcome. There may well only be a one-in-a-million chance of the error giving rise to a visible fault in the program's operation, and with odds like this you may have to wait days or even weeks before the fault will recur. And any changes you make to the program to get more information about the source of the error will affect the program's timing. This might easily perturb the situation to make it less likely for the fault to occur, or even shift the point at which it occurs to a different part of the program.

Project 4.3

Write a program with two or more threads where each thread repeatedly copies a global variable, adds 1 to the copy and then stores the copy back in the original variable. Find a way of detecting lost updates (for example, count the total number of updates and compare this to the number of updates that have actually been made to the variable). Estimate the probability of an update being lost in your program. (Note: if you use Java, you will need to do the copy/modify/write as a sequence of separate statements, since Java threads only get rescheduled between statements.)

4.5 ☐ MUTUAL EXCLUSION

A sequence of instructions which can lead to erroneous results if more than one thread executes it at the same time is known as a **critical section**. What we need is some way of signalling that a thread is executing inside a critical section so that any other threads that want to execute inside that critical situation can wait until the critical section is free.

4.5.1 MUTEXES

A simple solution is to use a **lock variable**, often referred to as a **mutex** (short for 'mutual exclusion'). Most processors (certainly all modern processors) provide some sort of **test-and-set** instruction which can be used for this. For example, consider an instruction that tests whether a variable is zero and at the same time sets it to 1. Use 0 to indicate that the critical section is free and 1 to indicate that it is in use. Here is some pseudocode that illustrates how this works:

```
while (test_and_set(mutex) == 1) {
  // do nothing
}
critical_section();
mutex = 0;
```

To enter the critical section, use the test-and-set instruction to discover whether the critical section is free. If it is, the test-and-set instruction will indicate that the original value of the mutex was 0, and at the same time it will also have changed the value of the mutex from 0 to 1. If another thread does the same thing, the mutex will be set to 1 again, but the test-and-set instruction will indicate that the original value was also 1. When this happens, the thread will go round the loop again and repeat the test-and-set instruction. When the first thread leaves the critical section, it resets the mutex to 0. When the second thread executes the test-and-set instruction again, it will now see the original value of the mutex as 0, indicating that it is now safe to execute the critical section, and at the same time will have set it to 1 to prevent any other thread from entering the critical section.

Notice that this requires a single instruction to test and set the mutex. A two-step solution (test, and then set) produces a race condition; there is a risk that two threads will both test the mutex at the same time before either has had the chance to set it to 1. Operations like this that must be performed as a single indivisible step are referred to as **atomic** actions.

Exercise 4.2

On the processor you are using, find out what instructions are available that will test the value of a variable in memory and change it in a single operation.

One major drawback to using a test-and-set instruction like this is that it uses **busy waiting**; that is, a thread waiting to enter a critical region is wasting processor time by keeping the processor busy executing a loop which repeatedly tests the mutex. Of course, until some other thread gets a chance to run, the value of the mutex cannot possibly change. A simple solution is to suspend the thread (giving some other thread a chance to run) if the mutex is set:

```
while (test_and_set(mutex) == 1) {
    suspend();      // an operation which asks the system
}                   // to execute a different thread
critical_section();
mutex = 0;
```

A better solution is if suspend is a blocking operation, so that the thread will not be considered for execution by the operator system scheduler until it is explicitly unblocked, and to explicitly unblock the first waiting thread on exit from the critical section. That way the scheduler will not waste time starting threads that will just suspend themselves again. The mutex will need to keep a list of waiting threads so that it can find the first one that is waiting, and there will need to be a way to mark threads as being blocked. This will be discussed further in Chapter 7.

4.5.2 SEMAPHORES

A **semaphore** is a generalisation of a mutex devised by Dijkstra which has an integer value that is greater than or equal to zero. There are two operations on semaphores, usually called wait and signal. Dijkstra's original paper [7] refers to these operations as P and V, standing for the Dutch words 'proberen' and 'verhogen'. These can be roughly translated as 'down' and 'up' respectively (think 'probing' and 'heightening'); 'down' and 'up' are alternative names for these operations which are sometimes used instead of wait and signal. The wait operation suspends the thread if the semaphore's value is zero, and otherwise decrements the semaphore value (i.e. moves its value 'down'). The signal operation increments the semaphore value (moves its value 'up'), and wakes up any thread which was suspended by a wait operation on that semaphore. The wait operation can be implemented using a 'test and decrement if not zero' operation, which decrements the semaphore value if it is not already zero and then returns the original value of the semaphore before it was decremented. This is illustrated in the following pseudocode:

```
wait(Semaphore s) {
  while (test_and_decrement_if_not_zero(s) > 0) {
    suspend();
  }
  // the original value of s was > 0, so it's safe to proceed
}
```

Notice that the number of threads that can enter a critical section is the same as the initial value of the semaphore. If the initial value was 3, then three threads would be able to enter the critical section before the semaphore value reached zero, but a fourth thread would then be prevented from entering. In particular, a semaphore with an initial value of 1 is the same as a mutex. Also, as with a mutex, the 'test and decrement if not zero' step at the heart of the wait operation needs to be executed atomically. If the processor does not have a suitable atomic instruction to do this (and most processors do not), a mutex can be used to create a critical section which protects the instructions it takes to do it, as shown by the following pseudocode:

```
int test_and_decrement_if_not_zero(Semaphore s) {
  lock(mutex);            // protect operstions on the semaphore
  temp = s;               // make copy of original value
  if (s > 0) {            // semaphore is non-zero
    s = s - 1;            // so decrement it
  }
  unlock(mutex);          // unlock the mutex
  return temp;            // and return the original value
}
```

Allowing more than one thread to pass a wait operation might not seem terribly useful, since the whole idea of critical sections is to allow only one thread at a time to enter, but there is one common idiom that uses precisely this technique: the **bounded buffer**. Bounded buffers are normally used to iron out differences in speed between separate threads, where one thread (the **producer**) produces data which is consumed by another thread (the **consumer**). If the producer and consumer work at basically the same speed, but sometimes the producer is faster than the consumer and vice versa, excess production can be stored in the buffer until the consumer is ready to deal with it. A bounded buffer has a fixed size, which needs to be calculated based on the maximum number of items that can possibly be produced by the producer thread before a single one is consumed by the consumer thread. The producer stores items into the next available space in the buffer, 'wrapping round' to the beginning of the buffer when the end is reached. Similarly, the consumer removes the next available item from the buffer, wrapping round to the beginning when the end of the buffer is reached. This is illustrated in Figure 4.7.

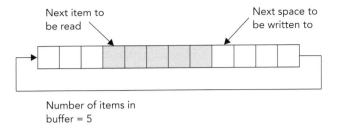

Figure 4.7 A bounded buffer.

The bounded buffer has two basic operations: insert(item), which adds an item to the back of the queue of items, and remove(), which removes an item from the front of the queue and returns it to the caller. Since these both operate on the same buffer, they need to be synchronised so that only one process at a time can be either adding or removing items at any one time. Pseudocode for the two operations is shown in Figure 4.8.

```
insert(Item i) {                Item remove() {
    wait(spaceAvailable);           wait(itemsAvailable);
    wait(mutex);                    wait(mutex);
    doInsert(i);                    Item i = doRemove();
    signal(mutex);                  signal(mutex);
    signal(itemsAvailable);         signal(spaceAvailable);
}                                   return i;
                                }
```

Figure 4.8 Operations on a bounded buffer.

Assuming a buffer size of N, a maximum of N items can be added to an empty buffer before it becomes full. Similarly, when the buffer is full, a maximum of N items can be removed before it will become empty. By starting with an empty buffer and setting the initial value of spaceAvailable to N and the initial value of itemsAvailable to 0, a consumer thread trying to remove an item from the empty buffer will be blocked. A producer thread which tries to add an item to the buffer will pass the initial wait, decrementing spaceAvailable to N-1 as it does so. After adding the item to the buffer, itemsAvailable will be incremented to 1 by the signal operation at the end, and a waiting consumer thread will be allowed to proceed past the initial wait. If there are no consumer threads, the producer thread will be able to add a total of N items to the buffer (thereby filling it up) before the value of spaceAvailable reaches zero. If the producer thread tries to add another item to the buffer, it will be blocked until a consumer thread removes an item from the buffer and then calls signal to increment the value of spaceAvailable above zero again.

Note that whenever spaceAvailable is incremented, itemsAvailable is decremented and vice versa. This means that the sum of the values of the two semaphores remains constant; that is, they should always add up to a total value of N. This is as it should be, since all the elements in a buffer of size N should be either in use or free at any one time.

The semaphore mutex prevents multiple threads performing these two operations at the same time. For example, if the buffer were half full, it would be perfectly possible for a producer thread to be putting an item into the buffer at the same time as a consumer thread was trying to take one out. Initialising mutex to 1 ensures that only one thread at a time can execute the internal operations (doInsert and doRemove) that manipulate the shared internal data structures; in other words, mutex is a semaphore which is being used to implement a normal two-valued mutex.

Project 4.4   Implement a bounded buffer in a language which supports multithreading.

4.6 ❑ SYNCHRONIZATION IN HIGH-LEVEL LANGUAGES

Semaphores (including mutexes, since semaphores can be used in place of mutexes) solve the problem of concurrent access to critical sections, but they are a very low-level mechanism. They must be used wherever a shared data item is accessed, so it's much too easy to get things wrong. You might forget to use a semaphore in one case but not in others; you might use the wrong semaphore; or worst of all, you might call wait but forget to call signal, in which case the critical section will stay locked forever and everything will come to a grinding halt. Another classic mistake would be to reverse the order of wait operations in the bounded-buffer code shown earlier. An empty buffer will cause a thread which calls remove to block on the itemsAvailable semaphore. If the operation wait(mutex) is performed before wait(itemsAvailable), the mutex semaphore will be kept locked while the thread is blocked waiting for an item to become available. This means that any threads trying to insert items into the buffer will not be able to get into the critical section; they too will be blocked, and once again we shall come to a grinding halt. This situation is known as a **deadlock**, and is discussed in more detail later in this chapter.

Anything this error-prone is a very bad idea in a multithreading system. It can lead to race conditions where the error may only manifest itself as a fault once in a blue moon. Errors like this which are time-dependent and cannot be reproduced reliably can be really hard to track down. This does not mean that semaphores are a bad idea; it's just that they need to be used as a low-level building block that can be used to construct higher-level mechanisms that are safer to use.

A better approach is to encapsulate the shared data together with the methods that access it, and to make sure that all the methods are executed in a mutually exclusive manner. This requires building high-level mutual exclusion mechanisms into high-level languages, so that compilers can ensure that the correct code is always generated. The earliest such mechanism was the **monitor**, developed in slightly different forms by Hoare [9] and Brinch Hansen [3]. These ideas have been adopted and refined by many modern high-level languages, including two that I will discuss here: Java and Ada 95.

4.6.1   SYNCHRONIZATION IN JAVA

Java is a modern object-oriented language with built-in support for multithreading. All objects in Java have an internal mutex. You can lock an object's mutex using a `synchronized` block which looks like this:

```
synchronized (object) {
  // critical section
}
```

The compiler will generate the correct code to lock the object's mutex at the beginning of the block and unlock it at the end. Inside the critical section, there are three methods that can be used to control things further:

- `object.wait()`: release the lock on the object's mutex and suspend the thread on the object's list of waiting threads
- `object.notify()`: wake up one of the threads from the object's list of waiting threads, if there are any. The thread that gets woken up is chosen arbitrarily (there is no guarantee that it will be the thread that has been waiting longest, for example) and it will then have to reacquire a lock on the object's mutex before it can continue.
- `object.notifyAll()`: as for `object.notify()`, except that all the threads in the object's list of waiting threads are woken up, if there are any. Each one will have to reacquire a lock on the object's mutex before it can continue.

As well as synchronized blocks as described above, the methods of a class can be marked as 'synchronized'. A synchronized method locks the mutex of the object it belongs to, so only one thread at a time can be executing any of that object's synchronized methods.

Figure 4.9 shows how semaphores can be implemented in Java. A new object of class Semaphore with an initial count of 3 can be created and used like this:

```
Semaphore sema = new Semaphore(3);
sema.doWait();
sema.doSignal();
```

The object sema has a private field (an integer called count) which only the methods of the class can access. Only one thread at a time will be able to lock the object so it can call any of the synchronized methods of sema. Once a thread has locked the object, it can call any of its synchronized methods, and one synchronized method can call another one without any problems.

When a thread calls doWait() it will wait inside the loop if the count is zero, releasing its lock on the object as it does so. This will allow another thread to call

```
class Semaphore {
  private int count;
  public Semaphore (int i) {
    count = i;
  }
  public synchronized void doWait () {
    while (count == 0)
      wait();
    count--;
  }
  public synchronized void doSignal () {
    count++;
    notifyAll();
  }
}
```

Figure 4.9 A semaphore implemented in Java.

doSignal(), which will call notifyAll() to wake up any waiting threads. Once the thread inside doWait() is woken up, it will have to reacquire its lock on the object before it can continue executing, which means it will not be able to resume until the other thread exits from doSignal() and releases its lock on the object.

Using synchronized methods is better than using synchronized blocks, because the synchronization is localised within the class itself rather than being distributed to the points where the object is accessed. This avoids the risk that the synchronization will be omitted at some of the points where the object is used, but of course it is still necessary to decide whether methods should be synchronized when the class is being designed; you can have a mixture of synchronized and unsynchronized methods in a class, and unsynchronized methods can be called at any time, even when another thread is executing a synchronized method. And there is nothing to stop you making fields like count public, so that anyone can access them directly.

Project 4.5   Write code to implement a bounded buffer in Java using semaphores as defined above.

4.6.2 SYNCHRONIZATION IN ADA 95

Ada 95 provides a more flexible construct to achieve mutual exclusion, known as a **protected record**. A protected record contains some private data to be protected, and a collection of public operations to access it. Three kinds of operation are allowed: **functions**, **procedures** and **entries**. A function has read-only access to the data; because of this, it is safe to allow more than one thread to be executing functions in the same protected record at the same time. Procedures and entries have read/write access, so they can perform updates and thus they must have exclusive access to the data. Even executing a function at the same time as a procedure or entry might be unsafe, because some of the data that the function reads may have been updated while other parts of the data might not have been updated yet. If a thread attempts to call any of the protected record's operations while another thread is executing one of its procedures or entries, it will be put in a queue of threads awaiting access to the record.

An entry is like a procedure, except that it has a **guard condition** which must be true before the entry can be called. Once a thread has gained access to a protected record to call an entry, it tests the entry's guard condition. If the guard condition is false, the thread will be suspended and placed in a queue associated with the entry (which will also allow another thread to gain access to the record). The guard conditions will be re-evaluated whenever a procedure or entry call completes, as only a procedure or entry call can alter the data and so possibly change the value of the guard condition.

A protected record to implement a semaphore is shown in Figures 4.10 and 4.11. It consists of two separate parts: a specification headed by 'protected type' and a body headed by 'protected body'. Note that there is no need for any operations like Java's wait or notify. The guard condition on the Wait entry will block any thread that tries to call Wait until the count is greater than zero, and the condition will be re-evaluated every time Signal is called. The Get operation returns a copy of the count; any number of threads can call Get safely at the same time as long as neither of the other two operations is being executed at the same time.

We can define objects of this type like this:

```
Sema : Semaphore(3);   -- a semaphore with an initial value of 3
```

and then call the operations of the object like this:

```
Sema.Wait;
I := Sema.Get;
Sema.Signal;
```

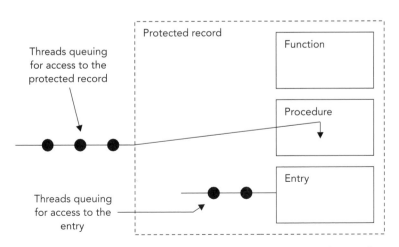

Figure 4.10 Threads queuing for access to a protected record.

```
protected type Semaphore (N : Integer) is
   function Get return Integer;
   entry Wait;
   procedure Signal;
private
   Count : Integer := N;
end Semaphore;

protected body Semaphore is
   function Get return Integer is
   begin
      return Count;
   end Get;
   entry Wait when Count > 0 is
   begin
      Count := Count - 1;
   end Wait;
   procedure Signal is
   begin
      Count := Count + 1;
   end Signal;
end Semaphore;
```

Figure 4.11 A semaphore implemented as an Ada protected record.

The compiler enforces the language rules (making sure that the data components are private and are not written to by functions) and generates code which implements the guard evaluation and queuing policies. Unlike Java, the queuing policy in Ada is well defined; queues are processed in a first come, first served order by default, with threads held in an entry queue taking precedence over threads queuing to access the protected object. Different queuing policies can also be specified if an application has any unusual requirements.

Project 4.6   Write code to implement a bounded buffer in Ada using semaphores as defined above.

4.6.3   OTHER MECHANISMS

Another approach to interprocess communication is to use **message passing**. This is essentially what happens when an event such as a mouse click occurs in Windows: a message describing the event is constructed and added to a queue of events associated with the appropriate thread. The Win32 GetMessage function waits until there is a message in the queue. When there are any messages in the queue, it removes the first one from the front of the queue and returns a copy of the message to the thread that called GetMessage. Unix pipes are another message-passing system, where the messages are the individual characters being written to and read from the pipe.

For text-based applications, Unix pipes are ideal. Two processes can be connected together in a pipeline and text can be transferred between them through the pipe. However, this is not much use if you want two graphical applications to communicate with each other. Having one such application control another requires a higher-level mechanism which allows structured messages to be passed between the two applications.

Windows provides a mechanism known as **COM** (the Component Object Model) which, among other things, allows one application to expose selected functions to another. It is based on the use of **interfaces**, an object-oriented programming concept which is supported directly in languages like Java and C#. A class can **implement** one or more interfaces if it wishes to, and the idea is that an interface defines a set of operations that must be defined by any class which implements that interface. If you use an object belonging to a class which implements a particular interface, you can guarantee that the operations defined by that interface will be available. You don't have to know what type of object it really is; any object will do as long as it supports the interface you require. The actual object that you end up with may have additional operations in addition to the ones you are interested in, but you won't know about them unless you know the actual class that the object belongs to; the interface just gives you a particular restricted view of the object's properties. For example, a clipboard might be designed as a class which implements a Clipboard interface, which specifies required operations like cut, copy, paste and clear. Any object that implements these operations can be used as a clipboard, regardless of what extra qualities it may have.

The COM specification requires that all COM objects support an interface called IUnknown. This interface provides operations which let you find out what interfaces the object supports, and to get a reference to the object as one which implements any one of its supported interfaces so that you then have access to the operations of the object as defined by that interface. For example, you could query an object to check whether it supports the Clipboard interface, and get a view of it as a Clipboard object if it does so that you can use the cut and paste operations defined by the Clipboard interface.

To use a COM component, you get a reference to it by using COM operations to look up its name in the system registry. This will load the code for the component into memory and return a reference to it as an object implementing the IClassFactory interface. The IClassFactory interface defines an operation called CreateInstance which you can use to create an object implementing the IUnknown interface. You then use the IUnknown interface's QueryInterface operation to get a reference to the object as one that implements the interface you're interested in. This is illustrated in Figure 4.12. It may seem like an elaborate process, but it avoids you having to know anything about the object you are dealing with except the interface you want to use. The object may be in a library which is loaded into the address space of the current process, or it may be running in a separate process, or it might even be running on a separate machine. All you know to start with is that it will be something which supports the IUnknown interface, and you can then use the

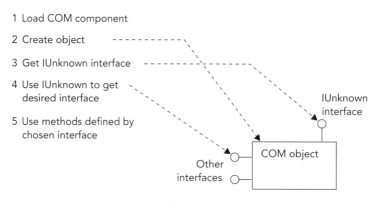

1 Load COM component

2 Create object

3 Get IUnknown interface

4 Use IUnknown to get desired interface

5 Use methods defined by chosen interface

IUnknown interface

COM object

Other interfaces

Figure 4.12 Using a COM object.

QueryInterface operation to get a different view of it and access a different set of operations. You can use it just like any other objects that your program might create without having to know any of the implementation details, and you can use it to manipulate structured data items rather than amorphous streams of raw bytes of data.

4.7 ❑ DEADLOCK

The mechanisms in languages like Java and Ada can provide reliable access to data which is shared between threads, eliminating common race conditions. However, there are still a number of problems which are specific to multithreaded systems which even these mechanisms cannot solve.

Deadlock is where two or more threads prevent each other from proceeding. Each thread holds some resource that the other needs to be able to proceed; so each thread is preventing the other from making any progress. Since neither thread can proceed any further without the resource it is waiting for, neither thread will be able to get to the point where it will release the resource it already holds. The result is that both threads will be stuck like this forever.

A simple example that illustrates deadlock is to imagine two trains travelling towards each other on the same track, as in Figure 4.13. When the trains meet, they will both have to stop because they cannot go any further. Each of the trains controls a resource (a section of track) that the other needs to be able to continue. Until one of the trains can somehow release the resource it controls by moving to a different section of track, the deadlock will continue.

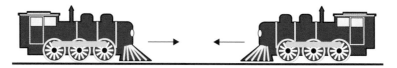

Figure 4.13 Two trains colliding on a single track.

```
insert(Item i) {                    Item remove() {
    wait(spaceAvailable);               wait(mutex);
    wait(mutex);                        wait(itemsAvailable);
    doInsert(item);                     Item i = doRemove();
    signal(mutex);                      signal(mutex);
    signal(itemsAvailable);             signal(spaceAvailable);
}                                       return i;
                                    }
```

Figure 4.14 A bounded buffer which causes a deadlock.

We saw an example of deadlock at the beginning of Section 4.6, in connection with the semaphore-based solution to the bounded buffer problem. A version of the code from Figure 4.8 is shown in Figure 4.14, but here a bug has been introduced by reversing the order of the wait operations in the code for remove. This error will result in a deadlock whenever the buffer is empty; the thread calling remove will have locked the mutex semaphore and will be waiting on itemsAvailable, while a thread calling insert will end up waiting on mutex and so will be unable to signal itemsAvailable to release the other thread. The fact that misusing semaphores like this can lead to deadlock so easily means that they must be used with great care; it is usually preferable to use higher level constructs which are built in to a programming language, since the compiler will not make mistakes like the one described above.

Deadlock is a problem that has been thoroughly analysed over the years. There are four necessary and sufficient conditions for deadlock to occur:

- The resources involved cannot be shared; only one thread at a time can use a particular resource.
- Once a resource has been allocated to a thread, that resource cannot be **preempted** (i.e. taken away) by another thread. Threads hold on to the resources they have been allocated until they release them voluntarily.
- Threads can request additional resources at any time.
- There must be a circular chain of two or more threads, each waiting for a resource held by the next thread in the chain.

In the case of two trains heading towards each other on the same track, you can see that each of these conditions is true. The threads are the trains, and the resources involved are sections of track. The first condition means that you cannot have two trains at exactly the same place at the same time. The space occupied by one train cannot simultaneously be occupied by another train. The second condition means that a train may not be pushed aside or otherwise forcibly removed from the section of track that it is on. The third condition means that a train (which already occupies a section of track) can occupy another section of track by moving forwards. The fourth condition occurs when the two trains meet head-on; they are both stuck waiting for an opportunity to move forward onto the section of track occupied by the other, while at the same time occupying the section of track that the other needs. The circular chain is that the first train is waiting for the second train to get out of the way, while at the same time the second train is waiting for the first train to get out of the way. Neither train can occupy the same space as the other, and neither can push the other out of the way.

Exercise 4.3

Convince yourself that all of the above conditions are indeed necessary for deadlock. What would happen if any of the conditions did not hold?

Since these are necessary and sufficient conditions, the deadlock can be broken if any one of them is denied. For example, if the trains could somehow pass through each other (ghost trains perhaps?) then the first condition would be denied since the trains could then occupy the same section of track at the same time. Similarly, if one train could push the other backwards down the track, it would be preempting the use of the section of the track that the other was occupying, thus denying the second condition. The third condition could be denied by forcing both trains to claim all sections of the track at once before going on to the beginning of the track. This is in fact how single-track railways are managed. Before proceeding, each driver must wait for a signal indicating that the entire track is clear all the way to the next passing place. The fourth condition is denied if both trains are going in the same direction, since the train in front never needs to use a section of track occupied by the train behind.

Project 4.7

Write a program involving two or more threads that uses the synchronization mechanism of your chosen language to create a situation that can lead to deadlock (for example, nested synchronized blocks in Java where each thread synchronizes on the same objects but in a different order). Use another thread to monitor the state of each thread to detect deadlock (for example, set variables in each thread to record which resources are held and which are being waited for). How long does it take before deadlock actually occurs?

4.7.1 DEADLOCK PREVENTION

In an operating system, it is impossible to predict what individual processes will try to do. Deadlock can be prevented by making it impossible for one or more of the four necessary conditions to occur, but this might be impossible or unfeasibly restrictive. Preventing the first condition would mean making all resources shareable. This is possible in some circumstances but not in others. The classic example of making an unshareable resource shareable is **print spooling** (Figure 4.15), which was mentioned in Chapter 1. A printer is an unshareable resource because if it were shared, the output of the different processes using it would be jumbled together. Even limiting it so that only one process could print on a particular page would be

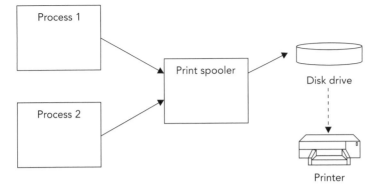

Figure 4.15 Processes sharing a printer via a print spooler.

unacceptable, as the output would consist of a number of interleaved pages that would somehow need to be sorted into the separate piles for the various processes that produced them. The solution is to virtualise the printer by introducing a **print spooler** process which has exclusive access to the printer. Each process that wants to use the printer sends the document to be printed to the print spooler, which stores the documents on disk and deals with them in sequence. However, you cannot do this with every unshareable resource; for example, critical sections are resources which are designed to be unshareable (only one thread at a time should be able to execute within a critical section), so making them shareable would not be feasible.

To prevent the second condition occurring, resources must be preemptible. However, it is not practical to forcibly remove a thread from the middle of a critical section, or to take a printer away from a process partway through printing a page, so this is not generally possible. The third condition, that threads can request additional resources at any time, could be prevented from occurring by requiring each thread to request all the resources it might need when it gets to the point where it needs to request the first such resource. Once the resources had been allocated, it would not be possible to request any more until they had all been released. This would work if you could predict in advance what resources would be required, but this is not always possible. The resources needed might depend on what commands are issued by the user of a program. Also, resources will be tied up unnecessarily; for example, consider a process which uses an unshareable resource such as a modem to dial a particular telephone number and download data for several hours, as well as using another unshareable resource such as an unspooled printer to print error messages. This would tie up the second resource (the printer) from the moment the process started using the modem, and would keep it tied up (perhaps unnecessarily) for several hours, even if no errors occurred and the printer never needed to be used.

The final condition, that there is a circular chain of processes requesting resources, could be prevented by arranging the unshareable resources in a particular order and requiring that they be requested in that order. In this approach, each resource is given a number, and you can only request a resource whose number is higher than the highest-numbered resource that you already hold. However, it is generally impossible to find an ordering that will satisfy everyone. If a high-numbered resource is required for a long time with occasional use of a lower-numbered resource, the lower-numbered resource will need to be requested first and held until a time it can be guaranteed that it will no longer be needed. This can lead to the same inefficient use of resources as if all resources had to be requested at once.

4.7.2   DEADLOCK AVOIDANCE

If none of the four necessary conditions for deadlock can be definitively prevented from occurring, deadlock is always a possibility. However, it is in principle possible to avoid deadlocks by predicting whether it is safe to allocate a particular resource; that is, whether allocating the resource could possibly lead to a deadlock. This relies on all threads declaring in advance which resources they might need. Figure 4.16 illustrates how a collision between two trains can be foreseen based on a possible sequence of resource requests.

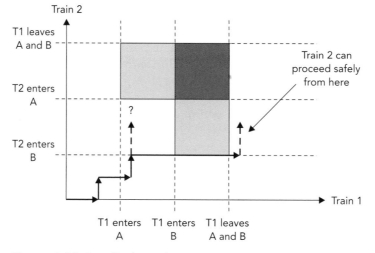

Figure 4.16 Deadlock prediction.

Trains 1 and 2 both declare in advance that they will want to use track A and track B at some point. The axes show the distance travelled by each train at a given moment in a situation where Train 1 will request track A and then track B, while Train 2 will request track B and then track A. Train 1 advances for a while, then Train 2 advances while Train 1 is stopped. Train 2 stops while Train 1 advances some more. Train 1 reaches the point where it enters track A. Train 2 then reaches the point where it is about to enter track B. Is it safe to proceed?

Figure 4.16 shows the places where a deadlock would happen as the lightly shaded areas in the diagram; that is, those areas where either:

- Train 1 is on track A and wants to enter track B while Train 2 is on track B and wants to enter track A, or
- Train 1 is on track B and wants to enter track A while Train 2 is on track A and wants to enter track B.

The darker shaded area towards the top right of the diagram is impossible to reach; it is where both trains have each entered both sections of track.

The danger zone is the area below and to the left of the two deadlock zones which Train 2 is about to enter. If Train 2 enters it, either Train 2 will reach the deadlock zone above it, or Train 2 will stop and let Train 1 proceed, in which case Train 1 will enter the deadlock zone to the right. Since neither train can go backwards, the only possible paths forward lead to deadlock. To avoid the deadlock, Train 2 must be prevented from entering the danger zone; in other words, its resource allocation request must be denied or delayed. Only if Train 1 can continue until it reaches the right-hand edge of the deadlock zones (that is, the point where it releases both sections of track) will it be safe for Train 2 to continue.

One well-known approach to deadlock avoidance is the Banker's Algorithm, which relies on knowing the maximum possible set of resources that each thread might request. The name arises from the idea of a banker who has promised loans at some future time (potential resource allocations) to a number of people, and when one of these people requests a loan the banker has to consider whether there will then be sufficient funds left to cover all the agreed commitments if everyone else asks to borrow the maximum amount at the same time. Requests are only granted if they do not lead to a situation where a future request might have to be denied due to insufficient funds.

Whenever a resource is about to be allocated, the Banker's Algorithm provides a way to test whether there is a possible sequence of allocations which would prevent the requesting thread from continuing. The impending disaster can be deduced from a matrix showing the resources that each thread might use. When considering a request to allocate a resource, the algorithm works like this:

- **Step 1**. Check whether there will be enough remaining resources after granting the request to satisfy the requirements of at least one thread. If not, a deadlock is possible.
- **Step 2**. Pick a thread whose resource requests can all be satisfied and consider what the situation will be if it terminates and releases all its resources. Repeat from Step 1 if there still some threads to consider.

If Step 2 reaches the position where there are no threads left to consider, the situation is safe. It means that, after granting the request, there is some sequence where each thread can request its maximum allocation of resources and run to completion, thereby freeing the allocated resources. On the other hand, if granting the request means that it is impossible to grant any other thread its agreed maximum allocation, a deadlock would result if the worst case happened and every thread tried to claim the agreed maximum.

Exercise 4.4   Consider the situation where the maximum loans agreed by the banker for four clients (A, B, C and D) are $6,000, $7,000, $8,000 and $9,000 respectively. Each client has borrowed $3,000 so far. The bank has $5,000 available in cash. What is the maximum additional loan that can be granted safely to each of the clients?

One problem here is that the result is very conservative. Threads might be held up for long periods to avoid a deadlock that is in actuality highly unlikely and would only arise if threads tried to claim all the resources they need at once. For example, the Banker's Algorithm would prevent two trains travelling in the same direction along a single-track railway. The result will be a much slower and less responsive system. The really big problem is that the algorithm relies on threads declaring their resource needs in advance, and this is not usually possible for systems where users can run any program they feel like whenever they want.

4.7.3   DEADLOCK DETECTION AND RECOVERY

The approach adopted by most operating systems (including Unix and Windows) is to assume that deadlock is possible, but that it is a low-probability risk, and to do nothing to prevent deadlocks occurring. This has the advantage that no restrictions are placed on any of the processes in the system, and the assumption is that this advantage outweighs the disadvantage of an occasional deadlock occurring. This approach values simplicity over safety; in life-critical systems (for example, the control system in an aircraft) one would hope that safety would always take precedence over simplicity. In such systems it will be necessary to adopt one of the methods discussed above for preventing or avoiding deadlock entirely, or finding a rigorous proof that deadlock is impossible in a particular system. However, a user of a Unix or Windows system is not usually (and certainly should not be!) using the system in a life-or-death situation.

If deadlock is allowed to occur, it is first of all necessary to detect when a deadlock has occurred, and then to recover from it somehow. The simplest approach is to leave it all to the user (what Tanenbaum calls the 'Ostrich Algorithm': the operating system sticks its head in the sand and pretends that there isn't a problem). With this approach, deadlock detection consists of a user noticing that nothing much is happening. Recovery consists of the user killing one or more processes until the problem goes away. The problem with this is that there might be another reason apart from deadlock why nothing visible is happening; the application might be waiting for a response to a request it has sent to a remote machine, for example.

A better approach is to automate deadlock detection by using a separate process (which needs to be guaranteed to be deadlock-free!) to monitor the state of the system. It needs to scan the internal tables which record the state of each process (including which resources they each hold and, if they are waiting, what they are waiting for). If it discovers that there is a circular chain of waiting processes, then there is a deadlock.

The next question is what to do in order to recover from the deadlock. The simplest way to do this is to apply *force majeure* by killing one or more of the dead-locked processes, thus releasing whatever resources they currently hold. This could be done by asking the user to select a process to be killed, or simply be killing one of the deadlocked processes at random and waiting to see if the deadlock goes away. If it doesn't, then kill another process, and keep killing processes until there is no more deadlock. This is the approach adopted by VMS. Provided that the processes that are killed can be restarted, it is generally acceptable. For example, a compilation can always be restarted from the beginning with no ill effects. On the other hand, killing an editor where many changes have been made to a file but the changes have not yet been saved would be extremely inconvenient (although many editors deal with this, as well as the possibility of the entire system crashing, by automatically saving changes at regular intervals so that they can be recovered automatically).

In the case of a shared database, killing a process that has updated the database might leave the database in an inconsistent state. Restarting the process would only make matters worse; if the process had incremented a value in some record, restarting it would increment it a second time. A solution to situations like this is to take a **checkpoint** of each process after an important update. The checkpoint is a snapshot of the state of the entire system. This is saved on disk so that the process can be **rolled back** to the latest checkpointed state rather than all the way back to the beginning. This is a fairly expensive solution which requires a lot of disk space for storing checkpoints, so it is generally only used in critical systems where any failures, no matter how rare, are unacceptable, but where occasional interruptions while a rollback and retry take place are acceptable.

Database updates are normally treated as **atomic transactions** which do not cause any changes to the database until the entire transaction is **committed**. By checkpointing a process after an update has been committed, any incomplete changes after that point can be discarded. It is somewhat more complicated to roll back a process to an even earlier checkpoint, as the last committed transaction will need to be undone, which may involve rolling back other processes to an earlier state if they have made use of the transaction data that is being revoked. In the worst case, this can lead to a cascade of rollbacks, eventually rolling back each of the processes involved to the very beginning.

4.8 ☐ LIVELOCK

Livelock is a situation that is similar to deadlock except that the threads involved are able to continue executing. However, they prevent each other from doing anything useful while they are executing. A simple analogy is the situation which sometimes arises when two people are trying to pass each other in a corridor. Both people step to the same side of the corridor, blocking each other. In an attempt to correct the situation, both people then step to the other side of the corridor, blocking each other again. If both people were perfectly synchronised, this situation could continue indefinitely. However, differences in timing will normally resolve the situation quite quickly; one person will start to step aside before the other, and the other person will see this and stay where they are.

The difference between livelock and deadlock is that there is still some activity. When two trains meet on the same railway track, they have to stop. When two people meet in a corridor, they can keep moving, but only from side to side. There is still movement, but it just isn't achieving anything useful. Livelock is not usually a major problem since timing variations will normally resolve the situation fairly quickly; it only becomes a problem in real-time systems, where processes must respond to events by a fixed deadline. If livelock can occur in a real-time system, the unpredictable delay involved before the livelock gets resolved means that it is impossible to guarantee how long it will take a process to do anything.

Ethernet is a famous example of dealing with livelock. An Ethernet network uses a single cable to connect several machines together, as shown in Figure 4.17, and messages are sent by broadcasting them along the cable. All machines receive each message that is sent, but only the machine whose address is given in the message will take any notice of it. Whenever one machine wants to send a message to another machine, it monitors the state of the data traffic on the cable and if necessary waits until the line is idle, with no other machine transmitting. Once the line is idle, it can then transmit its message.

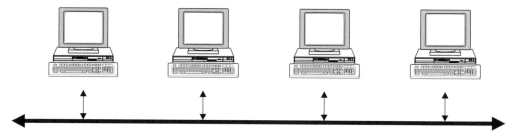

Figure 4.17 An Ethernet network.

However, it is perfectly possible for two machines to simultaneously detect that the line is idle and start transmitting at the same time. When this happens, the two messages are said to **collide**. This is not a collision in the sense of two trains crashing together, but of the messages interfering with each other. The data that will actually be transmitted along the cable will typically be a mixture of the two messages; if one machine is transmitting 00000... while the other is transmitting 11111..., the result will be a mixture of 0s and 1s.

A machine which is transmitting a message is also able to receive its own message by monitoring the data on the cable. A collision is detected whenever the message being transmitted does not match the data on the cable. A machine which detects a collision can **back off** by stopping its transmission, waiting for the line to be idle again, and then retransmitting. However, when a collision occurs, both the machines that were transmitting will back off, and when they start transmitting again another collision might occur. To prevent this happening, each machine waits for a random period of time (up to a maximum limit) before retrying. This will normally prevent a second collision, but further collisions are still possible, especially when the network is heavily loaded with machines which are all trying to send messages to each other. The solution to this is known as **exponential backoff**, where the maximum limit for the random delay period is doubled after each collision. For example, the first collision might result in a delay of anything up to 1 ms; if there is a second collision, the delay chosen will be anything up to a maximum of 2 ms. If there is a third collision, the delay will be anything up to 4 ms, and so on. On a heavily loaded network, the result will be that the competing machines back off for longer and longer periods, which increases the chance that one of them will successfully manage to transmit a message. As the load increases, the network performance will drop gradually rather than ceasing entirely. This is known as **graceful degradation**, where the performance is degraded in a graceful way rather than failing abruptly in a distinctly graceless way.

4.9 ❑ STARVATION AND PRIORITY INVERSION

It is often desirable to give different priorities to different threads, so that high-priority threads will be given preference by the scheduler when it chooses which thread to run next. For example, a thread which is displaying frames from a real-time video which has to wait while each frame is received should normally be given preference over a long computation that does little or no input or output. A thread like the one displaying the video is referred to as **I/O bound**, since the maximum speed of the thread is limited by the speed of the input and output it depends on and it has processor power to spare. A long computation with no I/O restrictions is referred to as **compute bound** or **processor bound**, since the maximum speed of the thread is limited by the amount of processor time it can get to perform the computation. I/O bound threads should normally be given a higher priority than processor bound threads since they will frequently execute blocking I/O requests which will give lower-priority threads a chance to execute, whereas a high-priority processor-bound thread will only rarely give any other thread a chance to run.

When threads can have different priorities, some additional problems can occur. One such problem is that of **starvation**, where a low-priority thread is competing for resources with a set of high-priority threads. If a high-priority thread releases a resource that it holds, another high-priority thread will be able to acquire it before the low-priority thread gets a chance to run. The high-priority threads will be able to pass the resource back and forth between themselves, and the low-priority thread will not get a chance to grab the resource for itself.

Another situation where starvation could occur would be in a naïve implementation of Ada's protected record mechanism (described in Section 4.6.2 above). In a protected record, multiple calls to functions within the record are possible simultaneously, but procedures or entries require exclusive access. If a function is being executed, a procedure call will be blocked until the protected record is not in use. If another thread calls a function in the same protected record, the first function call can complete but the procedure call will still be unable to proceed. If there is a continual stream of function calls, the procedure call will be blocked forever. In this case, the problem arises from the fact that function calls are effectively given a higher priority than procedure calls. A simple way to fix the problem is to allow function calls to proceed only if there is no pending call to a procedure or entry; in other words, procedure and entry calls should always take precedence over any function calls.

A related problem is where a low-priority thread holds a resource that a high-priority thread needs. The high-priority thread will be unable to proceed, and the low-priority thread will be able to execute at the expense of the high-priority thread. If there are other high-priority threads running, the low-priority thread will also be unable to proceed. This situation is known as a **priority inversion**, where a low-priority thread is able to block the progress of a high-priority process. Even worse, if the high-priority process keeps trying to acquire the resource rather than blocking until it is available, the result is a deadlock. The high-priority process has the use of the processor but not of the other resource it needs; the low-priority process has the resource but is prevented from being able to use the processor to execute by the presence of the high-priority process.

A solution to the problem of priority inversion is to assign a priority to each resource. While a resource is in use, temporarily raise the thread's priority to the same priority as the resource itself, so that it will be executed preferentially and will release the resource as quickly as possible. Combining this with a requirement that threads can only request resources with a priority higher than the thread's current priority guarantees that deadlocks are prevented, since circular chains of resource requests will be impossible. A thread holding a high-priority resource will run at a high priority, and cannot be blocked by a lower-priority thread. The lower-priority thread will only have low-priority resources allocated to it (if it had a high-priority resource then it too would be a high priority thread) and the high-priority thread cannot want any of these resources because of the rule that threads can only claim resources whose priority is higher than their own. This is known as the **Immediate Ceiling Priority Protocol** (ICPP).

Question 4.1   What is the relationship between priority inversion and deadlock? Why is ICPP guaranteed to be deadlock-free?

4.10 ❑ THE DINING PHILOSOPHERS PROBLEM

The Dining Philosophers Problem is a famous problem which illustrates deadlock, livelock and starvation in a single situation. It involves five philosophers seated at a circular table in a Chinese restaurant (Figure 4.18). Between each pair of

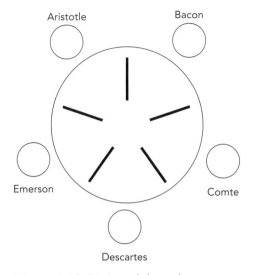

Figure 4.18 Dining philosophers.

philosophers is a single chopstick. Each philosopher alternates between eating and thinking (probably about why there are only five chopsticks for five people!). A philosopher needs to pick up the two chopsticks on either side in order to eat, and puts them back down afterwards before settling down to do some thinking.

If each philosopher adopts the same algorithm for picking up the chopsticks and picks up the left chopstick before the right chopstick, there is a possibility that all five philosophers will simultaneously pick up their left chopsticks. This will mean that none of them will be able to eat (since they each need two chopsticks to be able to eat). Assuming that hungry philosophers will not put down their chopsticks until they have eaten, they will be stuck in a classic deadlock. The chopsticks are resources which, once acquired, are not released until the action they are required for has been completed.

The deadlock is fairly easy to break by denying one or more of the four necessary conditions for deadlock:

- The circular waiting condition can be avoided as shown in Figure 4.19 by having one extra chopstick. The philosophers to either side of the two chopsticks never have to wait for each other to put down their chopsticks, since there will always be a chopstick available on one side. This is topologically equivalent to seating the philosophers along one side of a long table, as shown in Figure 4.20, in which case they are no longer in a circle.

- Allowing resources to be preempted would mean allowing the philosophers to snatch the chopsticks out of each other's hands. There is still a risk that all five philosophers will simultaneously snatch the chopsticks from their neighbour to the right, thus losing their own left chopstick in the process, and then simultaneously snatch back the chopstick from their neighbour to the left, which puts them back where they started. However, this is now a livelock situation rather than a deadlock, and it will presumably be resolved by the strongest philosopher

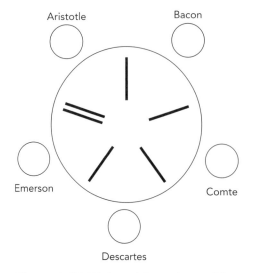

Figure 4.19 Dining philosophers with an extra chopstick.

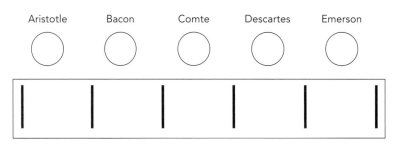

Figure 4.20 Dining philosophers in a row.

managing to hold on to his own chopstick while snatching the other one he needs, in which case he will be able to eat and then put down both chopsticks.

- Allowing resources to be released before they have been used would mean allowing the philosophers to put down a chopstick before eating if the other chopstick is not available. Again, there is a risk of livelock if all philosophers put down their chopsticks and then simultaneously pick them up again. This will presumably be resolved by timing variations; the philosopher with the fastest reflexes will get the chopsticks sooner or later.

- Making chopsticks shareable would allow each philosopher to eat using his neighbour's chopstick as well as his own. (If anyone can think of a way to make chopsticks shareable, please let me know....)

As you can see from this, livelock can still occur even when the conditions required for deadlock are not satisfied. Livelock will only occur when there is a circular chain of threads trying to access the same unshareable resources, but it can still occur even if the resources can be released or preempted. Using a technique like the Ethernet exponential backoff approach will break a livelock situation eventually by perturbing the coincidences in timing which lead to livelock, but there is no way to guarantee when 'eventually' will be. The only way to guarantee that livelock does not occur is to avoid circular chains of threads or unshareable resources.

There are other ways to resolve the deadlock, by introducing additional elements to the scenario. One variation is to introduce a bottle of soy sauce, and require that philosophers pick this up before they try to pick up the chopsticks. Once they have picked up both chopsticks (or picked up one and put it down again) they must release the bottle of soy sauce. This breaks the circularity by preventing more than one philosopher from trying to pick up their chopsticks at the same time; the bottle of soy sauce acts as a mutex for chopstick acquisition since only once philosopher at a time can pick it up.

Another apparently plausible approach is to require both chopsticks to be available before attempting to pick up either of them. However, this does not actually solve the problem; if all the chopsticks are on the table, all philosophers see both of the chopsticks they need and so they can each pick up the one to their left, leading to deadlock. In fact, this makes things worse, because it makes starvation possible – literally so in the case of the dining philosophers! If at least one of your two neighbouring philosophers is always eating, you will never get the chance to pick up either of the chopsticks you need since at most one chopstick will be available at any time. You will never see both chopsticks on the table at the same time and you will starve. Being able to pick up one chopstick at a time means that you will be able to prevent one of your neighbours from eating, and then you will just have to wait for the other chopstick to become available.

Project 4.8 Devise a solution to the Dining Philosophers Problem in a language which supports multithreading.

4.11 ❑ SUMMARY

Being able to run multiple processes at the same time can be extremely useful, as can running multiple threads within a single process. However, care needs to be taken in situations where more than one thread might try to update the same data. In such situations it is possible for **race conditions** to arise where the outcome of the update operations might be time-dependent and hence unpredictable. These problems can be overcome by using **mutexes** or **semaphores** to restrict access to the **critical sections** of code which perform the updates. However, semaphores are a very low-level and error-prone mechanism, and it is a lot safer to use languages like Ada 95 or Java, which provide higher-level mechanisms.

There are several other problems that can arise as soon as it is possible for one thread to prevent another from entering a critical section. The most serious is **deadlock**, where a set of threads are mutually blocking each other's progress. It is possible to prevent deadlock by making it impossible for one or more of the four necessary and sufficient conditions to occur, but this is often impractical. Predicting and avoiding deadlock is also possible but generally impractical. Most systems rely on detecting deadlock when it occurs and breaking the deadlock with brute force.

Other problems are livelock and starvation, which are much harder to detect since the threads involved are still active, even though they might not be doing anything useful. These problems arise from coincidences in timing within a group of threads. Livelocks and starvation situations generally resolve themselves as the result of timing variations between the threads involved, so these are not generally treated as serious problems except in real-time operating systems, where it must be possible to give firm guarantees about response times.

4.12 ❑ ADDITIONAL RESOURCES

Semaphores were originally described by Dijkstra in [7], a classic paper in which he also presents a solution to the bounded buffer problem and describes the Banker's Algorithm. The Dining Philosophers Problem was also first described by Dijkstra in [8]. Deadlock was exhaustively analysed by Coffman *et al.* in [6], a paper which defines the now-famous four necessary and sufficient conditions for deadlock to occur. Livelock and starvation are dealt with in some detail by Burns and Welling [5].

This chapter used Ada 95 and Java as examples of modern languages which support concurrency using variations of the monitor concept developed by Hoare [9] and Brinch Hansen [3]. Ada 95 is defined as an ISO standard in [10], while Java is defined by Joy *et al.* in [11]. A useful introduction to Ada programming in general is given by Barnes [2], while Burns and Welling [4] is a book specifically concerned with concurrency in Ada. There are many good general books about Java, including Arnold *et al.* [1].

4.13 ❑ GLOSSARY

atomic action   an action which is performed as a single, non-interruptible operation.

atomic transaction   in database systems, a set of updates and other operations which is treated as a single operation which either succeeds or fails completely.

Banker's Algorithm   an algorithm for predicting potential deadlocks.

blocking operation   an operation which prevents a thread from continuing until the operation is complete.

busy waiting   waiting for a resource by continually checking the state of the resource in a loop, thereby keeping the processor busy while the thread is waiting.

checkpoint   in database systems, a snapshot of the state of the database which can be used to restore the database if an error occurs later.

clipboard a metaphorical storage device used to transfer information between applications in a GUI system.

COM (Component Object Model) a mechanism developed by Microsoft and DEC which is used extensively on Windows systems to allow communication between objects which may be located in separate processes.

commit in database systems, completing a transaction and finalising any database updates.

critical section a section of code which can only be executed safely by a single thread at a time.

deadlock a situation where two or more threads block each other so that neither can proceed.

Dining Philosophers Problem a famous problem used to illustrate deadlock and related problems.

DLL (Dynamic Link Library) the name used for a shared library on Windows systems.

exponential backoff a technique for breaking a livelock by retrying an operation at ever-increasing intervals.

graceful degradation a gradual worsening of performance rather than an abrupt failure.

guard condition in Ada, a condition used to block or allow access to an entry in a protected record.

ICPP (Immediate Ceiling Priority Protocol) a deadlock-free technique used to avoid priority inversions.

interface a specification of the services provided by an object which does not define how those services are implemented.

I/O-bound job a job which spends most of its time waiting for input and output.

livelock a situation similar to deadlock in that two or more threads prevent each other from performing any useful work, although the individual threads are not blocked and can continue executing.

monitor a structured mechanism for mutual exclusion.

mutex a simple binary mechanism for ensuring mutual exclusion.

mutual exclusion where one thread excludes other threads from executing the same critical section.

priority inversion a situation where a low-priority thread blocks the execution of a higher-priority thread.

processor-bound job a job which uses the processor intensively.

protected record a mechanism used in Ada 95 for mutual exclusion.

race condition an anomalous situation whose outcome depends crucially on the timing of events, and which can have different results at different times.

rollback in database systems, restoring a database to an earlier checkpointed state after a failure.

scheduler the part of the kernel which manages the switching of control between different threads and processes.

semaphore a mechanism for mutual exclusion and synchronization based on a non-negative counter.

shared library a module containing library functions which is loaded into memory once by the first process which requests its use, and is shared by any other processes that request it subsequently.

starvation a situation where a thread is prevented from proceeding by the combined actions of two or more threads.

synchronized method a mechanism used in Java for mutual exclusion.

test-and-set instruction a machine instruction which tests the value of a variable and sets it to a specific value as a single atomic action.

thread a component of a process which executes independently of other threads, analogous to an emulation of a processor within a computer system.

4.14 ❑ REFERENCES

[1] Arnold, K., Gosling, J. and Holmes, D. *The Java Programming Language.* Addison-Wesley (2000)

[2] Barnes, J. G. P. *Programming in Ada 95.* Addison Wesley (1998)

[3] Brinch Hansen, P. The programming language Concurrent Pascal. *IEEE Transactions on Software Engineering,* **SE-1** (Jun 1975), 199–207

[4] Burns, A. and Wellings, A. *Concurrency in Ada.* Cambridge University Press (1998)

[5] Burns, A. and Wellings, A. *Real Time Systems and Programming Languages.* Addison-Wesley (2001)

[6] Coffman, E. G., Elphick, M. J. and Shoshani, A. System deadlocks. *ACM Computing Surveys,* **3**(2) (Jun 1971), 67–78

[7] Dijkstra, E. W. Cooperating sequential processes, In Genuys, F. (ed.) *Programming Languages.* Academic Press (1965). Available online at
`http://www.cs.utexas.edu/users/EWD/ewd01xx/EWD123.PDF`

[8] Dijkstra, E. W. Hierarchical ordering of sequential processes. *Acta Informatica,* **1**(2) (1971), 115–138. Available online at `http://www.cs.utexas.edu/users/EWD/ewd01xx/EWD310.PDF`

[9] Hoare, C. A. R. Monitors: an operating system structuring concept. *Communications of the ACM.* **17**(10) (Oct 1974), 549–547

[10] International Organization for Standardization. *Reference Manual for the Ada Programming Language.* ISO/8652–1995 (1995)

[11] Joy, B., Steele, G., Gosling, J. and Bracha, G. *The Java Language Specification.* Addison-Wesley (2000)

BENEATH THE DESKTOP

OVERVIEW: BENEATH THE DESKTOP

Now that we have looked at what operating systems do and the mechanisms they need to provide to do it, this part looks at how these mechanisms can be implemented. The implementation issues include how memory is managed to provide each process with a separate address space, how the hardware and kernel interact with each other, and how the kernel interacts with device drivers to manage the various peripheral devices available. Normal programs cannot deal with any of these issues; they require the use of specialised privileges and facilities that are not accessible to ordinary users of the system.

Chapter 5 begins by examining memory management, since an understanding of this is central to understanding how the operating system manages processes. Facilities like memory management require close cooperation between the kernel and the underlying hardware, so Chapter 6 looks at hardware issues, and in particular the facilities that the hardware must provide to support the needs of the system kernel. Chapter 7 then looks at the kernel itself and describes how the kernel uses the facilities provided by the hardware to manage processes. The other major implementation issue is how the kernel deals with the variety of peripheral devices available in modern systems, so Chapter 8 deals with device drivers and explains how the kernel interacts with device drivers to manage hardware resources in the system.

5

MEMORY MANAGEMENT

In this chapter, we begin to look at some of the implementation details which allow the operating system to provide programmers with an environment which is, in effect, an emulation of an idealised computer system. At the heart of this 'emulation' is the way that memory is managed so that each process is given the illusion that it has its own memory which is completely separate from the memory belonging to other processes, in the same way that separate computer systems each have their own separate memories.

5.1 ☐ ADDRESS SPACES

A process can be thought of as a model of a complete computer system, with its own processor, memory and I/O devices. Like a real computer system, the range of addresses that can be accessed (the **address space**) is determined by the number of bits the processor uses to represent an address. For example, the 6502 processor used in the Apple II used 16 bit addresses, giving a maximum of 2^{16} different possible addresses. The Intel Pentium family uses 32-bit addresses, giving a maximum of 2^{32} different addresses. In both cases, the smallest addressable unit of data is the byte, so the 6502 can support a maximum of 2^{16} bytes of memory (65,536 bytes, or 64 KB) while the Pentium can support up to 2^{32} bytes of memory (4,294,967,296 bytes, or 4 GB).

Of course, not all possible addresses have to correspond to an actual memory location. Most present-day machines have much less than the full complement of memory installed, so that most of the addresses in the processor's address space will not correspond to any location in physical memory.

5.1.1 PROCESS ADDRESS SPACES

Like a real computer, a process has an address space determined by the number of bits used by the processor to represent an address. In an emulation of an Apple II, the address space is 64 KB as a result of the 16-bit addresses used by the 6502 processor being emulated. If the emulation is being done on a Pentium processor with 512 MB of memory, it is no problem to emulate a large number of Apple II systems; simply reserve some memory for the emulator itself, and divide the remaining memory into 64 KB blocks, one per emulation. The addresses accessed by a particular emulation can be treated as an index into the 64 KB array which represents the memory of the emulated machine, as Figure 5.1 shows.

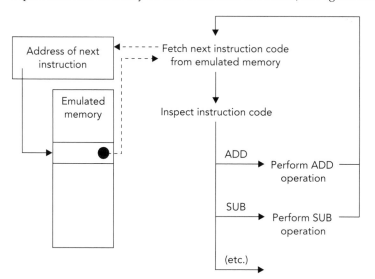

Figure 5.1 Emulating an Apple II on a Pentium.

In an operating system, the problem is more difficult. The 'emulated' processor used by each process is the real processor with a few restrictions on the instructions that the process can execute. It therefore has exactly the same architecture as the real processor, and in particular the address space of each process is the same size as the address space of the real processor. On a Pentium-based machine, this means that every process uses 32-bit addresses, so each process has an address space of 4 GB. Considering that the available physical memory usually occupies only a fraction of the available address space, dividing the physical memory among a large number of processes is more difficult than it is in the case of an emulator for a simpler processor, since the physical memory is not enough to fill the address space of even a single process.

The operating system will need to translate addresses within the address space of a process into the corresponding addresses in physical memory, just as an Apple II emulator needs to translate the addresses used by a program into references into a 64 KB array. As we will see, there are a number of ways that the address space of a process can be **mapped** (translated) to corresponding addresses in physical memory. However, this address translation process is the heart of any memory management technique; the addresses referenced by a user process are always translated into a corresponding physical address by a hardware unit (the **memory management unit**) situated between the processor and the memory.

5.1.2 FIXED-SIZE MEMORY ALLOCATION

One way of sharing the physical memory among several processes is to divide the available memory into a number of fixed-size blocks; for example, a 512 MB physical memory might be divided into four blocks of 128 MB: one for the operating system and the remainder for three processes. Each process will have an address space of 4 GB; 128 MB will correspond to the allocated memory, and the rest will be unused. Each process will appear to be a separate Pentium-based computer with 128 MB of memory.

Using fixed-size blocks is a solution which has the benefit of simplicity. The emulation of memory that the operating system performs for each process simply needs to treat an address referenced by an individual process as an index into the 128 MB array representing the memory available to that process. The operating system just needs to keep track of the **base address** of the memory allocated to each process so that it can do this. Address translation can be done by checking that the address is within the 128 MB limit, and if it is, adding the base address of the 128 MB array to the address referenced by the process to give the corresponding address in physical memory. This is shown in Figure 5.2.

A reference to an address outside the 128 MB limit can be treated as an error condition and which can be reported by generating an exception which the

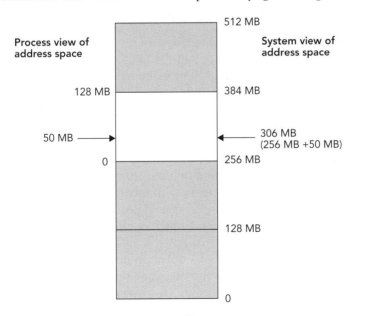

Figure 5.2 Fixed-size memory allocation.

operating system can deal with in some way. After all, a reference to an out-of-range address probably signifies a bug in the program that made the reference. The operating system designer then has the freedom to report the error to the user or to take some other action.

The fixed-size blocks approach has some drawbacks arising from its simplicity. The operating system will only be able to manage a maximum of three concurrent processes, and each process will have a fixed allocation of 128 MB of memory. If the program being run in a particular process only requires 32 MB of memory, the other 96 MB of memory allocated to it will be wasted. One solution is to divide the available physical memory into a number of blocks of different sizes. For example, instead of three blocks of 128 MB each, there might be one block of 128 MB, two blocks of 64 MB, and four blocks of 32 MB. This would mean that each program would have to state its memory requirements in advance so that the operating system could decide which block of memory to allocate, and in addition to recording the base address for each process, the operating system would need to store the size of the allocated memory block so that it could check whether addresses referenced by the process fell within the allocated limit. Even so, it is likely that much of the memory would be wasted, as the requirements of particular programs are unlikely to match the available block sizes exactly. It would also be impossible to execute a program requiring more than 128 MB of memory, even though there may be enough free memory available to accommodate it. Despite the drawbacks, several early operating systems used fixed-size block allocation schemes like these.

5.1.3 VARIABLE-SIZE MEMORY ALLOCATION

A better solution is to allocate blocks of memory on demand. If a program requires 115 MB of memory, allocate a 115 MB block to the process if one is available, and record the base address and limit value (the maximum valid address) in the same way as before. This means that it would be possible for a user to run one large program using all the available memory or lots of small programs. This is better, but there are still drawbacks. One is that the available memory will become **fragmented** if lots of small programs are run; when a process finishes executing a small program, the memory that it used can be marked as being available to be used by another process. The problem that results from this is that if a large program needs to be executed, there may be many small blocks of free memory but no single block which is large enough. For example, Figure 5.3 shows a system with 50 MB of free memory. However, the largest block is only 15 MB in size, so a 20 MB program could not be loaded.

One possible solution is to **defragment** the memory when this happens by moving the contents of memory for each process (and adjusting the corresponding base address) so that all the allocated memory blocks are brought together at the start of the physical memory and all the free blocks are coalesced into a single large block of free memory at the end of the allocated area, as illustrated in Figure 5.4.

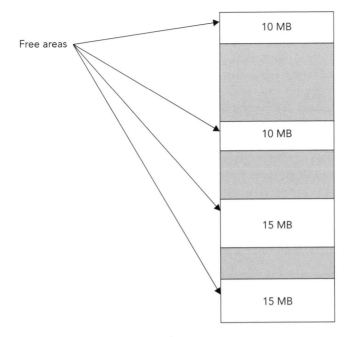

Figure 5.3 A fragmented memory system.

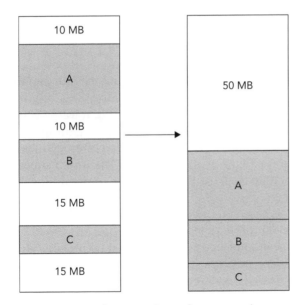

Figure 5.4 Defragmenting a fragmented memory.

This process is sometimes picturesquely referred to as 'burping'. It will be invisible to the processes that are moved; they will continue to reference the same addresses as before but the address translation will now yield different physical addresses than it did before. The downside is that copying large amounts of memory around like this will slow things down quite a bit if it needs to be done too often, and all the processes involved need to be suspended while they are being moved.

Another problem is that programs still need to declare their memory requirements in advance. For many programs, this simply is not practical. The amount of memory required by, say, a word processor program depends on the size of the documents that it is being used with. This is essentially the same problem as we faced earlier; we might want to edit several small documents or one large one.

One solution is to allow programs to allocate additional blocks of memory on demand. The operating system would need to record several pairs of base/limit values for each process (one pair for each block of allocated memory) and the address translation algorithm would become more complicated. However, this would allow a process to start with a minimal memory allocation and increase it as necessary as the program runs.

Exercise 5.1   Describe how address translation would be performed if there are multiple base/limit values. How could you organise a table of base/limit pairs to allow additional entries to be added at any time?

5.2 ☐ VIRTUAL MEMORY

Most modern systems now use a scheme known as **virtual memory** as the standard memory management technique. Virtual memory was originally introduced in about 1960 on the Manchester Atlas computer, but it was expensive to implement, and as a result it was only used in top-of-the-range 'mainframe' systems until fairly recently. In the last decade or so, advances in technology have allowed processor designers to integrate memory management units which support virtual memory onto the processor chip itself, so that virtual memory can now be used on even the cheapest of systems.

Virtual memory is based on the scheme described above, where processes are able to allocate extra memory on demand, and the operating system keeps track of the blocks that have been allocated to each individual process. However, in a virtual memory system, memory is always allocated in fixed-size blocks known as **pages**. The advantage of using fixed-size blocks as the allocation unit is that it simplifies the problems of allocating memory and performing address translations. Allocation is easy, because any request for additional memory can be satisfied by allocating an appropriate number of pages to the requesting process, without having to find a single block which is large enough to satisfy the request. The pages do not need to be contiguous; they can be scattered around anywhere in memory, as Figure 5.5 shows. This is much the same as the way that files are stored on a disk; the blocks making up a file don't have to be stored together, but they are still treated as a continuous sequence when you read the file. It also does away with the

Program to be loaded   Memory

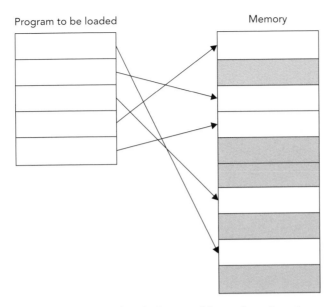

Figure 5.5 Pages loaded into arbitrary locations in memory.

problem of fragmentation, since it doesn't matter where the blocks being allocated are actually located; there is no longer any need to coalesce all the free blocks into a single free block so that a request for a large block can be satisfied.

As an analogy, consider the way that rooms are numbered in a hotel. A room number such as 205 identifies the fifth room on floor 2; room 305 is probably in the same position as room 205, but directly above it on the third floor. The room number can be treated as a combination of a floor number (which tells you which button to press when you get into the elevator) and a number which tells you where to go when you get to the right floor. Of course, in any sensible hotel, the floors are numbered according to their physical position within the hotel. However, it doesn't have to be like this; the hotel management could number their floors in an arbitrary order (Figure 5.6) provided that they also rewired the control panel in the elevator to match the chosen numbering scheme. As long as pressing the button marked '2' in the elevator takes you to the floor which has room 205 in it, it doesn't really matter whether that floor is actually the second physical floor in the building.

The blocks of physical memory that are allocated to hold individual pages are known as **page frames**. The operating system needs to maintain a **page table** for each process which keeps track of which page frame in physical memory is allocated to each of the pages belonging to the process, just as the rewired elevator control panel in the hotel described above keeps track of which floor is which. Address translation is done by dividing the address by the page size to give a page number, and by using the page number as an index into the page table the corresponding physical address can be determined. For example, if the page size was 1000 bytes, addresses 0000 to 0999 would be in page 0, addresses 1000 to 1999 would be in page 1, addresses 2000 to 2999 would be in page 2, and so on.

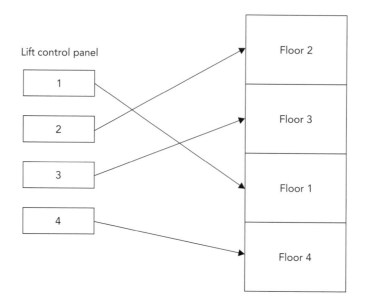

Figure 5.6 A hotel that doesn't number its floors sequentially.

Discarding the last three digits (dividing the address by 1000) gives the page number in each case. The last three digits (the remainder from the division) give you a value between 000 and 999 which tells you which byte of the page frame to access. So if page 1 were stored in page frame number 5, the **virtual address** 1486 (byte 486 of page 1) would be translated into the **physical address** 5486 (byte 486 of page frame 5).

Question 5.1   How does this approach relate to your solution to Exercise 5.1 above?

Since addresses on real computers are binary values, using a page size which is a power of 2 makes it easy to divide by the page size. On Pentium-family processors, the standard page size is 4K (2^{12}) bytes. This is a compromise between having large pages which will waste memory if only a small amount of memory is actually needed, and having small pages which will mean having more entries in the page table. The page number for an address on a Pentium system is determined by dividing the address by 2^{12}, which can be done by discarding the last 12 bits, just as dividing by 1000 in decimal (10^3) can be done by discarding the last three digits. A 32-bit address can therefore be treated as a 20-bit page number followed by a 12-bit **offset** value giving the location of the byte within the page, just as a four-digit address in Figure 5.7 can be treated as a one-digit page number followed by a three-digit offset into the page.

The page number is used as an index into the page table. The selected page table entry contains the corresponding page frame number, which gives the physical

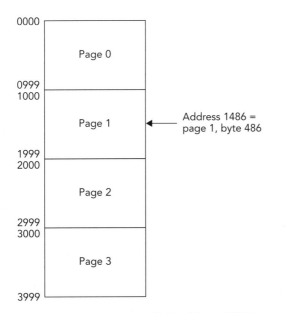

Figure 5.7 A program divided into 1000-byte pages.

location of that page. The page number in the virtual address is replaced by the page frame number from the page table to give the corresponding physical address. The offset is unchanged, as the position that it specifies within the page corresponds directly to the position within the selected page frame. This is shown in Figure 5.8.

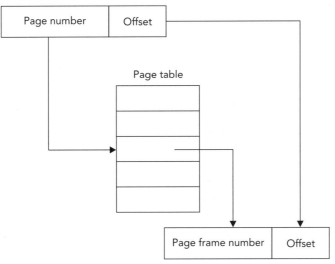

Figure 5.8 Virtual to physical address translation.

Since not all possible addresses in the address space will correspond to memory which has been allocated to the process, the page table entry will need to indicate whether the entry is valid or not (that is, whether the entry refers to a page which corresponds to some allocated memory). A single bit will suffice for this.

5.3 ❑ DEMAND PAGING

One of the major features of virtual memory is that it allows processes to increase their memory allocation at will by requesting extra pages. However, these extra pages do not actually need to be allocated until they are referenced for the first time. When a process requests an extra page of memory, the operating system can just reserve it by recording in the page table that the corresponding page in the virtual address space is in use. Only when the page is accessed for the first time will a page frame be allocated in physical memory. This approach is known as **demand paging**. With demand paging, it is no longer necessary for a program to have to request a particular amount of memory in advance. All programs can request as much memory as they want at any time, but only the memory they actually use will be physically allocated.

The page table can be used to keep track of what state the individual pages belonging to a process are in. The basic states are:

- **Unused:** a reference to an unused page is treated as an error condition, in exactly the same way as all the other schemes described earlier in this chapter.
- **Reserved:** the page has not been allocated a page frame yet. A reference to a reserved page means that it is time to allocate some physical memory to the page. Once this has been done and the page table has been updated to record which page frame was allocated, the page is marked as 'committed' and another attempt can be made to reference the page.
- **Committed:** the page corresponds to some specific page frame in physical memory, and a reference to a committed page is translated into a reference to the corresponding page frame.

When a page is reserved, it might be intended to be used to hold some data that is stored on disk (part of the program, or data from another file). The page table entry for a reserved page acts as a placeholder for a page in the virtual address space which has not yet been allocated a page frame. The page frame number portion of the page table entry is not used until the page is committed, so an entry for a reserved page can use it to hold the location of the corresponding data on the disk. This could be done by storing the disk address in the page table entry itself if a page table entry has enough space to hold a disk address. If this is not the case, the page table entry can be used to hold an index into another table containing the corresponding disk address. When the page is eventually committed by being referenced for the first time, the data can be loaded automatically from disk as part of the committal operation. A special value (typically zero) in the page frame number can be used to indicate that a reserved page is a 'blank page' which does not need to be loaded from disk when the page frame is allocated.

Question 5.2   Unused and reserved pages both alert the operating system that a page has been accessed for which there is no corresponding physical memory. How can the page table entry be used to distinguish between the two cases?

Demand paging makes it easy to load a program when a process first starts up. When the process is created, its page table is initialised to show that the pages corresponding to the program code are reserved and that they correspond to the appropriate locations on the disk where the code is stored. The size of the data area initially needed will be specified in the file containing the program, and a set of blank pages can be reserved for this. All other pages can be marked as unused. The very first instruction to be fetched when the process starts running will be on a reserved page and this page will therefore be loaded into memory automatically as part of the committal operation. As the instructions on this page reference instructions and data on other pages, they too will be loaded into memory. And if some part of the program is never executed (for example, code to deal with errors that do not actually occur, or code to print a document if the document is never printed) the code for that part of the program will never be loaded at all!

5.4 ☐ SWAPPING

With demand paging, a program can be executed even though it is not all resident in memory at once. The program can in fact be larger than the size of the available physical memory. Unused portions of the program are kept on disk and only loaded when they are needed. Problems will only arise when all the page frames in physical memory have been allocated and a new page needs to be allocated a page frame.

Once all the physical memory has been allocated, it will be necessary to free one or more pages that are no longer needed. I'll describe how you can determine whether a page is no longer needed in a moment. Given that you can identify pages that are no longer needed, you can **swap out** these pages by writing them to the disk. Linux systems use a separate disk partition (the **swap partition**) for this purpose, while Windows uses a **swap file**, typically a hidden file in the filesystem on the primary disk. By marking the page table entry as 'reserved' and recording the address where the pages were written to on the disk, you guarantee that if these pages are ever referenced again, they will be reloaded automatically from the disk.

Exercise 5.2   Different versions of Windows use different names for the swap file. Find out what the swap file is called on as many different Windows systems as you can.

Of course, if the page has never been written to when it needs to be swapped out there is no need to write it to the disk since a copy will already exist on the disk (or else it is a 'blank page' which is still blank, in which case a new blank page can be allocated if it is referenced again). The memory management system will need to keep track of the disk address from which each page was loaded so that the page table entry can be changed to indicate a reserved page at the appropriate address on disk.

The disk therefore acts as an extension of main memory. The term 'virtual memory' refers to this use of disk space as an extension of main memory; as a user, you do not need to distinguish the two and do not need to be aware of how the space is being juggled on your behalf. It all happens invisibly, transparently, behind the scenes. The effect is that all the space behaves as if it really were main memory, and it appears as if you had a much larger main memory than you really do. Each process can behave as if it really does have 4 GB of memory at its disposal.

5.5 ❑ THE PAGE TABLE

In a virtual memory environment, the operating system needs to maintain a page table for each process. The information in the page table needs to record whether or not a page is valid (that is, whether it corresponds to some physical memory or not), and if it is valid, the corresponding page frame address.

There is however a problem with the size of the page tables. A 32-bit address using 4 KB pages will be treated as a 20-bit page number and a 12-bit byte number. The 20-bit page number means that the page table will have 2^{20} (slightly over one million) entries. On Pentium-family processors, a page table entry is 32 bits (4 bytes) in size; this means the page table will be 4 MB in size. And that's just for a single process; other processes will have their own address spaces and thus their own page tables. A lot of memory would be used up just to hold the page tables.

For this reason, most processors use multiple levels of page tables. For example, a Pentium processor uses two levels of page table, as shown in Figure 5.9. The first 10 bits of an address are used as an index into the first-level page table whose physical address is stored in a dedicated processor register. This register is only accessible to the operating system kernel and the memory management unit. Since the index into this table is only 10 bits wide, only 1024 (2^{10}) entries are needed, and since each entry is 4 bytes wide, this means a total of 4 KB are needed (which is exactly one page!).

The selected page table entry in the first-level page table gives the address of a second-level page table, and the next 10 bits of the address are then used as an index into this second-level table. Again, since the index is 10 bits wide and each entry is 4 bytes wide, this means a total of 4 KB are needed, so each second-level table will also occupy exactly one page. The page table entry selected from the second-level page gives the location of the page being referenced, and the last 12 bits of the address select one of the 4 KB within the page.

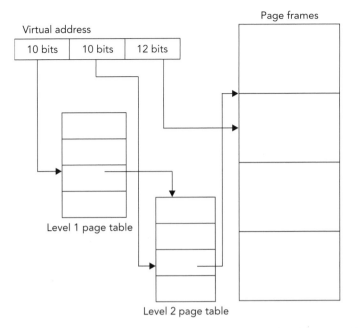

Figure 5.9 Address translation using two levels of page table.

Exercise 5.3

Show the steps involved in translating the hexadecimal address 0x5036FF01 to a physical address on a Pentium processor.

The first-level page table needs to be kept in memory whenever the process is executing, but the second-level page tables can be allocated like any other pages. They are reserved and committed when they are needed, and can be moved in and out of memory on demand. If the first-level page table references a second-level page table that is not already in memory, it will be swapped in from disk in the same way as any other non-resident page would be. Although a process can use its full address space and therefore require the full 4 MB of page table space to be allocated, this rarely happens in practice; most programs have much more modest memory requirements. And even if it does happen, not all of the second level page tables need to be present in memory at the same time.

Newer generations of processors use 64-bit addresses, which makes it increasingly difficult to use the same multi-level page table scheme as can be used for 32-bit addresses. For example, the Alpha 21164 processor developed by DEC uses 64-bit addresses internally, and has three levels of page table. In fact, only 43 bits of the address are used when accessing memory. The page size is 8 KB, requiring a 13-bit offset, and the remaining 30 bits of the address are divided into three 10-bit page table indexes, which means that the individual page tables need to contain 1K entries each. Each entry is 64 bits (8 bytes) in size, so once again an individual page table occupies exactly one page (8 KB). However, it would be much harder to use multi-level page tables if all 64 bits of the address were used.

A solution which is used on some 64-bit processors is to use an **inverted page table** with one entry per physical page of memory containing the corresponding page number, rather than a conventional page table with one entry per page which contains a page frame number. The disadvantage of this approach is that it makes virtual address translation much harder, since the only way to find the physical page frame which contains a particular page is to search the inverted page table for an entry which contains the required page number. This can be done by using a data structure such as a **hash table** to make the process of searching for a particular page more efficient.

A hash table uses a **hashing function** to convert the page number into a small integer (say in the range 0 to 255). The hashing function should distribute the page numbers fairly evenly throughout the table, so that consecutive page numbers do not all generate the same value. Taking the last 8 bits of the page number might be a satisfactory hashing function in this case, and it has the virtue of simplicity.

The value produced by the hashing function is used as an index into the hash table, which in this case will have 256 entries. Each hash table entry then points to a list of page numbers that the hashing function maps to that position in the table, together with the corresponding page table entry. This is illustrated in Figure 5.10.

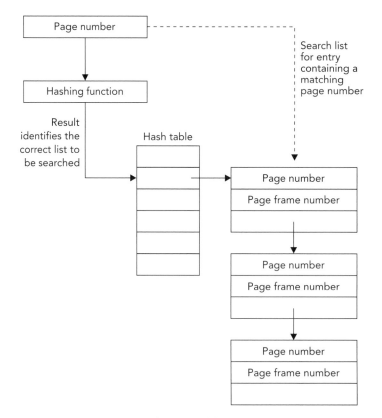

Figure 5.10 An inverted page table.

In this case the list will contain all known page numbers whose last 8 bits match the one being searched for. Having located the hash table entry, the list it points to must be the one that contains the desired page number if it is present. The list is then searched sequentially to find the desired page number, and the corresponding page table entry associated with it. If the page number is not found, it means that the page is unused and that there is no page table entry for it. If the result of hashing the page numbers is evenly distributed, the individual lists will be quite short and can be searched quite quickly. The effect is to cut the search time down by a factor of 256 because only the page numbers whose last 8 bits are the same are looked at. This sounds quite inefficient, but additional specialised hardware could be used to help speed up the search.

5.6 ❑ SHARED MEMORY

Virtual memory also allows memory to be conserved by sharing common pages between processes. If two copies of the same program are loaded and executed, the program code will be the same in both cases. Modern programs do not generally use 'self-modifying code', where the program modifies itself as it runs, so you can guarantee that all the pages which contain program instructions (**code pages**) will be identical. If one of these pages is loaded into memory, the page table entry for the page in each of the two processes can be set to refer to the same physical page frame. Each process will think that it has a separate copy of the page, but in fact it will be shared. As long as neither process modifies the page, the illusion will be preserved.

A common use for shared pages is for sharing common libraries used by many different programs. On Unix systems, these are referred to as **shared object libraries**, normally stored in files with a '.so' suffix, while Windows refers to them as **dynamic link libraries** (DLLs). For example, the code to draw user-interface objects such as windows and buttons is required by nearly all Windows programs, so the code to do this is held in a DLL. When a program tries to load a particular DLL (Figure 5.11), the operating system checks to see whether a copy of the corresponding file has already been loaded into memory. If it has, the page table for the requesting process is updated to refer to the existing copy rather than loading another copy. The operating system also needs to keep a **reference count** for each shared library, indicating how many processes are using each one, so that when the last process which is using the library terminates or explicitly releases the library, the library can safely be removed from memory.

Question 5.3   Do shared areas of memory need to be mapped to the same virtual addresses in each process? Consider what happens when memory addresses are stored in the shared area itself. Consider also what happens if the virtual address is already in use in one of the processes.

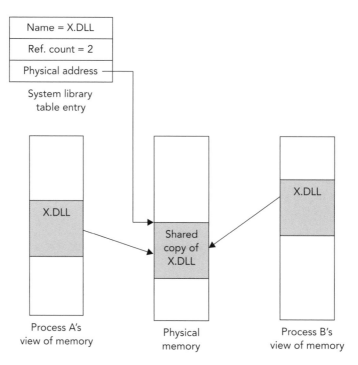

Figure 5.11 Sharing libraries between two processes.

The ultimate shared resource is, of course, the operating system itself. Every program will need to use system calls to access operating system facilities such as input and output, so on most systems the operating system itself is mapped into the address space of every process. The core of Windows itself consists of three DLLs which are always loaded into memory:

- KERNEL32.EXE: the system kernel.
- GDI32.EXE: the graphical device interface, which provides functions to draw graphical objects on the screen.
- USER32.EXE: operations intended for direct use by user programs, including API operations like CreateWindow, CreateProcess, RegisterClass, GetMessage, and input and output functions.

On both Windows and Linux, the last gigabyte of the 4 GB address space in every process appears to contain a complete copy of the operating system itself. However, matters need to be arranged so that this memory is not normally accessible, and is only accessible when a system call transfers control to the operating system. This is to prevent a process (either deliberately or accidentally) changing anything within the operating system which would impact on other processes. A couple of extra bits in the page table entry can be used to record what types of access are allowed to each page (reading, writing, both or neither). This is discussed further below.

It is also possible to arrange for processes to share data pages which can be modified; one process can then communicate with another by modifying a variable within a shared page. This can be done by mapping a file into memory, which is effectively what happens when an executable program file or DLL is loaded. On Windows, this is done with the `MapViewOfFile` API function; the corresponding function on Linux is called `mmap`. A block of pages is marked as reserved, with corresponding disk addresses referring to the file. Referencing any page within the file's mapped area causes the page to become committed by loading the relevant section of the file. If a second process maps the same file, the two processes will share a copy of the file in memory. Mapping a file into memory is also an extremely efficient way to read a file into memory; it is generally much better than allocating a block of memory, opening the file, reading it sequentially into memory, and then closing it.

Exercise 5.4   Devise a scheme which allows shared memory to be dealt with in processors which use inverted page tables.

5.6.1   ACCESS PERMISSIONS

On most systems, the page table entries contain a few bits to specify what types of access (e.g. read access or write access) are permitted for each page, and an illegal access can be reported as an error. For example, the Pentium uses two bits in the page table entry (the user/supervisor and read/write bits) to indicate the type of access a user process has to the page: read and write (user, write), read-only (user, read), or no access (supervisor). The operating system always has full access to all pages (both read and write access). The format of a Pentium page table entry is shown in Figure 5.12. Other processors have similar schemes, with minor

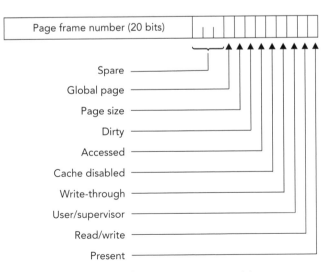

Figure 5.12 Format of a Pentium page table entry.

variations. For example, some processors distinguish instruction fetches from data reads ('execute' access rather than 'read' access) so that code pages cannot be read as data, and hence copied, while readable data pages cannot be executed as code.

Code pages can be marked as read-only (or execute-only, on processors that support this) to prevent processes from modifying them. The operating system code itself can be made inaccessible by marking the corresponding pages as 'no access' (which does not prevent the operating system itself from accessing them, of course). Inaccessible pages can also be used to catch common errors in programming languages like C. In C, **pointer variables** can hold the addresses of data elsewhere in memory, and by convention the address 0 is used to designate a **null pointer**, in other words a pointer that does not point to a valid address. A common error in C programs is to forget to check whether a pointer is null before using it, which can result in the data at address 0 being treated as valid data. This can lead to all sorts of trouble. By making page 0 unreadable, it is possible to trap any attempt to access address 0 and report the attempt as an error.

5.6.2 EXAMPLE: WINDOWS ADDRESS SPACE LAYOUT

On Windows, the address space (Figure 5.13) is normally divided into a 2 GB user area followed by a 2 GB shared system area (although it can also be arranged as a 3 GB user space and a 1 GB shared system area, which is how Linux systems are organised). The first and last 64 KB blocks of the user area are always marked as inaccessible (addresses 0x00000000 to 0x0000FFFF and 0x7FFF0000 to 0x7FFFFFFF). Making the first 64 KB inaccessible means that inadvertent references to address 0 can be trapped, and similarly making the last 64 KB inaccessible guards against defining a buffer (array) which starts at an address in the user area but straddles the boundary into the system area.

The 64 KB area before the inaccessible block at the end of the user area (addresses 0x7FFE0000 to 0x7FFEFFFF) is also inaccessible except for the first 4 KB of it (addresses 0x7FFE0000 to 0x7FFE0FFF). This 4 KB region is a read-only page which

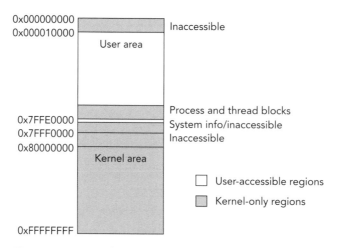

Figure 5.13 Windows address space layout.

is mapped to the same physical address as a page in the system area which contains useful information such as the system time, version number and so on. This lets user processes read this information directly without having to execute a system call to get it from the system area, which would be much slower.

The page immediately before this (prior to address 0x7FFE0000) is used for the **process environment block**, a system data structure which contains all the information needed by the system to suspend and restart the current process, and the pages preceding this are used for the **thread environment blocks** for each thread within the process (of which there is always at least one).

5.7 ❑ PAGE FAULTS

What happens if a page is referenced which is not actually in memory? As described above, an exception (a **page fault**) will be generated; this will abort execution of the current instruction and enter the operating system's page fault handler. A page fault will also save an error code indicating why the page fault occurred (for example, the page is not in memory, or access to the page is denied) and the address that caused the fault. The page fault handler can try to rectify the fault and then re-execute the failed instruction. Normally, the fault occurs because the page needs to be loaded from disk into memory; in other words, the page table entry is marked as reserved. The operating system needs to find an unused page frame, load the contents of the page from disk, and then update the page table to record the newly allocated page frame address.

When the system first starts up, this is easy to do because most of the physical memory is unused. As the system becomes busier, there may not be enough physical memory available to satisfy the demand, and the operating system will need to free up one or more page frames before it can load any other pages. This means there must be some strategy for choosing pages as candidates for replacement.

This is another example of how operating systems separate **mechanisms** from **policies**. The implementation of virtual memory as described so far is almost entirely a hardware **mechanism**, with few implications for operating system design other than the need to provide a page fault handler to load missing pages into memory and to keep the page tables up to date as it does so. However, the page replacement **policy** used by the operating system to choose which pages it should replace is entirely a software matter, and it can have a major influence on overall system performance. A policy which frees pages which are almost immediately referenced again will cause an excessive amount of disk traffic as pages are swapped in and out of memory. Since disk accesses are typically about a million times slower than memory accesses, frequently waiting for a page to be loaded from disk will slow things down quite drastically.

The operating system will of course be able to suspend a thread which has generated a page fault until the faulted page becomes available, and resume execution of some other thread instead. If servicing a page fault takes as long as it takes to execute a million instructions, we would like to be able to execute at least that many instructions between faults. Otherwise, the disk is constantly being accessed to service page faults. In the worst case, if not enough instructions can be executed before another page fault occurs, we have a situation known as **thrashing**, where the disk is constantly busy but the processor is idle a lot of the time, unable to proceed until a page is fetched from disk and almost immediately having to wait again for another vital page. The visible symptom of this is that the overall system throughput falls (the system visibly slows down) while the disk is being accessed continuously (and usually audibly).

Since page faults are determined by the dynamic behaviour of the programs being executed, it is impossible to implement a perfect replacement strategy. A perfect strategy would require miraculous clairvoyant powers to predict what pages would be accessed in the future. The best we can hope for is a **heuristic** policy which will make reasonable guesses about the future behaviour of the program based on recent behaviour. This requires some consideration of what typical program behaviour looks like in the majority of cases.

Most systems base their strategy on the idea that pages that have been referenced recently are likely to be referenced again in the near future, a notion which is rather grandly referred to as the **principle of locality**. If an instruction on a particular page is executed, subsequent instructions on the same page are likely to be executed next. Loops in programs can mean that instructions on the same page (or neighbouring pages) will be executed repeatedly for relatively long periods of time. The data items that a program refers to are typically close together (local variables near the top of the stack, elements of the same array, and so on).

When a program first starts, it will generate a flurry of page faults because none of the pages it needs is in memory. After a while, enough pages will be resident in memory to allow long stretches of uninterrupted processing to take place with only occasional page faults. When this happens, we say that the program has a **working set** of pages available. There will be further flurries of page faults whenever control moves to a different part of the program and a new working set of pages is assembled. Once a working set has been established (when the average rate of page faults is low) there is little benefit in allowing the process to claim extra page frames, as this will not significantly reduce the rate of page faults and will instead reduce the number of frames available to other processes to establish working sets of their own. If there is not enough memory to hold the working sets of all the processes being executed, the system will start thrashing; for example, you can run Windows NT on a machine with only 16 MB of memory, but it will tend to thrash at the slightest provocation. Increasing the amount of available main memory will generally cure this.

One approach is to allocate a fixed number of page frames to a program's working set, and have each program recommend a working set size when it is first loaded. This can cause problems; if the space allocated is too small to hold the program's working set, the resulting page faults will cause the entire system to run more slowly. On the other hand, if it is too large, page frames that could be used elsewhere will be wasted. Approaches based on dynamically varying the number of frames allocated are therefore more widely used. The size of the working set will vary somewhat during execution, and a variable allocation strategy can adapt to these changes and use the available resources more efficiently as a result.

5.7.1 FREEING PAGES

If a process needs to load a page and the request makes the number of unused frames fall below a certain minimum level (in the simplest case, when there are no more unused frames), the system must start identifying which frames are possible candidates to free up for reallocation. A special system process (known on Unix systems as the **kernel swap daemon**) is responsible for doing this; this process runs at regular intervals and tries to free up some page frames if the amount of free space has dropped below a certain minimum level. Some frames must not be considered; for example, frames into which a disk transfer is pending and indeed the frames which contain the page fault handling code. Such frames are marked as being **locked** and are never considered for replacement. Frames that have been written to are **dirty** and must be saved on disk before they are reused. Frames that have not been written to are **clean**, because they are the same as they were when they were last allocated: either initialised to zeros or copied from a known location on disk. The memory management hardware will need to set a bit in the page table entry whenever a page is written to in order to keep track of whether pages are dirty or clean.

Exercise 5.5

Page swapping can be based on a global replacement strategy, where pages belonging to any process can be swapped out to create a free page, or a local replacement strategy, where only pages belonging to a particular process will be swapped out to allocate a new page to that process. What are the advantages and disadvantages of each approach?

Clean pages are much cheaper to reuse than dirty ones, since nothing needs to be written back to the disk before the frame can be reused. If there are no clean pages, the kernel swap daemon can build up a list of dirty pages and start writing them back to disk and then mark them as clean (since an up-to-date copy now exists on disk). The result is a list of clean page frames that can be allocated to any process that needs them. Of course, if any of these pages are referenced again before they have been allocated elsewhere, their entries can simply be removed from the list of free pages and reallocated to their original owners.

Exercise 5.6

Consider a memory management unit which does not support a 'dirty' bit which is automatically set when a page is written to. How could a 'dirty' bit be implemented in software, and would it be worth the effort? Explain your answer.

5.7.2   SWAPPING POLICIES

So how can the operating system choose which pages to add to its list of free pages? A simple strategy is **FIFO** (first in, first out; see Figure 5.14): that is, to choose the oldest pages (i.e. the ones which have been resident for the longest time). However, a page that has been resident for a long time might still be in active use, in which case it will be referenced again almost immediately. In this case, it will usually still be in the list of free pages and can be reallocated immediately, as described above, with little or no overhead. When this happens, it will now be the youngest (most recently loaded) page, so the system will not consider it again for some time as a candidate for replacement.

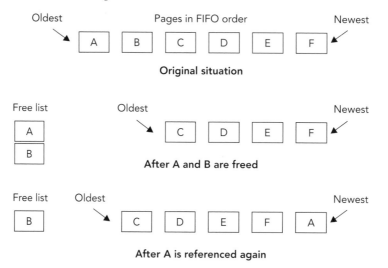

Figure 5.14 Behaviour of a FIFO replacement policy.

The behaviour of this scheme is often suboptimal, and there is an overhead in the need to keep track of the order in which page frames were allocated (e.g. using a linked list of page frame addresses). An alternative strategy is **LRU** (least recently used), a strategy which appeals to the principle of locality: the page which has been used least recently is least likely to be referenced again. This should give much better performance, but the overhead is much worse: a list of page frame addresses could be used as described above to keep track of the order in which pages are referenced, but every reference would require the corresponding entry to be moved to the front of the list. There are other ways of recording the history of page references, but they all involve a substantial overhead for every page reference.

Although it would be impractical to keep a complete history of page accesses, there are schemes (generally known as **clock policies**) which give a good approximation to LRU, and whose only overhead is an extra bit in the page table entry. This technique (Figure 5.15) requires a **usage bit** which the memory management hardware sets to 1 whenever the corresponding page is referenced in any way (including when it is first loaded into memory). This is used to record whether the

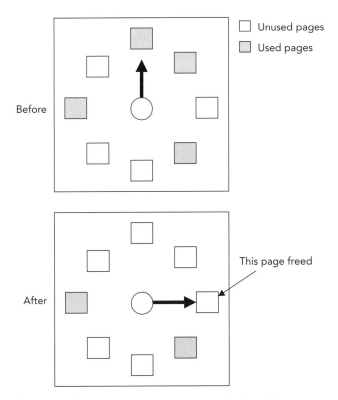

☐ Unused pages
☐ Used pages

Before

This page freed

After

Figure 5.15 Freeing pages using a clock policy.

corresponding page has been referenced since the last time it was considered. To identify a page which is suitable for replacement, the kernel swap daemon scans the page tables looking for entries whose usage bit is 0. As the scan proceeds, any entries that are examined whose usage bit is 1 have their usage bits reset to 0. Each page encountered whose page table entry has a usage bit set to 0 (i.e. not referenced since the last scan) is added to either the list of free pages if it is clean, or to the list of dirty pages waiting to be written to disk otherwise. The pages whose usage bits have been set to 0 will be freed the next time they are considered unless they have been referenced in the meantime, which will have set their usage bits back to 1. The scan continues until the kernel swap daemon has enough free pages at its disposal, and it can then go back to sleep again. The next time it needs more free pages, the scan will start from the point where the previous one left off. The scanning is done repetitively, so that the scan resumes from the beginning once the last entry has been scanned.

Note that this scheme degenerates into something like FIFO if every page has its usage bit set to 1. During the scan, all pages considered will have their usage bits reset to 0; eventually, the scan will return to the first page again and, as its usage bit is now 0, it will be chosen for replacement.

Exercise 5.7   If a clock policy is used locally (where each process is dealt with separately) how can this be used to manage the working sets of the processes? What does having every usage bit set to 1 imply?

5.8   ❑   COPY-ON-WRITE

As I mentioned earlier, the Unix fork system call creates a new process by making an exact copy of the process which called fork. I also said that process creation on Unix systems was quick and easy. So how do I reconcile these two assertions?

The solution is to use an elegant technique based on page sharing. When fork creates a new process, all it really has to do is to make a copy of the page table. The page tables of the two processes now point to exactly the same physical pages. However, the writable pages in the two processes are changed to mark them as **copy-on-write** pages. When either process attempts to write to a page, the page is copied, and the page table entries in each process are updated to refer to the two separate copies as normal writable pages. Copies are only made when absolutely necessary, so this approach maximises efficiency by minimising the time and space needed for making copies of pages.

Copy-on-write can be implemented using a single spare bit in the page table entry to indicate whether the page is copy-on-write or not. As shown in Figure 5.12, the Pentium has three spare bits in the page table entry that the operating system can use for its own purposes, so one of these can be used as a copy-on-write bit. A copy-on-write page is marked as read-only but with the extra copy-on-write bit set as well. Attempting to write to the page will generate a page fault because the page is marked as read-only, and the page fault handler can check whether the faulting page is marked as a copy-on-write page, and then either copy the page if it is or generate the normal 'access violation' exception if it is not. When the page is copied, the page table entry is updated to point to the copy as a normal writable page. This is discussed further in Chapter 7.

5.9   ❑   SEGMENTATION

Some processors (including the Pentium) provide another level of memory management known as **segmentation**. However, since many processors do not support this, operating systems which are designed to be portable to a variety of different processor architectures (including Windows and Linux) do not make any use of the Pentium's segmentation facilities. In some ways this is a pity, since modern Pentium processors have a 36-bit address bus which allows up to 64 GB of physical memory to be connected to them, although this has to be treated as a number of separate segments of up to 4 GB each as a result of the internal 32-bit architecture imposed by the use of 32-bit registers for specifying memory addresses.

In a segmented system, the available memory is divided into a number of separate address spaces, each of which has a specified size. For example, one segment might be 10 MB in length while another might be 50 MB. The valid addresses in the first segment would be 0 to 10 MB – 1, while the valid addresses in the second segment would be 0 to 50 MB – 1. Address 0 in the first segment refers to a completely different location from address 0 in the second segment. Attempting to access beyond the end of a segment causes a 'segmentation violation' exception to be reported. An address in a segmented memory system has two parts: a segment number and an address within the segment.

Each memory reference on a Pentium uses one of six **segment registers**. The three main ones are CS (the code segment, used for instruction accesses), DS (the data segment, used for data accesses) and SS (the stack segment, used for references to data stored on the stack). Three others (ES, FS and GS) have no dedicated purpose, and can be used as an alternative to the normal segment register in any individual instruction by prefixing the instruction with a 'segment override' code prefix. Each segment register contains a 16-bit value which acts as an index into a **segment descriptor table** maintained by the operating system, which allows for up to 64K different segments.

Question 5.4   Look at Question 5.3 again. How can segmentation be used to allow shared blocks of memory to be loaded into different virtual addresses in different processes?

The entries in the segment descriptor table specify the base address and limit value (size) of the segment, as well as some status and permission bits which are similar to those in a page table. This is shown in Figure 5.16. The limit value is a 20-

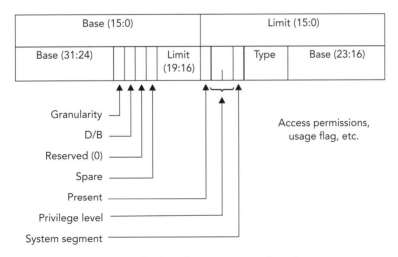

Figure 5.16 Format of a Pentium segment descriptor.

bit value which is measured either in bytes or in 4K pages depending on the setting of the 'granularity' bit, so each segment can be up to 4 GB in size. The base address is a 32-bit value measured in 'paragraphs' of 16 bytes each, giving a physical address space of up to 4 'gigaparagraphs' (64 GB). Interestingly, on the Pentium, segment descriptors distinguish 'read' accesses from 'execute' accesses, although page table entries do not. The type field specifies one of four sets of access permissions: read-only, read/write, execute-only and execute/read.

Segmentation has many advantages. It allows different program components to be segregated into separate address spaces; for example, a data structure such as an array could be put into a segment of its own, which would mean that bounds checking for array accesses would be handled by the memory management system, rather than having to check explicitly whether an array index was valid each time the array was accessed. An awful lot of operating system bugs are due to 'buffer overrun' errors where data is written to a position beyond the end of an array, overwriting something else instead. Segmentation can allow errors like this to be detected automatically without the need for any extra code to check for valid accesses in software.

However, because many processors do not support segmentation, both Windows and Linux adopt a 'flat address space' approach. The available memory is treated as being a single segment which is 4 GB in size, and all the segment registers are initialised so that they all refer to this one segment. This effectively disables segmentation; only the operating system is able to access the segment registers or segment descriptor tables to change this setup, and it simply doesn't do this.

5.10 ❑ SUMMARY

Memory management (and virtual memory in particular) is at the heart of how an operating system manages processes. On Pentium systems, each process has a separate 4 GB address space which appears to contain its own personal copy of the operating system kernel. Each page of the address space can be given its own set of access rights to prevent read-only code or data from being modified or to prevent user processes accessing the kernel directly. Memory areas can be shared between processes, and this can particularly improve memory usage when shared libraries are involved. In particular, all processes share a common copy of the system kernel. Accesses to unallocated regions of the address space will generate exceptions which can be used to guard against common programming errors.

Virtual memory allows processes to run programs that are bigger than the available physical memory, which it does by only loading pages from disk when they are referenced. A kernel process ensures that there are sufficient free pages at all times to satisfy requests to load a page, using a policy which tries to free up pages that are unlikely to be required in the near future. Modified pages will need to be written back to the disk before they can be freed, but copies of unmodified pages will already exist on disk so that they can just be marked as free. For this to work, the memory management hardware will need to assist the operating system by keeping track of which pages have been referenced and which have been modified.

5.11 ❑ ADDITIONAL RESOURCES

Fotheringham [4] and Kilburn *et al.* [7] describe the original virtual memory implementation for the Manchester Atlas, while Denning provides a detailed survey of virtual memory in [3]. Another paper by Denning [2] introduced the notion of the working set. A more recent paper by Jacob and Mudge [5] describes implementation issues for virtual memory systems on modern processors.

Solomon and Russinovich [10] describe how virtual memory is handled in Windows, while Aivazian [1] and Rusling [9] both include some information on virtual memory management in Linux systems. Love [8] also includes a section on Linux memory management. Jacob and Mudge [6] describe how virtual memory is implemented on a selection of modern 64-bit processors.

5.12 ❑ GLOSSARY

address translation   the translation of the virtual addresses used by a process into the corresponding physical addresses used by the underlying physical memory.

address space   the range of addresses that can be referenced by a process.

base and limit registers   a simple system of virtual memory where the base register specifies an offset used to calculate a physical address and the limit register defines an upper bound for the address space of the process.

clock policy   a policy used to choose pages to swap out where pages are considered in a cyclical order.

committed page   a page to which some physical memory has been allocated.

copy-on-write   a mechanism for minimising the duplication of pages, where pages are shared and only copied when they are written to.

demand paging   a mechanism whereby reserved pages are only committed (loaded into memory) when they are referenced.

dirty page   a page which has been written to and for which there is no corresponding copy on disk.

heuristic   a rule of thumb which will produce a reasonable answer most of the time. Heuristics are generally used in situations where there is no algorithm that will always produce the 'correct' answer.

inverted page table   a technique used on systems with large address spaces to minimise page table size, mapping page frames to pages rather than pages to frames.

locked page   a page which must remain resident in memory and must not be swapped out to disk.

memory management unit   the hardware unit responsible for address translation.

page   a fixed-size block of addresses within the address space of a process.

page fault   an exception reported by the memory management unit when a page which is not present in memory is referenced.

page frame a physical block of memory allocated to hold a page.

page table an operating system table which maps page numbers to page frames for each process.

physical address an address in physical memory.

principle of locality the principle that, if an address is referenced, it (or a nearby address) is likely to be referenced again in the near future.

reserved page a page which has been allocated within the address space of a process but which has not yet been allocated a corresponding page frame in physical memory.

segmentation a rarely used memory management technique which involves providing a process with multiple logically separate address spaces, each of which can be a different size.

swapping copying pages between memory and disk.

thrashing a condition arising from excessive swapping, where page faults are happening faster than the system can load the corresponding pages.

virtual address an address within the address space of a process, which can correspond to different physical addresses at different times as pages are swapped in and out of memory.

virtual memory a technique for managing memory using fixed-size pages which are independently mapped to page frames in physical memory.

working set the set of pages that a process needs to be resident in memory in order to avoid excessive numbers of page faults.

5.13 ❑ REFERENCES

[1] Aivazian, T. *Linux Kernel 2.4 Internals*. The Linux Documentation Project (Mar 1996). Available online at http://www.tldp.org/LDP/lki/

[2] Denning, P. J. The working set model for program behaviour. *Communications of the ACM*, **11**(5) (May 1968), 323–333

[3] Denning, P. J. Virtual memory. *ACM Computing Surveys*, **2**(3) (Sep 1970), 153–189

[4] Fotheringham, J. Dynamic storage allocation in the Atlas computer, including an automatic use of a backing store. *Communications of the ACM*, **4**(10) (Oct 1963), 435–436

[5] Jacob, B. and Mudge, T. Virtual memory: issues of implementation. *IEEE Computer*, **31**(6) (Jun 1998), 33–43

[6] Jacob, B. and Mudge, T. Virtual memory in contemporary microprocessors. *IEEE Micro*, **18**(5) (Jul/Aug 1998), 61–75

[7] Kilburn, T., Edwards, D. B. G., Lanigan, M. J. and Sumner, F. H. One-level storage system. *IRE Transactions*, **EC-11**(2) (Apr 1962), 223–235

[8] Love, R. *Linux Kernel Development*. Sams (2003)

[9] Rusling, D. A. *The Linux Kernel*. Linux Documentation Project (Jan 1998). Available online at http://www.tldp.org/LDP/tlk/

[10] Solomon, D. A. and Russinovich M. E. *Inside Microsoft Windows 2000*. Microsoft Press (2000)

CHAPTER 6

H A R D W A R E   S U P P O R T

In the previous chapter we looked at how memory is managed to provide each process with the illusion that it has its own private memory. Features like this are implemented using a combination of hardware and software. The software side of virtual memory management involves updating page tables and swapping pages in and out of memory. On the hardware side, there needs to be specialised memory management hardware which will perform address translation and which will generate page fault exceptions if the translation cannot be done for any reason. The operating system cooperates with the hardware to provide the information it needs to do its job (page tables, in this case) and the hardware cooperates with the operating system by using the page tables to do address translation and by modifying the page table entries to keep track of which pages have been accessed and which have been modified. All this is completely hidden from anyone using the system.

Most of the work that the operating system does involves dealing with the underlying hardware. Conversely, the hardware must be designed so that it provides the facilities that the operating system needs to manage the machine efficiently. This chapter looks at the specialised hardware that an operating system relies on to be able to fulfil its purpose, which is to provide individual processes with the illusion that they are running on an idealised computer system that is separate from any other processes running at the same time.

6.1 ☐ HOW COMPUTERS WORK

Up until now, I have been somewhat hazy about many of the actual implementation issues in writing a working operating system. This chapter starts to address some of these issues by looking at the difference between a software emulation of a process environment and how modern processor designs support operating system requirements in hardware. To begin with, I need to review some of the basics of computer operation.

The heart of any computer system is the processor. The processor carries out a repetitive cycle of fetching the next instruction and executing it, as shown in Figure 6.1. To do this, it needs to keep track of where the next instruction is located in memory, and it uses an internal **register** usually called the **program counter** to hold the address of the next instruction. Pentium processors use 32-bit addresses, so the program counter is a 32-bit storage unit referred to as EIP. Unlike everyone else, the Pentium uses the term 'instruction pointer' (IP) rather than 'program counter', but I'm going to stick to the standard terminology that everyone else uses.

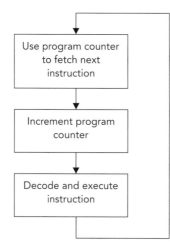

Figure 6.1 The fetch–execute cycle.

There are a number of other registers within the processor which are used for temporary storage and various other purposes. On a Pentium, the registers are all 32 bit storage units. The main ones are called EAX, EBX, ECX, EDX, ESI, EDI, EBP and ESP. There is also a 32-bit **status register** called EFLAGS, which consists of a set of values reflecting the current state of the processor. On many processors this is referred to as the **program status word** (PSW). There are also six **segment registers** (CS, DS, ES, FS, GS and SS) which I will ignore for now. The programmer's view of a Pentium processor is illustrated in Figure 6.2.

The processor normally executes instructions sequentially, but the sequence can be altered using **jump** (or **branch**) instructions which alter the value of the program counter. This is how loops and conditional statements in high-level languages are implemented. To implement functions and procedures in high-level languages, additional **call** and **return** instructions are used. A call instruction is like a jump instruction, except that the **return address** (the address of the instruction following the call instruction) is saved, so that the return instruction can reload the program counter from the saved value. The next instruction to be fetched will be the one whose address is given by the program counter, so execution will resume at the instruction after the call instruction.

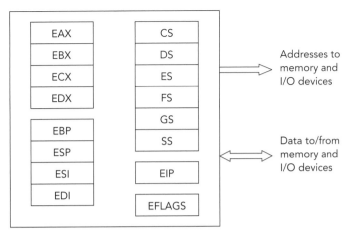

Figure 6.2 Programmer's view of the structure of a Pentium processor.

6.1.1 THE STACK

The return address from a call instruction is stored on the **stack**, which is a block of memory that allows new items to be 'pushed' onto it, and items to be removed by 'popping' them off the top of it. The usual analogy is with a stack of plates in a canteen; when you put a plate on top of the stack, it pushes the rest of the plates down. When you remove a plate, a spring pops up another plate. (Stack terminology also makes a handy 'geek test'; if you ask someone what the opposite of 'push' is, anyone who says 'pop' rather than 'pull' is a geek.)

The position of the top of the stack is given by the **stack pointer** register (ESP on a Pentium processor). Special **push** and **pop** instructions add items to the stack and remove items from it, as do the **call** and **return** instructions. Pushing a value onto the stack decrements the stack pointer to point to an unused location and writes the value into the address specified by the stack pointer. The stack therefore grows downwards from the top of the address space towards the program and data located at the bottom of the address space. Popping an item off the stack copies the value whose address is specified by the stack pointer and then increments the stack pointer so that it points to the next item on the stack. Figure 6.3 shows how this works. Note that a value popped off the stack is not actually removed from memory, but it is no longer part of the stack because the stack pointer has been adjusted to point to the next item. It will be overwritten with a new value the next time something is pushed onto the stack.

6.1.2 THE INSTRUCTION SET

The instruction set that a processor supports also has a significant effect on its ability to support the functionality required by an operating system. In recent years there has been a movement away from **complex instruction set computers** (CISC) in favour of **reduced instruction set computers** (RISC). The CISC philosophy is to provide a rich set of powerful instructions that implement a lot of

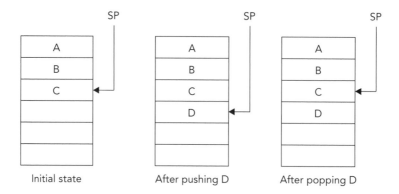

Figure 6.3 Pushing and popping a stack.

functionality in hardware (or rather, in **microcode**). The Pentium is an example of this approach. The RISC philosophy is that smaller building blocks can be implemented more efficiently and the structures built from these building blocks can be optimised more effectively; processors such as the SPARC used in Sun workstations exemplify this approach. Nevertheless, there is some general agreement on the building blocks that a processor's instruction set must provide to support a modern operating system.

There are some obvious requirements that any processor should satisfy. I've already mentioned the need for an instruction that can be used to implement system calls (for example, the INT instruction on Pentium processors or the TRAP instruction on Motorola 680x0 processors). A test-and-set instruction or something similar is needed to implement mutexes, particularly on processors designed for use in multiprocessor systems. There are a number of other instructions which are described elsewhere in this chapter and the next which are provided for use by the operating system kernel.

Exercise 6.1   For a particular processor, identify the instructions that can be used to implement a mutex, and explain how they can be used for this purpose.

6.1.3 MEMORY AND I/O DEVICES

The processor specifies a memory location or I/O device that it wants to access using its **address**. The range of available addresses is known as the **address space**, but not all addresses will correspond to a valid memory location or I/O device. The Pentium processor uses 32-bit addresses, giving an address space of 2^{32} addresses (up to 4 GB of memory). Usually, only a fraction of the available addresses actually correspond to valid memory locations On the computer I am using, the processor has an address space of 2^{32} bytes (4 GB), but there is only 512 KB (2^{19} bytes) of memory actually installed, which occupies only one-eighth of the available address space.

I/O devices can share the same address space as memory (known as **memory-mapped I/O**) or use a separate address space that is accessed by a special set of instructions (**port-based I/O**). Pentium-based systems can use either approach; there are special IN and OUT instructions which specify a 16-bit **port address** for an I/O device, or I/O devices can be given addresses in the same 4 GB address space as memory and accessed using the same instructions that are used to access memory. A 16-bit address as used by an IN or OUT instruction specifies one of 64K I/O port addresses, which bear no relationship to the addresses used for accessing memory.

In a memory-mapped system (Figure 6.4), a keyboard might be set up to respond to a pair of addresses. One will correspond to the keyboard's **status register**, which returns a byte of data indicating whether a key has been pressed, whether the shift key is down, and so on. The other will correspond to the keyboard's **data register**, which gives the binary code corresponding to the key that was most recently pressed. The only visible difference between an address corresponding to an I/O device and one corresponding to a memory location is that a value being read from an address corresponding to an I/O device will depend on the state of the external device, rather than being a copy of the last value that was written to the address.

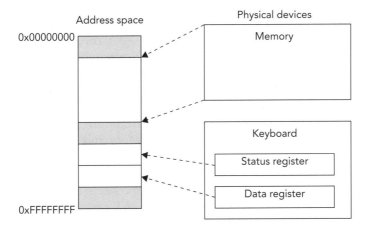

Figure 6.4 A memory-mapped keyboard.

Reading a character from the keyboard could be done by repeatedly reading from the address corresponding to the status register until its value 'spontaneously' changes to indicate that a key has been pressed. The key code for the key that has just been pressed can then be read from the data register, and usually the act of reading the data register will automatically reset the 'key pressed' indicator in the status register.

The processor is connected to the rest of the system by a **data bus**, which is used to transfer data to and from the rest of the system, and an **address bus**, which is used to broadcast addresses to the rest of the system (Figure 6.5). The term 'bus' is

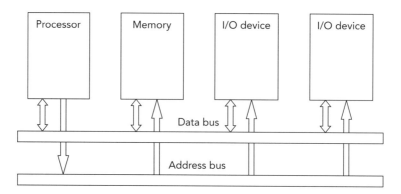

Figure 6.5 Data and address buses.

used here in its electrical engineering sense of a set of parallel electrical conductors (wires, or tracks on a printed circuit board). Each conductor can carry one bit of information at a time, so the number of conductors making up a bus (the 'width' of the bus) determines the number of bits it can carry. The Intel Pentium family of processors have a 32-bit data bus and 32-bit address bus, so data can be transferred in units of up to 32 bits in a single operation, and addresses are 32 bit values, as mentioned earlier.

When a processor tries to read a byte of data from a particular address, it uses the address bus to broadcast the address to the rest of the system and then, after a short delay, samples the data bus to get the resulting value. If the address corresponds to an existing memory location or I/O device, the corresponding device will respond with the data it contains. If not, nothing will respond to the broadcast address, and there will be no valid data returned by any part of the system. Depending on the way the data bus hardware is designed, the result might be zero, or all ones, or some essentially unpredictable value. Similarly, when the processor wants to write a byte of data to a particular address, it broadcasts the address on the address bus and the data on the data bus and then it waits for a short time to allow some other part of the system to respond. If the address corresponds to an actual memory location or I/O device, the corresponding memory or I/O device will respond by storing the data being broadcast. If not, nothing will respond to the address and the data will be ignored. A read-only memory device (**ROM**) is similar to normal memory in that it allows its contents to be read in the usual way, but any data written to it will simply be ignored.

Thus the address space is simply the range of possible addresses. Not all addresses need to correspond to an actual memory location, and the result of reading from an unused address will in general be unpredictable, while the result of writing to an unused address (or an address in a read-only memory) is that the data being written will simply be ignored. The memory management system provides predictability by trapping references to invalid memory addresses and reporting them as exceptions.

6.2 ❑ USER AND KERNEL MODES

We've already seen that the view of the processor and memory is somewhat different from the point of view of a process to the underlying reality as seen by the operating system. Ordinary processes can't execute certain instructions, like the 'halt' instruction on a Pentium processor, and some areas of memory are not accessible to them, notably the shared area where the operating system is loaded.

To implement this, the physical processor needs to be able to operate in two different **modes**, normally referred to as **user mode** and **kernel mode** (or **supervisor mode**). Some processors provide more than two modes of operation, with different levels of capabilities (for example, the Pentium has four different modes), but since some processors only satisfy the minimum requirement of providing two different modes, operating systems that are designed to be portable to different processors (like Windows and Linux) use only two of the Pentium's four modes; the least privileged mode for user mode, and the most privileged mode for kernel mode.

Question 6.1   Why might more than two modes be useful?

In user mode, only a subset of the processor's facilities can be used. Other facilities (such as the 'halt' instruction) can only be used when the processor is operating in kernel mode. Attempting to use one of these **privileged instructions** will generate an **exception**, which will transfer control to an operating system routine which will deal with it in some appropriate way. System calls are also implemented the same way; the 'system call' instruction just generates a specific exception that the operating system handles by performing the requested operation.

Exercise 6.2   For a particular processor, identify the privileged instructions that it provides and try to categorise them. Why do they need to be privileged? Why would it be unsafe for user processes to execute them?

6.2.1 EXCEPTION HANDLING

When an exception occurs (Figure 6.6), the processor performs what is essentially a self-generated **call** instruction, except that in addition to saving the return address that identifies where the exception occurred, status information including the current processor mode is also saved. In some cases extra information will also be saved; for example, when the memory management unit reports a page fault, the address which generated the page fault and the type of access being attempted are

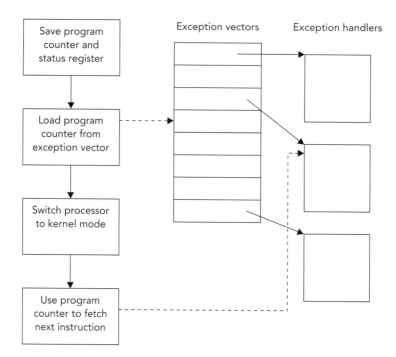

Figure 6.6 What happens when an exception occurs.

also saved, as well as an error code indicating whether the fault occurred because the page was not present in memory or because the type of access being attempted was not allowed.

Once all the necessary status information has been saved, the processor switches into kernel mode and transfers control to a specific address within the operating system kernel. Each possible exception has a specific number, and the exception number is used as an index into a table of **exception vectors**. An exception vector contains the address of the kernel routine which will deal with the corresponding exception (the **exception handler**). One of the first things the kernel does when the system is starting up is to initialise the exception vector table with the addresses of the appropriate exception handling routines within the operating system kernel. The address of the table itself is usually specified by a processor register which is only accessible in kernel mode (that is, the instructions which access the register are privileged instructions, only usable when the processor is operating in kernel mode).

Exercise 6.3   For a particular processor, find out how exceptions are handled. What does the hardware do in response to an exception? What different categories of exception are there, and are they dealt with differently?

At the end of dealing with the exception a special form of the **return** instruction (called IRET on Pentium processors) will restore the original processor mode as well as the return address, so the process will continue executing from the point where the exception occurred in the same mode as it was in at the time it occurred.

The important thing to realise here is that when an exception occurs, the current thread does not stop executing so that the 'operating system' can start executing instead. The same thread is still running, but it's now running in kernel mode rather than user mode. There is no separate 'operating system' thread as such. Ordinary threads switch back and forth between kernel mode, and one of the kernel routines (the **scheduler**) transfers control from one thread to the next when necessary. But there is always a thread running. Most of the work of the operating system is done by ordinary threads when they are executing in kernel mode.

So, threads spend some of their time executing in user mode and some of their time in kernel mode, executing operating system routines which deal with system calls and other exceptions. When a thread is executing in kernel mode, it has the ability to do absolutely anything. It can access I/O devices, halt the processor, switch control to another process, or do anything else it wants to do. However, the only way to switch the processor from user mode into kernel mode is by generating an exception; instructions that would switch modes are privileged, and will just generate an exception if they are executed in user mode. This means that you can't just execute any code you please in kernel mode; you can only switch into kernel mode if, at the same time, you go to one of a limited number of kernel entry points as specified in the exception vector table.

6.2.2   INTERRUPTS

An **interrupt** is an exception which is generated by an external device rather than as a result of some action performed by the processor. Interrupts occur at unpredictable times in response to external events, such as mouse movements or keypresses. What happens is that when an external device has an event to report, one of the control signals used to connect the device to the processor is activated. The processor checks the state of this control signal before fetching each instruction, and if it is active, it generates an interrupt exception (Figure 6.7). This makes the processor save the address of the instruction it was about to execute, switch into kernel mode, and reset the program counter register to the address specified by the exception vector for the interrupt. The processor then uses the program counter to fetch and execute the next instruction, which will be the first instruction of the **interrupt service routine** (ISR).

One problem is that the interrupt signal is still active, and will stay active until the device has been dealt with. We don't want the same interrupt to be recognised again before the processor fetches the next instruction of the interrupt service routine, so a bit in the processor status register (the **interrupt flag**) is used to specify whether the processor will check for interrupts between instructions or not. As part of the response to an external interrupt, this bit is cleared to disable the recognition of any further interrupts. This means that no further interrupts will be

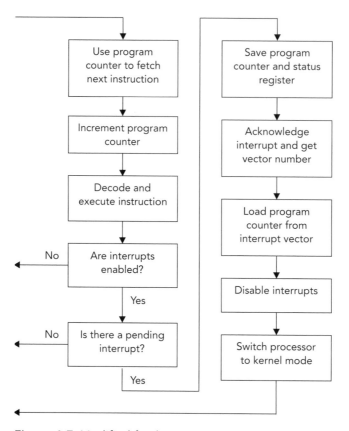

Figure 6.7 Modified fetch–execute cycle including interrupt recognition.

acted upon until the interrupt service routine reaches a point where it is prepared to allow interrupts to be recognised. Privileged instructions (called CLI and STI on Pentium processors) are provided to clear and set the interrupt flag explicitly. These can only be used in kernel mode, as otherwise a user-mode process could just disable all interrupts, and there would be no way to interrupt the process to allow any other process to run. The interrupt service routine doesn't need to enable interrupts explicitly; returning from the interrupt handler will restore the original value of the status register (including the original setting of the interrupt flag), so interrupts will be re-enabled automatically at the end of the interrupt handler.

As an example, consider what happens when a process wants to transmit a block of data to a character-oriented device such as a modem. The processing involved is shown as pseudocode in Figure 6.8. The process issues a system call specifying the address of the block of data and its length, and these are stored in some variables that the interrupt handler can access. The first character of the block is then sent to the device, and the thread which issued the system call is suspended so that some other thread can be executed while the data transfer is taking place.

When the modem has finished transmitting the character, it will generate an interrupt. The interrupt service routine will read the modem's status register to determine the reason for the interrupt, and this will also deactivate the interrupt

```
Start_Transfer:
    pos = 0;
    count = buffer.length;
    modem.send (buffer[pos]);
    thread.suspend();

Interrupt_Handler:          // called after each send completes
    if (error) {
        reportError();
    }
    else if (count > 0) {
        pos = pos + 1;
        count = count - 1;
        modem.send (buffer[pos]);
    }
    else {
        thread.resume();
    }
```

Figure 6.8 Transmitting data using interrupts.

from the device. If this is an 'operation complete' interrupt, it then decrements the block length that was saved earlier, which gives the number of characters remaining to be sent. If the block length is still greater than zero, it advances to the next character in the block and sends that character to the device. It then continues executing the thread that was interrupted.

Successive interrupts will be generated after each character has been transmitted until eventually the block length will reach zero, indicating that all the characters have been sent successfully. At this point, the original thread can be woken up and allowed to continue from the point where it was suspended, which will be at the point immediately after the original system call.

The above has assumed a single interrupt handler, and presumably a single interrupting device. Of course in reality there will be many devices that can generate interrupts: the mouse, the keyboard, modems, printers, network cards, disks, and so on. One solution is to use an external device to multiplex the interrupt signals from the various possible sources onto a single interrupt signal to the processor. IBM PCs used a device called a PIC (Programmable Interrupt Controller; Figure 6.9) to do this which could have up to eight devices connected to it. It had an 8-bit status register which the processor could read to discover which of the eight devices generated the interrupt, with the status of each device shown by a separate bit, as well as an 8-bit control register where each bit enabled or disabled interrupts from one of the eight interrupt sources. Most systems had two PICs; the first one multiplexed eight devices into a single signal, and the second one multiplexed this signal together with interrupt signals from seven other devices to give 15 different interrupt sources altogether. On Pentium processors the same functionality is integrated into the processor chip itself.

In a system like this, interrupt handling happens in two stages. The PIC generates an 'interrupt' signal, and when the processor recognises the interrupt it activates an 'interrupt acknowledge' signal. The PIC responds by putting the exception number for the interrupt on the data bus, and the processor reads this and then generates the requested exception. While the interrupt is being serviced, any

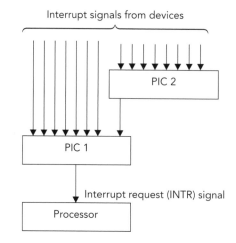

Figure 6.9 Using PICs to multiplex interrupt sources.

interrupts at the same or lower priority will be 'masked' (blocked) until an 'end of interrupt' command is written to one of the PICs control registers.

In contrast, Motorola 680x0 processors use seven different priorities of interrupt. Whereas the Pentium has a single 'interrupt flag' bit in the status register, there are three bits in the 680x0 status register which indicate the current interrupt priority (1 to 7, with 0 used to indicate 'no interrupt'). When an interrupt occurs, the return address and status register are saved, and these three bits are set to reflect the priority of the interrupt. Only interrupts with a higher priority than is specified by the status register will be allowed, so that if an interrupt with a priority of 4 occurs, any interrupts with priorities between 1 and 4 will be ignored while it is being serviced. However, an interrupt at priority 5, 6 or 7 will be able to interrupt the priority 4 interrupt handler. This is illustrated in Figure 6.10. On an IBM PC interrupt priorities are managed by the PIC rather than by the processor.

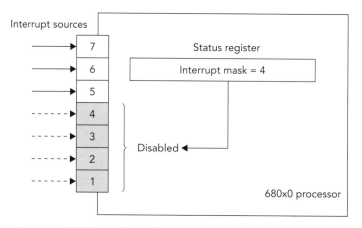

Figure 6.10 Motorola 680x0 interrupt priorities.

Exercise 6.4   For a particular processor, find out how interrupts are handled. Are there different priority levels? How many priority levels are there? How are interrupts masked when servicing an interrupt?

Where there are more devices than interrupt signals, some devices must share a single interrupt signal. For example, there are two interrupt signals reserved for use by serial ports on an IBM PC, so on systems with more than two serial ports the same interrupt will be generated by more than one serial port. When a serial port interrupt is recognised, the interrupt handler has to begin by identifying which of the serial ports was responsible. This has to be done by interrogating the control register of each serial port in turn.

6.2.3   TIMERS

Most systems include a **timer** which can generate interrupts at regular intervals. This guarantees a constant sequence of interrupts which can keep the system ticking over even when nothing else is happening. On a Pentium processor, the interrupt controller (which is integrated onto the same chip as the processor itself) includes a timer that can generate interrupts with a resolution of a microsecond or less.

Timer interrupts are normally used to switch between one thread and another, but they are also useful for scheduling operations to be performed at a particular time in the future. For example, a thread might be waiting for an update to a file to take place and then taking some action when it sees that it has been updated. To avoid wasting system resources, it may wish to check the file once a second or so. The timer allows a thread to go to sleep for a period of one second, and can wake it up after a timer interrupt if the specified period has elapsed.

The timer can also be used to keep track of the current date and time, although there is usually a separate **real-time clock** to do this. A real-time clock is typically powered by a small battery, which means that it will keep track of the passage of time even when the system is turned off, so the date and time will not have to be reset every time the system is turned on.

6.3 ☐ KERNEL MEMORY

So where is the operating system while a process is executing? It mustn't be in any memory which is accessible to user-mode processes, since this would be another potential loophole that would allow one process to interfere with another. On the other hand, many system calls need to be able to access the memory allocated to the process; for example, the *read* system call has to be able to transfer data into a memory buffer specified by the process. In an emulation, system calls like *read* can be implemented as 'magic' instructions which perform operations which are otherwise impossible to do. In an operating system, the magic has to be performed using essentially the same processor and memory as the process that requested the operation.

The normal solution to this involves putting the operating system into an area near the end of the address space, in a block of memory that is normally disabled (so that attempting to access it will generate an exception). As noted in the previous chapter, the types of access to pages in a virtual memory system can be controlled by their page table entries. On a Pentium processor, a page can be specified as one of read-only, read/write or inaccessible. However, to the operating system (that is, when the processor is in kernel mode) all pages are readable and writable. So a page which is marked as inaccessible when the processor is in user mode will be accessible in kernel mode

In both Windows and Linux, the kernel is always mapped into the end of the address space of each process. Windows gives 2 GB to the user process and 2 GB to the kernel, whereas Linux uses 3 GB for the user process and 1 GB for the kernel (Figure 6.11). Windows can also be configured to run in the same way as Linux. All the memory in the kernel's region of the address space is marked as inaccessible while the process is executing in user mode. When an exception occurs, the processor switches into kernel mode, which makes the memory in the kernel region accessible, and the process starts executing the appropriate routine within the kernel to deal with the exception.

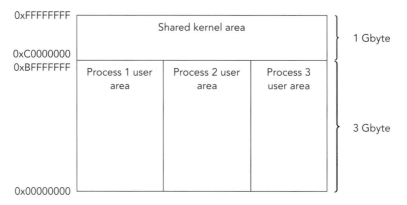

Figure 6.11 Processes sharing a copy of the kernel.

6.3.1 PROTECTING I/O DEVICES

There are two ways to connect I/O devices, as mentioned earlier. Either they can be **memory-mapped**, sharing the same address space as the memory, or they can be **port-based**, using a separate set of addresses which are completely unrelated to addresses in the memory address space. Either way, it is possible to make them inaccessible when a process is executing in user mode but accessible when the process is executing in kernel mode.

In the case of memory-mapped I/O, all we need to do is to map all the external devices to addresses within the shared kernel region of the address space. This means that, like the rest of the kernel, they will be completely inaccessible in user mode, but accessible when dealing with an exception in kernel mode. The processor will also be switched into kernel mode when an external device generates an interrupt, and the kernel routine to handle the interrupt will be able to access the device in order to determine the reason for the interrupt.

In port-based I/O, special IN and OUT instructions are needed to access the I/O port addresses, since they are not part of the memory address space that all the other instructions operate on. If these instructions are privileged so that they can only be executed in kernel mode, we are safe once again.

Question 6.2   Does your computer use memory-mapped or port-based I/O? Explain how you found the answer to this.

The Pentium uses a more elaborate system for protecting I/O port addresses; it uses a **permission bit map** to choose which devices are accessible in which mode. A single bit is used for the status of each port address (so the map can be up to 64 Kb in length, or 8 KB). If an I/O device is accessed in user mode and the corresponding bit in the permission bit map is set to 0, the access is allowed. If the bit is set to 1, an exception is generated. This means that individual I/O devices can be made directly accessible from a user mode process if required, and each process can have its own permission bit map which is activated whenever the process resumes execution so that access to I/O devices can be granted or denied selectively to individual processes.

6.4 ❑ SYSTEM CALLS

Of course, there must be an instruction which can be used to implement system calls. This just needs to be an instruction that generates an exception so that it switches into kernel mode and calls a corresponding exception handler. Any privileged instruction (such as 'halt') will generate an exception, so any such instruction could potentially be used. However, it is also convenient to allow system calls to be made in kernel mode, so co-opting an instruction like the 'halt' instruction would not be a good idea; if you did this, a system call made when the processor was executing in kernel mode would halt the processor completely!

Modern processors will always provide an operation specifically designed for use as a system call instruction. The Motorola 680x0 processor family provides a 'trap' instruction which includes a 4-bit code identifying one of 16 possible exceptions to be raised (TRAP #0 to TRAP #15) which the operating system can use to perform whatever extra operations it might need; the Intel Pentium family has an 'interrupt' instruction with an 8-bit code identifying one of 256 possible exceptions (INT 00 to INT FF, using hexadecimal notation) which can be used in the same way. For example, the Windows API on a Pentium-based machine uses the instruction INT 2E as the 'system call' instruction, with the number of the API function in one register and the address of a parameter block in another register. Linux uses INT 80 for the same purpose. Results are passed back to the calling process via processor registers, one of which is always a code that indicates whether or not the requested operation was performed successfully. (The Pentium also has a 'call gate' facility which was specifically designed for implementing system calls, but Windows and Linux both use the INT instruction instead.)

6.5 ❑ MEMORY MANAGEMENT HARDWARE

In an emulator, the address translation process of a virtual memory system would need to be implemented in software by the emulator program. Each instruction fetched from memory, and each data item referenced by those instructions, would require the emulator to execute several instructions to perform the address translation. In an operating system, additional hardware is needed to perform address translations so that it does not impose this sort of performance penalty. This hardware is referred to as the **memory management unit** (MMU). Keeping the address translation mechanism as simple as possible keeps the complexity of the hardware to a minimum and also minimises the time taken to do address translations.

The variable-block allocation strategy described in Chapter 4 translates addresses by adding a base register to the address and at the same time comparing the address to a limit register, generating an exception if the address is beyond the allowed limit. This can be implemented with a very simple MMU attached to the processor's address bus, as shown in Figure 6.12. There is a control signal from the processor which enables or disables the MMU. This can be connected to an output from the processor indicating whether the processor is in kernel mode or not, so that the

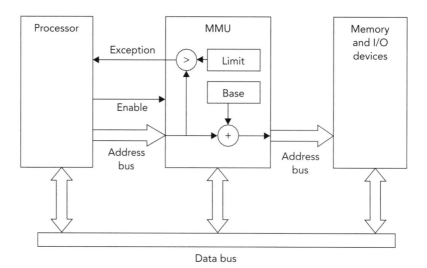

Figure 6.12 Connecting a memory management unit.

MMU is enabled in user mode and disabled in kernel mode. When it is disabled, the MMU passes all addresses unchanged to the memory subsystem, except for a couple of addresses which correspond to its internal base and limit registers. This allows the operating system to load and save values into these registers. When the processor switches into user mode, the MMU is enabled and it then translates addresses by adding the base register to them before passing them on to the memory subsystem. At the same time, the address is compared to the limit register and another control signal is used to generate an exception if the address is out of range.

As with the simple base-and-limit scheme described above, the memory management unit in a virtual memory system is responsible for translating virtual addresses to physical addresses. However, the operating system is responsible for allocating memory and constructing the corresponding page tables for each process. The page table must therefore be accessible to both the operating system and the memory management unit. The memory management unit needs to be given the (physical) address of the page table; on the Pentium processor, the page table address is stored in a special processor register called CR3, which can also be accessed by the MMU. The page table address register is another part of the process state that needs to be saved when the operating system switches to another process.

At least part of the format of a page table entry will also be determined by the memory management hardware. For example, demand paging requires a single bit in the page table entry to say whether the page is committed or not (the 'present' or 'valid' bit). When a process references a page, the MMU needs to inspect this particular bit to determine if the page is present, and if necessary generate a **page fault** exception so that the operating system can load the corresponding page. Similarly, when a page is written to, the MMU must set the 'dirty' bit in the page table entry to record that the page has been modified. Any bits in the page table entry which are not used by the MMU can be used by the operating system for its own purposes; for example, an otherwise unused bit can be used to indicate a 'locked' page which should never be swapped out to disk. As Figure 6.13 shows, there are three spare

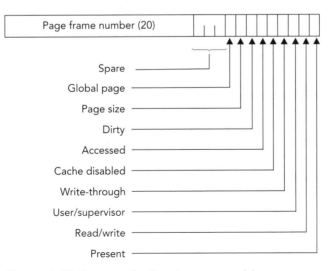

Figure 6.13 Format of a Pentium page table entry.

bits in the page table entry, as well as bits to specify whether the page has been accessed or is dirty and whether it is present in memory.

Question 6.3   Which pages would you want to be locked, and why?

6.6 ☐ CACHING

A difficulty with virtual memory is the cost in terms of hardware performance. Each memory access in a virtual memory system on a Pentium-based machine involves accessing both the first- and second-level page tables in addition to the requested page, a grand total of three accesses. This means that without special hardware support, the main effect of providing virtual memory would be to reduce the overall speed of the system by a factor of three.

These costs can be made manageable by **caching** copies of frequently used data. One simple modification is to include a **physical program counter** register in the processor which holds the physical address corresponding to the virtual address in the program counter (or at least the page frame number corresponding to the virtual page number). This only needs to be set up when the first instruction on a new page is executed, so the cost of translating the program counter to a physical address is reduced from once per instruction to once every few hundred instructions, assuming fairly normal dynamic behaviour for the program being executed. Similarly, the memory management unit normally incorporates a **translation lookaside buffer** (TLB) which holds copies of the most recently accessed page table entries, so that accesses to page table entries in main memory can be minimised.

The TLB is normally implemented in hardware using an **associative memory** (Figure 6.14), where each memory cell contains its own comparison hardware. This means that searching for a particular value is as simple as asking all the cells simultaneously to compare their contents with that value and having the first matching

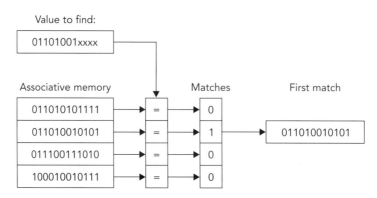

Figure 6.14 An associative memory.

cell deliver its value. Associative memories are much more expensive than conventional memories, but a TLB only needs to contain a few dozen cells to give a high **hit rate** (the proportion of searches which find a matching value). Most TLBs have space for about a hundred entries.

The time taken to access the TLB is much less than the time required to access main memory, and the TLB search can be overlapped with the time it takes to set up the read operation to fetch the page table entry from memory. The term 'lookaside' here means that the MMU 'looks to the side' at the TLB while it starts up the memory access to the page table. If the TLB contains a copy of the required page table entry, the read operation can be abandoned; if not, the read operation continues and the page table entry is fetched from memory. When it has been fetched from memory, it is stored in the TLB so that it will be found if the same page table entry is referenced again in the near future.

Updating the TLB can be done automatically in hardware whenever a TLB miss occurs, but on some systems the TLB entries are updated in software. A TLB miss generates an exception which the operating system handles by finding the correct page table entry and storing it in the TLB. This has to be done very quickly, and is only acceptable if the TLB is large enough that misses are fairly rare. To speed things up, a much larger list of recently used page entries can be kept in memory to avoid searching page tables and possibly causing yet more TLB misses. Many modern RISC processors, like the SPARC processors mentioned in Section 6.1.2, use this approach. It also allows the operating system to predict possible patterns of activity and preload the TLB with the relevant page table entries to further reduce the risk of misses.

Both the physical program counter and the TLB are special cases of a more general mechanism, the **cache**. Even with a TLB, page table entries will still need to be fetched from memory from time to time, adding to the overall time required to access data and instructions in memory. Virtual memory will thus give an overall performance that is worse than the direct use of physical memory due to the need for extra page table accesses, albeit occasional ones. However, if copies of recently accessed data and instructions are kept in a cache (in a similar way to the way that the TLB stores recently accessed page table entries), the need to access main memory can be drastically reduced.

Exercise 6.5   On Windows, the system Performance Monitor can be used to inspect many system performance metrics, including the number of page faults per second and the number of cache misses per second. Find out how to use the system performance monitor by consulting the help system, and see how the rates are affected under different system loadings (for example, playing music or video and/or downloading a file from the Internet and/or using a word processor). How do you explain what you see happening under the different circumstances?

Most modern systems include a cache which operates much faster than main memory and which can hold recently accessed data and instructions, with a typical capacity of about 512 KB to 1 MB on most PCs. For example, a typical cache might be 512 KB in total, organised as four banks (**sets**) of 128 KB each. Each set might be organised as 4096 blocks (**lines**) of 32 bytes each, together with the corresponding address from which each line was loaded. While preparing to read from main memory, the cache can be searched in a similar way to the way the TLB is searched. If the address being accessed is already in the cache, the data can be taken directly from the cache rather than from main memory. The cache usually operates an order of magnitude faster than main memory, so assuming a reasonably high hit rate the average access time will be substantially reduced.

Question 6.4   Assuming that it takes 50 ns to access main memory but only 5 ns to access the cache, that the value being accessed is found in the cache 90% of the time, and that there are two levels of page table so that each memory access requires two page table accesses plus one data access, what is the average time for a memory access?

To keep costs down, there is normally only one address comparator per cache set, but all four sets can perform a search at the same time. This organisation is described as a **4-way set associative cache** and requires only four comparators instead of several thousand. Five bits of the address are used to select one of the 32 bytes in a line, but instead of using the remaining 27 bits to search every location, as in a fully associative memory, 12 bits are used to identify one of the 4096 available lines in each set where the data will be stored if it is present, and the remaining 15 bits are used as a **tag** to identify the address where the line was loaded from. The data could be held in that particular line in any one of the four sets, so the tag part of the address is simultaneously compared with the tags in the selected line in each of the four sets to see if one of them matches, as shown in Figure 6.15. If it isn't there, a block of 32 bytes is read from memory and put into the appropriate line in one of the sets. The sets are usually updated in sequence for the sake of simplicity, so that the first block that is read goes in the first set, the next block goes in the second set, and so on.

Question 6.5   Why use four sets, rather than one or two or eight?

Most systems have multiple levels of caching (Figure 6.16); for example, a Pentium system includes a **level 1 cache** of about 32 KB which is physically incorporated into the processor chip itself, with a slower but larger **level 2 cache** which is external to the processor, situated between the processor and main memory. When a memory access is made, the level 1 and level 2 caches are both checked to

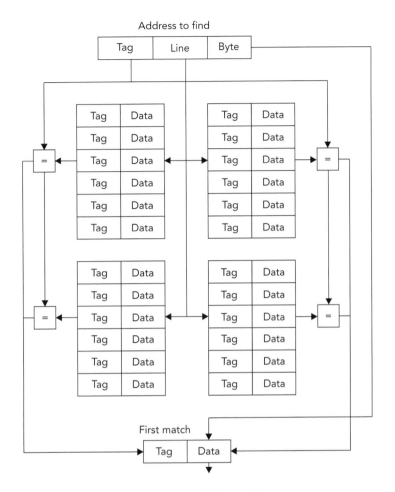

Figure 6.15 A 4-way set-associative cache.

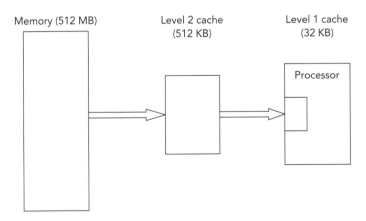

Figure 6.16 A two-level cache.

see if the data is there. The level 1 cache is the fastest, so it will respond first it the required data is there. If it isn't in the level 1 cache but it is in the level 2 cache, the level 2 cache will be the first to respond, and the level 1 cache will then be able to update itself with the required data as it is transferred in from the level 2 cache. If all else fails, the access to main memory will proceed to completion, and both caches will update themselves when the data is transferred.

Exercise 6.6   Find out the sizes of the caches on the system that you are using (level 1, level 2, TLB and any other). What are the relatives speeds of these compared to main memory?

6.7 ❑ POWER MANAGEMENT

Another hardware issue that is becoming increasingly important is power management. This is particularly true in the case of battery-powered portable devices such as laptop computers, handheld PCs and mobile phones. Battery technology has improved dramatically in recent years, but battery life will always be an issue. The questions that need to be addressed are how can power consumption be minimised, and what action should be taken in the case of a power failure? These questions are also important for mains-powered systems. Minimising power consumption is not as critical as it is in battery-powered systems, but it is still desirable for ecological reasons. The likelihood of a power failure depends very much on where in the world you are, but even in places with a reliable power supply it is still necessary to deal with the possibility of a power failure for server systems that need to be continuously available or for high-reliability systems that must shut down safely. London and New York each have a power supply system that is normally completely reliable, but both of these cities suffered major power failures in the summer of 2003.

The problem with a power failure is that is there is a possibility of data loss or corruption. Storage devices can be divided into two major categories: **volatile** storage that requires a power supply in order to preserve stored data, and **non-volatile** storage that does not require a continuous supply of power. Processor registers, cache and main memory in current designs are all volatile, whereas devices such as disks, CDs and flash memory cards are all non-volatile. You can unplug a disk drive or remove a CD without losing the information it contains, but doing the same to main memory will destroy its contents. It was not ever thus; machines in the 1960s used magnetic storage technologies for main memory ('core store') which would retain its contents even if power was turned off, and it is of course possible that the future development of memory technologies such as flash memory will make them fast enough and cheap enough to be used as main memory. At present, only handheld devices like cameras, mobile phones and palmtop computers use flash memory. On such devices, speed is less of an issue than the need for non-volatile storage in the absence of disk drives or any other stable storage devices.

The danger with a power failure is that there may be data in volatile memory which is waiting to be recorded on a non-volatile device such as a disk. If the power is lost, so is this data. It may be that some of the data gets stored on disk but not all of it. For example, writing data to a file might involve allocating an extra storage block. Related data structures will also need updating, notably the list of free disk blocks and the list of blocks allocated to the file. If the data has been written to a newly allocated block but that block has not been marked as belonging to the file, the data is effectively lost. If the block has not been marked as being in use, it may be overwritten when the system is restarted. Power might fail halfway through a disk write, so that only part of a disk block gets written correctly.

The common solution for systems where reliability is important is to use an **uninterruptible power supply** (UPS). What a UPS does is to monitor the incoming voltage level from the mains supply and generate an interrupt if the voltage drops below a certain threshold. This is illustrated in Figure 6.17. It also incorporates what is effectively a backup battery that is kept charged by the power supply while it is operating. This will provide enough power to keep the system operational for a period of time: possibly hours (to keep the system running normally until power is restored) or a few seconds or minutes (to allow time for an orderly shutdown).

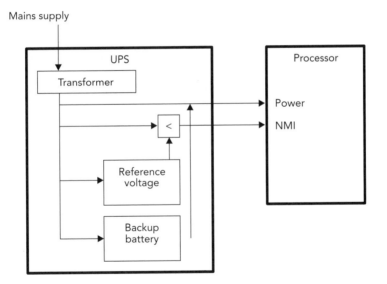

Figure 6.17 An uninterruptible power supply (UPS).

The interrupt generated by a UPS must take priority over everything else in the system. It doesn't matter what else is going on; if the UPS reports an imminent power failure, the operating system must respond immediately. Processors provide a special interrupt for this purpose, known as a **non-maskable interrupt** (NMI), which cannot be disabled. The processor will always respond to an NMI even if all other interrupts are disabled. The operating system can deal with an NMI by going into its shutdown procedure, flushing all unsaved data from memory to disk. Windows also provides a **hibernate** option as an alternative to a normal shutdown. This just saves the entire contents of memory to disk, allowing the memory image to be reloaded so that work can be resumed from the point at which it was hibernated.

Most modern systems also use intelligent power supplies which are controlled by software. Pressing the on/off switch on a system like this will not turn the power off directly; instead, it will generate an interrupt which the operating system can respond to by initiating an orderly shutdown as before. Once the system is in a safe state, the processor sends a signal to the power supply which then turns itself off. For power supplies that provide this feature, Windows allows you to choose how the system will respond to the power button, either by shutting down normally or by hibernating.

Another possibility on battery-powered systems such as laptops is for the system to go into a **standby** state. This is a state that minimises power consumption by turning off devices such as the disk and screen which consume a lot of power, so that the only part of the system that draws any power is the processor and memory. This allows the system to be restarted very quickly. However, power is still being consumed, and measures are needed to minimise this consumption.

The standard semiconductor technology currently used in modern systems is known as CMOS (Complementary Metal-Oxide Semiconductor) which has a very low power consumption when devices are idle. The only significant power consumption is when transistors are changing state, either turning on or turning off. The amount of power used when a transistor changes state also depends on the voltage used to power the transistor. This means that the power consumption for CMOS devices depends on the system voltage and clock speed (ultimately, the speed at which transistors are being switched on and off). A processor whose speed is measured in gigahertz draws quite a lot of power and will flatten a fully charged battery within a very few hours. A solution is to lower the processor's voltage and clock speed when the system is idle. This reduces the system performance, but if it is idle this doesn't matter. This is what happens in the standby state; the system clock speed is reduced to a minimum and the supply voltage is also reduced, thereby minimising the power consumption and maximising battery life.

Ideally we would like to stop the clock entirely, which would reduce the power consumption to near-negligible levels. Unfortunately this is not possible with modern processors and memories. Volatile memory can be further subdivided into **static** devices and **dynamic** devices. Static devices store data in a way that is stable as long as power is available; dynamic devices need to be **refreshed** at regular intervals to prevent data loss. Dynamic memories store data using unstable devices (tiny devices called **capacitors** which can be charged up like batteries but which will gradually lose that charge if it isn't refreshed) and they provide stability by refreshing the devices at regular intervals, effectively by reading the contents of the memory and then writing it back again to top up the charge on the capacitors. Static devices are slower and more expensive than dynamic ones, so most systems use dynamic memory rather than static memory. This limits the minimum clock speed; it still needs to be high enough to keep all the dynamic system components refreshed. However, with the clock operating at its minimum speed and dynamic refreshes as the only activity, a laptop battery will usually be able to keep the system in standby mode for several weeks.

Power management is generally linked to the timer and interrupt controller. The timer is used to measure how long the system has been idle for, which is basically how long it has been since the last interrupt from anything but the timer. No interrupts means no activity, and most systems will initiate power-saving measures after a given idle time. Even if the system does not go into a standby state there are a number of measures which can reduce power consumption. This includes turning off disks, which consume quite a lot of power when they are kept spinning; and either turning off the screen or activating a 'screen saver' program which generates a continually shifting display. This is also useful as a security measure; most systems can be set to require a password to be typed in when a machine is woken up, which means that you can walk away from a machine without logging out and be sure that no-one else will be able to use it while you are away.

The original idea of screen savers was to prevent a fixed, unchanging screen image from being 'burnt into' the phosphor coating of the screen itself, although with modern screens this is no longer the problem that it used to be. However, many people like their computer to display soothing geometrical patterns or pictures of fish swimming back and forth when it is not in use. Screen savers can also make productive use of the processor power that would otherwise be wasted when the machine is idle. One popular screen saver that actually does something useful is available from the SETI project (the Search for Extra-Terrestrial Intelligence). This downloads chunks of data from the SETI project and processes it while the machine would otherwise be idle, looking for patterns that might indicate signals from intelligent races elsewhere in the universe.

When an interrupt occurs (typically when a key is pressed or the mouse is moved) the system wakes from its slumbers, speeding up the clock and restoring the display. Disks are generally not restarted until they need to be accessed, but this causes a noticeable delay when they do need to be accessed. It is also very audible as the disk whines back to life.

6.8 ☐ HARDWARE FAILURE

Hardware devices aren't perfect, although it is easy to forget this. They don't usually fail very often, but when they do, it is almost guaranteed to happen at the worst possible moment. Processors can overheat, disk drives can develop mechanical failures, and floppy disks can be demagnetised. (Or, as I discovered while writing this book, laptop computers can be stolen....) Keeping backup copies of data as described in Chapter 3 is often sufficient to reduce the problem from a disaster to a minor inconvenience. However, some systems are required to run reliably 24 hours a day, 365 days a year, and any **downtime** (periods of unavailability) can be hugely expensive. For example, downtime in a banking system can cause transactions to be lost or delayed, which can end up costing a lot of money.

Systems like this tend to use redundant components to ensure continuous availability, so that a spare component is always ready to take over if anything fails,
which allows the system to keep running while the fault is repaired. This is similar
to the idea of keeping a spare tyre in a car; if you get a puncture, the spare will at
least get you to the nearest garage.

6.8.1 RAID

Disk drives are probably the components most at risk of failure in any system. They
are mechanical devices which are prone to wear and tear and they are also heavily
used. Although a faulty disk can be replaced and restored from a backup copy, this
is a less-than-perfect solution for systems which need to be available 24 hours a
day, 365 days a year. Replacing a faulty disk and restoring it from a backup will
inevitably require some system downtime. As disk prices have dropped, it has
become fairly cheap to use a 'Redundant Array of Inexpensive Disks' (RAID) as a
way of solving this problem. The 'I' in RAID has since been redefined to mean
'independent' rather than 'inexpensive', perhaps because manufacturers didn't
like the implication that their disks were cheap. The idea behind RAID is to write
multiple copies of each file to multiple disks, so that if one disk fails it can be
removed and replaced. If **hot-swappable disks** are used, which can be physically
removed without halting the system, no downtime will be required.

There are seven different forms of RAID, known as 'levels' even though there is
no hierarchy involved. RAID level 0 (Figure 6.18) is intended as a way of increasing
performance rather than reliability; when a file is written, it is distributed across
several disks, which allows disks to be written to (and read back) in parallel. For
example, an 8 KB block can be written as four 2 KB blocks, with one block being
stored on each of four disks. Each of the sub-blocks is referred to as a **stripe**. There is
no redundancy involved here, so the term RAID is a bit of a misnomer in this case.

The simplest version of RAID that provides data redundancy is RAID 1 (Figure
6.18), where a copy of the data is written to more than one disk. When reading data
back from the disk, different parts of the file can be read from different disks in
parallel, so it is possible to use this technique to improve read performance. For the
truly paranoid, it is possible to read from all of the disks in parallel, comparing the

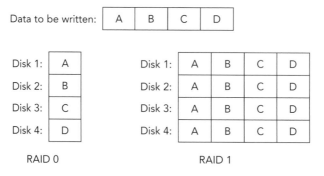

Figure 6.18 RAID 0 and 1.

data to detect any inconsistencies. If three or more disks are used, a majority voting system can be used to determine which disk is faulty if the data is inconsistent.

RAID level 2 is much more ambitious. Instead of writing a block of bytes to each disk, each byte is split into eight separate bits and the different bits are written to different disks. Redundancy is achieved by adding a few parity bits to allow for error detection and correction which are computed from the data bits; each parity bit is set so that the total number of bits set to 1 in a particular group of bits is always even (or always odd). This requires a substantial number of disks which must be kept rotationally synchronised, and it also requires the parity bits to be verified for every byte of data read from the disks. As a result, this is rarely seen in practice.

RAID level 3 uses a simplified version of the same basic idea, with only a single parity bit which is set so that the total number of 1s in each byte is always even. This provides error detection but no error correction, unless of course you know which drive has crashed! As soon as you know that, you can reconstruct all the data on the faulty drive by reconstructing it from the parity bit. If all the other bits (including the parity bit) contain an odd number of 1s, the value for the faulty disk must have been 1; if there is an even number of 1s, it must have been 0. However, although this is a lot simpler than RAID 2, you still need to keep the disks rotationally synchronised.

RAID level 4 (Figure 6.19) goes back to writing data in stripes, but with an extra parity stripe computed from the stripes written to each of the other disks. Thus, if four disks are used with a fifth parity disk, a block of 8 KB could be written as four stripes of 2 KB each. The four stripes are then combined together to produce a parity stripe that can be used to reconstruct any single disk that fails, just as with RAID 3. However, because data is written in stripes rather than bit-by-bit, the disks do not need to be rotationally synchronised. This makes it a much more practical solution.

The only problem with RAID 4 is that the parity disk must be written to whenever the data in any individual stripe is changed. With four disks plus parity, this means that the parity disk suffers from four times as much wear and tear as the other disks. RAID level 5 (Figure 6.19) solves this problem by alternating the parity stripe on different disks, so that the first disk is used for parity for the first set of stripes, the second disk is used for parity of the second set of stripes, and so on. The disk that

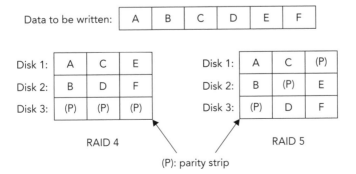

Figure 6.19 RAID 4 and 5.

contains the parity stripe can easily be calculated from the stripe number. It takes a bit more effort to reconstruct a failed drive because each set of stripes is stored differently, but it eliminates the problem of undue wear and tear to any individual drive.

As disks become larger, and larger disk arrays are used in RAID systems, the possibility of multiple disk failures increases. The problem with RAID 5 is that you can reconstruct a single failed disk from the parity information on the other disks, but a multiple disk failure cannot be corrected. RAID 6 is designed to address this for larger RAID arrays; it is essentially the same as RAID 5 except that a more complex error-correction code is used instead of a simple parity code.

6.9 ❑ SUMMARY

Modern hardware has been designed hand-in-hand with modern operating systems. The two are interdependent; operating systems require specific hardware facilities such as interrupts and separate supervisor and user modes, and specialised hardware, such as memory management units, requires an operating system which can use its features effectively. The primary hardware requirements for a modern operating system are:

- Separate user and supervisor modes, with certain privileged instructions only available when the processor is operating in supervisor mode.
- The ability to respond to interrupts and other exceptions.
- Instructions which support the needs of an operating system to do things like enabling and disabling interrupts, performing and returning from system calls, test-and-set instructions, and so on.
- A timer to provide a guaranteed source of interrupts to keep things ticking over, as well as maintaining a continuous timebase which can be used to measure time and to control timed events.
- A memory management unit which provides memory protection by allowing the address space of individual processes to be mapped onto the underlying physical memory.

For high-reliability systems where continuous availability is necessary, redundant hardware can be used to guard against hardware failures. This increases the price of the overall system, so the cost of a potential failure needs to be weighed against the cost of the extra hardware involved.

6.10 ❑ ADDITIONAL RESOURCES

Tanenbaum [13] is an excellent introduction to computer architecture in general. For more processor-specific information, the architecture of the Pentium 4 processor is defined in a three-volume set available from Intel [6–8], while by way of comparison the Motorola 680x0 architecture is described in [10]. Clements [2] describes hardware design and assembly language programming using the Motorola 68000 family. A good general introduction to assembly language programming for 8086-family processors (including the Pentium family) is given by Hyde [5].

The idea of RISC processors was originally presented by Patterson and Séquin [11]. Patterson also introduced the idea of RAID storage in [12], and a more extensive survey of RAID designs is given by Chen *et al.* [1].

Cache memory has been around since the early 1960s, although the name 'cache' was first used by Conti *et al.* [3]. Cragon [4] contains a thorough treatment of cache and memory design. Software TLB management is described by Uhlig *et al.* [14], and Jacob and Mudge [9] describe a variety of TLB design approaches used in some modern 64-bit processors.

6.11 ❑ GLOSSARY

address bus a set of electrical connections used to transmit addresses from one hardware device to another.

associative memory a form of memory whose contents are accessed by matching a value against the contents of each cell, rather than by specifying a positional address.

bus a set of related electrical connections.

cache a fast memory used to keep copies of data which has recently been accessed from a slower memory to avoid the delay in accessing the slower memory if the data is needed again.

call instruction an instruction used to call subroutines, which stores the return address before jumping to the beginning of the subroutine.

CISC (Complex Instruction Set Computer) a processor which provides a set of instructions which can combine several low-level operations such as accessing memory and performing arithmetic operations.

data bus a set of electrical connections used to transmit data from one hardware device to another.

dynamic memory a form of memory whose contents need to be refreshed at intervals to prevent the data from being lost.

exception a condition which unexpectedly changes the flow of control in a program, often as the result of an error.

exception vector a value specifying the address to which control should be transferred when a particular exception occurs.

hibernation an alternative to shutting down a computer, where the contents of memory and other relevant state information is saved to disk so that the machine can be restarted later in exactly the same state.

hit rate   the proportion of accesses to a cache which successfully retrieve the data being sought.

hot-swappable disk   a disk unit which can be removed and replaced while the machine is running.

interrupt   an exception generated by an external hardware device.

jump instruction   an instruction which transfers control to a different part of the program, breaking the normal flow of control from one instruction to the next.

kernel mode   an execution mode where any instruction, including privileged instructions, can be executed, and which also allows access to protected regions of the address space.

level 1 cache   a small cache built in to the processor chip which caches values from the level 2 cache.

level 2 cache   a larger cache external to the processor which caches values from main memory.

line   the unit of data transfer to or from a cache.

MMU (memory management unit)   a hardware device responsible for performing address translation and checking access permissions.

memory-mapped I/O   input/output devices whose addresses are located in the same address space as memory.

non-maskable interrupt   an interrupt which is always enabled, used to report system-critical events such as power failures that should never be ignored.

page fault   an exception generated by the MMU in a virtual memory system when a page is accessed which is not present in memory.

physical program counter   a cached copy of the physical address corresponding to the virtual address held in the program counter register.

port-based I/O   input/output devices whose addresses are in a separate address space from memory, which are accessed using special 'in' and 'out' instructions.

privileged instruction   an instruction intended for use by the operating system only, which will generate an exception if an unprivileged user program attempts to execute it.

program counter   the processor register which is used to hold the address of the next instruction to be fetched from memory.

program status word   a processor register containing a variety of status information, usually including condition codes set by the previous instruction, the processor mode and interrupt mask bits.

RAID (Redundant Array of Inexpensive/Independent Disks)   a set of disks used as a single volume arranged to provide data redundancy in case of the failure of any single disk.

register   one of a small number of high-speed storage locations within a processor which are used to hold status information and temporary values.

return address the address to which control should return at the end of a subroutine.

return instruction an instruction used at the end of a subroutine to transfer control to the return address.

RISC (Reduced Instruction Set Computer) a processor which provides a set of simple instructions which, because of their simplicity, can be executed extremely quickly.

set associative cache a cache consisting of a number of sets of lines, where a particular line in each set can be matched associatively in a single operation against the address being sought.

stack a region of memory used for temporary storage, including local variables and return addresses within subroutines.

stack pointer the processor register which identifies the top (most recently used location) on the stack.

standby a processor mode which reduces power consumption by switching off all the hardware except that needed to keep dynamic memory refreshed.

static memory a form of memory which does not need to be refreshed regularly, unlike dynamic memory.

stripe a segment of a block of data, so that each segment of the block can be written to a separate disk in a RAID system.

subroutine an independent section of a program which can be called from many different places within the same program, usually referred to as a 'procedure' or a 'function' in most high-level languages.

tag the part of the address used to verify that a cache line contains the data being sought.

TLB (Translation Lookaside Buffer) a cache within the MMU which is used to hold recently accessed page table entries.

UPS (Uninterruptible Power Supply) a power supply which can maintain the power to a system for a certain amount of time in the event of a failure in the mains supply.

user mode an execution mode which restricts the actions that can be performed. Attempting to execute privileged instructions or access restricted regions of the address space result in an exception.

volatile memory memory whose contents are lost in the absence of a power supply.

6.12 ☐ REFERENCES

[1] Chen, P. M., Lee, E. K., Gibson, G. A., Katz, R. H. and Patterson, D. A. RAID: high-performance, reliable secondary storage. *ACM Computing Surveys*, **26**(2) (Jun 1994), 145–185

[2] Clements, A. *Microprocessor Systems Design: 68000 Hardware, Software and Interfacing.* Wadworth Publishing (1987)

[3] Conti, C. J., Gibson, D. H. and Pitkowsky, S. H. Structural aspects of the System/360 Model 85, Part 1: General Organization. *IBM System Journal*, **7**(1) (1968), 2–14

[4]   Cragon, H. G. *Memory Systems and Pipelined Processors*. Jones and Bartlett (1996)

[5]   Hyde, R. *The Art of Assembly Language*. No Starch Press (2003). Available online at
      `http://webster.cs.ucr.edu/`

[6]   Intel Corporation. *IA-32 Intel Architecture Software Development Manual vol. 1: Basic
      Architecture*. Order no. 245470-012 (2003). Available online at
      `ftp://download.intel.com/design/Pentium4/manuals/24547012.pdf`

[7]   Intel Corporation. *IA-32 Intel Architecture Software Development Manual vol. 2: Instruc-
      tion Set Reference*. Order no. 245471-012 (2003). Available online at
      `ftp://download.intel.com/design/Pentium4/manuals/24547012.pdf`

[8]   Intel Corporation. *IA-32 Intel Architecture Software Development Manual vol. 3: System
      Programming Guide*. Order no. 245472-012 (2003). Available online at
      `ftp://download.intel.com/design/Pentium4/manuals/24547012.pdf`

[9]   Jacob, B. and Mudge, T. Virtual memory in contemporary microprocessors. *IEEE Micro*,
      18(5) (Jul/Aug 1998), 61–75

[10] Motorola Corporation. *68000 Family Programmer's Reference Manual*. Document
      M68000PM/AD (1992) Available online at
      `http://e-www.motorola.com/files/archives/doc/ref_manual/M68000PRM.pdf`

[11] Patterson, D. A. and Séquin, C. H. RISC 1: a reduced instruction set VLSI computer.
      Proceedings of the 8th International Symposium on Computer Architecture, ACM Press
      (May 1981), pp. 443–457

[12] Patterson, D. A., Gibson, G. A. and Katz, R. H. A case for redundant arrays of inexpensive
      disks (RAID). *Proceedings of the ACM International Conference on Management of Data*,
      ACM Press (1988), pp. 109–116

[13] Tanenbaum, A. S. *Structured Computer Organization*. Prentice Hall (1999)

[14] Uhlig, R., Nagle, D., Stanley, T., Mudge, T., Secrest, T. and Brown, R. Design Tradeoffs for
      Software-Managed TLBs. *ACM Transactions on Computer Systems*, **12**(2) (Aug 1994),
      175–205

7

THE KERNEL

Having looked at the hardware required to support a modern operating system, we now turn our attention to the software side of things. This chapter looks at the system kernel: the layer of software that is closest to the hardware and is the basis for the rest of the operating system.

7.1 ☐ KERNEL RESPONSIBILITIES

In earlier chapters I have compared the role of an operating system to that of an emulator. An emulator models one computer system in software using the hardware of another; an operating system models processes running on an idealised, virtualised version of the underlying hardware but uses real hardware to do this. The kernel is the heart of an operating system: it is where contact is made with the full power of the underlying hardware, as well as where all the nasty unvirtualised aspects of the hardware become apparent. However, some systems (including Windows) isolate hardware-dependent parts of the kernel in a separate **hardware abstraction layer** (HAL), which means that the rest of the kernel can be made more machine-independent and hence more easily portable to different systems.

All processes need access to facilities provided by the kernel. Whenever a process needs to use some feature that involves real hardware, it has to use the kernel to interact with the hardware on its behalf. This might be reading from a file, creating a window on the screen, or allocating some memory within its address space. An emulator can provide extra 'magic' instructions to do these things; an operating system provides an API using a 'system call' instruction which is provided by the underlying hardware to achieve the same effect. A system call is a specialised form of 'call' instruction: it remembers where to continue by storing the return address and current processor mode on the stack, switches the processor into kernel mode, and transfers control to a particular address within the kernel. A system call differs from a normal subroutine call in that a normal subroutine call instruction can transfer control to any point in memory; a system call instruction can only transfer control to the location defined by the corresponding exception vector. The instruction used to implement system calls (INT 2E for Windows, INT 80 for Linux) always transfers control to a common system call handler within the kernel.

Parameters are passed in the processor registers, including a code which identifies the operation to be performed. The kernel uses this as an index into a table holding the addresses of the kernel routines which implement each of the different possible system calls and goes to the specified address to carry out the requested operation. Results are passed back to the calling process via the processor registers, including a code to indicate whether or not the requested operation was performed successfully.

Since the processor is operating in kernel mode during a system call, the individual system call routines must be careful to validate the parameters supplied by the user. For example, the *read* system call, which reads a block of bytes from a file, requires parameters specifying the address of the buffer in the user-mode address space where the data should be read into, as well as the number of bytes to be read. The routine which implements this system call must begin by checking that all the addresses in the range specified by these two parameters are actually writable in user mode. Since the system call is being executed in kernel mode, it can write to any address in the user-mode address space, even if it would not be writable in user mode. Specialised instructions are provided by the hardware to do this checking; for example, Pentium processors provide instructions called VERR ('verify read') and VERW ('verify write') which check whether the requested access would be allowed in user mode. This prevents a system call which has been given an inappropriate address from overwriting memory that would otherwise be inaccessible to users (including the kernel address space itself). The sequence of events for a system call is illustrated in Figure 7.1.

In most operating systems, the kernel of the operating system is made to appear as though it is part of each individual process. For example, Linux on Pentium-family hardware uses the lower 3 GB of the address space (addresses 0x00000000 to 0xBFFFFFFF) for user-mode code and data; the last gigabyte of the address space (addresses 0xC0000000 to 0xFFFFFFFF) for kernel-mode code and data, as shown in Figure 7.2.

The kernel-mode part of the address space is not directly accessible while the process is executing in user mode, but a system call instruction will put the calling thread into kernel mode and transfer control to a specific address within the kernel-mode portion of the address space.

Once in kernel mode, the thread is able to access any hardware devices (including the memory management system), so it can issue commands to a disk to read a particular block of data into a particular address in the user-mode portion of the address space. It can also use the memory management system to make the memory belonging to another process visible within the user-mode address space in place of the memory of the process that issued the system call. In fact, this is how the operating system is able to suspend one process and resume another.

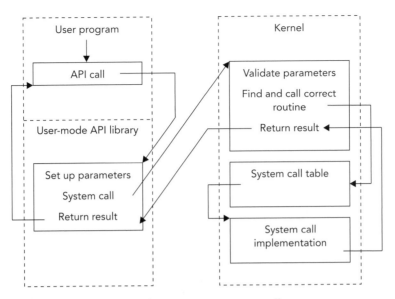

Figure 7.1 Sequence of events in a system call.

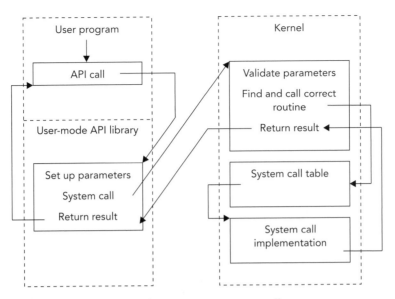

Figure 7.2 Processes and their address spaces.

Of course, the kernel is not physically duplicated in each individual process. A single copy of the kernel code is shared by all processes, together with any kernel data that is not specific to a particular process. The memory map of each process is set up so that the top gigabyte of the address space in each process refers to the same set of physical memory locations.

7.2 ☐ IMPLEMENTING THREADS

Threads are similar to processes in that they are executed concurrently, so the processor has to switch between threads at regular intervals to maintain concurrency. It does this by saving enough information to resume the thread later (the **thread context**). The only real difference between a thread and a process is the amount of extra state information that must be saved, such as file descriptors for any open files and the page table base address. Because of this, threads make a good introduction to the way that concurrency is implemented. Also, threads do not have to be implemented by the operating system. It is quite easy to implement threads by hand in an ordinary user-mode program. For example, Linux does not support threads natively, but the pthreads ('portable threads') library can be used to provide multithreading in a similar way to the method described here without having to write it all yourself.

Each thread will need an area of memory to be set aside for use as a stack. Each thread needs its own stack, as each thread will need to store its own local variables and temporary values separately from the other threads in the system. In addition you have to have a data structure for each thread (a **thread descriptor**) which is used to store the thread context and which links to the descriptor for the next thread to be executed. In the simplest case, the thread descriptor needs to hold a copy of the stack pointer register (ESP); all the other context information can be stored on the stack itself, as shown in Figure 7.3.

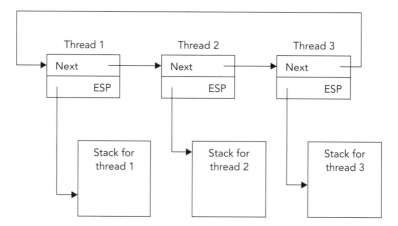

Figure 7.3 Thread descriptors.

The stack and the thread descriptor between them are used to store the state of the processor (that is, the contents of the processor registers) so that the state can be restored later. The processor state includes the program counter register, which gives the address of the next instruction that the thread is about to execute, and the stack pointer, which gives the position of the top of the thread's stack.

Switching to another thread can be done by calling a suspend procedure, which stores the processor registers in the thread descriptor for the current thread and reloads them from the thread descriptor for some other thread. For example, imagine two threads (A and B). When thread A calls the suspend procedure, the current state of the processor registers are saved and thread B is resumed. When thread B calls suspend, the saved register values for thread A are restored and execution continues from the point at which thread A called suspend. If each thread calls suspend at regular intervals, the threads will proceed concurrently.

The easiest place to store the contents of the processor registers is on the stack itself. When suspend is called, the call instruction will push the program counter on the top of the stack, so there is no need to save the program counter separately. Saving the other registers on the stack just requires a sequence of 'push' instructions; in fact, the Pentium provides instructions called pushad and popad which will push or pop all the registers in a single operation, and most other processors provide something similar. The flags register needs to be saved as well; separate pushfd and popfd instructions must be used to push and pop the flags register on a Pentium.

The next thing to do is to store the stack pointer itself, so that when the thread is resumed we can locate the saved copies of the registers and pick up from where the thread was suspended. This must go in the thread descriptor. We can assume that there is a global variable called current which contains the address of the current thread's descriptor. Since all the processor registers have been saved, we can load the value of current into any convenient register and use it to write the stack pointer into the current thread descriptor.

The final step is to get the next thread to be run and restore its state. The address of the descriptor for the next thread must be taken from the current thread's descriptor, and this will become the new current thread descriptor. Next, the new thread's stack pointer must be restored. The thread's saved registers can then be popped off the stack with a popad instruction, and finally a return instruction pops the saved program counter off the stack, which resumes execution at the point in the thread just after suspend was called.

In this simple case, the thread descriptor only needs to hold a copy of the corresponding thread's stack pointer and the address of the next thread descriptor. Here is the complete Pentium assembly language code for a simple version of suspend, with some explanatory comments:

```
SUSPEND:
    PUSHAD                    ; save all the registers
    PUSHFD                    ; save the flags register
    MOV   EBX,[CURRENT]       ; get the current thread descriptor
    MOV   4[EBX],ESP          ; save the stack pointer in it
    MOV   EBX,0[EBX]          ; get the next thread descriptor
    MOV   [CURRENT],EBX       ; make it the current thread
    MOV   ESP,4[EBX]          ; restore its stack pointer
    POPFD                     ; restore the flags register
    POPAD                     ; restore the other registers
    RET                       ; return to the point of suspension
```

The instruction MOV X,Y means 'move (copy) the value Y into X'. The notation [CURRENT] means 'the contents of the variable CURRENT', so the first MOV instruction will copy the value of the variable CURRENT into register EBX. The notation 4[EBX] means '4 bytes further on from the address held in the EBX register', so the second MOV instruction copies the stack pointer (ESP) into the second 4-byte slot in the thread descriptor. I'm assuming here that the thread descriptor is 8 bytes in size;

the first four bytes hold the address of the next thread descriptor, and the last four hold the saved stack pointer, as was illustrated earlier in Figure 7.3.

There are some extra complications I've glossed over. The Pentium also has a number of extra registers which are part of the processor's floating-point unit, and these would need to be saved and restored as well. This would increase the amount of space taken up on the stack by suspend, so it might be better to store all the registers in the thread descriptor itself to avoid running out of space on the stack.

Creating a thread involves allocating a block of memory for the stack and another one for the thread descriptor. The stack needs to be filled with initial values for all the registers in the correct order, and especially the program counter value which will determine where the thread will begin its execution. The descriptor needs to be initialised with the correct stack pointer value and linked in to the list of existing threads. When the previous thread in the list calls suspend, the registers will be loaded with their initial values using the values stored in the stack.

A thread can be terminated by calling an exit routine that deallocates the stack space for the thread, removes the descriptor for the current thread from the list of threads, deallocates the descriptor and then resumes the next thread in the list. To make life easier, we can extend the thread descriptor to include the base address and size of the block that was allocated for its stack. When the thread is created, it is also a good idea to put the address of the exit routine on the stack below the initial values for the thread's registers, so that if the thread executes a return instruction the place it will return to will be the exit routine.

Project 7.1   Implement functions to create, suspend and terminate threads as described above. Test it by writing a program that creates three threads, each of which executes a loop that prints a message identifying the thread and then suspends.

7.3 ☐ KERNEL OBJECTS

The kernel basically comprises the services which are essential for the rest of the operating system to function. These include:

- **Process management**. This includes managing data structures for processes and threads, including a **scheduler** which is responsible for switching from one thread to another in a similar way to the suspend routine described above. It also includes synchronisation primitives like mutexes and semaphores.

- **Memory management**. This involves managing the list of free page frames, keeping track of the working set size of each process, and allocating memory to processes on demand.

- **Exception handling**. This includes interrupt handling and system call handling.

- **Device management**. This involves providing a way for system calls to identify the correct device driver to carry out I/O operations, and loading and unloading device drivers when necessary.

Although many operating systems are not explicitly based on an object-oriented design, the best way to think of the kernel is as a collection of interacting **objects**. Each object encapsulates a data structure which it is responsible for managing as well as a set of externally accessible operations which can be invoked by other objects to operate on that data structure. In an object-oriented system, each object belongs to a particular **class** which defines what externally accessible operations each object of that class must provide. A class can **inherit** characteristics from a **parent class** and can extend those characteristics with additional externally accessible operations. It can also provide a different implementation of any of the operations it inherits from its parent. In operating systems terminology, objects are often referred to as **descriptors** since they 'describe' the state of the corresponding item; for example, a **thread object** is often referred to as a **thread descriptor** because it describes the state of the corresponding thread. The operations that a class of objects supports is often referred to as the **protocol** of the class, as it defines a standard way to invoke those operations.

As an example, consider mutexes and semaphores. Each **mutex object** belongs to a **mutex class** which defines the operations provided by the object. For a mutex, these are the wait and signal operations described in Chapter 4. Internally, there will be a flag indicating whether or not the mutex is in use and a list of **thread objects** that are waiting for the mutex to become free. A **semaphore object** belongs to a **semaphore class** which is basically the same except that a semaphore uses an integer counter rather than a Boolean flag. It also provides wait and signal operations, but these will be implemented differently from the corresponding mutex operations. It might also have an additional operation to return the current value of the internal counter.

One way to implement this would be to derive the semaphore class from the mutex class as shown in Figure 7.4, redefining wait and signal and adding the integer counter and any extra operations. Alternatively, both the mutex class and the semaphore class could be derived from a common **synchronisation** class which defines the abstract behaviour of all synchronisation objects, as shown in Figure 7.5.

Another important concept in object-oriented designs is **polymorphism**. Assuming that mutexes and semaphores are derived from a parent synchronisation class, we could write a function that takes any synchronisation object as a parameter and uses its wait and signal operations. The actual synchronisation object that the function is supplied with could be either a mutex or a semaphore, both of which are guaranteed to provide wait and signal operations, either inherited from the parent class or redefined in the derived class. When the function wants to call wait, it gets the address of the object's internal wait operation from a table defined in the class it belongs to and then calls that operation, as illustrated in Figure 7.6. We came across this concept in Chapter 3, where the Linux virtual filesystem provides operations like open, read and write which are passed on to the corresponding operations in either the FAT

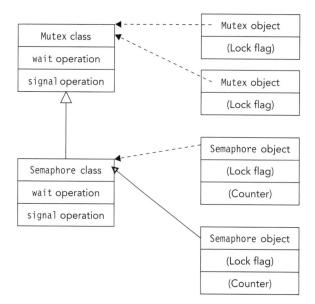

Figure 7.4 Mutex and semaphore objects.

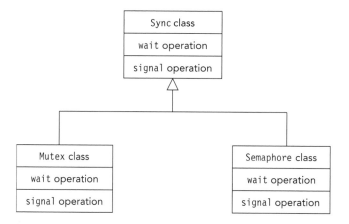

Figure 7.5 Inheritance schemes for mutexes and semaphores.

filesystem, the ext2fs filesystem or an ISO-9660 (CD-ROM) filesystem. Each of these filesystems is represented by an object which defines its own implementations of each of the required operations.

In some cases, kernel objects each have a fixed size and there are a known, limited number of them, in which case a fixed-size array of objects can be used. An example of this is the exception vector table, whose size is determined by the number of different possible exceptions. Another example is the Unix file descriptor table belonging to each process, which normally holds 20 file descriptors to allow each process to have up to 20 files open at any one time. More commonly, the individual

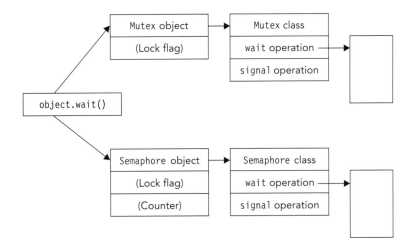

Figure 7.6 Polymorphism.

objects are linked together using pointers in arrangements which can change over time, such as the **queues** and **trees** illustrated in Figure 7.7.

The kernel must have a pool of available memory from which it can allocate new objects as they are needed, and one of the most fundamental memory management operations is the management of this pool of memory. Most kernel objects are quite small, so this is a separate issue from allocating and deallocating entire pages of memory. One common approach used to allocate and deallocate objects efficiently is to use a technique known as **buddy blocks**. In this scheme, memory is always allocated in blocks whose size is a power of two. The system keeps a list of available blocks of various different sizes and tries to allocate a block of the appropriate size when requested. For example, a request for a block of 26 bytes would be satisfied by finding a block of 32 bytes (the next highest power of two). If there is no block of 32 bytes available, a block of 64 bytes is allocated and split into two blocks of 32 bytes, one of which will be used to satisfy the original request and the other of which will be added to the list of available 32-byte blocks. Similarly, if

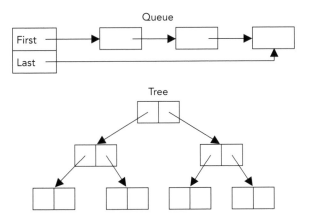

Figure 7.7 Queues and trees.

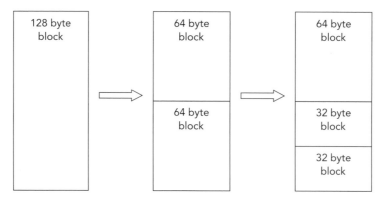

Figure 7.8 Buddy blocks.

there are no 64-byte blocks available to do this with, a 128-byte block is split into two 64-byte blocks, and one of those can then be split into two 32-byte blocks, as shown in Figure 7.8.

Freeing blocks when they are no longer needed is easy to do with this approach. When a block of 32 bytes is freed, the neighbouring 32 byte block is checked to see if it is also free. The neighbouring block can be identified by dividing the block address by its size. For example, consider two 32-byte blocks which are allocated at addresses 0 and 32; dividing the address by the block size gives an even result if it is the first block of a pair or an odd address if it is the second block of a pair. If the neighbouring block is free, the two can be coalesced into a single block of 64 bytes. Each allocated block will need to use the first couple of bytes of the block to indicate its size, and this can include a single bit to indicate whether it is free or not.

Project 7.2   Write a class or set of functions to implement a buddy block allocation system, with `allocate` and `release` operations to allocate blocks of a particular size and free them again.

There are some common properties that practically all objects will share, and it makes sense to encapsulate these in a root parent class (traditionally called Object) from which all other classes are ultimately derived. Common properties might include the size of the object, a pointer to the next object of the same type to allow all such objects to be enumerated, a pointer to a table of operations for that object (which can also be used to identify the object type), and possibly an object name.

Another common requirement is to organise objects into **queues**; for example, a queue of **thread objects** which are waiting for access to a mutex or a queue of **memory objects** describing pages which are waiting to be written out to disk. Queues can be represented by **queue objects** which contain pointers to the first and last objects in the queue and a count of the number of objects in the queue, with operations add to add an object to the back of the queue and remove to remove objects from the front of the queue. Any objects which can be added to a queue (which may well be every object) will need to include a pointer that will be used to point to the next object in the same queue and possibly a pointer to the queue object itself, so that it is possible to identify which queue an object is attached to at any time.

The add and remove operations on queues are quite simple to implement. Removing an object from the front of the queue is done as shown in Figure 7.9 by taking a copy of the pointer to the first object in the queue, and then modifying the queue header's pointer to the first object to point to the next object after the one just removed.

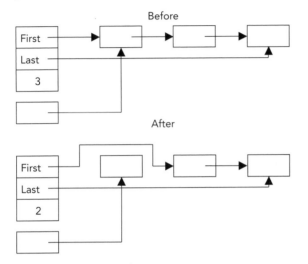

Figure 7.9 Removing an object from a queue.

Adding an object to the end of a queue is done as shown in Figure 7.10 by modifying the 'next' pointer of the last object in the queue to point to the object being added, and then resetting the queue header's pointer to the last object to point to the object being added.

Project 7.3   Write add and remove operations to manipulate a queue in a language with which you are familiar.

Operations on queues, like memory allocation and deallocation, are fundamental operations in any kernel. These fundamental operations will be called on from many places in the kernel code. It is also perfectly possible that they will be called from within interrupt service routines as part of the processing of an interrupt from an external device. The danger here is that the queue that the interrupt service routine attempts to operate on might already be being operated on at the

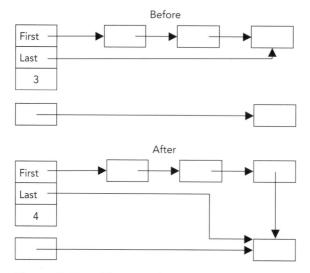

Figure 7.10 Adding an object to a queue.

time, and this could leave the queue in an inconsistent state. The solution in a user program would be to use a mutex to protect the queue operations, but this is not acceptable in the kernel; for one thing, mutex operations themselves involve suspending threads in a queue! Since queue operations are only a few instructions long, it is perfectly acceptable to protect them by disabling external interrupts during those few critical instructions so that they execute as atomic operations which cannot be interrupted. However, this won't work on a multiprocessor system where disabling interrupts for one processor has no effect on the other processors. This is discussed further in Chapter 9.

7.3.1 MICROKERNEL DESIGNS

Some operating systems are based around a **microkernel** design, where the kernel is kept as small as possible and processes running in user mode do as much of the work as possible. For example, a device driver might run as a process in user mode which has access to the corresponding device by mapping the I/O address of the device into the user-mode address space of the process, or by setting the appropriate I/O permission bits for port-based I/O on a Pentium. The ultimate responsibilities of the kernel in a microkernel design come down to process creation, thread scheduling, memory management and interprocess communication. Everything else can be done using normal processes which have access to specialised resources such as I/O devices. All you need is a set of specialised server processes which provide services such as device management to any client program that wants to use those services, as illustrated in Figure 7.11. This reduces the size and complexity of the kernel, making it easier to understand and maintain, and it also makes it easy to add, remove or modify the server processes which handle everything else.

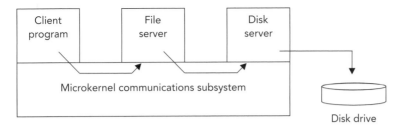

Figure 7.11 User-mode servers in a microkernel.

So why aren't microkernels the rule, rather than the exception? A lot of arguments have been advanced for and against microkernels, but in the end most of the arguments against the idea are based on efficiency considerations. Calling a kernel function from user mode means that the calling thread has to switch into kernel mode and back again, but communicating with another process to do the same job involves several context switches between user mode and kernel mode to send the message to the server process, schedule the server process to do the work and generate a response, and switch back to the original thread in the original process so that it can deal with the response from the server.

Switching between processes like this can be a lot of work, especially if it is done frequently. When executing a system call in a conventional kernel, the same thread executes the call (unless it is a blocking operation) with only mode changes from user mode to kernel mode and back again to worry about. Switching to a new process involves much more work: you have to switch to a different set of page tables, for one thing, and this might generate a series of page faults if the selected process has been swapped out. The situation might change; whenever an argument has been fought between simplicity and elegance on the one hand and efficiency on the other hand, the simplicity-and-elegance approach has always won out eventually as technological advances erode the efficiency considerations. We will have to wait and see how things develop in this particular case.

Question 7.1   What are the advantages and disadvantages of the microkernel approach?

7.3.2 EXOKERNELS

An even more extreme design approach is to use an **exokernel**, with an even more minimal kernel providing secure access to machine resources and the ability to deallocate resources on demand (or by force if necessary). The exokernel deals with resource allocation, but all the resource management functions (including processor scheduling and memory management) that a traditional kernel provides are then delegated to user-mode libraries. With this approach, what would traditionally be considered to comprise an operating system simply becomes another user-mode API, and multiple 'operating systems' can be supported on a single machine by applications which use different libraries.

The proponents of this approach claim that the low-level nature of the operations provided by an exokernel allows those operations to be combined into higher-level operations by individual applications in a more flexible way than is possible with a fixed set of high-level kernel operations. The small size of the exokernel also makes it easier to build and test. As for efficiency, the fact that most work is done in user mode means that relatively few mode switches between user and kernel modes are needed.

Engler *et al.* [4] describe an experimental exokernel called Aegis developed at MIT. This is reported to be several times faster than a traditional Unix implementation running on the same hardware. However, systems like this are still highly experimental.

7.4 ❑ PROCESS MANAGEMENT

Processes and threads are managed by the kernel using objects which are used to record their state. As we have already seen, thread objects will need to hold the contents of processor registers, as well as other information such as the thread priority, a reference to the process object for the process which owns the thread and an indication of the current state of the thread. Thread objects can to some extent be seen as extensions of the process object they belong to; the process object defines the overall environment for the threads its owns, including such aspects as the address space within which the threads operate, a list of all the threads owned by the process, and the environment variables and opened files that the threads can access. Each thread object belonging to a particular process describes the current state of executing some program within the process environment, which includes the values of the processor registers, the queue of pending events arising from windows created by the thread, and so on.

Threads go through a number of different states as they execute. These states include:

- **Running**: the thread is the one that is currently executing. On a multiprocessor system there will be one running thread per processor.

- **Ready to run**: the thread is not currently executing, but it can be chosen to resume its execution when the currently running thread is suspended

- **Blocked**: the thread is waiting for some operation to complete before it can proceed, and should not be considered when looking for a thread to execute. The thread descriptor is put in a queue associated with the operation.

The **scheduler** is one of the most important parts of the kernel. It is responsible for choosing a new thread to execute when the currently executing thread is suspended, and for performing a **context switch** from the suspended thread to the new current thread. A context switch involves saving processor registers for one thread and reloading them from the descriptor for another, in a similar way to the suspend routine described earlier in this chapter. The process that the new thread belongs to must also be made active if it is not already the active process. This will primarily involve ensuring that the appropriate address space is accessible by making the process page tables accessible. As a result, the processor is now executing instructions 'in the context of' the new thread, or in other words with the appropriate register values for the thread and the appropriate virtual memory layout for the process that it belongs to.

Thread objects can be attached to a variety of system queues, where each queue contains threads in a particular state. There needs to be at least one queue of ready-to-run threads, and the scheduler will choose one of these to run next. The usual approach is to have a separate queue for each of the possible thread priority levels, as shown in Figure 7.12; the scheduler can inspect these queues in order, looking for a non-empty queue. The first thread in the first non-empty queue is the one that should be started next. This scheduling mechanism is thus fairly simple, which makes it highly efficient. However, the scheduler must also be fair, sharing out the available processor time in an equitable way. This is a matter of scheduling policy, which in this approach is determined by the order in which thread descriptors are placed in the ready-to-run queues. Again, we see here a distinction between **mechanism** and **policy**.

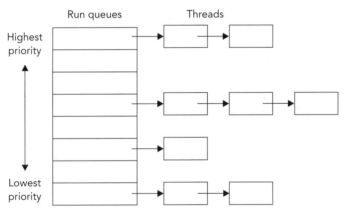

Figure 7.12 Run queues.

Exercise 7.1   Find out the number of priority levels that are supported by the operating system you are using.

When a new thread is created, a new thread object is allocated from the kernel's pool of available memory and initialised to describe the initial state of the thread, with appropriate values for the processor registers and so on. This is then added to the queue of ready-to-run threads which corresponds to the initial priority of the thread. At some point the scheduler will start it running, and it will execute until a timer interrupt occurs (indicating that it has used up its allocated time slice), or until it performs a blocking operation such as waiting for an input event or trying to enter a busy critical section, or until it terminates. In the first case the thread is returned to the 'ready-to-run' state and its descriptor is added to an appropriate queue according to its priority; in the second case it enters the 'blocked' state and its descriptor is added to a queue associated with the event source or mutex that it is waiting for. In the last case the memory for the descriptor is freed, and if it is the last thread in the process the process is also terminated and its descriptor freed. The transitions between thread states are illustrated in Figure 7.13. On Unix systems each process has to report an exit code to the parent process that created it, so it may be necessary for the process descriptor to be kept in a so-called **zombie** state (where the process is not yet officially dead, but it is also no longer alive because it has no active threads) until the parent process has accessed its exit code.

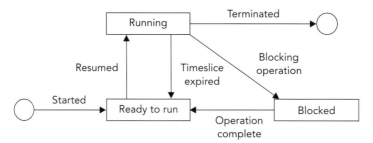

Figure 7.13 A thread state transition diagram.

Blocking operations in the kernel result in the descriptor for the active thread being added to some queue associated with the blocking operation. For example, if a semaphore had a value of zero, a wait operation on that semaphore would result in the descriptor for the calling thread being added to the queue associated with the semaphore. When this happens, the scheduler must be executed to choose a new thread to run. Blocking operations use a kernel suspend routine to suspend the current thread and add it to a specified queue. The suspend routine doesn't return; it just jumps to the start of the scheduler once it has suspended the thread. However, the return address from the call to suspend will be stored in the thread descriptor as the address of the next instruction for that thread to execute when it is unblocked.

Hopefully, a blocked thread will sooner or later be unblocked. For example, a thread blocked on a semaphore wait operation should at some point be unblocked by a corresponding signal operation. The signal operation will make the first thread in the semaphore's queue (if any) ready to run by transferring it to the scheduler's ready-to-run queue. When the scheduler eventually chooses this thread to run, it will be at the point where it would return from the suspend operation inside the code for the wait operation.

As a concrete example, consider how a mutex is used to control access to a critical section:

```
while (test_and_set(mutex.value) == 1) {
  suspend(mutex.queue);
}
critical_section();
mutex.value = 0;
if (not_empty(mutex.queue)) {
  resume(mutex.queue);
}
```

This is a slight modification of the code shown in Chapter 4. Assuming that the mutex has been locked by another thread, a thread executing this code will enter the initial loop and be suspended in the mutex's queue. Later, the thread executing the critical section will emerge from it, setting the mutex value to zero and resuming the suspended thread by moving it back into the ready-to-run queue. When the thread that was suspended resumes execution, it will be inside the loop at the point immediately after the call to suspend, and it will continue by going around the loop and trying to lock the mutex again. Some other thread might have got into the critical section before this happens, in which case the thread will be suspended again. Eventually it should succeed in locking the mutex and it will then be able to enter the critical section.

7.4.1   THE TIMER QUEUE

Another important system queue is the **timer queue**, which can be used to schedule particular threads to run at a specified time. The entries in the queue specify the time to wait, and a pointer to the thread object for the thread to be resumed when the specified time expires. The time to wait is normally held as a time difference between the wake-up time of the preceding queue entry and the wake-up time of the current entry, as shown in Figure 7.14. For example, if two threads are to be woken up after 15 and 20 seconds respectively, the first entry in the timer queue will give the time until the first thread needs to be started (15 seconds), and the second entry will give the time between the two threads (20 – 15 = 5 seconds). The value associated with the first entry in the timer queue is reduced

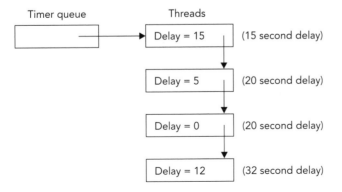

Figure 7.14 A timer queue.

whenever a timer interrupt occurs. After 15 seconds have elapsed, the value associated with the first entry in the queue will have reached zero, and when this happens the first thread will be removed from the queue and made ready to run, leaving the other thread as the first thread in the timer queue. This thread will now wait a further 5 seconds before it is resumed, which means that it will have waited 20 seconds altogether. Note that if two threads want to sleep until the same time, the time difference between them will be zero, so when the counter for the first sleeping thread has reached zero and the process has been resumed, the next item in the queue will have a delay time of zero and should therefore be resumed at the same time.

The system timer generates interrupts at fixed intervals. This interval is known as a **clock tick** (known in Linux as a **jiffy**). Times will need to be measured in clock ticks, rather then in seconds. The timer hardware generates an interrupt every clock tick, and the timer interrupt handler deals with any time-related activities that need to be carried out. This includes decrementing the time delay for the first item in the timer queue, and waking up any threads at the front of the queue whose time delay has reached zero. The timer interrupt handler is also responsible for rescheduling if the time slice for the current process has expired, and for any other time-related activities, such as updating counters in the thread descriptor which record the amount of processor time it has used.

Exercise 7.2   Find out the size of a clock tick on the system you are using.

7.5 ❑ SCHEDULING

A basic scheduling mechanism was described earlier. The queues of ready-to-run threads are inspected in order of decreasing priority, and the first thread in the first non-empty queue is the one that resumes execution. The fairness of the scheduler depends critically on the policies used to decide how threads are ordered within these queues.

The simplest approach is known as **round-robin scheduling**. In this scheme, when a thread is started, the system timer is programmed to generate an interrupt after a fixed time period (typically something like every 10 or 20 milliseconds), known as the thread's **quantum**. If the thread is still running when the timer interrupt occurs, it is moved to the back of the queue of ready-to-run threads, as shown in Figure 7.15. Where all threads have the same priority, this is a simple technique that will share out the processor time fairly. However, where there are multiple priority levels there may be a single high-priority thread and several lower-priority threads. While the high-priority thread is running, the corresponding ready-to-run queue will be empty since this is the only thread with a high priority. If the high-priority thread uses up its full time quantum, it will be moved to the back of the

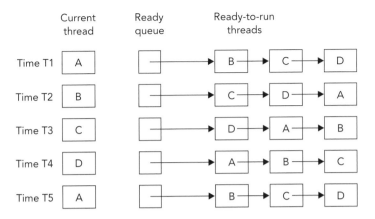

Figure 7.15 Round-robin scheduling.

(empty) high-priority ready-to-run queue, so that when the scheduler tries to find a thread to execute it will find the same high-priority thread that was just suspended. The lower priority threads will then be starved of processor time.

A way to avoid this is to allow thread priorities to be dynamically adjusted according to their behaviour. A thread that uses up its full time quantum without blocking can have its priority reduced, so that it will eventually drop below the priority of the other threads in the system. Similarly, a thread that is made ready to run after it has been blocked can have its priority raised so that it will stand a better chance of being scheduled. It could be raised to a fixed level, or it could be increased by a value inversely proportional to the amount of processor time it used before blocking. With the latter approach, a thread that executed for a very short time before blocking would have its priority raised more than would be the case for a thread that executed for most of its quantum before blocking. This requires the time to be stored in the thread descriptor when the thread is blocked so that the scheduler can use this information to calculate the new priority.

There are many other approaches to scheduling. The basic idea is to share out the processor time equally between all the threads in the system. A different approach that can be used to achieve this is known as **lottery scheduling**. In this approach, each thread is given one or more 'lottery tickets'. When the scheduler wants to select a new thread to run, it chooses a lottery ticket at random and resumes the thread which holds that lottery ticket. Priorities can be implemented by giving threads multiple lottery tickets, which will increase their chances of winning the lottery. The scheduler needs to keep track of the available lottery ticket numbers and the threads to which they correspond, rather than keeping threads in queues. The chance that a thread will be scheduled will be in direct proportion to the number of lottery tickets it holds.

Threads may be allowed to exchange lottery tickets if they wish, so that a client requesting a service from a server process can give the server process its lottery tickets while it is blocked waiting for the server's response. This will increase the chances of the server process running, and hence the speed with which the server will deal with the client's request. When the request has been dealt with, the server process can return the lottery tickets it was given to the client thread.

Lottery scheduling makes it easy to solve scheduling problems that are quite difficult to solve by other means. For example, if one thread needs to be able to process 30 events per second and another needs to be able to process 50 events per second, giving the first thread 30 lottery tickets and the second thread 50 lottery tickets will ensure that the available processor time is (on average) shared out in the ratio 30:50.

On multi-user systems, the scheduling policy also needs to share the available processor time fairly between different users, not just between different threads. A user who starts up ten threads should not be given ten times more processing time than a user who only starts up a single thread. It is normal to allocate each user the same proportion of the total available time, and share the user's time allocation between the threads for that user. This is another problem that is easy to solve using lottery scheduling. All the scheduler needs to do is to allocate every user a fixed number of lottery tickets (say 1000 each) for the user's initial process, and the processor time will be shared equally among all the users. The operation to create a new thread needs to transfer a certain number of lottery tickets from the parent thread to the child thread. These can be returned to the parent thread when the child thread terminates.

7.5.1 EXAMPLE: THE LINUX SCHEDULER

Linux divides processes into two categories: *normal* processes and *real-time* processes. Real-time processes have a higher priority than normal processes so that any real-time processes that are ready to run will always be scheduled in preference to a normal process. They will be scheduled using either a round-robin approach, where each process is moved to the back of the queue after it has been run, or a FIFO (first in, first out) approach, where the processes are run in the order in which they were added to the queue, and this order never changes.

Normal processes have a priority which also determines how long they will be allowed to execute for before being pre-empted. Each such process has a counter which is initially loaded with the value of the process priority. Whenever a timer interrupt occurs, the counter for the active process is decremented, and the scheduler is called when the value of the counter reaches zero. The scheduler is also called when the current process suspends itself, or at the end of certain system calls (for example, at the end of a fork system call when a new process has just been created).

The scheduler searches the run queue for the process with the highest counter value and starts it running. This means that the highest priority process will be run initially, but as it runs its effective priority decreases (as given by the value of its counter). Even low-priority processes will get a chance to run as soon as the counters for the high-priority processes drop to small enough values. Eventually, all the runnable processes will have been executed and all their counters will have reached zero. When this happens (when the scheduler cannot find a process with a non-zero counter), the scheduler resets all the counters back to their original values based on the corresponding process priorities and then scans the list again looking for the highest-priority process.

More recent versions of the kernel use a more complex scheduling algorithm than the one described above, largely due to the introduction of support for multiprocessor systems. The latest kernels compute a 'goodness' measure for each runnable process based on a variety of factors including the processor which was last used by the thread and the processor to which it will be allocated, and it is the process with the highest 'goodness' measure that gets chosen. This is described in more detail in Chapter 9. However, the basic idea is very similar.

7.6 ❑ EXCEPTION HANDLING

Exception handling is one of the core elements of the kernel. When an exception occurs, the kernel has to identify the appropriate handler to deal with it. From a hardware point of view, all that happens is that the processor calls a kernel routine whose address is contained in the appropriate entry in the **exception vector table**, a table which the kernel sets up. This is one of the first things the kernel does when it first starts up, before any processes are created which might generate any exceptions.

Question 7.2   When handling an exception such as a system call or interrupt, the kernel switches to a different stack in the kernel-mode address space. Why is this necessary?

However, as noted earlier, there may be several external devices which can all generate the same interrupt. Moreover, device drivers for new devices can be installed at any time, so it must be possible to add new interrupt service routines at any time. A solution is to maintain a list of **interrupt handler** objects, and to fill in the exception vector table with the address of an **interrupt dispatcher** routine which will work its way through this list, calling each interrupt handler in turn until the interrupt has been dealt with. A device driver can add interrupt handler objects to the list when it is loaded into memory, and can remove them from the list when it is being unloaded from memory.

One possibility is to have an interrupt handler return a code which indicates whether or not the interrupting device has been dealt with, and call each handler in turn until one reports that it has dealt with the interrupt. Another possibility is to just call every handler on the list. However, at least one handler must deal with an interrupt, otherwise at the end of the whole process the interrupt will still be active, and will be recognised again as soon as interrupts are re-enabled. This would indicate an unknown interrupt source, and it would be a fatal system error (what Linux calls a 'kernel panic') that would require the entire system to halt. If the system were allowed to proceed, it would just be continually interrupted and be unable to do anything useful; the only other possibility would be to run with interrupts disabled, which would prevent the system from being able to switch between user processes or respond to any other interrupts. On Windows, a kernel panic produces the well-known 'Blue Screen of Death', where the system halts after displaying an error message in white text on a blue background. It is done this way because trying to use the graphical interface to display an error message may not be possible while inside the kernel.

Question 7.3   Why might it not be safe use the normal graphical interface under these circumstances?

On a Windows system, the interrupt vector contains the address of an **interrupt object**, as shown in Figure 7.16. The beginning of this object is initialised with a handful of machine code instructions which call the real interrupt dispatcher, passing the address of the interrupt object as a parameter. This allows the interrupt dispatcher to obtain information about the interrupt object that called it. The interrupt dispatcher then processes the list of interrupt objects, calling the interrupt service routine specified in each interrupt object in turn. The use of interrupt objects makes it easy to add and remove interrupt service routines as device drivers get loaded into memory or unloaded from memory. There is a separate object for each individual device that can generate a particular interrupt. They might be the same type of device, in which case they will use the same interrupt service routine, but the interrupt object being used allows the interrupt service routine to identify the specific device that it should deal with. For example, if two serial ports share

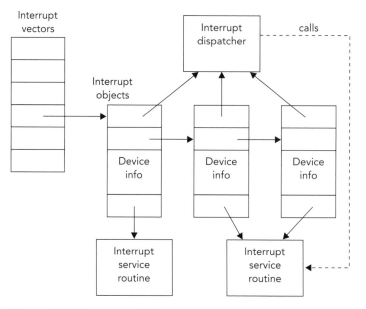

Figure 7.16 Interrupt objects.

the same interrupt, there will be an interrupt object for each port but they will both identify the same interrupt service routine. However, each interrupt object will contain the I/O address of the port that it is intended to deal with, and perhaps other information such as the address of a buffer to be used. The interrupt service routine will use this information to access the correct device and transfer data to or from the correct buffer.

After all the interrupt objects have had a chance to deal with the interrupt, the thread's original interrupt priority is restored so that lower-level interrupts can take effect.

7.7 ❑ MEMORY MANAGEMENT

The memory management system will need to control a number of kernel objects to be able to operate efficiently. For example, when a process allocates some extra memory within its address space, the memory manager must find an unused range of addresses that it can map the newly allocated pages into. Remember that the memory manager doesn't build page tables until they are actually needed, so it cannot easily search the page tables for a block of unused addresses. Windows and Linux both use a fairly typical approach to get around this problem, by maintaining a set of **virtual address descriptors** for each process which describe the status of the process address space. For each allocation request, a virtual address descriptor is created to store the range of addresses that were allocated and their status (read-only, copy-on-write, and so on). This makes it easy to identify unused blocks of address space to use for satisfying memory allocation requests.

On Windows, the virtual address descriptors are organised as a binary tree so that searching can be done efficiently; each descriptor points to a descriptor whose range of addresses precede its own and to a descriptor whose range of addresses follow its own. An example is shown in Figure 7.17. When looking for the descriptor corresponding to the address 0x3FE00000, the memory manager starts at the root of the tree, which in the example tree describes the range 0x20000000 to 0x2000FFFF. Since the address being searched for is after this, the memory manager uses the right-hand pointer to go to the next descriptor. This describes the range

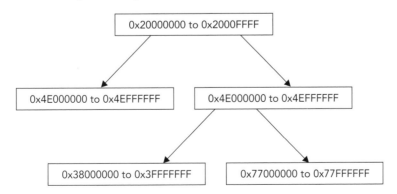

Figure 7.17 A tree of virtual address descriptors.

0x4E000000 to 0x4EFFFFFF, so this time the left-hand pointer is followed to get to a descriptor for addresses which precede this. This time, the descriptor describes the range 0x38000000 to 0x3FFFFFFF, which includes the address 0x3FE00000 that we are looking for.

The address descriptors are used to fill in page table entries when they are accessed for the first time. When a page fault occurs as the result of accessing an invalid page table entry, the memory manager needs to discover whether the page being accessed is unallocated (and report it as an error if so) or is reserved but not committed (as when it is accessed for the first time). An unallocated page will not have a corresponding descriptor; a reserved page will have a descriptor, and the information in the descriptor can be used to commit the page from disk and to fill in the page table entry.

The memory manager also needs to keep track of the status of each page frame in physical memory. Windows uses a **page frame database** for this, with one entry for each physical page frame, linked together into six linked lists as shown in Figure 7.18. There are eight possible states that pages can be in:

- **Zeroed:** pages that are free and have been filled with zeros so that they can be allocated in response for committal requests for blank pages.

- **Free:** free pages that have not been filled with zeros. They can be used to commit pages which are being loaded from disk, or can be filled with zeros and transferred to the zero page list. A kernel thread (the equivalent of the Unix **kernel swap daemon**) is responsible for keeping a certain minimum number of zero and free pages at all times.

- **Standby:** unmodified pages that have been freed but have not yet been transferred to the free list. If a reference to a page in the standby list is made, it can be transferred back to its original owner.

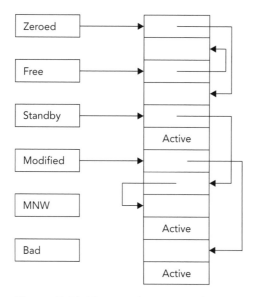

Figure 7.18 The Windows page frame database.

- **Modified:** modified pages that have been freed but not yet written to the disk. After they have been written to the disk, they are transferred to the standby list.

- **Modified no write:** modified pages which should not be written to the disk. This is used to delay writing these pages to disk until some other action has taken place.

- **Bad:** pages which have generated hardware errors and which should not be used.

- **Active:** this is a list of page frames which are in use. The entry for an active page frame also contains a **reference count** of the number of processes which have mapped this page into their virtual address space. These do not appear on any list.

- **Transition:** pages which are in the process of being transferred to or from disk. These do not appear on any list.

The reference count for an entry in the active list is used to implement the copy-on-write mechanism described in Chapter 5. When a page is copied using copy-on-write, the reference count in the corresponding page frame entry is incremented to show that there is now an extra process which references it. Each time the page is written to, a physical copy of the page is made in a new page frame and the entry for the original page frame is decremented. When the reference count shows that only one page table entry now refers to the page, the page table entry is changed to mark it as a normal writable page rather than making a separate copy of it.

7.8 ☐ KERNEL PROCESSES

When the operating system starts up, a few processes are created that perform operating system functions, which always execute in kernel mode. Processes like this do not require a user-mode address space (the bottom 2 GB of the address space on Windows, or the bottom 3 GB on Linux systems); they spend all their time executing within the kernel. For example, Windows has a **system process** which is home to a number of kernel-mode threads. These include memory management threads to write dirty pages out to disk, fill unused pages with zeros, swap processes in and out of memory, and so on. Linux has a number of such processes, including the **kernel swap daemon** (kswapd) which is responsible for swapping pages in and out of memory, as well as other memory management activities such as keeping the number of free pages above a system-defined minimum.

One important kernel-mode process is the **idle process**. This is a process which has a thread which is always ready to run, so that there is always at least one thread available to the scheduler at all times. The idle process can do anything it wants to do, as long as it doesn't try to perform any blocking operations that might make it unable to be scheduled for execution; the idle process must be available to run at all times. On multiprocessor systems, the idle process must provide a separate idle thread for each processor.

The idle process has the lowest priority of all, so that it only runs when there is nothing else to do. In fact, it might not be implemented as a real process at all; it might simply be a tight loop at the end of the scheduler that is reached if there is no other runnable thread and continues looping until some other thread becomes runnable. Once the idle process starts executing, it will need to continue executing until some external event occurs (an interrupt from an external device) which changes the state of some other thread in the system. A convenient way to implement the idle process on many processors is to use a 'halt' instruction at the end of the scheduler which will only be reached if there are no processes ready to run. The 'halt' instruction halts the processor until an interrupt occurs. After the interrupt has been serviced, execution resumes at the instruction after the halt instruction, and this can be a jump instruction which goes back to the start of the scheduler code to try to schedule a new thread for execution. Battery-powered systems can also use this opportunity to reduce the processor clock rate and voltage to minimise power consumption while the processor is halted.

Question 7.4   Could the idle process be used to perform deadlock detection? Would this be a good use for the idle process? Explain your answer.

<h2>7.9 ❑ DAEMONS</h2>

In addition to kernel processes, there are usually a number of other processes that are created automatically when the system is first started which provide background services that can be accessed by other processes. Examples include web servers, database managers, print spoolers, plug-and-play device management, performance monitoring and error logging services. Unix systems refers to processes like this as **daemons** (a 'daemon' being a friendly spirit, as opposed to a 'demon' which is an evil spirit) while Windows refers to them by the more prosaic name of **services**. On a microkernel nearly everything except thread scheduling, memory management and interprocess communication would be implemented in this way.

There is nothing particularly special about daemon processes except that they are normally completely invisible. They have no user interface; there are no standard input or output channels that a user can interact with directly. They must keep running at all times in order to provide the services they are intended to provide, which means that they need to intercept any exceptions that arise during execution. Errors and other status messages are generally recorded in a log file so that events can be reviewed at a later date, and there is often a configuration file which the service reads when it first starts up to parameterise its behaviour; for example, a web server needs to know which directories to make accessible, which network ports to use, and so on. The popular Apache web server (httpd, meaning 'HTTP daemon') is organised like this, with a configuration file called httpd.conf that specifies, among many other things, a directory into which it will write its log files, including an error log called error.log.

It may be necessary for the system administrator to stop and restart daemons as the result of configuration changes. For example, if the web server's configuration file is changed, the server must be restarted to force it to re-read its configuration file. This can be done by manually stopping and restarting the process, for example by using the Unix kill command to send a 'quit' signal to the daemon and then typing in the command which will start the daemon running again. Most daemons are written so that they will stop and restart in response to a particular signal; on Unix systems, the 'hangup' signal (SIGHUP) is usually used for this purpose. Exception handlers for signals like 'quit' and 'hangup' allow the daemon to be shut down in an orderly manner and or to be shut down and restarted.

Exercise 7.3   Find out how to display a list of all the processes running on the system that you are using. How many correspond to visible applications, and how many to daemon processes?

7.9.1   LINUX SYSTEM STARTUP

When the operating system is first loaded, it needs to initialise the various kernel data structures that it will use, create an initial process and start this first process executing. This first process will be responsible for completing the system initialisation by loading device drivers and creating daemon processes.

On Linux this initialisation process is performed by a process called init. The configuration file for this process is stored in the file /etc/inittab. After completing the system initialisation by loading device drivers and other kernel modules, mounting the root filesystem and so on, init creates a number of other processes as defined by /etc/inittab. This file defines the system **runlevel** (which can be overruled when the kernel is first booted if necessary). For each possible runlevel, /etc/inittab specifies which processes should be started. The standard runlevels are:

- **Single user.** This logs in the system administrator on the default system console. This is intended for emergencies only (such as forgetting the root password).

- **Multi-user.** A process running the getty program is created for each terminal, allowing a user to log in at each terminal.

- **Multi-user without NFS.** This is the same as multi-user but without any access to networked filesystems.

- **X.** This starts an X server running on the default X display and starts an X client process which runs a program to display the X login prompt. It also starts a few text-mode login processes just in case some 'behind-the-scenes' management is needed, such as restarting the X server if it crashes (perish the thought!).

- **Halt.** This just halts the system at this point

- **Reboot.** This initiates an immediate reboot.

The last two of these are provided for diagnostic purposes, and should not normally be used. Most Linux systems are set up to start X running on the system console.

In the standard configurations, /etc/inittab also creates a process running a shell script called /etc/rc.d/rc. This script is responsible for starting and stopping daemons such as web servers and print spoolers. It is given the runlevel as a parameter and runs a set of scripts held in the directory /etc/rc.d/init.d according to the runlevel. These scripts take a parameter which is any of start, stop, restart or status. Startup is actually managed by looking in a directory called e.g. /etc/rc.d/rc5.d for runlevel 5 and running all scripts whose names begin with 'S'. The scripts are called things like S16apmd, and are actually soft links to selected scripts in /etc/rc.d/init.d. These scripts are executed in ascending order according to the number after the initial 'S'. The rest of the name is an indication as to what it actually does; for example, apmd is the Advanced Power Management daemon, which controls the power management system to minimise power consumption, as described in Chapter 6.

7.9.2   WINDOWS SYSTEM STARTUP

On Windows, the equivalent of the entire suite of Unix /etc/rc.d scripts is held in the **registry**, a tree-structured database which holds most of the information relating to system configuration. Unlike configuration files on Unix systems, the registry is a binary file rather than a text file so it cannot be hand-edited to make configuration changes. Instead, a tool called regedit is provided to allow the registry to be inspected and edited in a human-readable form. An example of the registry as shown by regedit is given in Figure 7.19. Nearly all application programs use the registry to save their settings.

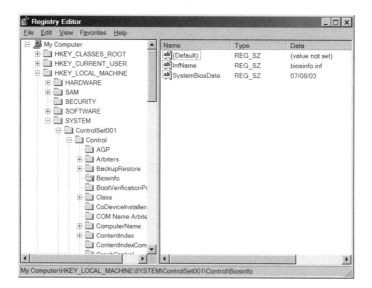

Figure 7.19 The Windows registry.

The registry actually consists of two separate files. One is the **system registry** held in a file called SYSTEM.DAT, and the other is the **user registry** held in a file called USER.DAT. Each user has a separate user registry, which contains per-user configuration information like the desktop background and contents, the 'sound scheme' listing the sounds to be made when windows are opened or closed, the screensaver settings and so on. The system registry contains global information which applies to the system as a whole rather than to individual users, including the device drivers to be loaded and so on. The system registry is read into memory at an early stage and is amalgamated with the user registry when a user logs in to form a single tree-structured database which will remain in memory at all times. Because of the critical importance of the registry, backup copies of the two registry files are saved in files called SYSTEM.DA0 and USER.DA0 in case anything nasty happens to the original files.

One of the first processes to be started is the **system process**, which consists of a number of kernel-mode threads which do things like monitoring the number of free memory pages. One of these kernel threads is responsible for creating the first user process, known as the **session manager**. The session manager creates several other processes, including the **logon process** which allows a user to log in to the system. When a user logs in, the user registry is loaded into memory and a number of new processes are created. These include the **service controller**, which uses information from the registry to start the service (daemon) processes and the **user initialisation** process. The user initialisation process creates a process to run the user's designated shell program and then terminates. The shell then makes it possible to create processes to run particular application programs as required by the user.

7.10 ☐ SUMMARY

The kernel is basically a collection of interacting **objects** which represent the state of the various parts of the system and which provide operations that are executed in response to exceptions (including interrupts and system calls) which switch the current thread into kernel mode. The objects are often organised as queues and trees of objects and are allocated dynamically as they are needed from a pool of available kernel memory. The objects (often known as **descriptors**) describe processes, threads, files, regions of memory and all the other resources that the kernel is responsible for managing.

There are a few special kernel-mode processes which always execute in kernel mode to perform system housekeeping tasks, but most of the work of the kernel is done by ordinary user processes when they are executing in kernel mode as the result of a system call or an interrupt from an external device. One of the most important routines within the kernel is the **scheduler**, which is responsible for choosing and switching to another thread. Other processes, known as **daemons** or **services**, are started automatically when the system first starts up and run invisibly to provide services such as web servers, although these are not part of the kernel itself.

Since Windows is a proprietary system, it is not possible to examine the kernel source code to find out its secrets. The next best thing is given by Solomon and Russinovich [8], a book which provides quite a lot of detail about the workings of the Windows kernel. On the other hand, the Linux kernel source code is readily available (it is supplied as part of the standard Linux distribution), so it is in principle possible to discover many of the finer details of kernel design by reading the source code. In practice, the source code can be quite hard to find your way around. Fortunately, there are many excellent references around to help you get started. Love [6] is an excellent up-to-date guide to the internals by one of the kernel developers. Bovet and Cesati [3] also gives a detailed coverage of the main aspects of the kernel, while Aivazian [2] and Rusling [7] each give less detailed but very worthwhile descriptions of major kernel structures.

Knuth [5] gives a thorough description of queues, lists, trees, buddy blocks, and many other data structures used in operating systems kernels.

For information about more exotic kernel designs, the Mach microkernel is described by Accetta *et al*. [1], while exokernels are described by Engler *et al*. [4].

7.12 ❑ GLOSSARY

buddy blocks a memory allocation system which uses blocks whose sizes are a power of two. Blocks can be split into two halves if a smaller block is needed, and are recombined into larger blocks when they are freed.

clock tick the interval between updates of a hardware timer.

context switch a switch from the execution of one thread to another, where the context (state) of the old thread is saved and replaced by the saved context of the new one.

daemon a program which is usually started when the system first starts, runs invisibly and lies dormant waiting for some event to happen.

HAL (Hardware Abstraction Layer) in Windows, a layer of software between the kernel and the hardware which encapsulates the machine-dependent portions of the kernel code.

idle process a process (or thread) which is executed only when there are no other processes ready to run, which is used to ensure that there is always at least one process (or thread) that is ready to run.

interrupt dispatcher a mechanism which calls each interrupt handler associated with a particular interrupt in turn.

interrupt handler the part of a device driver which handles interrupts originated by a particular device.

kernel swap daemon on Linux systems, a daemon process which maintains a minimum number of free memory pages. Other systems have a corresponding process or thread.

lottery scheduling a scheduling mechanism involving issuing each process or thread with a set of 'lottery tickets', one of which is chosen at random to select the next process or thread to run.

microkernel a kernel which provides a minimal set of facilities, all other aspects of the operating system being provided by server processes with no special privileges.

page frame database in Windows, a mechanism for keeping track of the status of each physical page frame. Other systems have an equivalent facility.

process descriptor a data structure describing the state of a process, including the saved context, which can be held in any of several system queues depending on the process status.

protocol an agreed standard which allows one system to communicate meaningfully with another.

quantum the period of time that a thread will be allowed to run before a context switch will be forced.

registry in Windows, a central repository holding system configuration information.

round-robin scheduling a scheduling policy where each process in turn is allowed to run.

scheduler the part of the kernel which is responsible for choosing a new process to run and resuming it.

service the name used on Windows systems for a daemon process.

thread context the information needed to resume execution of a suspended thread, notably the contents of the processor registers.

thread descriptor a data structure describing the state of a thread, including the saved context, which can be held in any of several system queues depending on the thread status.

timer queue a queue of processes or threads which have asked to be suspended until a specified time.

virtual address descriptor a data structure describing a block of virtual memory allocated to a process.

7.13 ☐ REFERENCES

[1] Accetta, M., Baron, B., Golub, D., Rashid, R., Tevanian, A. and Young, M. Mach: a new kernel foundation for UNIX development. *Proc. Summer '86 USENIX Conference* (1986), pp. 93–112

[2] Aivazian, T. *Linux Kernel 2.4 Internals*. The Linux Documentation Project (Mar 1996). Available online at http://www.tldp.org/LDP/lki/

[3] Bovet, D. P. and Cesati, M. *Understanding the Linux Kernel*. O'Reilly & Associates (2002)

[4] Engler, D. R., Kasshoek, M. F. and O'Toole J. Exokernel: an operating system architecture for application-level resource management. *Proceedings of the 15th ACM Symposium on Operating Systems Principles* (Dec 95), pp. 251–266. Available online at `http://www.pdos.lcs.mit.edu/papers/exokernel-sosp95.ps`

[5] Knuth, D. E. *The Art of Computer Programming vol. 1: Fundamental Algorithms*. Addison-Wesley (1997)

[6] Love, R. *Linux Kernel Development*. Sams (2003)

[7] Rusling, D. A. *The Linux Kernel*. The Linux Documentation Project (Jan 1998). Available online at `http://www.tldp.org/LDP/tlk/`

[8] Solomon, D. A. and Russinovich, M. E. *Inside Microsoft Windows 2000*. Microsoft Press (2000)

8

DEVICE DRIVERS

Device drivers are the essential operating system modules that are responsible for managing particular hardware devices. They are therefore intimately linked with the hardware they are designed to control. New devices can be added to a computer system and existing devices can be removed, so it is necessary to be able to load and unload device drivers while the system is running. Device drivers normally execute in kernel mode, primarily for efficiency reasons, but are not really part of the kernel itself, although the drivers for some standard devices such as the keyboard and mouse might be built into the kernel rather than being loaded separately.

Device drivers are also responsible for managing logical resources such as the filesystem rather than managing actual hardware devices. In fact, any module can be loaded as a device driver as long as it supports the protocol that the operating system uses to communicate with a device driver. The device driver protocol defines a mechanism by which any software module can be hooked into the basic kernel.

Device drivers are often very dependent on the exact version of the operating system that they are written for. The Linux kernel underwent some major changes in this area in version 2.4, and the organisation of Windows device drivers has changed dramatically with each new version of Windows, although a standard (**WDM**, the Windows Driver Model) was established beginning with Windows 2000.

8.1 ❑ THE I/O SUBSYSTEM

From a user's point of view, input and output are done using a set of standard library functions. In languages like C++, there are many such functions. For example, to output a message which includes an integer value i in C++, you might write something like this:

```
cout << "The value of " << i << " squared is " << (i*i);
```

This uses various flavours of the output operator '<<' to format the output into a sequence of characters and it then sends the resulting sequence of characters to the standard output stream. In particular, the values of i and the expression i*i (typically 32-bit binary integers) get translated into the appropriate sequences of characters, so that if the value of i were 25, the message displayed by the command above would be:

```
The value of 25 squared is 625
```

On Unix systems, this string of characters is ultimately transmitted to the standard output stream using the write system call, which takes three parameters:

- A **file handle** which specifies the file or device that the character string is to be sent to. This is an integer which can be used to locate a corresponding file object which identifies the file itself, the device driver responsible for handling file operations, the current position in the file, and so on.
- A pointer to a **buffer** where the string has been constructed.
- The number of characters to be written (i.e. the length of the string).

Something very similar happens on a Windows system, with a few minor differences in detail.

Question 8.1   How is this done on the system that you are using?

The write system call puts the address of its parameter list in a processor register, puts a number meaning write in another register and then issues the 'system call' instruction (INT 2E for Windows on a Pentium processor, INT 80 for Linux on a Pentium processor). This instruction saves the return address on the stack together with the current value of the status register (the Pentium EFLAGS register or equivalent), and generates an exception which switches the processor to kernel mode and transfers to a specific address within the kernel address space.

The system call exception handler begins by using the function code for write (which was earlier put in a processor register) as an index into a table which gives the address of each system call routine. It then jumps to the routine in the kernel that actually implements the write operation. This checks that the parameters are valid; in this case, that the addresses whose range is specified by the buffer address and its length are all readable in user mode. It then uses the file handle to select a **file object** from a table of files which the process has opened. There is a separate table maintained for each process; on Unix systems it can typically hold 20 entries,

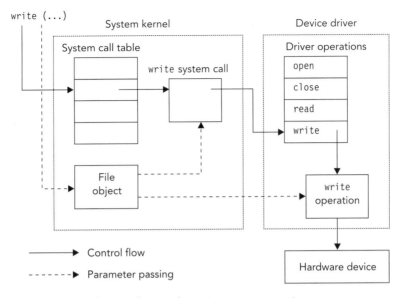

Figure 8.1 Calling a device driver's write operation.

allowing each process to open up to 20 files at any one time. The file object is initialised when a file is opened and contains information about the file's location and the current position in the file. It also identifies the **device driver** responsible for dealing with the data transfer.

Once the device driver has been identified, the next step is to look up the device driver's internal write operation from a table of operations supported by the device driver and then use the internal operation to output the string. The device driver's write operation uses information from the file object to identify the actual device to be used (since a device driver might be responsible for dealing with more than one device of a particular type) and interacts with the underlying hardware to carry out the necessary data transfer. If necessary, the thread which initiated all this will be suspended in a queue associated with the device driver while the hardware performs the operation and will only be woken up again when the hardware operation has been completed.

The steps involved are illustrated in Figure 8.1. This is a fairly elaborate sequence of events, but it shields the user-mode program from having to know anything about the hardware device that the standard output stream (cout in the example above) is actually connected to.

8.2 ❑ WHAT ARE DEVICE DRIVERS?

Due to the variety of different hardware that a computer system may use, it is impractical for an operating system to cater for every possible hardware device. It is usual for the operating system to support only those devices that are actually present in a particular system. The other problem is that the hardware configuration of a particular machine can change, with new devices being added and old ones removed from time to time. To accommodate this range of possibilities, each type of device has its own **device driver** which deals with the capabilities of that particular device type.

To allow the operating system to deal with a new type of hardware device, it must be possible to add an appropriate device driver (usually supplied by the hardware manufacturer) to an existing system. Device drivers are therefore not part of the operating system *per se*, but are essential if the operating system is to be able to cope with a variety of hardware configurations.

In the days before computers became just another piece of consumer electronics, computer systems were supplied together with an operating system tailored to the hardware configuration. Changes to the hardware configuration were relatively rare, and when it happened a new version of the operating system would need to be compiled with the correct device drivers for the new configuration. This would be impractical now; the idea of recompiling the operating system just so that you could plug in a digital camera would horrify most people. (It would also horrify companies like Microsoft, who would have to release their proprietary operating system's source code to allow it to be recompiled!) The only practical solution is to allow device drivers to be installed and uninstalled in the same way as any other piece of software.

Exercise 8.1   Most modern systems support 'plug and play', where new hardware, such as USB devices, is automatically identified when it is plugged in and new device drivers installed as needed. Find out how this is done.

Since it must be possible to add and remove device drivers from an existing system, the operating system needs a well-defined **protocol** which it can use to communicate with the device drivers that are present; **WDM** (the Windows Driver Model) is one such protocol. The operating system uses some sort of configuration file (for example, the Windows registry) to tell it which device driver modules need to be loaded into memory when the system starts up, and a standard way to ask device drivers to carry out particular operations. All device drivers need to support a standard protocol that allows any thread which can access the device driver to perform operations like reading and writing data.

Some drivers for essential devices like the keyboard, screen and disk are often built into the kernel code so that they are available from the moment the system starts up, but these are the exception to the rule. In general, device drivers are just shared modules, which are loaded into memory like any other shared library modules (Unix shared libraries or Windows DLLs). The main difference between device drivers and shared library modules is that they need to be accessible at all times, and this is normally done by loading them into the common kernel-mode address space, as shown in Figure 8.2. Because they are in the kernel-mode address

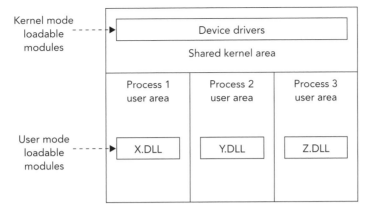

Figure 8.2 Kernel and user modules.

space they also need to execute in kernel mode. In fact, device drivers could be written to execute in user mode if the kernel provided a sufficient set of system calls to access I/O ports and so on, but they normally run in kernel mode for efficiency reasons, as this avoids the time-consuming requirement to continually switch back and forth between user mode and kernel mode inside the device driver, with all the accessibility checks that need to be performed each time that this happens. This is the case in both Windows and Linux.

Because device drivers run in kernel mode, there are some things you must be aware of when writing device drivers. Firstly, only kernel functions can be used; standard libraries intended for use in user mode must not be used, as the system calls they use can lead to deadlock if a critical section in the kernel has already been locked by the device driver or by the kernel code that invoked the device driver. Secondly, although interrupts can be disabled in kernel mode, they should only be disabled for short periods of time. And thirdly, device drivers need to be written so that they can be used on multiprocessor systems, This is not an issue for user processes, which each execute in a separate address space, but for code executing in the shared kernel-mode address space it is necessary to cater for the fact that other processors might be executing exactly the same piece of code and accessing exactly the same data. Finally, device drivers need to be bug-free, because any errors arising from bugs in a device driver executing in kernel mode can have consequences that might crash the entire system, and potentially corrupt entire filesystems and lose data.

Device drivers are generally the only way for user-supplied code to be executed in kernel mode. On Windows systems, they are sometimes used simply to gain access to internal kernel data structures. This can be done in conjunction with a normal user-mode program that calls operations such as read to ask the device driver to obtain information from the kernel, as illustrated in Figure 8.3. On Unix systems, the /proc filesystem is used in a similar way. Kernel modules can register themselves to appear as named files within the /proc filesystem, with I/O operations such as read and write. Although the 'files' in this directory can be accessed in the normal way, they are actually interfaces to kernel modules whose read and write

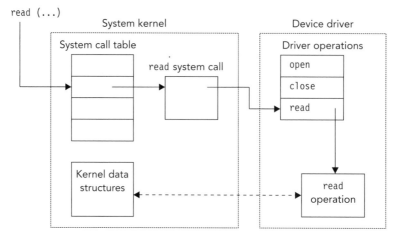

Figure 8.3 Using device drivers to access kernel data.

operations dynamically generate data to be read by the user, or process the data written by the user in some way. This mechanism makes it possible to write normal user-mode programs which can display system information such as the state of all the running processes, memory usage and so on, since all they have to do is read the information from the appropriate 'file' in the /proc filesystem.

8.3 ❑ TYPES OF DEVICE

Different hardware devices tend to work in completely different ways from each other. However, they can be divided into certain broad categories. Linux recognises three distinct categories of device: **character devices**, **block devices** and **network devices**. These are managed internally in quite different ways, but they all support a standard set of operations, including these:

- open: open the device for reading and/or writing
- close: close the device
- read: read a number of bytes from the device
- write: write a number of bytes to the device
- seek: shift to a different position in the stream of bytes handled by the device. This makes sense on disks and other direct-access devices, but for most other devices (e.g. a keyboard) the seek operation will just report an error.
- ioctl: perform some device-specific I/O control operation, such as setting the baud rate for a modem.
- mmap: map the device's stream of bytes into memory. Again, this works well with disks but not so well with keyboards.

As the list above implies, not all devices will support all operations. A printer does not support read or seek operations, nor does a CD-ROM support write operations. In these cases, the operations are still provided, but they just return an 'invalid operation' error code if they are called.

Although it may not explicitly be implemented as such, this can be thought of as defining a 'device' interface like the Java interface specification shown in Figure 8.4 whose protocol includes the operations above, and derived 'character device', 'block device' and 'network device' classes which implement the operations in different ways. All you have to know is that you are dealing with some kind of device and you then know that you can invoke operations like read or write. Each device driver will implement this interface and will thus be obliged to provide all the operations specified by the interface, but the implementations of these operations will be quite different for each type of device.

```
public interface Device {
    int open  (int mode);
    int close ();
    int read  (byte[] buffer, int length);
    int write (byte[] buffer, int length);
    int seek  (int position);
    int ioctl (int setting, int value);
    // ... and so on.
}
```

Figure 8.4 A Java device interface specification.

Character devices are devices like keyboards, printers and modems where the unit of data transfer is a single character at a time. These are the simplest type of device. Block devices are devices like disks where the basic unit of data transfer is a fixed-size block of data (typically 512 or 1024 bytes). Data is always read or written in multiples of this block size. Block device drivers have a queue of pending requests which they can process in any way they like; for example, a disk driver can rearrange the sequence of a set of pending transfer requests to minimise the delays involved in moving the disk heads across the disk surface. Network devices are devices which read and write packets of data, such as Ethernet controllers. These are similar in some ways to block devices, but they will be considered separately in Chapter 10.

When a device driver is loaded into memory, it must be initialised, and when it is about to be unloaded, it must be closed down. It must therefore include entry points that the operating system can call to perform these operations. On Linux systems, all kernel modules (including device drivers) must provide two operations called init_module and cleanup_module to start up and shut down the module. Initialisation in effect creates a 'device driver object' by passing a table containing the addresses of the functions that the device driver provides (the set of operations for the driver object) to the operating system. Cleaning up before the device driver is removed from memory will involve deregistering these functions (that is, destroying the device driver object).

It is in principle possible to transmit characters one at a time to many devices (for example, modems), but it would be incredibly inefficient in practice. To see why, just think what would happen if the interaction with the device driver as described at the beginning of this chapter had to be carried out for every individual character. The processor runs millions of times faster than most I/O devices, so it makes sense to give the device driver a group of characters in one go and let the device driver deal with them autonomously, sending them out as quickly as possible.

This involves the driver marshalling the characters to be written to a device into a storage area known as a **buffer** so that as many characters as possible can be dealt with at once. The buffer can be stored in the user-mode address space, but since the real work takes place in kernel mode it is usually better to use an intermediate buffer within the kernel-mode address space which can be accessed directly by the device driver. Since most I/O operations take a relatively long time to complete, the thread which initiates an I/O operation is normally suspended until the operation is complete, which means that a different thread (and possibly a different process) will be chosen for execution instead. As the transfer proceeds, the device driver may need to access the buffer. If a different process is executing when this happens, the user-mode address space of the original process may not be accessible; it might have been swapped out to disk, for example. Using a buffer in the shared kernel-mode address space ensures that the buffer will be accessible at all times, regardless of which process is executing when the device driver needs to access it.

Many systems use **double buffering**, where two kernel-mode buffers are used, as shown in Figure 8.5. When writing to a device, data can be transferred between the user-mode address space and one of the kernel-mode buffers while at the same time data is being transferred between the other kernel-mode buffer and the hardware device. This avoids conflicts in having the device driver and a system call both trying to access the same buffer. Conversely, when reading from a device, one buffer can be copied into the user-mode address space while the device driver is filling the other buffer. Either way, the idea is to avoid conflicts between the need to fill one buffer with the need to process the contents of the other. It is also possible to use double buffering on the user-mode side of the divide, so that the

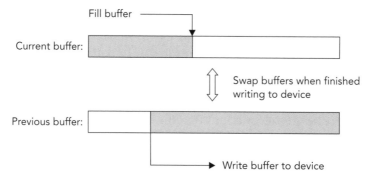

Figure 8.5 Double buffering.

user thread can fill a buffer and give it to the kernel to be dealt with while it carries on filling the other buffer.

8.5 ❑ DEVICE DRIVER STRUCTURE

Many devices are interrupt-driven, so device drivers must be able to respond to interrupts from their corresponding devices. An interrupt from a device will cause an **interrupt service routine** (ISR) to be executed to deal with it. For example, when a byte of data arrives from a modem attached to a serial port, an interrupt will be generated by the serial port hardware. The serial port device driver's ISR will need to read the incoming character into a buffer somewhere and tell the device to turn off ('dismiss') the interrupt signal it is generating.

One of the difficulties that must be considered is that when an interrupt occurs, the process that gets interrupted may not be the one that initiated the original I/O request. ISRs are executed by whatever process is active at the time. As mentioned earlier, actions like storing a character in a user-mode buffer are problematical because the buffer may be in a totally different address space from the one in which the ISR is being executed. This means that ISRs must be written in such a way that they do not depend on being executed within the context of a particular process. For example, a serial port ISR may use a buffer which is located in the common kernel-mode address space, so that it is guaranteed to be accessible at all times. However, at some point the data from this buffer will need to be transferred to a buffer in the user-mode address space of the process that requested it; this will only be possible when the process is actually executing so that its user-mode address space is accessible.

There are also timing constraints to be considered. While the ISR is executing, interrupts at the same or lower priority levels will be disabled. On return from the ISR, the original interrupt priority will be restored and any pending interrupts that were disabled while the ISR was executing will now be allowed to interrupt the processor. For example, a serial port may be delivering characters every few hundred microseconds, so any processing that takes longer than that amount of time runs the risk of missing the next interrupt and losing characters as a result. A timer interrupt might not only involve updating the operating system's time counter, but also rescheduling sleeping processes that need to be woken up and rearranging the system process queues. It is difficult, if not impossible, to put an upper bound on the time it might take to do this, as it depends on the number of processes in the various system queues. Where it *is* possible to derive an upper bound for the time it will take to service an interrupt, it is also necessary to take into account the possibility that execution of the ISR may be interrupted by a higher-priority interrupt.

For these reasons, interrupt service routines need to be kept short and sweet. The time-intensive and process-dependent parts of handling the interrupt need to be dealt with in some other way. In Linux systems, the part of a kernel module that deals with these aspects of interrupt processing are referred to as the **bottom half** of the module (the **top half** being that part of the module that is called directly by a user process to initiate an operation). In Windows, similar mechanisms called **deferred procedure calls** (DPCs) and **asynchronous procedure calls** (APCs) are used.

Exercise 8.2   List some of the operations that an interrupt handler might need to perform that are best suited to a separate 'bottom half' routine.

The idea is that the address of the bottom-half code is stored in an object which is added to a system queue, and a flag is set to indicate that some bottom-half processing is required. This is shown in Figure 8.6. When the scheduler is about to choose which process to execute next, any pending bottom-half routines are executed first. In the case where a bottom-half routine needs to execute in the context of a particular process (for example when the bottom-half routine needs to copy data to or from the user-mode address space), the object containing the address of the bottom half routine is added to a queue belonging to that specific process. When the scheduler chooses this process to resume execution, its context is restored in the normal way, but the pending bottom-half routines in its queue are executed before returning to the point in the process where normal execution should resume. In Windows, DPCs correspond to bottom-half routines and APCs correspond to bottom-half routines that need to be executed within the context of a specific process.

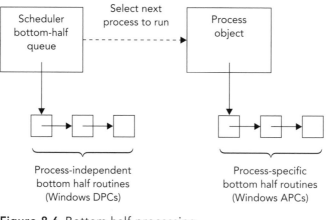

Figure 8.6 Bottom half processing.

Exercise 8.3   List some of the operations that an interrupt handler might need to perform that must be executed in the context of a particular process.

From the point of view of an interrupted process, bottom-half routines will be called at unpredictable points during process execution, just like interrupt service routines. Unlike interrupt service routines, they can if necessary run in the context of that particular process so that they can access the address space of the process. Any user-mode memory that they access (e.g. I/O buffers) will be subject to sudden volatile changes at unpredictable intervals.

8.6 ❑ LINUX DEVICE DRIVERS

As mentioned above, a device driver in Linux is a loadable module, and as such it must provide a function called `init_module` which will initialise the device driver. For character devices, this just involves calling a system function `module_register_chrdev` to register the device with the operating system, which returns a **major device number** used to identify the driver. Similarly, the module must provide a function called `cleanup_module` which should call `module_unregister_chrdev` to unregister the driver, as identified by its major device number.

Each registered driver is assigned a different major device number, and each individual device controlled by that driver is assigned a **minor device number**. For example, in the case of a serial port driver which controls a number of different serial ports, each serial port would have the same major device number which identifies the driver responsible for controlling it, but each would have a different minor device number. The `mknod` command can be used to create a device 'file' which can be used to refer to the device driver. For example, the following command creates a character device file called /dev/foo with a major device number of 15 and a minor device number of 1:

```
mknod /dev/foo c 15 1
```

Once this has been done, all operations on the 'file' /dev/foo will be routed to the character device driver which was assigned the major device number 15. For example, to read from this device, you would just use the `read` system call on the file /dev/foo. The code for the *open* system call in the Linux virtual filesystem will look up the directory entry for /dev/foo, which will identify it as referring to a character device. The major device number will be used to locate the correct character device driver, and the file descriptor created by `open` will be set up to refer to this. When you read from the 'file', the device driver's own `read` operation will be called to do the actual work. Each operation is passed a structure as one of its parameters which contains fields giving the major and minor device numbers for the device being accessed. This can be used to identify the particular device being accessed in drivers which control multiple devices.

The `module_register_chrdev` function requires a `file_operations` structure as one of its parameters, which consists of a table of pointers to functions (the 'methods' of the device driver, in object-oriented terms) which implement the functionality required for all character devices. Any operations which are not supported by the device can be specified as a null pointer, in which case an error code will be reported if the corresponding function is called. For example, when the read system call looks up the pointer to the read operation in the device driver, it will check if it is a null pointer and return an error code to the user if it is.

To prevent the device driver being removed from memory while it is in use, there is a **module usage counter** which will typically be incremented by the open operation and decremented by the close operation. Interrupt handlers used by the device driver can be installed using the request_irq function. This function specifies the interrupt number to be used, the address of a function to be called when an interrupt occurs, a value to be passed as a parameter to this function and flags which indicate whether the interrupt can be shared with another device driver.

When an interrupt occurs, the kernel's internal interrupt-handling code calls each of the registered interrupt handler functions in turn. There are some severe restrictions on what an interrupt handler can do, but it is up to the author of the interrupt handler to avoid doing anything unsafe. For example, it is unsafe to perform any blocking operation, since this would deadlock the system by preventing the interrupt handler from completing. It is also unsafe to access anything in the user-mode memory area, since the interrupt will be executed in the context of whichever process happens to be running at the time the interrupt occurs and so the contents of the user-mode address space cannot be relied on. Also, interrupt handlers must complete their processing as quickly as possible to allow other interrupts to be recognised.

Interrupt handlers can schedule work to be done later by adding the address of a bottom-half routine to a **task queue** using the queue_task_irq function. You can define your own task queues (in which case you are also responsible for processing any pending bottom-half routines at an appropriate time) or use one of a number of standard queues. One such queue is the **scheduler queue**, which is processed just before a new process is scheduled for execution. At this point it is safe to perform blocking operations (a blocking operation will just go back to the scheduler, which will start by processing any remaining bottom-half routines) and to undertake processing which is too lengthy to perform inside an interrupt handler. Another useful queue is the **timer queue** which is processed after every timer interrupt. Note that this is not the queue used to schedule work to be done at a particular time; it is instead a queue of bottom-half routines which all need to be executed at the next clock tick.

8.6.1 A BRIEF EXAMPLE

To illustrate more concretely how a device driver is constructed, the C++ code below gives the complete code for a driver to implement the Unix null device /dev/null, which ignores any data that you write to it and which always returns end-of-file when you read from it. This requires including a couple of header files provided with the kernel source code, as follows:

```
#include <linux/kernel.h>
#include <linux/module.h>
```

The first few functions implement the open, close, read and write operations. The open system call looks up the filename in the filesystem directory structure and creates a **file descriptor** which can be used to refer to the file. Because the file is a character device, it then calls the corresponding driver's open operation. All this operation needs to do is to increment the module usage count so that the module will not be removed from memory while it is in use.

```
int device_open (inode* i, file* f) {
  MOD_INC_USE_COUNT;
  return 0;
}
```

This function always returns a zero result (indicating success), and the open system call will then return a numerical **file handle** to the original caller which identifies the file descriptor that was allocated. This file handle can then be used in subsequent read, write and close system calls.

Closing the file just involves decrementing the module usage count; once this reaches zero it indicates that the module is not in use by anyone and can therefore be removed from memory.

```
int device_close (inode* i, file* f) {
  MOD_DEC_USE_COUNT;
  return 0;
}
```

The read operation is given a pointer to a buffer, the length of the buffer and an offset into the 'file'. It returns the number of bytes that were stored in the buffer. A result of zero indicates the end of the file has been reached, which is all that needs to be done in this case:

```
ssize_t device_read(file* f, char* buffer,
                size_t length, loff_t* offset) {
  return 0;         // number of bytes read = 0 (i.e. end of file)
}
```

Similarly, the write operation returns the number of bytes that were successfully written from the buffer. In this case, the buffer contents are ignored but the buffer length is returned to indicate that all bytes in the buffer have been dealt with.

```
ssize_t device_write(file* f, const char* buffer,
                size_t length, loff_t* offset) {
  return length;    // number of bytes written = length
}
```

The next step is to declare the file operations table, with null entries for all but the four operations above:

```
file_operations fops = {
  NULL,                // seek (not implemented)
  device_read,
  device_write,
  NULL,                // readdir (not implemented)
  NULL,                // select (not implemented)
  NULL,                // ioctl (not implemented)
  NULL,                // mmap (not implemented)
  device_open,
  NULL,                // flush (not implemented)
  device_close
};
```

The initialisation routine uses this table to register the device. A global variable is used to store the major device number, as this will be needed to unregister the device before the module is unloaded from memory. The registration function is given the desired major device number (zero in this case, meaning 'please allocate a new major device number'), a name which will appear in the list of devices (which can be accessed by reading the file /proc/devices), and the address of the table of file operations, and it returns the major device number or a negative error code.

```
int major;           // used to remember the major device number
int init_module() {
  major = module_register_chrdev (0, "null device", &fops);
  if (major < 0) {
    printk ("Init_module failed (%d)\n", major);
    return major;
  }
  return 0;
}
```

If registration is successful, this function returns a result of zero, indicating success. If not, an error message is printed using the special kernel-mode printing function printk. Unregistering the module is similar, using the major device number and the device name to identify the device. Again, a negative result indicates an error of some kind.

```
void cleanup_module() {
  int n = module_unregister_chrdev (major, "null device");
  if (n < 0) {
    printk ("Cleanup_module failed (%d)\n", n);
  }
}
```

And that's all there is to it!

Project 8.1   Write a Linux character device driver which stores the character most recently written to it and returns a series of copies of this character when you read from it. Return a null character if a read is performed before any writes have been performed.

8.6.2   THE /PROC FILESYSTEM

As mentioned earlier, Linux uses a pseudo-filesystem which is 'mounted' on the directory /proc to provide universal access to kernel data structures. In fact, /proc exists only in memory, and is really a collection of modules which provide read and write operations, just like character device drivers. When you read from a file in /proc (e.g. /proc/meminfo, which provides memory usage information, or /proc/devices which was mentioned earlier), the read operation in the corresponding module is called to fill the buffer you have provided.

Entries in the /proc directory are created using the proc_register_dynamic function, which takes a proc_dir_entry structure as a parameter. This contains things like the filename, access permissions, ownership details, and a pointer to an inode_operations structure, which includes a pointer to a file_operations table like the ones used by character device drivers.

The /proc filesystem contains some system wide information. For example:

- /proc/cpuinfo: information about the CPU, including the model name, speed, cache size and features supported.
- /proc/devices: information about device numbers for character and block devices.
- /proc/interrupts: information about each interrupt source, including the device name and the number of interrupts processed from each source.
- /proc/ksyms: the kernel symbol table, giving the address of each kernel routine.
- /proc/meminfo: information about memory, including the model name, speed, cache size and features supported.
- /proc/rtc: information from the real-time clock device.

There is also a directory for each process, where the process number is used as the directory name. The entries in each directory include:

- cmdline: the complete command line used to start the process.
- cwd: a symbolic link to the current working directory for the process.
- environ: a list of all the environment variables for the process.
- exe: a symbolic link to the executable file being executed by the process.
- fd: a directory containing symbolic links to the files to which the I/O streams opened by the process are connected, where the names of the links are the corresponding stream numbers.

- status: information about the status of the current process, including the current state (running, sleeping and so on), user and group ownership, and virtual memory usage.

Project 8.2   Write a module which provides the current date and time when it is read and install it as /proc/time. You will need to capture the current date and time as a string when the 'file' is opened and deliver it as a string followed by end-of-file as the 'file' is read. Write a program to test that it works.

8.6.3   BLOCK DEVICES

Block device drivers differ from character device drivers in that they can only transfer data to the corresponding device in multiples of the device's block size. This is for use with devices like disks and CD-ROMs. Also, only block devices can be mounted as filesystems. Read and write operations are implemented differently on block devices and character devices; for character device drivers the read and write system calls normally call the driver's internal read and write operations directly, whereas for block devices they do not. A read or write system call directed at a block device will instead be dealt with by adding an object describing the I/O request to a **request queue** associated with the device driver. This is illustrated in Figure 8.7. The I/O request object basically encapsulates the parameters that would have been passed to the read operation of a character device, and also includes a queue which the requesting thread can wait on until the operation is complete.

The request operation is the central operation provided by a block device driver. When a request is added to a driver's request queue by the read or write system calls, the driver's request operation is called to start processing the request queue if the queue was empty. If the queue already had one or more requests in it, the request operation will already have been called and will not need to be called again. Because requests can be added to the queue much more quickly than they

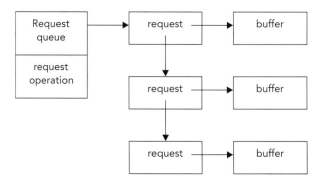

Figure 8.7 A Linux block device driver request queue.

can be dealt with, there will often be several pending requests in the queue. The request operation repeatedly processes requests until they have all been dealt with, using the driver's internal read or write operations to perform the I/O operation specified by each request block. The device driver can process the pending requests in its request queue in any order; for example, a disk driver may search the request list for the request whose disk address is nearest to the current disk head position, to minimise head movement.

After a request has been processed, the request object will be removed from the queue and the thread that made the request will be notified. The thread might have chosen to suspend itself while the request was being processed (a **synchronous** operation) in which case it needs to be woken up, or it might have carried on (an **asynchronous** operation), in which case a bottom-half routine will be needed to notify it when the transfer is complete. This could be done by setting a flag specified by the thread or by generating an exception.

Exercise 8.4   Find out how you can request an asynchronous file transfer in the operating system you are using, and how the device driver can notify you when the operation is complete.

To speed things up, it is normal practice to cache copies of recently accessed blocks in memory. Linux refers to this as the **buffer cache**. Bear in mind that memory is about a million times faster than a disk, so caching disk blocks is going to give you a performance boost even if you only rarely access the same block twice. Read operations for blocks that are already in the cache can be dealt with by returning a copy of the block from the cache rather than by accessing the device itself.

Caching also makes **lazy writing** a natural approach to take when writing to the disk. With lazy writing, a write operation just needs to update the cache (marking the cache block as 'dirty') and put a request in the request queue to write the cached block. When the data has been written to the device from the cache, the cached block can be marked as 'clean'. Requests to write a clean block will not require any device activity, although the thread that made the request will still need to be notified that the request has been dealt with. If several write operations are carried out on the same block, they will each update the cached copy of the block and add a request to the request queue. The first such request that gets dealt with will write the block to the device from the cache and mark it as clean, and each of the other requests will not do anything except notify the thread that made the request.

Question 8.2   If two separate threads perform synchronous write operations to the same disk block, does it matter in what order the disk driver carries out the operations? Explain your answer. Does the same argument apply if the write operations are asynchronous?

8.7 ❑ WINDOWS DEVICE DRIVERS

Windows device drivers are similar in concept to Linux device drivers, but there are many differences in the details. I/O operations in Windows are controlled by an **I/O manager**, which is responsible for packaging an I/O request into an object known as an **I/O request packet** (IRP) and passing it to the appropriate driver.

Information about the driver is encapsulated in a **driver object** which contains pointers to the various functions that the driver provides, in a similar way that a Linux major device number is used to access a table of operations. The driver object also has a list of **device objects** for the devices that it manages, which fulfil a similar role to Linux minor device numbers. The device objects all contain a pointer to the driver object that is responsible for dealing with them. This is illustrated in Figure 8.8. When a file is opened, a **file object** is created which contains a pointer to the corresponding device object. When reading from a file, the file object is used to locate the device object, which is then used to identify the device driver and invoke the desired operation. A reference to the device object is passed to the device driver so that the driver knows which device to deal with.

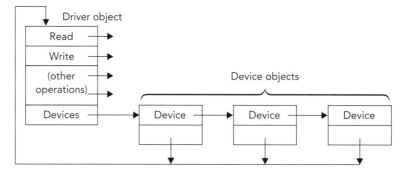

Figure 8.8 A Windows device driver.

As with Linux, a Windows device driver has an initialisation routine which is executed when the driver is first loaded, an unload routine which is executed if the driver is unloaded from memory, and a table of **dispatch routines** (open, close, read, write and so on). For many devices there will also be an interrupt service routine. When there is an interrupt service routine, there is usually also a **DPC routine** which corresponds to a Linux bottom-half routine. The interrupt service routine can add a **DPC request** object to the system DPC queue to complete the interrupt processing at a later time. Adding a DPC request to the DPC queue also generates a low-priority interrupt which will be recognised when any pending interrupts have been dealt with and the current interrupt priority drops to the level at which the DPC interrupt will be recognised. The DPC request identifies the DPC routine to be executed and any parameters it requires. Subsequent I/O requests to the device driver will be queued by the I/O manager until any DPCs queued by the driver have been processed.

There are also several other entry points that a Windows device driver can provide:

- A start routine which starts a data transfer to or from a device, in a similar way to a Linux block device driver's request operation.
- One or more completion routines which can be called by the I/O manager on completion of a lower-level request.
- A cancel routine which allows uncompleted I/O requests to be cancelled.
- A shutdown routine which will be called when the system is about to shut down, allowing the driver to do any last-minute cleanup.

Completion routines are normally used when one driver uses the facilities of another. As an example, consider a filesystem driver which issues its own I/O requests to a disk driver. A request to read the next few bytes of a file is sent to the filesystem driver, which determines the address of the corresponding disk block, issues an I/O request to the disk driver via the I/O manager and then suspends the calling thread. When the disk transfer is complete, the I/O manager calls the filesystem driver's completion routine which then transfers the requested data into the buffer provided by the suspended thread and wakes it up. Alternatively, rather than suspending the thread until the transfer is complete, the thread can be allowed to continue and the completion routine can send the thread a message (using the normal Windows message passing mechanism) to notify the thread that the operation has been completed.

Question 8.3   What are the similarities and differences between the Linux and Windows approach to requesting services from device drivers?

8.8 ❑ SOME SPECIFIC EXAMPLES

To provide some more concrete examples of how device drivers work, this section looks at some common devices and the way that the device drivers deal with them. I'll begin by looking at the keyboard, mouse and clock devices, and then move on to look at block devices such as disks.

8.8.1 KEYBOARD DRIVERS

The basic requirement of a keyboard driver is to collect characters typed at the keyboard and deliver them to any process that is interested in them. There is a bit more to this than meets the eye, because there is a certain amount of translation involved. A French keyboard is laid out differently from an English keyboard (AZERTY instead of QWERTY), so keys in the same position generate different characters. It would be possible to build completely different keyboards for different national markets, but it is easier to use standard keyboard hardware with differently labelled keys and let the operating system work out which character corresponds to which key. Because of this, keyboards just generate **keycodes** based on the position of the key that was pressed, and these are then translated into the appropriate characters under software control.

Also, it is often useful to be able to detect when a key is released as well as when it is pressed. One example of this is the 'auto-repeat' function that keyboards normally provide. When a key is held down, it generates a sequence of characters, so that pressing 'A' and holding the key down will generate a repeating sequence of As: 'AAAAA...'. This could be done entirely in hardware (and indeed it used to be done like this on older systems) but doing it in software is more flexible; for instance, you can use software to adjust the repeat rate to suit your own typing habits. If the keyboard generates interrupts when a key is released as well as when it is pressed, you can time the interval after a key has been pressed to see whether it is released within a certain time. If the auto-repeat time expires while the key is still held down, another copy of the character can be generated and the timer can be restarted. In fact, the 'A' key will be translated into either 'a' or 'A' depending on whether one of the shift keys has been pressed; the keyboard driver switches to upper case when a shift key is pressed and back to lower case when it is released.

Finally, some internal translation is normally done in text-oriented systems. For example, the 'backspace' key is used to 'rub out' the preceding character. Also, Unix systems expect the 'enter' key to generate a 'line feed' character, while other systems expect a 'carriage return' character. Unix systems allow a keyboard to be set into 'raw' mode where this translation is not done, or 'cooked' mode (the default mode) where the translation is done. This is done using an ioctl system call to the device driver. In 'cooked' mode, the keyboard driver buffers a complete line at a time, carrying out any necessary internal editing as it does so, and only starts delivering characters when a complete line terminated by the 'enter' key has been assembled. This is illustrated in Figure 8.9. In 'raw' mode the characters are delivered directly to the user's program, and no line editing or other processing is carried out.

The core of a keyboard device driver is the interrupt service routine. When a keyboard interrupt occurs, the keyboard ISR puts a keycode (a value identifying the key and an indication of whether it was being pressed or released) into an internal keyboard buffer. The keyboard buffer is usually a fairly small fixed size (32 characters or so), on the assumption that anyone interested in the keyboard will process it before this many keys have been pressed. Bear in mind that a fast typist going flat out will only press and release about 10 keys a second, so 32 key events will take at least about 1.5 seconds, which is fairly close to eternity at the speed at which a modern processor operates. If you take so long to process these key events that the buffer fills up, any subsequent key events will simply be discarded, although in practice it is quite difficult to make this happen.

When a request is made to read a character from the keyboard, the next key event in the keyboard buffer will be delivered. If the buffer is empty, the caller will be suspended until a keyboard interrupt puts something in the buffer. In the case of

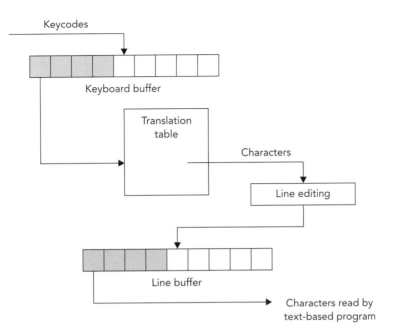

Figure 8.9 Keyboard handling in text-based systems.

Windows, keyboard events are delivered as messages which you can obtain by calling GetMessage. The system keeps track of which window (and hence which thread) has the keyboard focus, and any buffered key events are translated into messages and added to the appropriate thread's message queue.

From the point of view of a Windows application, key events are reported as messages of type WM_KEYDOWN (a key has been pressed) or WM_KEYUP (a key has been released). Normally the user's program will also translate WM_KEYDOWN messages into WM_CHAR messages by calling TranslateMessage before the WM_KEYDOWN message is processed, as illustrated in Figure 8.10. This translation is done using the currently selected keyboard layout. You can process or ignore any or all of these messages; the default action if you don't do anything with them yourself is to ignore them.

8.8.2 MOUSE DRIVERS

A mouse is a serial device that transmits a three-byte code whenever anything interesting happens; that is, the mouse is moved more than a certain minimum distance, or a mouse button is pressed or released. The three-byte value gives the distance moved horizontally, the distance moved vertically and the state of the buttons.

The mouse generates interrupts as these three-byte codes are generated. The mouse driver's interrupt service routine needs to calculate the new mouse position from the previous mouse position and the distance moved horizontally and verti- cally measured in units called **mickeys**. A mickey is approximately 0.1 mm of

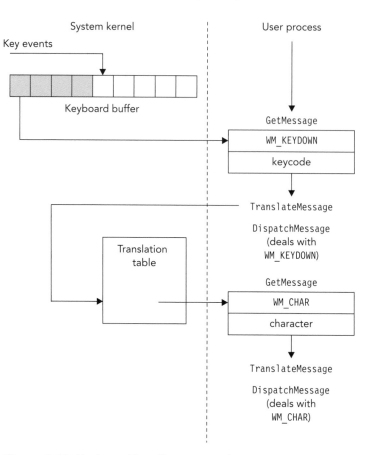

Figure 8.10 Keyboard handling in Windows.

mouse travel, but how this translates into the distance the mouse pointer moves on the screen is determined by an adjustable software setting (the **mickey-to-pixel ratio**). On a Windows system, the window corresponding to the current mouse position is identified and an appropriate message is added to the message queue for the thread that created the window. The mouse message (identified on Windows by names like WM_MOUSEMOVE, WM_LBUTTONDOWN, WM_LBUTTONUP and so on) contains the updated mouse position and button states.

The interrupt service routine's response to the mouse interrupt also needs to update the mouse pointer on the display, which is something that can be dealt with by sending a message to the display driver. The current shape of the mouse cursor also needs to be changed to the appropriate shape for the window; an arrow, an I-beam, a crosshair, a resize arrow or whatever. This is illustrated in Figure 8.11.

The thread which receives a mouse message can process it in some application-specific way, or it can pass it for the default handling to take place. The default handling for a mouse event checks for mouse clicks outside the current window and generates WM_ACTIVATE and WM_DEACTIVATE messages directed at particular windows to change the currently active window, and also translates multiple clicks

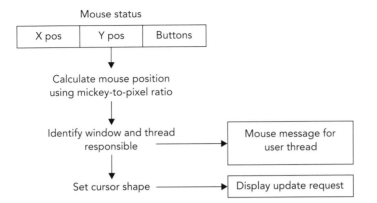

Figure 8.11 Mouse interrupt processing.

within a small area and a specified time period into double-click messages. The device driver itself is responsible for very little of this; the mouse driver itself is basically only responsible for keeping track of the mouse position and button state.

If the system becomes seriously busy, the display driver may not have time to deal with every mouse pointer update as it occurs. The result of this will be that the mouse pointer appears to move jerkily around the screen. If this happens, it indicates that the mouse position is still being tracked by the mouse driver, but the mouse position is not being updated often enough on the display to give the appearance of smooth movement. In really bad situations where the system stops reacting to position updates from the mouse driver (as the result of a system deadlock, perhaps) the mouse pointer can stop moving altogether. If this happens it is generally a sign that the system has crashed completely.

8.8.3 CLOCK DRIVERS

Timers (or 'clocks') are important because they allow time intervals to be measured and also allow work to be scheduled to be done at a later time. In a simple case, they can be used to delay a thread by suspending it for a specified period of time after which it will be resumed automatically.

The timer is a device that generates interrupts at regular intervals (the 'clock tick' period). Timer interrupts are responsible for a number of fundamental system activities, including these:

- Updating the current time of day (although keeping track of the date and time is usually handled by a separate real-time clock device).

- Expiring the time slice of the active thread and invoking the scheduler when necessary.

- Updating system usage statistics such as per-thread execution time.

- Running jobs that have been queued to be performed at a certain time.

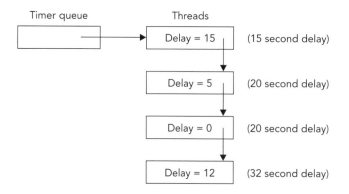

Figure 8.12 The timer queue.

Some of this can be done directly by the timer driver's interrupt service routine. For instance, updating the current time of day is normally just a matter of incrementing a counter. However, some timer-related processing involves more work than can be done within the interrupt handler itself, so it is mostly delegated to a bottom-half routine which will be executed after the primary interrupt processing has been dealt with.

Running scheduled jobs can be dealt with by maintaining a list of scheduling requests in a queue associated with the timer. Each request specifies the time interval that should elapse after the previous request has been dealt with and a reference to the thread which should be notified, as shown in Figure 8.12. There are several different possible ways to notify a thread, including generating an exception within the thread, waking the thread up if it has been suspended, or (in the case of Windows) sending the thread a WM_TIMER message which will also wake the thread up if it was suspended waiting for a message to arrive inside a call to GetMessage.

8.8.4 DISKS

As described in Chapter 3, disks are organised as a set of **cylinders**, each of which is composed of corresponding **tracks** on several platters. Each platter has its own **head** which is used to read and write data, and each track is divided into a number of **sectors** arranged around the track like slices of a pie.

Accessing a disk involves moving the heads to the appropriate cylinder, and the time it takes to do this is known as the **seek time**. There is then the time it takes for the disk to revolve so that the required sector is under the head (the **latency**) followed by the time it actually takes to transfer data to or from that sector. Seek time is the largest component in all this, so one of the goals of a disk driver is to minimise head movement.

Disks are block devices, so in both Unix and Windows the device driver maintains a queue of outstanding requests. These are likely to come from multiple sources; not just user processes trying to read and write files, but also the memory management system trying to swap pages in and out of memory. When a request is added to the queue, a flag associated with the driver is examined to see if the driver is already busy servicing a request. If the driver is idle, its request operation is called to start processing the request queue.

The request operation removes request objects from the driver's request queue one by one and processes them until the queue is empty. In the case of a disk, the time spent waiting for an access to signal that it is complete is enough time to do about a million memory accesses. While each individual request is being dealt with there is plenty of opportunity for other threads to run and to add more disk requests to the queue. As a result, the request operation will often have several requests to choose from. It can therefore search the queue for the most advantageous operation to perform out of those available (in particular, it can choose to deal with requests that can be satisfied from the buffer cache first).

The simplest approach is to process requests in a **first come, first served** (FCFS) order, but this approach will produce very sub-optimal behaviour for a device like a disk where the seek time dominates the time it takes to service a request. If disk requests are for sectors which are scattered all over the disk surface, the disk heads will have to be moved back and forth all the time. This will slow things down quite substantially if the system is heavily loaded and is performing a lot of disk accesses.

A better approach on a heavily loaded system is to search the queue for requests which are for addresses close to the current head position, and deal with the one which is closest to the current position first. The problem with this **closest block first** approach is that if requests are for disk addresses spread evenly across the disk, the average head position will be somewhere near the middle of the disk. It will therefore deal with accesses near the middle of the disk on either side of the current position in preference to accesses to the beginning or the end of the disk. The result is that requests for disk blocks near the beginning or the end of the disk will tend to be serviced less quickly than requests near the middle of the disk.

A simple modification can solve this problem. This modified approach is known as the **elevator algorithm**, as it is based on the way that elevators in tall buildings service requests. All that is needed is to record the current direction of head travel (in or out, rather than up and down as for an elevator), and service the nearest request in that direction. Once all the requests in a particular direction have been dealt with, the direction of travel is reversed and the nearest request in the new direction is chosen. The result is that the heads will tend to move inwards towards the centre of the disk, then outwards again.

To see how this works, consider a sequence of requests to cylinders 5, 23, 16, 27, 63 and 28 respectively. If the head is initially poised over cylinder 20, the head will have to move 15 cylinders to satisfy the first request, then 18 more for the next, then back another 7, then forward 11, then forward 36, then back 35. This gives a grand total of 122 cylinders that the head has to traverse.

If the algorithm chooses the closest block first, they will be serviced in the order 23, 27, 28, 16, 5, 63. The head moves three cylinders for the first request, then 4, 1, 12, 11 and 58 cylinders for each of the remaining requests, giving a grand total of 89 cylinders traversed by the head. This is much better than the first come, first served approach. The elevator algorithm will satisfy requests in the order 23, 27,

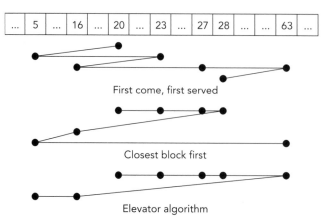

Figure 8.13 Behaviour of different disk block scheduling algorithms.

28, 63, 16, 5, for a grand total of 101 cylinders traversed. It therefore has a slightly worst performance than the closest block first approach, but is still considerably better than the first come, first served approach. The drop in performance is a trade-off in favour of fairness. Figure 8.13 illustrates the difference between these approaches.

Project 8.3   Write a program to implement the elevator algorithm, the first come, first served approach and the closest block first approach. Try them out with the same set of randomly generated requests. How does the total amount of head movement compare in each case? Are requests serviced fairly in terms of the average distance that the head must travel before a request is carried out?

8.8.5   FILESYSTEMS

Filesystems are naturally implemented as device drivers which provide the usual operations like open, close, read and write. These operations are implemented using the services of the appropriate driver for the physical device that the files are stored on. A call to open a file on a disk will generate a flurry of requests to the disk driver as directories are searched to locate the file's address on the disk (unless of course the directories are in the buffer cache). In the case of Unix filesystems, several different filesystem types can be built into a single hierarchical tree of names. Crossing a **mount point** (a directory where a separate volume has been mounted) will involve changing which underlying driver will be used in future requests. At the end of all this, a file descriptor will have been built which contains all the essential information needed to access the file in future. This will include a reference to the correct underlying driver to use and the current position within the file, which will initially be at the beginning of the first block.

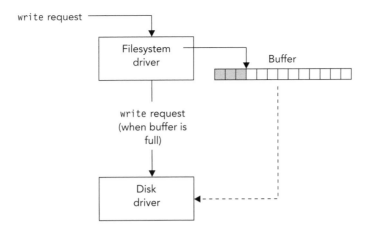

Figure 8.14 File system and disk driver interaction.

Operations like read and write just involve passing on the request to the underlying driver as illustrated in Figure 8.14, using the current position from the file descriptor to translate this into one or more requests for particular disk blocks. These requests can be issued asynchronously if they don't interfere with each other; for example, issuing requests to read several different disk blocks and then waiting until all of the requests have completed. The filesystem can make use of this by requesting the next few disk blocks in a file ahead of time and only waiting for the transfer to complete when or if the data is required. This lets the disk driver choose the most efficient way to service the requests.

One problem with disk drivers that do lazy writing is that the disk is always slightly out of date with respect to the cached copy, so the essential thing is to ensure that the filesystem's data structures on the disk are always left in a consistent state after every write operation, just in case the system crashes at that point. This means performing write operations to different parts of the filesystem's data structures in a particular order, waiting for each request to complete before issuing the next one in the sequence. This idea is taken further in the NTFS failure recovery scheme described in Chapter 3, which allows sequences of disk operations to be treated as atomic transactions where either all or none of the operations in the transaction will take place.

8.9 ❑ SUMMARY

Device drivers run in kernel mode, but they are not part of the kernel as such. Instead, they are loadable modules that can be loaded and unloaded while the system is running. Because they run in kernel mode they have the power to do almost anything, so correctness is essential; a buggy device driver can crash an entire system. Device drivers are also sometimes used as a 'back door' to allow user-supplied code to access kernel data structures.

Device drivers need to conform to a standard protocol; that is, they must be objects which provide a standard set of operations such as open, close, read and write. These operations are registered when the device driver is first loaded. This gives the rest of the system a standard way to ask any device driver to perform one of these operations.

Device drivers usually need to be able to respond to interrupts, so part of a device driver's initialisation involves registering an interrupt handler with the interrupt dispatching system. Interrupt service routines are executed when an interrupt occurs. Since interrupts can happen at any time, you cannot assume that the process that originally called the device driver will be the current process when the interrupt occurs, so interrupt service routines must not attempt to access the user-mode portion of the address space.

Interrupt service routines must be kept short and simple, since interrupts at the same or lower priorities will be disabled while the interrupt service routine is executing, so they are normally implemented as a **top-half** routine that performs the actual interrupt servicing and a **bottom-half** routine (known as an APC or DPC in Windows) that is executed at some later time when it is convenient to do so and which can perform any lengthier processing that is needed as part of the response to the interrupt. These can be scheduled for execution at points such as when a new thread is being scheduled or after the next clock tick. Where the bottom-half routine needs to execute in the context of a particular process, it can be scheduled to be executed when a thread from the required process is about to be resumed.

8.10 ❑ ADDITIONAL RESOURCES

Solomon and Russinovich [9] give a good explanation of how device drivers in Windows are organised. Mark Russinovich also maintains an excellent website (http://www.sysinternals.com/) with lots of information and tools, including source code. A brief article by Asche [1] describes how the organisation of device drivers has evolved in various different versions of Windows, and there are several books which deal with writing Windows device drivers in some detail, including Baker and Lozano [2] and Oney [5]. Additional books by Nebbett [4] and Schreiber [8] cover the largely undocumented native Windows API which provides essential facilities for writing device drivers.

A book by Rubini and Corbet [6] describes how to write Linux device drivers, and Salzman and Pomerantz [7] provides a brief guide to the same topics. Love [3] also describes how device drivers interact with the rest of the kernel. The Linux kernel source code is also worth exploring, since there are several simple device drivers (/dev/null and /dev/zero, for example) which are easy to understand and act as a template for building more complex drivers.

8.11 ❑ GLOSSARY

APC (Asynchronous Procedure Call) in Windows, a procedure that must be executed in the context of a particular process in order to complete servicing an interrupt.

asynchronous operation an operation which, once started, proceeds independently of its initiator.

block device an I/O device such as a disk which transfers data a block at a time.

bottom half in Linux, a routine which is queued for later execution in order to complete the servicing of an interrupt.

buffer a storage area used to marshal blocks of data being read or written to an I/O device.

buffer cache in Linux, a cache of recently accessed disk blocks. Other systems provide an equivalent facility.

character device an I/O device such as a modem which transfers data a single character at a time.

closest block first a disk scheduling algorithm which services the request closest to the current head position.

device driver a module (executed in kernel mode on both Linux and Windows) which controls a specific type of hardware device.

device object in Windows, a data structure representing a particular type of device.

dispatch routine an I/O function such as read or write in the device driver associated with the device being accessed, which is called via a table of pointers held by the driver object associated with the driver.

double buffering the use of two buffers to allow one buffer to be filled while the other is being emptied.

DPC (Deferred Procedure Call) in Windows, a routine which is queued for later execution in order to complete the servicing of an interrupt.

driver object in Windows, a data structure describing a device driver which contains pointers to the functions provided by the driver and a list of the individual devices managed by the driver.

elevator algorithm a disk scheduling algorithm which services the request closest to the current head position in the current direction of head travel. The direction of head travel is reversed when there are no more requests for blocks in the current direction.

FCFS (first come, first served) a disk scheduling algorithm which services requests in order of their arrival.

file handle a value used to identify a file which has been opened.

file object a data structure representing the state (current position etc.) of an open file, referenced via a file handle.

I/O manager   in Windows, the part of the kernel that routes I/O requests to the appropriate device driver.

IRP (I/O request packet)   in Windows, a data structure describing an I/O operation which is passed by the I/O manager to the appropriate device driver.

ISR (interrupt service routine)   a routine which is responsible for dealing with interrupts generated by a particular type of device.

kernel modules   software modules (such as device drivers) which are loaded by the kernel and which execute in kernel mode.

lazy writing   performing write operations by writing to a buffer which is only written to the device when it is convenient to do so.

major device number   in Unix, a number identifying a particular type of device (and hence a particular device driver).

mickey   the unit in which mouse movement is measured.

mickey-to-pixel ratio   the ration defining the relationship between the distance a mouse moves and the distance the mouse cursor moves on the screen.

minor device number   in Unix systems, a number identifying a single device out of a group of devices of this type, used by the device driver to identify the particular device being used.

mount point   in Unix, a directory which is overlaid with the root directory of another filesystem which is being mounted.

network device   an I/O device which is accessed via a network connection.

/proc filesystem   in Unix, a directory of pseudo-files associated with kernel modules which dynamically generate the data being read or consume the data being written. This is used to provide a simple mechanism for user processes to communicate with kernel modules.

protocol   a formal set of rules describing the format of data being transferred between software modules.

request queue   a queue of data structures describing pending disk transfers.

scheduler queue   in Linux, a queue of calls to bottom-half routines which should be executed before a new process is resumed.

synchronous operation   an operation which must complete before the caller can continue executing.

task queue   in Linux, a queue of calls to bottom-half routines.

timer queue   in Linux, a queue of bottom-half routines to be executed after the next timer interrupt (and also, confusingly, the name of a queue of processes which have suspended themselves until a particular time).

top half   in Linux, the part of an interrupt service routine which is executed immediately to service the interrupt.

WDM (Windows Driver Model)   in Windows, a standard for the way that device drivers are organised.

8.12 ❑ REFERENCES

[1] Asche, R. R. *The Little Device Driver Writer* (1994). Available online at
     `http://msdn.microsoft.com/developer/`

[2] Baker, A. and Lozano, J. *The Windows 2000 Device Driver Book: A Guide for Program-
     mers*. Prentice Hall (2000)

[3] Love, R. *Linux Kernel Development*. Sams (2003)

[4] Nebbett, G. *Windows NT/2000 Native API Reference*. Que (2000)

[5] Oney, W. *Programming the Microsoft Windows Driver Model*. Microsoft Press (2002)

[6] Rubini, A. and Corbet, J. *Linux Device Drivers*. O'Reilly & Associates (2001)

[7] Salzman, P. J. and Pomerantz, O. *The Linux Kernel Module Programming Guide*. Linux
     Documentation Project (Apr 2003). Available online at `http://www.tldp.org/LDP/lkmpg/`

[8] Schreiber, S. B. *Undocumented Windows 2000 Secrets: A Programmer's Cookbook*.
     Addison-Wesley (2001)

[9] Solomon, D. A. and Russinovich M. E. *Inside Microsoft Windows 2000*. Microsoft Press
     (2000)

PART **3**

BEYOND THE
DESKTOP

OVERVIEW: BEYOND THE DESKTOP

Until fairly recently, computers tended to be standalone systems with a single processor. Since processors are now so cheap, multiprocessor systems are becoming increasingly common. More importantly, the growth of the Internet and its associated networking technologies has meant that isolated computers are now extremely rare. The chapters in this section stop looking at computers as isolated single-processor systems and look at systems involving multiple processors instead.

Multiprocessor systems can be designed in a number of different ways. At one extreme there are tightly coupled systems with multiple processors sharing a common memory and common I/O devices. At the other extreme are loosely coupled systems built from networks of machines which each have their own separate memory and I/O devices. Chapter 9 looks at the design of such systems and the issues that arise when coordinating the parallel activities of multiple processors to perform coordinated computations.

The growth of the Internet means that most computers make use of network services provided by remote machines. Chapter 10 reviews networking technologies and common protocols used on the Internet, while Chapter 11 examines software technologies for dealing with distributed filesystems, distributed objects and distributed operating systems. Networked systems also raise a number of security issues, so Chapter 12 is concerned with safety and security.

CHAPTER 9

MULTIPROCESSOR SYSTEMS

Up until now, I have assumed an operating system which operates on a single machine with a single processor. Many operating systems still run on machines like this, but it is becoming increasingly common for machines to have multiple processors or to have network connections which allow them to act in concert with the other machines to which they are connected. This chapter explores some of the implications of an operating system running on a processor which is not an isolated unit, but is part of a larger system which shares resources with other parts of the system; other processors within the same machine, and other processors on separate machines linked by a communications network.

9.1 ☐ MULTIPROCESSOR SYSTEMS

Although processor power is continually increasing, there are still applications where even the fastest modern processors are inadequate. Examples include simulations used in fields such as weather forecasting, astrophysics, and aircraft and automobile design, where the goal is to simulate the behaviour and interaction of vast numbers of elements. For example, weather forecasting involves simulating how regions of the atmosphere interact with each other. The smaller the simulated regions are, the more accurate the forecast will be. Increases in processor power allow finer levels of detail to be modelled in the same amount of time (bearing in mind that it is necessary to produce weather forecasts before the weather actually happens!), but there can never be enough processor power available to provide a completely accurate and timely simulation. However, more processor power means better results.

One way to increase processor power is to use multiple processors. A machine with four processors will provide up to four times the processing power of a single processor. Up to four threads can be executed in parallel, one per processor. In practice, the increase in processor power is somewhat less than the theoretical maximum due to the overheads involved in coordinating the activities of the processors involved.

Most modern multiprocessor systems are **symmetric multiprocessor** (SMP) systems, where all the processors share the workload equally. An outline of SMP system organisation is illustrated in Figure 9.1. This is in contrast to asymmetric designs where there is a single 'master' processor which runs the operating system and controls a number of 'slave' processors which run user processes. In a typical SMP system, one processor will be started initially, and this processor must initialise the environment for each of the other processors in the system and then start them up when everything is ready. On Pentium systems this is done using an **interprocessor interrupt**. Once the other processors have been started they will all have equal status with the first processor.

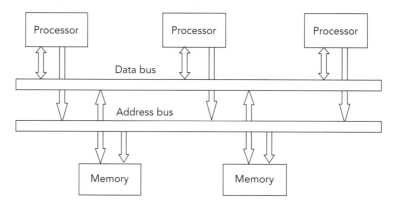

Figure 9.1 SMP architecture.

Question 9.1   What are the advantages and disadvantages of SMP systems compared to asymmetric multiprocessor systems?

In an SMP system, all the processors have equal access to the system's memory and usually I/O devices as well, and any processor can execute kernel code such as the scheduler. In some ways this makes life simpler: each processor executes a thread belonging to a user process until it becomes necessary to reschedule, and it then runs the scheduler in order to find a new thread to execute. Each processor therefore just executes threads from a common pool, or runs the idle thread when there are no other threads which are ready to run. In other ways the presence of multiple processors makes things much more complicated. For example, kernel routines such as the scheduler must be written with the possibility in mind that more than one processor will simultaneously try to execute the same code. In other words, the kernel needs to provide **reentrant** code which can be 'reentered' by another processor at any time. The alternative is to prevent more than one processor at a time from executing within the kernel by treating the entire kernel as a critical section. This was done in early versions of the Linux kernel, but it has a serious effect on overall system performance.

The problems here are similar in many ways to those of designing multithreaded programs compared to single-threaded programs. In a multithreaded program it is necessary to provide synchronization mechanisms such as semaphores to prevent multiple threads from entering critical sections which update shared data areas. Similarly, a kernel designed for use on an SMP system must provide synchronization mechanisms which will prevent more than one processor executing critical sections of the kernel. Ideally, the critical sections will be fairly small so that one processor won't block the others for any significant length of time.

The main limitation on SMP systems which are organised as shown in Figure 9.1 is **scalability**. The processors contend with each other for the use of the system buses, so the system buses become a major bottleneck. Only one processor at a time can use the buses, which means that as more processors are added the buses become busy more and more of the time, and processors are held up more and more waiting for access to the buses. The point where the bus is being used non-stop is usually reached with only a handful of processors. Once this limit is reached, additional processors cannot improve the system's performance, and might even make it worse.

Question 9.2   Assume an SMP system where each processor makes 100 million memory references per second for instructions and data, has a cache with an average hit rate of 90%, and a single set of buses connecting it to a memory subsystem with an access time of 20 ns. How many processors would the system be able to support?

9.1.1   CACHE COHERENCE

Caching can help to reduce the amount of contention between processors for access to memory. If a value can be supplied from the cache, there is no need to access memory. One problem in a multiprocessor system where each processor has its own memory cache is that the different caches can give an inconsistent view of memory. Suppose one processor has a particular value from memory in its cache and another processor updates that same value. If the first processor carries on using the value in its cache it will produce incorrect results. What is necessary is a way of achieving **cache coherence**, where all the processor caches reflect a single coherent view of the contents of memory.

This is of course a problem for the hardware designer, not the operating system designer. It is still worth considering in order to assess its impact on system efficiency. The big problem here is notifying processors when a memory location changes so that each processor can update its cache if necessary. A simple solution is to use a **write-through** cache, which immediately writes all updates to memory. The other processors can use **bus snooping** to detect when another processor is performing a write operation. They can use the values being broadcast on the address and data buses to update their own caches if they have cached that particular address, as shown in Figure 9.2.

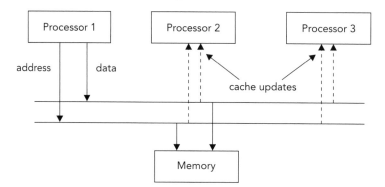

Figure 9.2 Bus snooping.

Unfortunately this reduces system efficiency. All write operations result in an immediate memory access which causes contention for the use of the system buses. It is more efficient to use a **write-back** strategy where writes are performed to the cache initially, and the bus management unit writes the updates back to memory when it is convenient to do so. If the value gets updated again before it has been written to memory, you have just saved a memory access. Unfortunately, an internal cache update is not visible to the other processors in the system. What is needed is a way to update any cached copies of the same address in the other processors, or at least to **invalidate** the cache entry in the other processors (that is, remove it from the caches in the other processors so that they will reload it if they need to access it).

Bus snooping can help here as well. Each processor can monitor the address bus to detect when another processor reads from an address that the processor has cached, and mark it in the cache as 'shared'. Writing to a shared cache location can then be done by writing the value through to memory immediately, which will ensure that all other processors can update their cache accordingly.

Question 9.3   In a system like this, how can the first processor let the second processor know that it has just accessed a shared location?

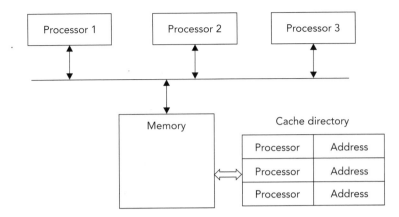

Figure 9.3 Directory-based cache management.

Another approach is to use a **directory-based** protocol, where a separate directory (a hardware unit which may be built into each memory module) keeps track of which processors have cached copies of which locations, so that when a processor fetches a value from memory it can be notified whether it is shared with other processors or not. This is illustrated in Figure 9.3. If a processor has the only copy of a particular location and another processor reads from it, a signal can be sent to the first processor to notify it that the address is now shared. Similarly, if a processor writes to a shared cached location, the processors holding copies of the location can be notified and can then invalidate the corresponding cache entry so that the data will need to be fetched from memory the next time it is needed.

9.1.2 SYNCHRONIZATION

Thread synchronization is much harder on a multiprocessor system than on a **uniprocessor** (single processor) system. On a single-processor machine it is possible to disable interrupts during short critical sections to ensure that the critical section is executed as a single indivisible unit where the thread that is executing the critical section cannot be interrupted or rescheduled. This simply won't work on an SMP system, because disabling interrupts on one processor will have no effect on any other processor. Mutexes using test-and-set instructions can still be used, providing the processor hardware guarantees that other processors will be unable to access memory until the test-and-set instruction completes (and that the operation is not just performed on a cached copy of the value). Modern processors which are designed to be used in SMP systems always provide 'interlocked' (atomic) test-and-set instructions which are safe to use in a multiprocessor environment.

Question 9.4   Why is interlocking needed? Why would processor designers choose to provide separate interlocked and non-interlocked versions of instructions like test-and-set?

Kernel mutexes are somewhat different from normal user-mode mutexes, which are used to synchronize access to a critical section by user-mode threads. Kernel mutexes are not needed for uniprocessor systems, where it is easy to ensure that only one thread at a time is executing inside the kernel. Also, a user-mode mutex has the option of suspending a thread which tries to acquire a locked mutex. If the critical section is part of the kernel, such as the scheduler or the suspend operation itself, it is not generally possible to do this. Instead, kernel mutexes are usually implemented as **spin locks**, which repeatedly test the mutex until it is free. This means that a processor which is blocked waiting for a kernel mutex to be unlocked cannot do anything else; it enters a 'busy waiting' state until it can lock the mutex. Of course this means that the blocked processor will be repeatedly accessing memory in order to test the mutex, and this will reduce the memory bandwidth available to the processor which is executing the critical section. For this reason, kernel critical sections need to be kept as short as possible to prevent other processors from being blocked for unreasonable periods of time.

Interrupt handling is also more complex in SMP systems than in uniprocessor systems. On a uniprocessor machine, all the interrupts are handled by the one processor. On a multiprocessor system, any interrupt can potentially be handled by any processor. One problem is preventing several processors from responding to the same interrupt. This is basically an issue for the hardware designer; one approach is to route each interrupt signal to a specific processor, which breaks the symmetry of an SMP system. A better solution is to use an intelligent interrupt controller such as the Intel IOAPIC [7] used in Pentium-based systems. This can choose which processor the interrupt will be routed to, as illustrated in Figure 9.4. What an IOAPIC does is to broadcast the interrupt request to the local interrupt controller (APIC) on each processor chip and then pass the interrupt to any local APIC that indicates that it is ready to accept it. While an interrupt is being serviced

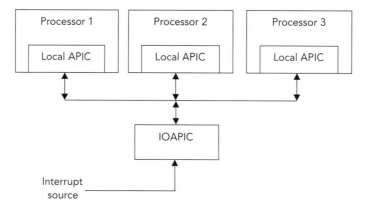

Figure 9.4 Connecting an IOAPIC.

by a particular processor, that processor's local APIC will ignore interrupt notifications at the same or lower priority than the current interrupt, but the IOAPIC will still accept them and other processors can be used to handle them.

9.1.3 SMP THREAD SCHEDULING

Scheduling on a multiprocessor system is a little bit more complex than it is on a uniprocessor. One obvious change is that the scheduler needs to be protected against being executed by more than one processor at a time. This could lead to the same thread being scheduled for execution by two different processors, or corruption of the list of ready-to-run threads. In other words, the scheduler needs to be a critical section protected by a kernel mutex.

Although exactly the same algorithms could be used as were described in Chapter 7, there will be a performance penalty if the presence of multiple processors is not taken into account. The reason for this is down to caching again. Once a thread has been executed by a particular processor, that processor will have relevant items in its cache and in the memory management unit's TLB. If the thread is then executed by a different processor there will be a penalty due to initial cache and TLB misses. The original processor will go on to execute a different thread, and it too will suffer from cache and TLB misses. In other words, both processors will suffer a drop in performance if a thread is moved from one processor to another. However, there will be times when the original processor is busy and the thread it was running has the highest priority, in which case the thread will need to be executed by a different processor. The scheduling algorithm must take all these factors into account.

The scheduler is therefore responsible for ranking the priority of the available threads *for a particular processor*, and it may give the same threads a completely different set of rankings on different processors. In SMP-aware versions of the Linux kernel, a function called goodness is used to calculate a priority for a particular thread on a particular CPU, and this is used in essentially the same scheduling algorithm that was described in Section 7.5.1.

What goodness does is to return a value which indicates the thread's ranking: over 1000 for a real-time process which should be run before any others (actually the thread's real-time priority + 1000), a lower positive value for a runnable thread, or zero if the thread's timeslice has expired. The thread's counter value (the number of clock ticks left in its timeslice) is used as a first approximation for its goodness, and bonuses are added to that if it was last executed on the same processor and also if it has the same address space as the previous thread that was run on the current processor. Adding a bonus for the same processor encourages the use of processors which may already have relevant data in the cache, and adding a bonus for the same address space encourages the use of processors with relevant TLB entries.

9.1.4 BUS CONTENTION

Historically, processor power has doubled every 18 months or so. This was noted in 1965 by Gordon Moore, a co-founder of Intel. His observation is now immortalised as **Moore's Law**, and it still holds true today. Unfortunately, the speed of memory and disks has not kept pace with this. The number of processors that can be used in a multiprocessor system is ultimately limited by the need to share a common memory. As more processors are added, memory will be accessed more frequently until it is in use 100% of the time. When this happens there is no point in adding any more processors, as they will just be competing with the other processors for access to memory, and they will either be blocked by other processors accessing memory or they will block other processors with their own memory accesses. Either way, there will be no net gain in processing speed when another processor is added.

One solution is to provide multiple buses to allow each processor in the system to access a separate block of physical memory at the same time. This approach involves using a **crossbar switch** to connect a particular processor to a particular memory module. Figure 9.5 shows a crossbar switch connecting three processors and three memory modules, so that each processor can be connected to a different memory module at the same time. The big problem here is the cost. Each switch has to be able to connect an awful lot of signals. A 32-bit address bus and a 32-bit data bus, together with some control signals, means that each switch is responsible for making or breaking 70 or 80 different connections. And in a system with P processors and M memory modules, the number of switches required is $P{\times}M$. Adding an extra processor means adding another M switches. Advances in technology might change this situation; for example, by the use of optical crossbar switches which can handle multiple simultaneous data streams without interference.

Another approach is to use a multistage network of switches such as an **omega network** to connect processors to memory modules. Each switch in an omega network has two inputs and two outputs, and either input can be connected to either output. An omega network provides enough possible paths to connect any processor to any memory module. Figure 9.6 shows a three-stage omega network which connects eight processors to eight memory modules, and separate paths are

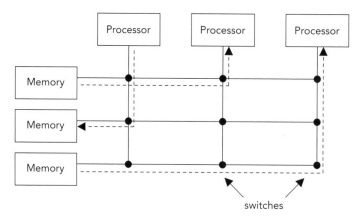

Figure 9.5 A crossbar switch.

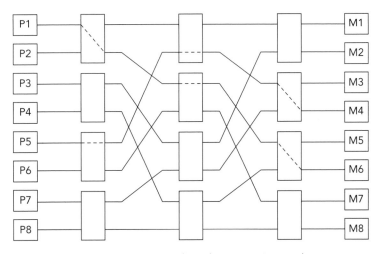

Figure 9.6 An omega network with two active paths.

shown from two of the processors to two of the memory modules (P1 to M6 and P5 to M4). Both of these paths can be in use at the same time.

In an $N \times N$ omega network there are $\log_2 N$ stages with $N/2$ switches in each stage. The multiple stages will inevitably increase the time it takes to access memory and increase the possibility of failures. Another problem is that an omega network is a **blocking** network. If any switch is in use for one path, it cannot be used simultaneously for a different path, and there is only one possible path between a particular processor and a particular memory module. Non-blocking networks are possible but they are much more expensive to construct.

Exercise 9.1   Find out about non-blocking network designs (e.g. Clos networks). How much more complex than omega networks are they? Compare the cost of doubling the number of processors and memory modules in each case.

Note that on any system using multiple buses it will be necessary to use a directory-based cache coherence protocol rather than bus snooping, since a memory access on one bus will be invisible to processors that are not currently connected to that bus. The individual memory modules must therefore keep track of which locations are accessed by which processors, and this will add yet more complexities to the design.

9.2 ☐ MULTICOMPUTER SYSTEMS

Rather than trying to pack more and more processors into a single machine, another approach to distributing the system workload is to share it between a number of separate machines (referred to as **nodes**), each with their own processor (or processors) and memory. Most machines now have network connections which allow them to be connected to other machines, so the network can provide a communications backbone to allow individual machines to request services from other machines, much as the kernel allows individual user processes to request services from device drivers on a standalone system.

The general structure of such a distributed system is shown in Figure 9.7. Using processors on remote machines to share the workload for computationally expensive jobs is an attractive idea. Most organisations have vast numbers of networked PCs which are idle for much of the time; they are often left switched on permanently, but they are usually completely idle at night and at weekends. Even during the day, a PC which is being used for typical office applications such as word processing, web surfing and reading email has a processor which is idle for more than 99% of the time. Considering the power of modern processors, that represents an awful lot of potential computer power that is just going to waste unless someone finds a way to use it.

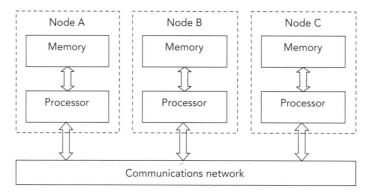

Figure 9.7 Distributed systems organisation.

Most networks these days use the communication protocols developed for the Internet, generally referred to as **TCP/IP**. What TCP/IP does is to define abstractions called **ports** which can be connected using **sockets**. Ports and sockets will be described further in the next chapter, but the important thing to realise is that they are abstractions built on top of an underlying networking system, in the same way that files are an abstraction built on top of an underlying disk or CD structure. Links can be established between ports on machines anywhere in the world, including ports that are located on the same machine. All you have to do is to create a socket connected to a specified port on a specified machine, using a 16-bit port number and a 32-bit machine number (the machine's **IP address**). For convenience, **domain names** like www.acme.com are usually used instead of IP addresses when referring to machines. This requires a **domain name server** (DNS) to convert the name to the corresponding IP address before it is used.

In the most recent version of the protocol (IPv6), IP addresses are 128 bits long, although this has not been widely adopted at the time of writing. A 32-bit IP address caters for about 4 billion unique addresses, whereas a 128-bit IP address allows for about 10^{38} unique addresses to allow every toaster and washing machine in the world to have its own unique IP address. In fact, 128 bits is more than enough to give every grain of sand its own IP address!

Exercise 9.2   Find out just how big 10^{38} really is. What is the mass of the Earth in grams? Is 10^{38} enough to give every gram of the Earth's mass its own IP address? Every milligram? Every atom?

TCP/IP actually provides two ways for ports to be connected. **TCP** (the Transmission Control Protocol) allows data to be transferred in continuous streams, in exactly the same way as files or Unix pipes provide streams of characters. As with reading or writing a file on a disk, you can assume that it's reliable; the data will either be transmitted correctly to the port at the other end of the connection or it won't be, but you'll be notified if it goes wrong. There is quite a large overhead in providing this reliability, so it is sometimes easier to use **UDP** (User Datagram Protocol), which is used to transfer individual messages called **datagrams** between two ports. The big difference is that each message is an individual item, rather than being part of a continuous stream of characters, and that there is no guarantee that a datagram will arrive at its destination. The communication system will do its best to deliver it for you, but you do not get any automatic response to tell you whether or not it got there. If it matters, you either have to get the receiver to send you back a datagram to acknowledge receipt, or use TCP instead, which handles all this sort of thing automatically.

The difference between TCP and UDP is similar to that between making a phone call and sending an email message. With a phone call (TCP), you know whether your call has got through because the person at the other end picks up the phone and talks to you, or you get an engaged tone or some other signal to tell you that the call failed. With email (UDP), you have no idea whether your message got there until you receive a reply. If you don't receive a reply, you can always send the message again if it's important. It might not be; you might for example be sending a regular newsletter to a subscriber, and it's up to the subscriber to contact you if they miss a copy of the newsletter. In this situation, you don't expect every subscriber to send you a message acknowledging receipt (in fact, you would be annoyed if they did).

9.3 ❑ CLIENTS AND SERVERS

Stream-oriented protocols like TCP make it as easy to connect to another machine as it is to open a file on the local machine. It may be slower than a local disk, but it's just as reliable. All you need is a program running on the remote machine that can interpret the messages you send and respond appropriately, in the same way that a shell interprets commands that you type. Programs like this running on a remote machine are referred to as **servers**, while the programs that you run that send requests to a server and deal with the server's reply are referred to as **clients**.

The client and the server need to share a common **application protocol** that allows the server to interpret requests from the client. For example, you could run a program on the remote machine that starts a shell on the remote machine, feeds your input to it and returns its output to you. From your point of view, it's just like typing commands to a local shell (but maybe a bit slower). From the point of view of the shell on the remote machine, it doesn't matter whether its input and output streams are connected to a local keyboard and display, to local files, or even to a machine on the other side of the world. And, surprise, there is already a standard application protocol called **Telnet** that does this for you.

Alternatively, you could run a server which, if you send it a filename, returns you a copy of the specified file. There is a standard protocol for this, too; it's called **HTTP** (the Hypertext Transfer Protocol) and it is the basis of the World-Wide Web. When you type a **URL** like `http://www.acme.comdir/file.html` into your web browser, the web browser connects to port 80 on the machine `www.acme.com` (port 80 being the standard port used by HTTP servers) and then sends a request for the file `/dir/file.html`. The server responds with a copy of the requested file, and your web browser displays it.

In fact, you can use a Telnet client to do the same thing. All you have to do is to type a command like this on your local machine:

```
telnet www.acme.com 80
```

This will open a connection to port 80 on `www.acme.com`, just as your web browser would. Now type this:

```
GET /dir/file.html HTTP/1.0
```

This command is interpreted by the HTTP server which is waiting for incoming requests on port 80 of `www.acme.com`, and it will return you something like this:

```
HTTP/1.1 200 OK
Date: Mon, 23 Jun 2003 13:52:08 GMT
Server: Apache/2.0.47 (Win32)
Content-Length: 1086
Connection: close
Content-Type: text/html;charset=utf-8

<!DOCTYPE HTML PUBLIC "-//W3C//DTD HTML 3.2 Final//EN">
<html>
<head>
  <title>The test file</title>
</head>
<body>
<h1>The test file</h1>
```

```
...
</body>
</html>
```

The first few lines are **headers** defined by the HTTP protocol standard. The very first line tells you the protocol version being used by the server and the result of your request as a numeric code and an explanatory string. In this case, it is '200 OK'; another possible response is '404 Not Found' to indicate that the server couldn't find a file with the name that you specified. After this comes a series of headers which in this case give the date, the name and version number of the server program, the length of the file being sent, the connection type, and the content type. In this case the content type is 'text/html', indicating a text file containing HTML content (Hypertext Markup Language). After this there is a blank line to mark the end of the headers, and this is followed by the file itself. Your web browser would receive exactly the same response, and it would use the content-type header to decide how to display the content of the file.

Exercise 9.3   Try using Telnet to access a web page that exists. Try it for a web page that does not exist, and for a directory name (without a trailing slash, e.g. /dir rather than /dir/). Compare the results.

So why isn't there just one standard, universal application protocol? The reason is that different protocols have different purposes, and different properties as a result. Telnet is a **connection-oriented** protocol. You establish a connection and then conduct a conversation with the server. The server has to deal with a series of requests from you and send responses to each request, keeping track of the overall state of the conversation as it does so. HTTP is a **connectionless** protocol which takes a single request and sends a single response in reply. Each request that you send is treated in isolation, with no connection to any earlier requests that you might have sent. These two approaches have quite different consequences, as we shall see later.

The other main reason is that the application domains for different protocols are quite different. Another common connectionless protocol is **SMTP**, the Simple Mail Transfer Protocol, which deals with sending email messages, and as such expects requests which specify a destination for the email you want to send, a subject line for the message, the message itself, message attachments and so on. Devising a common protocol which would deal with this as well as with file transfers like HTTP would be very difficult; you would end up with something very inefficient, and people would keep coming up with ideas for new features which the existing protocol couldn't handle. It's much easier to come up with a completely separate protocol which is designed to meet the needs of a specific application domain. Many applications also use their own special-purpose application protocols if none of the standard ones provide the necessary facilities.

9.4 ☐ DISTRIBUTED FILESYSTEMS

The big problem with this approach to networking is that it requires special-purpose client programs to communicate with the server. There is no integration with the facilities that the operating system provides. For example, you can use HTTP to copy a file from a server to a client, but you can't integrate the files provided on the HTTP server into your local filesystem. It is also impossible to copy an entire directory complete with subdirectories in a single operation; you have to resort to copying the files one by one, replicating the directory structure by hand. It's much nicer to be able to access remote filesystems transparently, so that you work with a centrally held copy of the file you're interested in rather than having to use a separate program to make a local copy. Apart from anything else, you will need to go through the whole process again if the centrally held copy on the server gets updated.

A much better approach is to allow a filesystem on a remote machine to be used as an extension of the local filesystem. This requires a filesystem driver which can be loaded alongside other filesystem drivers. Linux handles this using the VFS (Virtual File System), which routes requests for files to the appropriate filesystem driver. The filesystem driver then uses the facilities of another device driver to deal with the underlying hardware. A request for a local file on an ext2fs volume is passed to the ext2fs filesystem driver, which translates it into a series of requests to an underlying disk driver, as illustrated in Figure 9.8. A networked filesystem would translate the request into a series of requests to an underlying TCP/IP driver. And as we shall see later, the TCP/IP driver involves at least three layers of drivers in itself (a driver for TCP or UDP, which then uses a driver for the underlying IP protocol, which then uses a driver for an Ethernet connection or some other physical network).

There are several protocols which provide for networked filesystems, the commonest ones being NFS (Network File System) and SMB (Server Message Block).

open ("/dir/foo", ...)

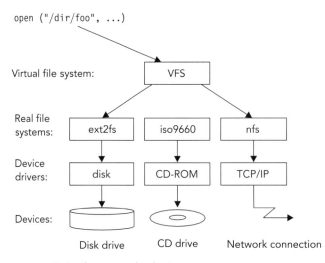

Figure 9.8 The Virtual File System.

From the point of view of a Unix client, an NFS or SMB directory tree is treated the same way as any other foreign filesystem; the remote filesystem is mounted onto any convenient local directory. When a file within this directory is accessed, the appropriate network operations are performed to access the remote file it refers to. On a Windows system, there are two approaches that can be used:

- The remote filesystem can be mapped to a drive letter so that it appears as one of the 'forest' of drives, in the same way as a local disk drive does. Names like R:\file\dir can be used to access the file file\dir on the remote filesystem mapped to drive R.

- A UNC (Uniform Naming Convention) name can be used, which uses the server name as a prefix to the path to the file. Names like \\server\dir\file can be used to access the file called dir\file on the remote filesystem of the server called server.

Question 9.5   What are the advantages and disadvantages of these two approaches?

One of the most important aspects of any filesystem design, whether local or remote, is reliability, including the ability to recover from errors. Designing reliable network protocols is difficult, and NFS and SMB use completely different approaches to deal with error recovery.

9.4.1   NFS

NFS is a protocol originally developed by Sun Microsystems, but is now a *de facto* standard which is widely used, particularly on Unix systems. It was originally developed for use with Unix systems, so NFS files have essentially the same set of file attributes that a normal Unix filesystem provides. This includes access permissions, owner and group identifiers, data and time of last modification, and so on. As with Unix filesystems, hardware devices on the remote machine can appear as files in an NFS filesystem, but NFS does not allow client machines to access hardware devices on the server directly; it is only possible to read and write normal files and directories.

NFS is a stateless, connectionless protocol implemented using the RPC (Remote Procedure Call) protocol, which is described in Section 9.5.1. From an NFS client's point of view, the NFS protocol is just a library of procedures that can be used to access remote files. Because the protocol is stateless, the server does not need to store any client-specific state; transactions are completely independent of each other. This means that the clients are insulated from the effects of server crashes or temporary network failures. If the server maintained state information for its clients, the clients would need to be aware of remote failures and then restore the state information on the server when service was restored. With a stateless server, the clients can just retry operations until they get a response from the server.

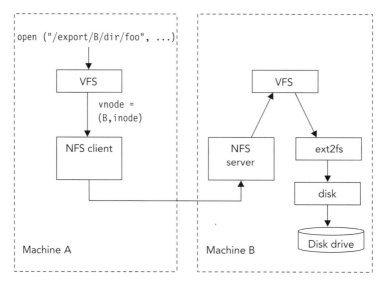

Figure 9.9 NFS and VFS.

On Linux systems, the virtual filesystem identifies files using **vnodes**, which are a combination of a server identifier and an inode number on that server. When the VFS is asked to access a file whose vnode identifies it as belonging to a remote machine, a request is sent via the NFS driver to the remote machine, as illustrated in Figure 9.9. Otherwise, a local file access is performed. The VFS can also deal with requests from remote machines in the same way; it sees a request for a local file and deals with it, sending back its response to whoever made the request. This may be the local NFS server, which has been contacted by the VFS of a remote machine.

An NFS server can make more than one of its directory subtrees available to remote clients. The NFS **mount protocol** defines how clients can interrogate a remote NFS server to discover what directory trees it exports. The client can then request access to a particular directory hierarchy, and the NFS server will return a **handle** which can be used to identify the root of that directory tree in future requests. The handle is a 256-bit value which is randomly generated by the server, although it may also encode information such as the date and time the handle was generated and a checksum to ensure that the handle is valid. On Unix systems, such values are referred to as 'magic cookies'; a **cookie** is a value which acts as a receipt for a transaction (in other words, a handle), and a **magic cookie** is one that has been created 'by magic', meaning that it is impossible for a client to manufacture a valid handle for itself, and it contains no information that the client can usefully interpret. The server may well be able to decode a handle quickly to identify what it refers to, but the client cannot. The handle might for example incorporate an inode number on a remote Unix filesystem, which will be completely meaningless except on the remote machine.

Once a client has obtained a handle and used it to create a mount point within the local filesystem, the remote filesystem becomes accessible. However, the client might not use the same naming conventions as the server; a Unix system will use '/ ' as a pathname separator where a Windows system will use '\'. To avoid this sort of problem, NFS does not allow pathnames to be used directly. If the client wishes to access a file called x/y/z on the remote server, it must first of all use the handle it was given for the remote filesystem and ask for a handle for the directory x. The server will return a new handle identifying directory x, and the client must then use this handle in a further request to obtain a handle for the subdirectory y. The handle for this subdirectory can then be used to open file z, which returns yet another handle that can be used to read and write the file. Figure 9.10 shows this sequence of events.

Because NFS is a connectionless protocol, the server does not retain any state information about the client's accesses to it. It treats each new request as completely unconnected with any previous requests; the only contextual information that it uses to identify a file being accessed is that which is encapsulated in the

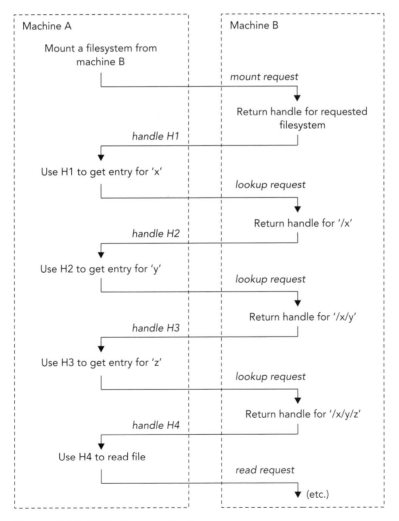

Figure 9.10 NFS directory lookups.

handle it provides for each file. As a result, the server does not keep track of the current position in the file for any particular client. The client is responsible for keeping track of the position itself and each read or write request must specify the position in the file to be read or written. This also means that seeking to a different position in the file is extremely efficient, as this doesn't involve any interaction with the server. The client keeps this information as part of the file descriptor which describes the file once it has been opened, so seeking to a new position is just a matter of updating this local information.

Exercise 9.4   Consider what will happen in the event of a crash at the server end. Show how recovery is possible at different points as a file is being created and written to. For example, is a file handle still going to be accepted as valid after a server crash?

NFS uses UDP as its underlying transport protocol, so it is possible that datagrams will be lost. If no reply is received for a particular operation, it may be that the original request has been lost (in which case the operation has not been performed) or the reply has been lost (in which case the operation has been performed). It is impossible for the client to tell whether it is the request or the reply that has been lost, which means that there is no way to tell whether the operation has in fact been performed. For this reason, NFS operations are designed to be **idempotent**, which means that they will have the same effect if they are repeated. An operation like appending a block of data to the end of a file is not idempotent, because if you append the same thing twice the file ends up storing two copies of the data. Writing a block of data to a particular position in the file is idempotent, because if the same write operation is repeated, the same position in the file will be overwritten with the same data. If a datagram is lost in transit the operation can just be retried.

Exercise 9.5   Prepare a list of possible operations on a file and identify which are idempotent and which are not. Can the non-idempotent operations you identify be implemented in an alternative way using idempotent operations?

9.4.2   SMB

SMB is a protocol originally developed jointly by Intel, Microsoft and IBM. SMB is the standard file and printer sharing protocol used on Windows systems, although SMB clients and servers are also available for Unix systems (for example, Samba). It is not really a distributed filesystem in the same sense as NFS, although it is often treated as such. Rather, it is a gateway protocol for accessing specific types of resource which are located on remote machines.

SMB was originally implemented on top of a networking protocol known as **NetBIOS** (Network Basic Input/Output System) which was developed in the early days of the IBM PC. NetBIOS provides an API for interfacing between programs and network hardware. IBM developed a mechanism for transmitting NetBIOS packets across Ethernet and token ring networks, known as **NetBEUI** (NetBIOS Extended User Interface), but these days NetBIOS is usually implemented on top of TCP/IP, using TCP or UDP to transport NetBIOS packets. Using TCP/IP is more flexible than NetBEUI as it allows NetBIOS packets to be routed across an internet, whereas NetBEUI is restricted to a single local area network. Microsoft has since developed an extension of SMB called **CIFS** (the Common Internet File System) which requires the use of TCP as its underlying transport protocol.

Whereas NFS is a connectionless protocol, SMB and CIFS are both connection-oriented. Both store state information about every open networked file on both the client and the server, so that the client can be notified if a file that has been opened by more than one client is updated by a different client. CIFS has also been designed to run well over slow connections, to accommodate users using modems to access the Internet over dial-up lines.

NetBIOS uses 15-character names to identify computers, and these are also used in CIFS. This means that there must be a mechanism for performing **name resolution** so that NetBIOS names can be translated into the corresponding IP addresses. IP broadcasting is the closest match to the original NetBIOS mechanism. When a client wants to connect to a server, it sends a broadcast request on the local network giving the server's NetBIOS name. The server responds with a message giving its IP address. Another approach is to use a **NetBIOS name service** (NBNS) server to keep track of machine names and the corresponding IP addresses. Microsoft used the name **WINS** (Windows Internet Name Service) for their NBNS implementation, and the name has passed into common usage so that it is now more commonly used than NBNS. If a WINS server is present, each client machine sends it a message containing its name and IP address which are recorded in a simple database on the server. Name resolution requests can then be handled by asking the WINS server to look up the name and respond with the corresponding IP address.

The SMB protocol defines a large number of commands (over 100 of them) relating to file and printer sharing. The commands are confusingly called SMBs (server message blocks!) although the name SMB is more commonly used as a name for the protocol itself. Clients issue commands to servers to perform operations like opening, closing, reading and writing files. Servers respond to each command SMB with a response SMB.

Clients need to be able to find out what servers are available so that they can connect to them. This is done by a process known as 'browsing'. The participating machines on a network hold an election to decide who will become the Local Master Browser (LMB), and the winner is responsible for maintaining a list of available services. This list is what appears when you click on the Windows 'Network Neighbourhood' icon, as illustrated in Figure 9.11. The services (remote printers and directory trees) are known as 'shares' in SMB terminology. Each share can be protected

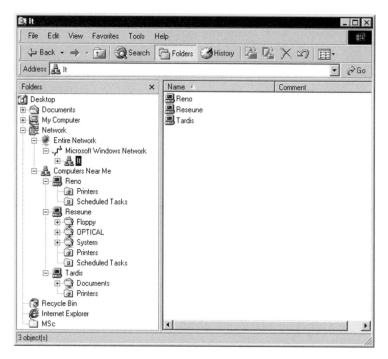

Figure 9.11 The Network Neighbourhood in Windows.

against unauthorised access using either 'share-level' authentication or 'user-level' authentication. Share-level authentication allows each share to be protected using a password, but there is no restriction on who can connect to the share. Anyone who knows the password is allowed to connect. User-level authentication allows access to be allowed or denied to individual users, and requires a username and password.

Because CIFS is connection-oriented, error recovery is more complex than it is in NFS. However, there are some advantages as well. Because the server knows about the connections that have been made, it can identify files that have been opened more than once. Files which are only opened by one user can be granted an **opportunistic lock** which means that the client does not have to write updates to the server immediately. Also, asynchronous operations are possible with CIFS, whereas NFS is basically synchronous due to its use of RPC to implement file operations. In CIFS, each request is given a 'multiplex ID' and a client can have multiple requests outstanding as long as they have different multiplex IDs. The multiplex ID is used to identify which request a response from the server refers to.

Exercise 9.6   List the steps that would be needed to recover form a CIFS server crash while a file was being created and written to.

9.5 ❑ DISTRIBUTED PROCESSING

The ability to share files between machines is very useful, but what if you want to run a program on a remote machine? As mentioned earlier, the Telnet protocol provides one way to do this. Unix systems also provide commands to allow you to connect directly to remote machines; these commands have names like `rlogin` (remote login) and `rcp` (remote copy). Unfortunately, if you wanted to capture the output of a program in a file you would have to use a file on the remote machine and then transfer a copy of the file to your local machine using a protocol like HTTP, or access it using NFS or SMB.

Most web servers provide a mechanism for executing programs on the server system which can be used in conjunction with HTTP. This is known as **CGI** (the Common Gateway Interface). A directory, which is traditionally called `cgi-bin`, is treated specially by the server. When you try to access a file in this directory, the web server executes it as a program rather than just returning a copy of it. Such programs are known as **CGI scripts**. The output of the program is what gets returned to you for display by your web browser. However, this is not a general-purpose mechanism for executing remote programs; it is intended as a way of providing dynamically created web pages rather than the static contents of an existing file. The output must include a 'Content-type' header line at the very least, and any header lines must be separated from the rest of the output by a blank line. If you don't do this, the web browser will not know what to do with the output.

9.5.1 REMOTE PROCEDURE CALLS

A more general mechanism for remote execution known as a **remote procedure call** (RPC) was developed by Sun Microsystems. As the name implies, it is a way to call individual procedures that are located on a remote machine. As mentioned above, the operations that NFS provides to open, close, read and write files are implemented using RPC. The basic idea is very simple; the client bundles together (**marshals**) a list of input parameters for the remote procedure, sends them to the server and then waits for a reply. The communication can be done using either TCP or UDP. The server unpacks (**unmarshals**) the parameters, calls the corresponding procedure and then marshals any output parameters. The outputs are then sent back to the client, which unmarshals them and stores them in the appropriate variables.

From the point of view of the client program, this behaves much like a normal procedure call except that it takes a bit longer. It calls a procedure with a list of parameters, and after the call has completed it continues. The only difference is that instead of the program being linked to a local copy of the procedure, it is linked to a **stub procedure** which is responsible for handling the communication with the server. On the server side there is a similar stub which unmarshals the input parameters and calls the actual procedure. The stub is actually in two parts: an **interface stub** which handles parameter marshalling, and a **communications stub** which handles the communication with the remote system. This is illustrated in Figure 9.12.

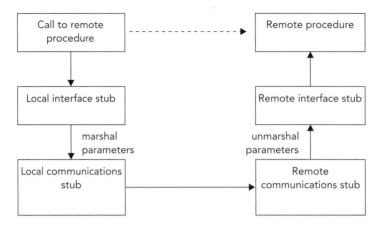

Figure 9.12 A remote procedure call.

Naturally, there are some complications. One is that the client and server do not share a common address space, so while a local procedure can communicate using global variables, a remote procedure cannot. More seriously, local procedures can make use of **pointer variables**, which can point to complex data structures in a common address space. A pointer variable would have no meaning for a remote machine, since it would have no way of accessing the corresponding data. Finally, the client and server machines might not be identical, so data items like floating-point numbers may not have identical binary representations on the two machines.

To overcome this, Sun has defined a standard **external data representation** (XDR) which can be used as a machine-independent way of transferring values of common data types between machines. These data types are listed in Table 9.1. They include integers and floating-point numbers of various lengths, Boolean values, strings, arrays (either fixed-size or with a count of the number of array elements), and structures containing a mixture of the other data types. If a complex data structure needs to be sent, the entire structure must be linearised into a structure built from the basic XDR types and sent as a whole to the server, rather than just passing a pointer to the structure.

Another problem is how to identify a particular remote procedure so that it can be called. You have to know which machine is acting as the server, and you have to have a way of identifying the particular remote procedure you want on the remote machine. A set of remote procedures is encapsulated in a program which is run on the server (for example, the NFS server program contains all the remote procedures that NFS provides). A particular procedure is identified using a 32-bit number to identify the program containing the procedure together with a program version number and a procedure number. Some program numbers have been reserved by Sun for well-known services; for example, all the procedures relating to NFS are encapsulated in a single program with the number 100003. The version number is useful to allow programs to be updated dynamically; there can be more than one version of a particular program running on the server machine at a time, so that

Table 9.1 XDR data types.

Data type	Size	Description
int	32 bits	signed integer
unsigned int	32 bits	unsigned integer
bool	32 bits	true (1) or false (0)
enum	arbitrary	enumeration type
hyper	64 bits	signed integer
unsigned hyper	64 bits	unsigned integer
float	32 bits	floating point
double	64 bits	floating point
opaque	arbitrary	sender's native data
string	arbitrary	ASCII characters
fixed array	arbitrary	fixed-size array
counted array	arbitrary	array with element count
structure	arbitrary	collection of data
union	arbitrary	choice of data
optional data	arbitrary	zero or more data items
constant	arbitrary	name and value
void	0	no data

existing clients of the old version can carry on using it while new clients can be directed to the latest version of the program.

The client also needs to know which port to connect to on the server machine. This is done by a service known as a **port mapper**. Whenever a program offering RPC services starts up, it must register itself with the port mapper. Clients can query the port mapper (normally via port 111) to get the port number for the server program.

Fault tolerance is an important aspect of RPC. Messages can be lost, and as was mentioned above, NFS deals with this by using idempotent operations that can be safely repeated if a message is lost. The RPC mechanism will automatically retry such operations if no reply is received within a specified time. However, for operations that are not idempotent, it is possible to specify that an RPC call is an **at-most-once** operation, in which case it will not be retried. The operation may not have been performed because the original request was lost, or it may have been performed but the reply was lost. In the latter case it would be unsafe to retry the operation.

Exercise 9.7   Some RPC systems allow for asynchronous request processing using 'futures', where a result is returned immediately to allow the caller to proceed. The server may not produce the actual result until some time later, but the caller will only need to block if it tries to use the result before the actual result has been produced. Explain how this could be implemented.

9.5.2   BUILDING A DISTRIBUTED PROGRAM USING RPC

A program can be a conventional program that just happens to use an existing RPC server program like the NFS server, or it can be built as a program whose functionality is intended to be distributed across a number of machines. This is quite complicated to do by hand, so there is a tool (rpcgen) which automates the process of building stubs for remote procedure calls.

To build a distributed program, the programmer has to decide which procedures will reside on which machines. For example, consider a simple program consisting of two procedures called A and B, where A will need to call B. In the normal, non-distributed, approach the two procedures might be compiled separately and then linked together to give a single executable program. In the distributed case, rpcgen must be used to generate stubs for the client and for the server. Procedure A will be linked to the client-side stub for B, while B will be linked to the server-side version of the stub. The interface stubs (one for the client and one for the server) must be written by hand, but the communication stub will be generated automatically by rpcgen.

To generate the communication stubs, you need a file called B.x containing an XDR specification of procedure B, which includes the program number and version number that you want to use for the RPC program containing procedure B. Running rpcgen on this file will generate the following files:

- B.h: declarations of constants and data types needed by both client-side and server-side stubs
- B_xdr.c: procedures for marshalling and unmarshalling parameters required by procedure *B*.
- B_clnt.c: the client-side communication stub
- B_svc.c: the server-side communication stub

The client application containing procedure A is compiled and then linked with the result of compiling B_xdr.c, the client-side communication stub B_clnt.c and the client-side interface stub. Similarly, the server program containing the real

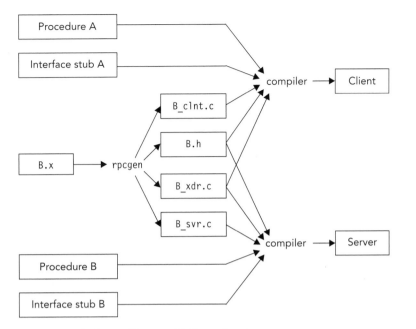

Figure 9.13 Compiling an RPC application.

procedure B is compiled and then linked with the result of compiling B_xdr.c, the server-side communication stub B_svc.c and the server-side interface stub. This is shown in Figure 9.13.

Sounds complicated? You're right, it is! But it's still a lot simpler than trying to do the whole thing by hand.

Project 9.1   Write a simple RPC program that provides a remote procedure to add two integers together and return the result.

9.5.3   WHY IS RPC USEFUL?

RPC is a general-purpose mechanism whereby one machine can offer services to anyone who wants to use them. This might be to allow clients to access a particular resource available on the server machine such as the filesystem, a database or a printer, or it might be used to distribute the processing load in computationally intensive applications. The rlogin and rcp programs on Unix systems that allow users to log in from a remote machine and copy files between machines are implemented using RPC.

Building an RPC program is harder than building a normal, non-RPC program because of the need to build stubs for each end of the connection, but once all the stubs have been generated they can be put in a library that any client program can make use of. The client program just calls particular procedures from this library without necessarily having to be aware that it is implemented using RPC.

One drawback to using RPC is the fact that only a limited number of data types can be used. Anything that needs to be used as a parameter must be expressed using these basic data types. In particular, data structures involving pointers must be linearised.

9.5.4 JAVA AND RMI

The Java programming language was designed with networking in mind. One common use for Java is to write **applets**, which are mobile application objects that can be embedded in web pages. When a web browser fetches a web page containing an applet, the code for the applet is fetched and executed by the web browser. This is made possible by the fact that Java programs are compiled into **bytecodes** for the Java Virtual Machine (JVM), and most browsers include a JVM emulator. The emulator executes the bytecodes in exactly the same way on any machine, regardless of the underlying processor architecture. The Java slogan is 'write once, run anywhere'.

Java also provides its own form of RPC known as **RMI** (Remote Method Invocation). This allows Java objects on one machine to call methods belonging to objects on a remote machine. RPC is designed so that it is language-neutral; it doesn't matter what language you write your programs in: the underlying communication with a remote procedure uses a limited set of XDR data types. Since RMI is specific to Java, any Java data type can be used as long as it is serializable, and most Java classes are serializable. Serialization involves converting an object into a stream of bytes that can be reconstituted at the other end. To make a class serializable, all you normally have to do is to state that the class implements the Serializable interface.

Java classes can implement one or more **interfaces**. An interface is a specification of a set of methods that must be provided by any class which implements that interface. For example, the following interface specification declares an interface called Adding which requires any implementing class to provide a method called add which takes two integer parameters and return an integer result:

```
public interface Adding {
  public int add (int a, int b);
}
```

A class which implements this interface might look like this:

```
public class Adder implements Adding {
  public int add (int a, int b) { return a + b; }
}
```

Since this class implements the Adding interface, it must provide an add method whose specification matches the one defined by the interface. Whenever an Adding object is required, an Adder object (or an object of any other class which implements the Adding interface) can be used instead, as it is guaranteed that it will provide all the methods required by the Adding interface.

Java relies heavily on pointers (known as **references**). Objects in Java are allocated dynamically and manipulated using references to the dynamically allocated memory. When the last reference to an object disappears, the memory for the object is automatically reclaimed (a process known as **garbage collection**). For example, strings in Java are implemented by instances of the String class. An object which contains a string will actually only contain a reference to a String object. To serialize such an object, the object itself and the String object it refers to must both be serialized, with the reference to the String object being replaced by a value which identifies the String object in the serialized data stream. Java serialization handles this automatically; it can also cope with circular chains of references or multiple references to the same object. It does this by recording which objects it has serialized so that it can avoid re-serializing an object that has already been dealt with. RMI works by sending a serialized copy of the parameters to the remote method and getting back a serialized copy of any object returned by the method, which can then be reconstituted as an object of the appropriate type on the client system.

Each Java object belongs to a particular class, and the class contains methods that can be executed on any object belonging to that class. The code for the methods can also be transmitted between the client and the server. This means that a server can return an object to the client which belongs to a class which is not known on the client system, simply by including copies of all the methods of the corresponding class in the serialized data stream. This is a very useful ability, as it allows a remote method to specify an interface as its return type and then return an object of any class that implements the interface.

The server class must be derived from the standard class RemoteObject or one of its subclasses (the simplest of which is UnicastRemoteObject) and must implement an interface derived from Remote which declares the methods that will be available to be called remotely. Most of the hard work involved in implementing RMI can be inherited automatically by deriving the server class from UnicastRemoteObject.

Locating a remote method is handled by an RMI **registry server** that runs on the server machine. When the server program starts up, it must register a server object and a corresponding name by which is can be accessed. The client obtains a reference to a remote object by contacting the registry server and specifying the name that was used to register it. Any of the methods defined by the server interface can then be called in exactly the same way as if the object were a local object.

9.5.5 A SIMPLE JAVA RMI EXAMPLE

To illustrate the use of RMI, this section gives a simple example based on the Adding interface described earlier. A few minor changes are needed. First, any remote object must implement the Remote interface, and any remote methods must specify that they might throw the exception RemoteException. The Remote interface does not define any methods; it is just a way of marking that the interface can be invoked remotely. The `Adding` interface now looks like this:

```
import java.rmi.*;
public interface Adding extends Remote {
  public int add (int a, int b) throws RemoteException;
}
```

The first line makes the names `Remote` and `RemoteException` visible (both of which are defined in the package `java.rmi`).

A class which implements this interface will need to be derived from `RemoteServer` or one of its subclasses. The class `UnicastRemoteObject` is the simplest one to use:

```
import java.rmi.*;
import java.rmi.server.*;
public class Adder extends UnicastRemoteObject implements Adding {
  public Adder () throws RemoteException { }
  public int add (int a, int b) throws RemoteException
    { return a + b; }
}
```

This defines `Adder` as a class derived from the `UnicastRemoteObject` class which also implements the `Adding` interface (and thus also the `Remote` interface which `Adding` is derived from). It has a **constructor** which does nothing but which might throw the exception `RemoteException`, and an implementation of the add method required by the `Adding` interface.

Finally, there needs to be a program which will register this class using the RMI registry:

```
import java.rmi.*;
public class AddServer {
  public static void main (String args[]) {
    try {
      Naming.rebind ("Adder", new Adder());
    }
    catch (Exception e) {
      System.out.println(e.getMessage());
    }
  }
}
```

This will create a new `Adder` object. It uses the method `Naming.rebind` to bind the object to the name 'Adder'.

The next thing to do is to create a stub for the client to use to call the methods defined by `Adder`, which is done using the `rmic` compiler tool included in the Java development kit. This creates a file called Adder_Stub.class. Now all that's needed is to start the RMI registry service and run the server:

```
rmiregistry &
java AddServer
```

The first line starts the RMI registry server running as a background process, and the second runs the server, which will contact the registry server when it executes the call to Naming.rebind. On a Windows system you would use the command start rmiregistry rather than rmiregistry & to run the RMI registry server in a separate process.

Finally, we need the client program. When this is compiled it will need a copy of the compiled code for the Adding interface and a copy of the client stub Adder_Stub.class that was generated by rmic. Here is the client program:

```
import java.rmi.*;
public class AddClient {
  public static void main (String args[]) {
    try {
      Adding adder =
            (Adding)Naming.lookup("//192.168.11.3/Adder");    // (1)
      System.out.println(adder.add(123,456));
    }
    catch (Exception e) {
      System.out.println("Exception " + e);
    }
  }
}
```

This uses Naming.lookup to contact the registry server at the specified IP address (in this case 192.168.11.3) to look up the name Adder on line 1. A domain name like www.acme.com can also be used instead of an IP address. The result is an object that implements the Remote interface, and we must convert this to the actual interface (Adding) so that its add method can be called. Once we have done this, we can use System.out.println to display the result of calling the object's add method, which in this case will be 579.

Exercise 9.8   Try this example to see whether it works as advertised. What happens if you make adder an Adder object (in other words, using the class directly rather than the Adding interface) and change the cast on line 1 to convert the result of Naming.lookup to Adder rather than Adding?

As you can see, this is much simpler than using RPC, and it is largely due to the fact that we don't have to use any language apart from Java. Most of the hard work is built in to the classes in the Java RMI library. The equivalent RPC code involves writing an XDR interface specification and hand-coding the interface stubs for both the client and the server.

9.6 ❑ DISTRIBUTED OBJECT FRAMEWORKS

Most modern software is designed using an object-oriented approach where the system as a whole is considered to be a community of interacting objects. In a traditional single-threaded design, these objects would be passive constructs which would encapsulate data and related procedures to access and manipulate that data. In a multi-threaded design, the objects can be active rather than passive, responding directly to events as they occur rather than passively waiting to 'speak when they're spoken to'.

Since such objects are self-contained units with a well-defined interface to the rest of the system which does not involve the direct use of shared data, it is an attractive idea to distribute the objects making up the system across a number of machines in a transparent way that makes it irrelevant whether the objects are located on the same machine or on different nodes of a distributed system. This section looks at some of the distributed object frameworks in common use that make this possible. Such frameworks are often referred to as **middleware**, as they occupy a position between applications and the underlying network services. It is important to realise that this section just gives a brief snapshot of some current technologies; rapid change in the range of accepted and established technologies is characteristic in this field at the moment.

One of the most important things that the frameworks described in this section have in common is a **naming service** of some sort, which allows clients to discover how to access the resources they require. Facilities like RPC and RMI rely on clients knowing where their resources are located, and the middleware systems described in this section build higher-level facilities by making the process of resource location as transparent and flexible as possible.

9.6.1 CORBA

CORBA (the Common Object Request Broker Architecture) is the oldest and most well-established of the technologies described in this section. It is defined by the OMG (Object Management Group), a consortium formed in 1989 by many of the major companies in the field, including IBM, Apple and Sun. The first CORBA standard was published in 1991.

CORBA was designed (like RPC) to satisfy the needs of heterogeneous systems comprising nodes based on a variety of hardware platforms, operating systems and communications systems. It is based around the use of an Object Request Broker (ORB) to connect applications to the services they require. The basic model

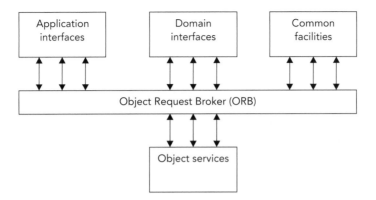

Figure 9.14 CORBA architecture.

underlying CORBA (the OMA, or Object Management Architecture) is illustrated in Figure 9.14.

The role of the ORB is to manage communications between clients and the objects they wish to use. It uses a protocol called IIOP (Internet Inter-ORB Protocol) which is layered on top of TCP/IP. There are four major categories of object that communicate via the ORB:

- **Object services**. These are common services which are required by most distributed programs. They include the Naming Service, which locates relevant objects based on their names, and the Trading Service, which locates objects based on their properties.

- **Common facilities**. These are also common services, but more application-specific than object services. For example, the Distributed Document Component Facility (DDCF) provides a common document model that allows spreadsheets to be linked into word-processed documents. It thus fulfils a similar role to OLE (Object Linking and Embedding) in older versions of Windows.

- **Domain interfaces**. These are oriented towards specific application domains; for example PDM (Product Data Management) for the manufacturing industry.

- **Application interfaces**. These are application-specific interfaces which, unlike the other categories described above, are not standardised. However, application interfaces that are sufficiently general and useful might end up migrating into one of the other categories.

The aim of CORBA is to hide information about object location, implementation, and the communication mechanism being used. When a CORBA object is created an **object reference** is returned which is used by the ORB to locate the corresponding object. These references are **opaque**, in that they contain no meaningful information that the client can use or modify. They can however be stored in files or databases for later use by converting them into equally opaque strings; that is, they are **persistent**. Objects references are usually created by **object factories** which manufacture new objects or by a **lookup service** such as the Naming Service, which finds an existing object.

When an object is created, the client is given a client-side stub known as a **proxy** which is used to marshal and unmarshal parameters and communicate with the remote object. The proxy can also report events generated by the remote object to the client, where the remote object 'pushes' an event notification via an event channel to its clients. The client-side stub can then report the event by raising an exception, by calling a client-side callback function, or by sending a Windows event to the client thread's event queue.

CORBA is intended to be language-independent and platform-independent, so in some ways it is similar to RPC's XDR; it needs to be able to specify data types and object interfaces in a way that is not dependent on any particular language or hardware platform. A language called IDL (Interface Definition Language) is used to specify the properties of CORBA objects in a portable way. Special compilers are used to convert IDL specifications into Java, C++, or any one of a variety of different languages. IDL specifications essentially fulfil the same role as Java interfaces; they specify the behaviour that an object is guaranteed to provide without providing any information about how this behaviour is actually implemented.

CORBA also supports a Dynamic Invocation Interface (DII) which allows you discover objects without having to know their names. An **interface repository** is used to hold interface specifications; a client can get a particular interface from the repository and get information about the methods it provides and the parameters it requires. It can then use this information to construct a call to a method of the remote object.

9.6.2   JINI

Jini is a Java-specific object framework implemented on top of Java's RMI facilities. The name is not an acronym, although it has been suggested that it stands for 'Jini Is Not Initials'. Jini is based around the idea of **federations** of services (devices and software components), where services can join or leave a particular federation as necessary. Services communicate using a **service protocol** defined as a set of RMI-based Java interfaces. Some standard service protocols are essential to the Jini infrastructure, but the design is open-ended so that new service protocols can be defined for specific purposes.

The **lookup service** is a central component of any Jini system. What a lookup service does is to map a particular interface to a set of objects that implement that interface. Additional descriptive entries can be associated with the services listed by the lookup service; for example, a request for a printer might result in a list of available printer services together with descriptions of their capabilities (resolution, speed, colour capabilities and so on). Requesting a particular service from this list will then load a **proxy object** into the client system, as shown in Figure 9.15. The proxy object handles all the communication with the remote object. Bear in mind that a Java object encapsulates both code and data; loading an object can involve downloading code as well as data. The code will be executed under the control of a **security manager** to prevent potentially dangerous operations from being performed on the client machine.

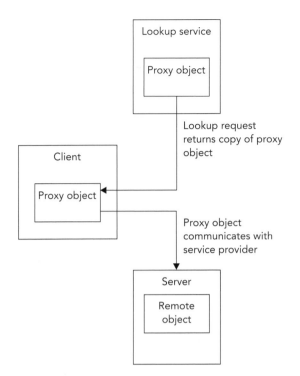

Figure 9.15 Jini service invocation.

Access to Jini services is generally based on **leases**. A lease entitles you to use the service for a particular period of time. It may also give you exclusive access to the service, where no one else will be able to use that particular service until you release it, or non-exclusive access, which allows the same resource to be shared concurrently with others.

A proxy object can simply pass everything to the remote object in the same way that a stub in RPC or RMI does (a **thin proxy**), or it can do some local processing on the client node before passing a request to the remote object (a **fat proxy**). For example, a proxy might validate parameter values locally before passing them to the remote object, giving more responsiveness at the client end (no waiting for a remote server to tell you that a value is out of range) and less loading at the service end (no need to validate parameters sent by the client). This provides a lot of flexibility to distributed system designers; the processing in a service can be divided between the proxy and the remote object in any convenient way. Proxies can also create local user interfaces; for example, a Jini-enabled printer might supply a proxy which displays a dialog box, allowing the user to choose the resolution, colour depth, paper size and so on. The proxy can then supply the user's chosen settings to the printer whenever the client wishes to print anything.

A service can register itself by using the **discovery** protocol to locate a lookup service. It can then use the **join** protocol to upload a proxy object to the lookup service together with any additional descriptive entries for the service. If a lookup service is already known then a direct TCP connection can be established to the relevant node, but if not a multicast UDP request is used to find one, as explained in the next chapter. Lookup services use a well-known port number (4160) so that clients that initially have no access to any Jini services can gain access to an initial service, although this is hidden in a Java class called LookupDiscovery which manages all this automatically.

Since the lookup service is itself a Jini service, a proxy object for the lookup service (a **registrar**) will be loaded into the client system when the initial contact is made with the lookup service. This proxy object will implement the **join** protocol which allows a new service to register itself with the lookup service. A lookup service can also register itself with a different lookup service, enabling lookup services to be distributed in the same way as any other service.

9.6.3 COM, DCOM AND .NET

COM (the Common Object Model) and DCOM (Distributed COM) are mechanisms developed by Microsoft which are heavily used throughout Windows. COM was briefly described in Chapter 4. Like CORBA and Jini, it relies on the use of interface specifications to define the properties of the objects it manages. DCOM is a natural extension of this idea, using the COM runtime system to act as a proxy on the client and server, as shown in Figure 9.16.

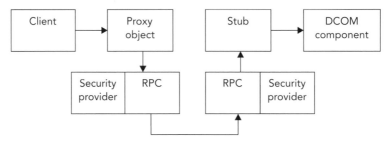

Figure 9.16 DCOM architecture.

COM and DCOM objects are identified using globally unique 128-bit identifiers. These are referred to as **class identifiers** (CLSIDs) and they are generated when a component is created, using information such as the time of day and the node's Ethernet MAC address to ensure uniqueness. CLSIDs are stored in the registry on the node where they are located and identify the file containing the implementation of the class. A remote DCOM object can be created by directing a request to a specific node if the client node has an entry in its local registry giving the CLSID and the corresponding remote node, or it can be done by looking up the location of the object on the network domain controller or by using a naming service such as Microsoft's Active Directory service. The remote node creates a process to execute the DCOM object and returns a proxy which the client uses to access the remote object. DCOM objects can also return proxies to other DCOM objects, which may or may not be on the same node. Like files in a filesystem, DCOM objects can have associated access rights which determine which users of a system can access them.

Like CORBA, DCOM uses an IDL (Microsoft IDL, or MIDL) to define the interfaces supported by the objects it manages. Unlike CORBA, the IDL is not compiled into a high-level language like Java or C++, but into a binary interface which is essentially a table of pointers to the functions that implement the methods required by the interface, similar to the table of file operations that a device driver provides.

COM uses reference counting to determine when objects are no longer required, but failures can occur in distributed systems. Each server 'pings' its clients at two-minute intervals, sending them an 'are you still there?' message. If a client fails to respond to three consecutive pings, the server assumes that the client has shut down and that it no longer requires the object. To avoid large numbers of 'ping' messages and their responses overloading the communications subsystem, the ping messages for a particular client system are grouped into a 'ping set' which is sent as a single message.

The main problem with COM and DCOM is that they are Microsoft-specific solutions which are not supported on other platforms. They have also been developed on an *ad hoc* basis from earlier interprocess communication technologies (DDE and OLE) with new features bolted on to existing features, which means that there are often several mutually incompatible ways to do the same thing. Nevertheless, the sheer size of the Windows market means that COM and DCOM are more widely used than any other distributed object system.

More recently, Microsoft has released its **.Net** platform, which uses industry-standard protocols to make objects available as **web services**. The .Net platform compiles objects written in any one of a variety of languages into a common intermediate language (Microsoft Intermediate Language, or MSIL) which is similar in nature to the bytecodes used by the Java Virtual Machine. This provides platform independence for .Net binaries. Each object is described by an XML (extended markup language) document which can be registered with a **discovery service** to allow clients to locate the objects they require. Another standard protocol (SOAP, the Simple Object Access Protocol) is used to transfer XML documents via HTTP connections. The discovery service is another standard (UDDI, the Universal Description, Discovery and Integration standard) which acts as an XML-based distributed registry.

Question 9.6   Why do all the systems described here use interfaces rather than the actual classes to define the types of remote objects?

9.7 ❑ SUMMARY

This chapter has looked at ways of increasing the scale of computer systems by using multiple processors within a single machine and also by harnessing the combined power of a set of networked machines to share the load of file storage and processing power between machines. To some extent this is getting away from the subject of operating systems, since middleware like CORBA and Jini is implemented as a set of user-level servers rather than being anything to do with the system kernel or device drivers. However, much of what was talked about in earlier chapters would be implemented in this way in a microkernel-based operating system. To some extent it is all a matter of where you choose to draw the dividing line between the operating system and user software.

Networking is implemented using device drivers, so it is usually regarded as part of the operating system, whereas web servers and middleware are usually not; they are just daemons (services) started before any user processes so that they are always available. However, Windows relies heavily on COM; many of its system management functions are implemented as COM components rather than being integrated into the kernel. This is done to provide flexibility and to make it easier to upgrade these components without having to upgrade the entire kernel. Adopting a modular design like this makes good sense, but it all makes it harder to draw a line between the operating system and user software.

The middleware technologies described here are still in their infancy and evolving rapidly, so it remains to be seen which will become dominant. CORBA is long-established but based on a set of special-purpose protocols; it is also more difficult to use than the alternatives, largely due to the need to produce language-neutral IDL specifications and then match them up with language-specific implementations. Jini is simpler to use, but it is limited by the fact that it is specific to the Java platform. COM and DCOM are similarly limited to Microsoft systems.

The newest technology among those described here is .Net. There is some suspicion about .Net because it is another Microsoft product, even though it is based on a number of open standards. At the moment, development tools and implementations of the MSIL runtime only exist for Microsoft systems, and to be really successful it will be necessary for tools and MSIL implementations to be made freely available for other platforms, particularly for open-source ones such as Linux.

9.8 ❑ ADDITIONAL RESOURCES

The Intel specification for multiprocessor systems is given by [7], and the IOAPIC data sheet [8] also contains some relevant material. Cache coherence issues are described by Dubois and Thakker [3]. Mudge *et al.* [9] discuss the use of multiple buses in multiprocessor systems, while Sawchuk *et al.* [16] describe optical crossbar switches and their potential impact on multiprocessor machines. Feng [5] provides a survey of interconnection networks including Omega networks and others.

Networking issues, including all the networking protocols discussed in this chapter, are described in publicly available discussion documents called **RFCs** (Requests For Comments), many of which have been adopted as standards. You should definitely read these if you are interested in the details.

NFS is described by Comer [2] and defined in RFC 1094 [20]. Hertel [6] gives a good detailed description of CIFS, and specifications are available for using NetBIOS over TCP/IP as RFC 1001 [10] and RFC 1002 [11]. RPC and XDR are also described in Comer [2], and the full specifications are also available. RPC is defined in RFC 1057 [19] and XDR in RFC 1014 [21]. A tutorial on RMI is given by Wollrath and Waldo [26].

Tanenbaum and van Steen [22] is an excellent book covering many of the issues in this chapter, including a number of middleware systems. The October 1998 issue of *Communications of the ACM* was a special issue on CORBA, and includes a good overview by Siegel [17]. Siegel has also edited a book on CORBA [18]. If you want the gory details, the CORBA specification is available from the OMG [12]. Waldo [24] gives an overview of Jini, and there is a book by Edwards [4] which explains how Jini works in much more detail. Again, the gory details are available: the Jini specification is detailed in Arnold *et al.* [1].

Rogerson [15] is a good description of how COM works, while Thai and Oram [23] describe how COM has been extended into DCOM. The workings of the .Net framework are described by Watkins *et al.* [25], who were involved in the development of .Net, and also by Richter [14]. Another book by Prosise [13] is more oriented towards .Net development. There is also a lot of material available at Microsoft's website (http://msdn.microsoft.com/netframework/).

9.9 ❑ GLOSSARY

application protocol a protocol used to enable two specific applications to communicate with each other across a network.

at-most-once operation an operation which must be performed once or not at all, which will produce an erroneous situation if executed more than once.

bus snooping in a multiprocessor machine, a mechanism for ensuring cache coherence by monitoring activity on the address and data buses generated by other processors.

cache coherence in multiprocessor machines, the problem of ensuring that the data held in each processor's cache is consistent with the data held in the caches of the other processors.

CGI script (Common Gateway Interface script) a program executed by a web server to produce dynamic content.

CIFS (Common Internet File System) an Internet-based filesystem derived from Microsoft's earlier SMB protocol.

COM (Component Object Model) a mechanism developed by Microsoft and DEC which is used extensively on Windows systems to allow communication between objects which may be located in separate processes.

communications stub in RPC, the part of a stub which is responsible for communicating a request across the network.

connection-oriented protocol a protocol involving a sequence of requests and responses.

connectionless protocol a protocol where each message is treated as a separate transaction from any other requests.

cookie a token identifying a transaction which allows later transactions to be related back to it.

CORBA (Common Object Request Broker Architecture) a protocol which defines a standard interface mechanism for accessing objects in a distributed system.

DCOM (Component Object Model) an extension of COM developed by Microsoft to deal with objects which are potentially distributed across the nodes in a distributed system.

directory-based protocol in multiprocessor systems, a mechanism for achieving cache coherence by using a directory to keep track of which processors have cached copies of which memory locations.

discovery protocol in Jini, the protocol by which clients discover the range of services available.

fat proxy a proxy which performs a substantial amount of local processing before passing a request to the remote object.

federation of services in Jini, a set of distributed objects which collaborate to provide a particular set of services.

garbage collection the reclamation of resources that can no longer be referenced.

HTTP (Hyper-Text Transfer Protocol) a standard Internet protocol used to transfer web pages and related items between machines.

idempotent operation an operation that can safely be performed several times, which leaves the state of the system unchanged when performed a second time.

IDL (Interface Definition Language) a language used to specify the interface between objects for use in a distributed object system such as CORBA.

interface a specification of the services provided by an object which does not define how those services are implemented.

interface stub in RPC, the part of a stub which is responsible for parameter marshalling.

interprocessor interrupt in a multiprocessor system, an interrupt sent from one processor to another.

invalidation marking a cache entry as being out-of-date (invalid).

timestamp a value used to indicate the time at which a message was sent.

Jini a Java-specific distributed object management system.

join protocol in Jini, the protocol by which a proxy is loaded to access a remote service.

lookup service a means of discovering available objects which implement a particular interface.

magic cookie a cookie whose value is encoded in a way that is meaningless to its recipient.

marshalling organising parameters for a remote procedure call into a form that can be transmitted across a network.

middleware a layer of software which acts as an intermediary between an application and a network.

mount protocol the protocol used by NFS for mounting remote filesystems.

name resolution the process of finding the object that a name refers to.

naming service a service providing a mechanism for name resolution in a distributed system.

NBNS (NetBIOS Naming Service) a mechanism used in SMB and CIFS for name resolution.

.Net Microsoft's cross-platform successor to COM and DCOM.

NetBEUI (NetBIOS Extended User Interface) a transport protocol used to transfer NetBIOS requests and replies across a network.

NetBIOS an API providing a set of commands for transmitting data between nodes on a network.

NFS (Network File System) a stateless connectionless distributed filesystem developed by Sun Microsystems.

node an individual machine in a distributed system.

opportunistic lock in CIFS, a file lock granted to allow increased efficiency when there are no other users of a file.

ORB (Object Request Broker) in CORBA, the mechanism used to connect applications to the services they require.

persistent object an object which can be saved in a file or database and restored later.

port mapper in RPC, a service to enable clients to discover the port to use for a particular remote procedure call.

reentrant code code which can be safely executed by more than one thread at a time without the actions performed by any thread having any effect on the behaviour of any of the other threads.

registry server in RMI, a name resolution service which allows objects to be located on a network.

RMI (Remote Method Invocation) the Java-specific equivalent of RPC, allowing methods of remote objects to be called.

RPC (Remote Procedure Call) a mechanism for invoking a computation on a remote node of a distributed system.

security manager in Java, a mechanism used to check that untrusted objects loaded from remote sites can be granted permission to perform potentially unsafe operations.

service protocol in Jini, a set of RMI interfaces defining a service.

SMB (Server Message Block) a protocol to enable file and printer sharing on a network, or a command defined by this protocol.

SMP (Symmetric Multi-Processor) a multiprocessor system where there is no special processor acting as a 'master' processor which is responsible for executing operating system code, where all processors are equally able to execute operating system code.

spin lock in multiprocessor systems, a mechanism for ensuring mutual exclusion between different processors.

stateless protocol a protocol which treats each request as an independent transaction unrelated to any previous transactions.

stub a proxy used in RPC and RMI to invoke a remote procedure or method.

TCP/IP TCP over IP, the stream-oriented reliable protocol suite used on the Internet comprising TCP as the transport protocol supported by IP as the network protocol.

Telnet the standard application protocol used for remote logins and terminal emulation on the Internet.

thin proxy a proxy which performs little or no local processing before passing the request to the remote object.

UNC (Uniform Naming Convention) a Windows naming convention that can be used to identify a file on a remote file server.

uniprocessor a computer system with a single processor.

VFS (Virtual File System) on Linux systems, a filesystem which provides unified access to files which may be stored on different devices or different machines.

vnode on Linux systems, the VFS equivalent of an inode specifying a server identifier and an inode number on that server.

WINS (Windows Naming Service) Microsoft's implementation of NBNS, a name which is now used commonly as a synonym for NBNS.

write-back cache a cache where information is written back to memory lazily, when it is necessary to do so.

write-though cache a cache where updates are written to memory immediately.

XDR (External Data Representation) in RPC, a data representation which is portable between different machine architectures.

9.10 ❑ REFERENCES

[1] Arnold, K., O'Sullivan, B., Scheifler, R. W., Waldo, J. and Wollrath, A. *The Jini Specification.* Addison-Wesley (1999)

[2] Comer, D. E. *Internetworking with TCP/IP Vol III: Client–Server Programming and Applications.* Prentice Hall (1996)

[3] Dubois, M. and Thakkar, S. Cache architectures in tightly coupled multiprocessors. *IEEE Computer*, **23**(6) (Jun 1990), 9–11

[4] Edwards, W. K. *Core Jini*. Prentice Hall (2000)

[5] Feng, T. A survey of interconnection networks. *IEEE Computer*, **14**(12) (Dec 1981), 12–27

[6] Hertel, C. *Implementing CIFS, the Common Internet File System*. Prentice Hall (2003)

[7] Intel Corporation. *Multiprocessor Specification*. Document no. 242016-006 (May 1997). Available online at http://www.intel.com/

[8] Intel Corporation. *82093A I/O Advanced Programmable Interrupt Controller*. Document no. 290566-001 (May 1996). Available online at http://www.intel.com/

[9] Mudge, T. N., Hayes, J. P. and Winsor, D. C. Multiple bus architectures. *IEEE Computer*, **20**(6) (Jun 1987), 42–48

[10] NetBIOS Working Group. *Protocol Standard for a NetBIOS Service on a TCP/UDP Transport: Concepts and Methods*. RFC 1001 (Mar 1987). Available online at http://www.rfc-editor.org/

[11] NetBIOS Working Group. *Protocol Standard for a NetBIOS Service on a TCP/UDP Transport: Detailed Specifications*. RFC 1002 (Mar 1987). Available online at http://www.rfc-editor.org/

[12] Object Management Group. *The Common Object Request Broker Architecture: Core Specification*. OMG document formal/02-12-02 (2002). Available online at http://www.omg.org/docs/formal/02-12-02.pdf

[13] Prosise, J. *Programming Microsoft .NET*. Microsoft Press (2002)

[14] Richter, J. *Applied Microsoft .NET Framework Programming*. Microsoft Press (2002)

[15] Rogerson, D. *Inside COM*. Microsoft Press (1997)

[16] Sawchuk, A. A., Jenkins, B. K. and Raghavendra, C. S. Optical crossbar networks. *IEEE Computer*, **20**(6) (Jun 1987), 50–60

[17] Siegel, J. CORBA and the OMA in enterprise computing. *Communications of the ACM*, **41**(10) (Oct 1998), 37–43

[18] Siegel, J. (ed.) *CORBA 3 Fundamentals and Programming*. John Wiley & Sons (2000)

[19] Sun Microsystems. *RPC: Remote Procedure Call Protocol Specification: Version 2*. RFC 1057 (Jun 1988). Available online at http://www.rfc-editor.org/

[20] Sun Microsystems. *NFS: Network File System Protocol Specification*. RFC 1094 (Mar 1989). Available online at http://www.rfc-editor.org/

[21] Sun Microsystems. *XDR: External Data Representation Standard*. RFC 1014 (Jun 1987). Available online at http://www.rfc-editor.org/

[22] Tanenbaum, A. S. and van Steen, M. *Distributed Systems: Principles and Paradigms*. Prentice Hall (2002)

[23] Thai, L. T. and Oram, A. *Learning DCOM*. O'Reilly & Associates (1999)

[24] Waldo, J. The Jini architecture for network-centric computing. *Communications of the ACM*, **42**(7) (Jul 1999), 76–82

[25] Watkins, D., Hammond, M. and Abrams, B. *Programming in the .NET Environment*. Addison-Wesley (2002)

[26] Wollrath, A. and Waldo, J. RMI. In Campione, M. (ed.), *The Java Tutorial Continued: The Rest of the JDK*. Addison-Wesley (1999). Available online at http://java.sun.com/docs/books/tutorial/rmi/

NETWORKING
TECHNOLOGIES

Networking is fundamental to most computer systems. Thanks to the growth of the Internet, practically every machine in the world can be connected to any other machine. To a large extent, computers have stopped being computing devices and have instead become communications devices. The previous chapter explored some of the ways in which networking can be used to distribute storage and processing requirements across a network of machines.

Before going any further we need to look in more detail at the communication technologies that a modern network relies on, and the limitations that it has. This chapter covers the basics of the networking technologies that are currently in common use, concentrating on Internet protocols and the use of Ethernet as the underlying network infrastructure.

10.1 ❑ NETWORKING

In the last decade or so, the thing that has undoubtedly changed the way we use computers more than anything else has been the spread of computer networks, and in particular the growth of the Internet. Connecting computers together is nothing new, but it only used to be seen in the context of 'satellite' computers connecting to a central **mainframe** system, as in Figure 10.1.

The advent of networking technologies such as Ethernet has allowed any computer on a network to connect to any other for such purposes as transferring files between machines. Rather than having a mainframe as a central hub around which all else revolves, you can in many cases use a decentralised network of

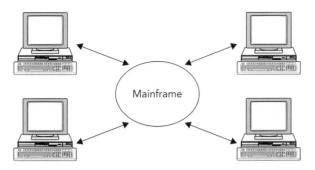

Figure 10.1 A mainframe with multiple terminals.

computers to provide the same facilities at much lower cost and with greater capabilities for expansion and adaptation.

Mainframes were used to provide central services: file storage, printing services, archiving and backup services, and software services such as database management. In a networked environment, these services can be devolved to lower-cost machines acting as dedicated **servers**: file servers, print servers, database servers, and so on. There is no longer a central machine which can bring everything else to a grinding halt if it crashes. Powerful machines are still needed for use as database servers and other systems with heavy processing requirements. However, a database server can be dedicated to the purpose, rather than having to provide all the other services of a mainframe as well.

The next step is **internetworking**. A **router** (or **gateway** system) which is connected to two or more separate networks allows messages from a machine on one network to be routed to a machine on one of the other networks, as shown in Figure 10.2. A collection of networks such as this is known as an **internet**, and

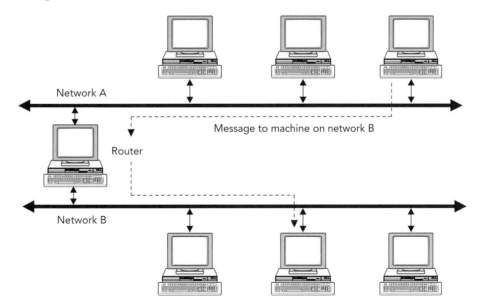

Figure 10.2 Internetwork routing.

inevitably as different networks became connected to internets, the whole thing came together as single global internet (usually called 'the Internet', with a capital 'I' to distinguish it from other, non-global, internets). Thanks to the Internet, practically every networked machine in the world is connected to every other.

In order to allow different types of network to be interconnected, additional protocol layers are needed to insulate programs from the differences in the underlying hardware. The protocol described in this chapter is the standard protocol used on the Internet, generally referred to as TCP/IP. This is in fact a suite consisting of a number of several separate but related protocols, and I will describe it in more detail later.

TCP/IP provides reliability and flexibility by using a technique known as **packet switching**. Long messages are broken up into smaller **packets** which are then routed independently to their intended destination. This means that there is no need for a point-to-point connection to be established between the source of the message and the destination machine (which is what happens in a conventional telephone call). If there are multiple routes available to the destination, different packets might be sent along different routes. This allows the load on individual network nodes to be balanced, with packets being diverted away from nodes that are heavily congested with network traffic. However, this also means that some packets might take longer to arrive than others, and there is also no guarantee that the packets will arrive in the order in which they were sent. The implications of this will be considered further in the next chapter.

10.1.1   IP ADDRESSES, DOMAIN NAMES AND URLS

As mentioned in the previous chapter, machines are identified by unique IP (Internet Protocol) addresses. For machines connected to the Internet, these need to be globally unique, and because of this there is a central authority (IANA, the Internet Assigned Numbers Authority) which is responsible for coordinating the use of IP addresses to ensure uniqueness. The version of IP that is still most widely used (IPv4) uses 32-bit addresses to identify machines, although a newer version of IP (IPv6) extends this to 128-bit addresses to accommodate the rise in the number of networked devices. It is rapidly getting to the point where not only computers, but also toasters and washing machines, will need their own IP addresses; however, I will only consider the original version of IP (IPv4) here.

IP addresses are traditionally written in 'dotted quad' notation, with four decimal values between 0 and 255 separated by dots, e.g. 192.173.10.125. IPv6 uses eight groups of four hexadecimal digits separated by colons, e.g. 4A36:5BFF:9017:38F2:7A77:4285:F3B0:178E. These addresses are obviously going to be much harder to memorise!

IP addresses are very rarely used by humans as a way of identifying machines. People find readable **domain names** like www.acme.com easier to remember and use, so there needs to be a way of **resolving** (looking up) a domain name to find the corresponding IP address. This is done using a **domain name server** (DNS). A name like www.acme.com indicates that it is somewhere in the com **domain** (commercial companies, with no geographical specification) and within that to acme.com, the subdomain of the particular company. Within that subdomain, the final prefix www again narrows it down to one specific machine (probably a machine acting as the company web server, since the www prefix is a commonly used convention to indicate a machine hosting a web server). The way that the DNS is used to map domain names to IP addresses is described in Section 10.3.4.

Exercise 10.1	Find out how to use the nslookup command on your system to map domain names to IP addresses. Try using it to look up the addresses of some different domain names around the world. Is there any pattern as to how IP addresses are organised, either geographically or by the organisation which uses them?

The World-Wide Web uses identifiers called **URL**s (Uniform Resource Locators) to provide a uniform notation for identifying individual resources anywhere in the world. An example of a URL is a name like http://www.acme.com/dir/file.html. This consists of the name of the protocol to be used to access the resource (in this case 'http', the Hypertext Transfer Protocol). The rest of the URL identifies the resource itself, which in the case of HTTP is the name of a specific file on a particular machine. For HTTP, the URL specifies the domain name or IP address of the target machine (the domain name www.acme.com in this case) and a name identifying the file on that machine (/dir/file.html in this case). The filenames follow the Unix conventions, even if they are being used to refer to files on non-Unix systems. There are many other possibilities; URLs are defined in full in RFC 1738 [1].

10.2 ❑ SOCKETS

From a programmer's point of view, the lowest level of access to network facilities is via the **socket** API. A socket is an endpoint for a network connection; it can be connected to a particular port on a machine elsewhere on the network, or even on the same machine. The socket API was originally developed for Unix systems at the University of California at Berkeley, but is now widely implemented (with minor variations) on other systems as well. The Windows socket implementation is commonly referred to as Winsock, and it adds a few features to the original design to support the event-driven programming style used by GUI-based Windows applications. Sockets are usually used for TCP/IP communication, but the API was designed in such a way that it could be used with other protocols as well. The description here concentrates on using sockets for TCP/IP.

Exercise 10.2	Find out what the differences are between Winsock and standard Berkeley sockets.

The model for using sockets to allow client applications to communicate with servers is similar to the way that the telephone system works. A client connects to a server by specifying the server's IP address and port number in much the same way as someone making a phone call dials the number of the person they want to speak to. A server waits for an incoming connection from a client application, which is just like waiting for a phone to ring. The server then accepts the connection, which is like picking up the phone. Once the connection has been accepted, the client and server can hold a conversation, and when the conversation finishes they both 'hang up' to break the connection.

A client wishing to communicate with a server must first of all create a socket using the socket API call. This can be either a TCP or a UDP socket, as specified by one of the parameters to socket. Next, it must establish a connection using the connect API call. This requires as a parameter a data structure which encapsulates the IP address and port number that the client wishes to connect to. Additional API calls provide several other useful operations; for example, gethostbyname translates a domain name like www.acme.com into the corresponding IP address, and getprotobyname translates the names of standard application protocols like 'http' into their well-known port numbers (port 80 in the case of HTTP).

The connect call returns an integer handle which identifies the stream in exactly the same way as the file handle which is returned when the open system call is used to open a file. On Unix systems, it makes no difference to the client program whether the stream is connected to a file or to a remote TCP port. Once a connection has been successfully established using connect, the client can send and receive data. UDP connections use send and recv system calls to send and receive datagrams. For TCP connections, data is transferred using read and write system calls, in exactly the same way as reading and writing any other I/O stream. Afterwards, the close system call closes the socket in exactly the same way as a file would be closed (although the Winsock implementation calls this function closesocket rather than close since file and socket operations on Windows systems are not implemented identically, as they are on Unix).

A server is slightly different from a client, as it must listen to a socket until an incoming connection request is received from a client. The socket is initially created in the same way as for a client, but it is then bound to a particular IP address and port number using the bind API call. The IP address is required because a single machine can have multiple IP addresses; for example, a machine acting as a router between two networks will have a separate network adapter for each network that it is connected to, and different IP addresses on each of those networks.

Standard protocols like HTTP and Telnet are assigned **well-known** (i.e. standardised) port numbers by IANA, the Internet Assigned Numbers Authority. For example, the well-known port for HTTP is port 80, while Telnet uses port 23. Non-standard protocols just have to pick a port that is not already in use, and clients have to know which port this is to be able to connect to the server. Ports 1024 and above should normally be used; in fact, most systems will prevent anyone but the superuser (system administrator) from using ports with numbers below 1024.

The next step is to call listen to start the server listening for incoming connections. This API function specifies the number of pending connections that will be queued before any further connection requests are denied. Finally, an incoming connection is accepted by calling accept. What accept does is to wait for an incoming connection and then create a new socket that will be used for that connection. From this point on, the server behaves just like a client application; it uses read and write (or send and recv) to talk to the client, and then closes the socket when the conversation is over. Since this is a different socket from the one that clients try to connect to, the original socket is still open, so the server can go back to accept the next incoming connection request. Figure 10.3 illustrates this sequence of events.

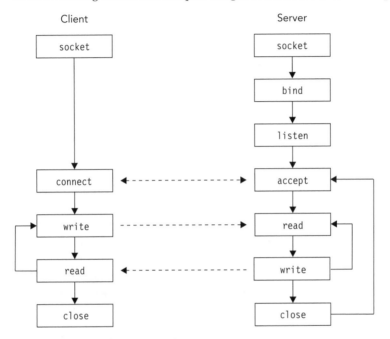

Figure 10.3 Basic client and server operation.

10.2.1 NETWORK BYTE ORDER

One minor complication arises when transferring multi-byte data items. For example, an integer is normally stored as a 32-bit (4 byte) value. Different machines store the individual bytes for such values in either 'big-endian' or 'little-endian' order. The terms were borrowed from the people in the story *Gulliver's Travels* who went to war over whether boiled eggs should be broken at the big end or the little end; big-endian means that the 'big end' (most significant byte) comes first, whereas little-endian means that the 'little end' (least significant byte) comes first. For example, Sun workstations use 'big-endian' ordering, whereas Pentium machines use 'little-endian' ordering. Thus the hexadecimal value 0x12345678 would be stored as the four byte sequence 0x12, 0x34, 0x56, 0x78 on a Sun workstation, but as the sequence 0x78, 0x56, 0x34, 0x12 on a Pentium machine. To avoid misinterpretation, a standard **network byte ordering** is used for all multi-byte data sent over a network. All multi-byte values must be translated to and from network byte ordering before and after transmission using API functions such as `htonl` (host-to-network, longword) and `ntohl` (network-to-host, longword) Network byte ordering is actually the big-endian ordering as used by Sun workstations, so functions like `htonl` and `ntohl` don't actually do anything on big-endian machines (but you should still use them for portability reasons).

Exercise 10.3   Devise an experiment which will show whether the machine you are using is big-endian or little-endian.

10.2.2   MULTITHREADED SERVERS

This basic server design described above only allows the server to deal with a single client connection at a time. If someone has already connected to the server, you will be put in a queue of waiting connection attempts, and your connection will only be established when all the previous waiting connections have been dealt with. This is like being put on hold when you try to telephone a computer supplier's helpline (although at least the server won't play muzak for you while you're waiting!). An **iterative server** design like this is probably acceptable for services which only take a short, fixed amount of time to complete, but most services take relatively long and unpredictable amounts of time to complete. For example, the time required to transfer a file from one machine to another will depend on the size of the file; transferring a short file might take a fraction of a second, but a large file might take several minutes. To avoid bottlenecks when a service takes a long time to complete, a **multithreaded server** design is normally used instead, as shown in Figure 10.4. A multithreaded server works by accepting

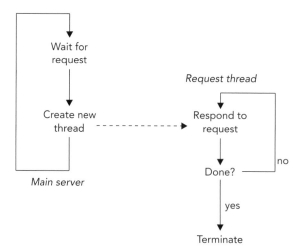

Figure 10.4 A multithreaded server.

connections on its assigned socket, but rather than dealing with the connection directly, it creates a separate thread to deal with the connection (the read, write and close sequence in the server shown in Figure 10.3). The main server thread then goes back to wait for another request while the earlier connection is serviced by the separate thread. This is similar to a telephone switchboard, where the switchboard operator connects you to someone on a separate extension who can deal with your problem, and then hangs up and waits for another call.

Of course it is possible to overwhelm the machine's capacity by sending it more requests than it can cope with. Faced with thousands of requests, the server would create thousands of threads to deal with them, which could easily grind the entire system to a halt. To avoid this problem, there is usually an upper limit on the number of simultaneous incoming connections that the server will accept. Most servers use a configuration file which defines details like this, so that it can be adjusted by the system administrator. Another way to deal with this is to create a fixed-size **pool** of threads when the server first starts up. Each thread in this pool will wait for a connection to be allocated to it, and it will then service the connection and go back to waiting for another connection. This is illustrated in Figure 10.5. When the main server receives an incoming request, it just passes it to any one of these threads which is not currently busy. If all the threads are busy, the incoming request is queued until one of the threads finishes serving an existing request and becomes free. This also has the advantage that the overheads involved in creating and destroying threads are avoided; the pool of threads is created once and for all when the server starts up.

There are many other features in the socket API, but the description above summarises the most important features. It is for example possible to use the select API call to check the status of one or more sockets to see if any incoming connection requests or data packets are available. This function can also specify a timeout value, which can be used to limit how long select will wait for something to happen before it gives up. It is also possible to send urgent messages (for example, requests to cancel a data transfer) using 'out-of-band' messages, which

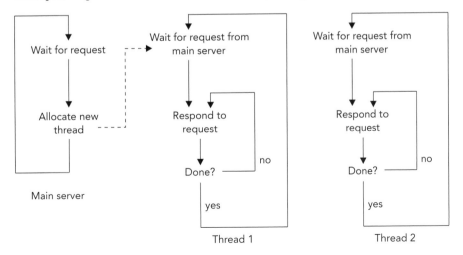

Figure 10.5 A thread pool.

will be delivered in preference to any other messages that may already have been sent.

10.2.3   A SIMPLE EXAMPLE IN JAVA

Java provides a number of standard classes for handling sockets, URLs and many other networking-related constructs. These classes encapsulate most of the hard work that is required when using the sockets API directly, and as a result a simple example can be written much more easily in Java than in most other languages. The following example implements a simple server and client. The idea is that the client will send a string such as 'world', and the server will respond by sending the traditional message 'Hello world!' to the client (or 'Hello John!' if the client sends the string 'John'). The client code is shown in Figure 10.6.

```java
import java.net.*;
import java.io.*;
public class Client {
   public static void main (String args[]) {
      try {
         Socket s = new Socket(args[0],2000);      // (1)
         InputStream  in = s.getInputStream();     // (2)
         OutputStream out= s.getOutputStream();
         String r = args[1] + "\n";                // (3)
         out.write(r.getBytes());
         int c;
         while ((c = in.read()) != -1) {           // (4)
            System.out.print((char)c);
         }
         s.close();                                // (5)
      }
      catch (Exception e) {                        // (6)
         System.out.println("Exception: " + e.getMessage());
      }
   }
}
```

Figure 10.6 Example Java client code.

The program requires two command line arguments: the server's domain name or IP address, and the string to be sent. The line marked (1) creates a TCP socket and connects it to port 2000 on the machine specified as the first command line argument. UDP sockets can be created using a separate class DatagramSocket. The two lines beginning at the line marked (2) get the input and output streams belonging to the socket. The two lines beginning at the line marked (3) create a string consisting of the second command line argument followed by a newline character. The characters in this string are then written to the stream. The loop beginning at line (4) reads characters one by one from the socket's input stream until the connection is closed (which is signified by reading the value –1). The socket is then closed on line (5). The lines beginning at (6) report any exceptions that might occur, such as a failure to connect to port 2000 on the specified machine.

```
import java.net.*;
import java.io.*;
public class Server {
   public static void main (String args[]) {
      try {
         ServerSocket a = new ServerSocket(2000);    // (1)
         while (true) {                              // (2)
            Socket s = a.accept();                   // (3)
            InputStream  in = s.getInputStream();
            OutputStream out= s.getOutputStream();
            out.write("Hello, ".getBytes());         // (4)
            int c;
            while ((c = in.read()) != '\n') {        // (5)
               out.write(c);
            }
            out.write('!');                          // (6)
            s.close();
         }
      }
      catch (Exception e) {
         System.out.println("Exception: " + e.getMessage());
      }
   }
}
```

Figure 10.7 Example Java server code.

The server code is shown in Figure 10.7. Line (1) creates a TCP server socket bound to port 2000 and then listens on it. Line (2) is the start of the server's main loop which accepts and responds to client requests. Line (3) accepts an incoming connection to the server socket and creates a new socket to handle the connection. As in the client code, it then gets the socket's input and output streams. The first part of the response is sent to the client at line (4), and the loop beginning at line (5) then echoes characters back to the client until a newline character is seen. Line (6) outputs the tail end of the response to the client and then closes the socket. The server will then loop back to wait for the next connection.

You can use this command to run the server as a background process on a Unix system:

```
java Server &
```

On a Windows system, you can start the server as a separate process like this:

```
start java Server
```

You can run the client program by typing something like this:

```
java Client 192.168.11.6 world
```

which will connect to port 2000 on the server whose IP address is 192.168.11.6 and send the string 'world'. The server should reply 'Hello, world!'.

Exercise 10.4	Try the example above to make sure it works as advertised.

You should compare the sequence of events in the client and server code shown here with the sequence of events shown in Figure 10.3. Many of the lower-level details are hidden by the Java socket classes; a ServerSocket encapsulates the socket/bind/listen part of the server's sequence, and a Socket encapsulates the socket/connect part of the client's sequence.

Project 10.1	Write a multithreaded server that accepts the name of a directory and produces a listing of the contents of that directory on the server system. Use Telnet as a client to test it.

10.3 ☐ TCP/IP

As mentioned earlier, TCP/IP is actually a suite of several different protocols. The name 'TCP/IP' means 'TCP over IP', and refers to the fact that the IP protocol is used for transferring TCP messages. The device drivers which deal with the various TCP/IP protocols are closely linked and arranged in layers, with higher protocol levels being implemented in terms of lower layers. The entire set of drivers is usually referred to as a **protocol stack** because of this layering. At the topmost level there are the **transport layer** protocols (TCP and UDP), which deal with port-to-port connections. These are implemented on top of the **network layer** protocol (IP), which transfers messages from one machine to another. This in turn is implemented on top of the **datalink layer** protocol, which is usually Ethernet. Above the transport layer is the **application layer**, which provides an application-specific protocol to allow a client and a server to understand one another. Telnet and HTTP are both examples of application protocols. There is also a **physical layer** below the datalink layer, which is concerned with the electrical properties of the physical cables used to connect machines together.

The way that networking protocols are implemented as a stack of drivers layered on top of each other is another example of the way that device drivers can use each other's facilities. Many drivers use other drivers to perform their work, rather than communicating directly with hardware; for example, the filesystem is implemented as a device driver, but it has to use the facilities provided by lower-level drivers for devices such as disks and CD-ROMs. However, the TCP/IP protocol stack is usually implemented as a single software module, rather than as a TCP module and a separate IP module, since IP is unlikely to be used in isolation. In fact, it is generally only possible for user processes to access facilities provided by the transport layer.

Question 10.1   What are the advantages and disadvantages of using a protocol stack comprising several layers of protocol rather than a single protocol layer?

From the point of view of each layer in the protocol, that layer on one machine appears to be talking directly to the corresponding layer on the other machine. The application layer appears to talk directly to the remote application layer, the transport layer appears to talk directly to the remote transport layer, the internet (IP) layer appears to talk directly to the remote network layer, and the data link (Ethernet) layer appears to talk directly to the remote data link layer. In fact, an application-layer message is packed into a series of TCP packets, which are wrapped up in IP datagrams, which are in turn wrapped up in Ethernet frames. The frames that arrive on the destination machine are unpacked to reveal the original IP datagram; the network layer unpacks the IP datagram to reveal a TCP packet; the transport layer unpacks and reassembles TCP packets to produce the original application-layer message. This is illustrated in Figure 10.8.

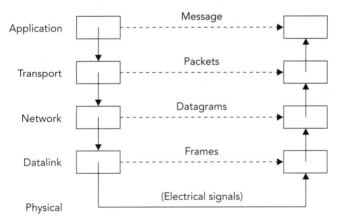

Figure 10.8 Protocol layering.

There are also several internal protocols that never manifest themselves at the application level. **ICMP** (Internet Control Message Protocol) is a protocol which you can think of as the IP layer's very own application protocol. It is used for control messages to test if a particular address is reachable, to measure routing delays, to report failures or congested routes, and so on. These messages are used to update the IP routing tables in each machine, among other things. They are generated directly by the IP layer and sent to the IP layer on the destination machine. When the datagram is unpacked at the destination, a message type field in the header of the data identifies it as a TCP packet, a UDP datagram, an ICMP control message or whatever. The IP layer uses the type field to choose the appropriate way to deal with the datagram's contents.

10.3.1 ETHERNET

As an example of networking technology, I'm going to describe Ethernet, which is probably the commonest networking technology in use today. Ethernet was originally developed at Xerox's Palo Alto Research Center, as were many other technological innovations that we take for granted today, including the mouse and window-based graphical user interfaces. Astonishingly, Xerox failed to capitalise on all this wealth of innovation, leaving it to companies such as Apple and Microsoft to introduce these ideas to the mass market.

Ethernet is a **broadcast** medium which allows any machine to broadcast a message which will be received by every other machine on the network, as illustrated in Figure 10.9. It is based on a high-speed serial connection using connections such as coaxial cable or twisted-pair wiring, with transmission rates up to 100 Mbps (megabits per second) using twisted-pair cables. Faster versions of Ethernet are also becoming available using fibre-optic technology.

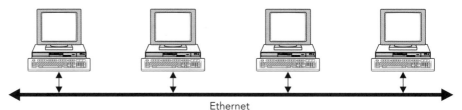

Ethernet

Figure 10.9 Ethernet topology.

With a centralised mainframe system, each satellite computer had its own separate communications link. In modern networks, there is no central system. With Ethernet, a single network cable is shared by several machines, so no single machine can be allowed to monopolise the cable for any length of time. Data is therefore sent in **frames** of up to 1500 bytes of data at a time, with longer messages being broken up into multiple frames. Each frame also includes a header specifying the source and destination address and the frame type, and there is a 32-bit checksum at the end to allow the frame's integrity to be verified. Each Ethernet controller card is manufactured with a globally unique 48-bit address, known as its MAC (Media Access Control) address, so that you can send a message to any machine as long as you know the MAC address of its Ethernet card.

Sending a message is handled by the associated Ethernet device driver. To send a frame, you first of all have to monitor the connection until the line is idle (no data is being transmitted). When the line is idle, you can start transmitting. This is known as **Carrier Sense with Multiple Access (CSMA)**. The frame that you transmit is received by every machine on the network (including your own), but only the intended recipient will take any notice, based on the destination address in the frame header. The frame also includes the sender's address to enable the recipient to send a reply back.

There is nothing to stop two or more machines monitoring the line, detecting that it is idle, and starting to transmit at the same time. If this happens, a **collision** is said to occur. The data will be corrupted, since if one machine transmits 0 and another transmits 1, the result might be seen as either 0 or 1. Each machine receives its own frames as they are being transmitted, and if the frame it receives is not identical to the frame it is transmitting, it backs off (stops transmitting) and tries again later. Thus, Ethernet is said to use **CSMA with Collision Detection (CSMA/CD)**. Livelock could occur if all machines were to back off, wait for the same amount of time and then try again, producing another collision and another backoff. To prevent this happening, each machine delays for a random time, up to a maximum delay specified in the Ethernet standard. If a second collision occurs, the maximum delay is doubled, and each subsequent collision redoubles the maximum delay. The randomness of the delays chosen will eventually break the livelock. Collisions are of course more likely if the network is heavily loaded, in which case throughput will decrease as the network load increases, but the network should never stop working entirely. This type of gradual failure is known as **graceful degradation**.

Wireless networking is also becoming increasingly popular, especially for mobile devices such as laptops and handheld computers. A number of standards have emerged; Bluetooth is a standard for short-range communication between devices such as handheld computers, mobile phones, digital cameras, and other portable devices. The IEEE (Institute of Electrical and Electronic Engineers) has also developed a set of standards known as 802.11 which are commonly used for wireless networking on laptops, and often referred to as 'Wi-Fi'. The most recently ratified version of this standard, 802.11g, allows transmission speeds up to 54 Mbps. It is essentially the same as Ethernet, but without the cables.

10.3.2 THE NETWORK LAYER

There are of course other networking technologies that could be used instead of Ethernet. An example is token ring networking, originally developed by IBM. In a token ring system, computers are arranged as a ring as shown in Figure 10.10 with connections between each adjacent pair of computers. A specially formatted frame (the **token**) is passed from each machine to the next. A machine that wants to transmit a frame has to wait for the token to arrive. It then transmits a single frame, followed by the token. Each machine forwards frames which are not addressed to it to the next machine in the ring.

An internet might connect an Ethernet network to a token ring network. In order to enable messages to be sent across networks of such different architectures, a higher-level protocol must be used which defines the format of messages that can be transmitted as frames across any network. The predominant protocol used for this purpose is the **Internet Protocol (IP)**.

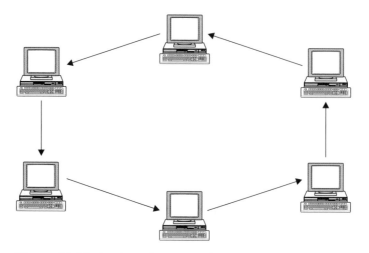

Figure 10.10 A token ring network.

An IP address encapsulates a network number and the number of a machine within that network. Originally, addresses were divided into separate **classes**; class A addresses began with 0 followed by a 7-bit network number and a 24-bit machine number (addresses 0.x.x.x to 127.x.x.x), class B addresses began with 10 followed by a 14-bit network number and a 16-bit machine number (addresses 128.x.x.x to 191.x.x.x), and class C addresses began with 110 followed by a 21-bit network number and an 8-bit machine number (addresses 192.x.x.x to 223.x.x.x). Other addresses were reserved for other purposes; in particular, the so-called class D addresses were allocated for multicasting, which is described further below. These different address classes are illustrated in Figure 10.11.

Using classes like this was a relatively inflexible scheme, as a class C network which grew to over 256 addresses would need to be allocated a brand new class B address, and this would be wasteful if only a few more addresses were needed. Instead, each machine on a network is allocated a unique IP address, together with a **subnet mask** which consists of a set of 1s followed by a set of 0s. This allows a class A, B or C network to be divided into a number of smaller subnetworks. The 1s correspond to the bits comprising the network number, and the 0s correspond to the bits comprising the machine number. For example, a class C network address would be equivalent to using the subnet mask 255.255.255.0.

Class A:	0	Network (7)			Machine (24)	
Class B:	1	0	Network (15)		Machine (16)	
Class C:	1	1	0	Network (23)		Machine (8)
Class D:	1	1	1	0	Multicast group (28)	

Figure 10.11 IP address classes.

There are several reserved addresses that are treated specially. The machine number 0 is reserved to denote the network itself. This is the value that you get from the logical AND of a particular machine's IP address and its subnet mask; for example, the logical AND of the 32-bit binary values represented by 192.173.10.125 and 255.255.255.0 yields 192.173.10.0. A machine number of all 1s is a **directed broadcast** address which can be used to broadcast a message to all machines on a particular network; for example, to send a broadcast to all machines on the class C network 192.173.10.0, you would use the address 192.173.10.255. The address consisting of all 1s (255.255.255.255) is the **limited broadcast** address which can be used to broadcast a message to all machines on the local network. An address of all 0s (0.0.0.0) means 'this machine', and can be used during startup when a machine does not yet know its own IP address. Addresses of the form 127.x.x.x (typically 127.0.0.1) correspond to the **loopback address**, which can be used to send messages between applications running on the same machine. This can be useful for debugging purposes; two communicating applications can be tested on a single machine, and they will behave in exactly the same way as if they were on different machines. There are also some **private network** addresses, such as 10.x.x.x, which are reserved for use by personal networks that are not connected to the Internet as a whole. Messages sent to one of the loopback addresses will never be sent to any other machine, and messages to a private network address will never be routed to a different network.

IP uses the underlying network to send **datagrams** from one machine to another. A datagram consists of a header containing, among many other things, the source and destination IP addresses, in the same way that an Ethernet frame header contains source and destination MAC addresses. An IP datagram will be encapsulated in an Ethernet frame for transmission, as shown in Figure 10.12. If the destination machine is on the same network, it can be delivered directly by looking up the Ethernet MAC address which corresponds to the IP machine number and directing the Ethernet frame containing the datagram to that address. If not, it must be sent to a router which can then route the datagram across another network towards its final destination. The network it is sent to might not be the intended destination, so the process needs to be repeated by routing it through yet another router. To deal with the possibility of datagrams being routed in a circle, the IP header contains a **time-to-live** (TTL) value which is decremented each time the datagram is routed between networks. If this value reaches zero, the datagram is discarded.

This whole process is managed by an IP driver which uses the underlying network driver to send the datagrams encapsulated in a frame. The network driver

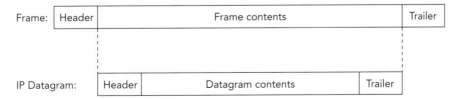

Figure 10.12 IP datagrams and Ethernet frames.

and the IP driver are the two bottom layers of the **protocol stack**, where successive layers of network protocols are implemented on top of lower-level protocols, forming a stack-like structure of drivers layered upon drivers. Among other things, the IP layer must maintain a **routing table** which maps network addresses to 'next hop' routers that can forward the message to an appropriate network.

An important point to note about IP is that it does not guarantee that a datagram will reach its destination. It provides a 'best effort' service, but datagrams can and sometimes do get lost in transit. To provide reliable communication it is necessary to add another protocol layer on top of IP.

Exercise 10.5   Find out how to use the traceroute command on your system. (Note that traceroute is called tracert on Windows systems.) Investigate the routing to a machine in a different country (e.g. nic.funet.fi in Finland or monash.edu.au in Australia). Is the route the same if you try it again? Is it the same a day later or a week later?

10.3.3   NAME RESOLUTION

IP uses IP addresses for identifying machines, but as mentioned earlier, people usually use more memorable **domain names** as machine identifiers which must be translated into IP addresses before they can be used at the IP level. Domain names are tree-structured, like the organisation of files in a hierarchical filing system, but with the most significant part of the name at the end rather than at the beginning.

As mentioned earlier, a **domain name server** (DNS) must be used to translate domain names into IP addresses. Each machine must know the IP address of a DNS that it can use. It is fairly normal to have at least two DNS addresses so that there is a secondary DNS that can be contacted if the primary DNS is unavailable. When a DNS lookup is performed, the primary DNS will be contacted first. If it does not respond then the next one will be tried instead, and this will be continued or there are no more DNS addresses to try. Each DNS has a list of domain names and their corresponding IP addresses. It will primarily be responsible for machines within the same subdomain as itself, but it may know other commonly used addresses too. Each entry in the DNS also has a 'type' code, so that the same name may resolve to different IP addresses depending on the type of service being sought (a mail server or a web server, for example). If the DNS knows the IP address corresponding to the name, it returns it in its reply. If not, then its passes on the query to another DNS that might be able to help. Domain name servers are arranged as a tree which basically reflects the domain name hierarchy itself, so the request is redirected up towards the root of the tree and then back down the appropriate branch. Each DNS is responsible for keeping track of all the names within its domain. An example DNS tree is shown in Figure 10.13, although in reality there is unlikely to be a separate DNS at all levels of the hierarchy, since a single DNS will be able to store millions of DNS entries. The real tree is likely to be much shallower than the one

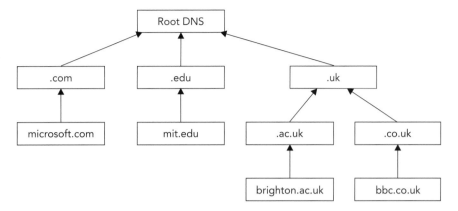

Figure 10.13 Domain name structure.

shown, although the tree in Figure 10.13 will serve here as a conceptual model of what goes on.

This approach is known as **recursive resolution**. When my machine wants to look up the domain name www.acme.com, it sends a request to its local DNS. This might have an entry for www.acme.com, but if not it will pass it up the tree towards the root DNS. Every DNS must therefore be configured with the address of a primary server further up the tree, and usually the addresses of additional secondary servers that it can try if the primary server is unavailable. The root DNS knows at least which DNS to contact for each of the top-level domains, such as com and edu and uk, so even if it cannot resolve the domain acme.com directly it can ask a DNS that deals with the com domain for the address of the acme.com DNS. This DNS will finally be able to resolve the name and respond with the corresponding IP address.

To make this more efficient, each DNS caches copies of recently accessed domain names in accordance with the principle of locality, since recently accessed domain names are quite likely to be accessed again in the near future. Replies are appended to the original request, so by the time the query has been resolved, my local DNS will not only know the IP address for www.acme.com, it will also know the address of a DNS for the acme.com domain. This means that it can send future requests directly to the appropriate DNS. The machine that made the original request will probably cache the IP address for www.acme.com so that it does not have to go through the whole process again later.

10.3.4 TCP AND UDP

The highest level of the TCP/IP protocol suite is the **transport layer** which implements two different protocols: **TCP** (Transmission Control Protocol) and **UDP** (User Datagram Protocol). The fact that TCP is layered on top of IP gives rise to the term TCP/IP, or 'TCP over IP'. In the same way that IP datagrams are encapsulated

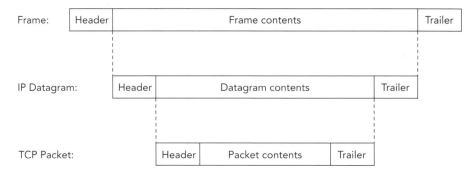

Figure 10.14 Packaging TCP packets into IP packets and Ethernet frames.

in Ethernet frames, a TCP **packet** or a UDP **datagram** is encapsulated within an IP datagram. This is illustrated in Figure 10.14.

Both TCP and UDP establish connections between two **ports** on the source and destination machines. A port is specified by a 16-bit value, which means that each machine has up to 65,536 ports available. An application which connects to a particular port will receive any messages sent to that port but none of the messages sent to a different port, so this allows each machine to participate in multiple simultaneous network interchanges.

UDP, like IP, is a best-effort unreliable datagram protocol which can be used to send short messages from one place to another with very little overhead. The only difference is that an IP datagram is routed from one machine to another, whereas a UDP datagram is routed from one port to another. TCP is a reliable stream-oriented protocol which, from the user's point of view, is very similar to reading and writing a file. A continuous stream of data is broken up into a series of packets which are transmitted individually inside IP datagrams and then reassembled at the other end. The individual packets may travel by different routes to the destination, so they may not arrive in the correct order. The destination machine will have to buffer the individual packets as they arrive if this happens until any missing packets arrive. Each packet includes a sequence number that can be used to reorder the original data stream correctly.

Reliability is achieved in TCP by having the receiver send acknowledgement packets back to the sender for each packet it receives. The acknowledgement packet includes the sequence number from the original packet. If a packet gets lost, no acknowledgement will be sent. The acknowledgement packet might also be lost. Either way, if the sender does not receive an acknowledgement, it will retransmit the packet. For the sake of efficiency, a **sliding window** protocol is used, where the sender will send a number of packets without waiting for acknowledgements. Figure 10.15 shows an example using a window size of 4, which means that four packets can have acknowledgements outstanding at any time. When the acknowledgement for the first packet of the window is received, the window slides along (hence the term 'sliding window') so that another packet can be sent while waiting for the remaining acknowledgements. If no acknowledgement for a packet is received within a reasonable time, the packet is assumed to have been lost and is

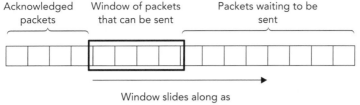

Figure 10.15 Sliding window protocol.

retransmitted. The packet may of course have been received, but the acknowledgement might have gone astray, in with case the receiver will receive duplicate copies of the packet when the sender retransmits it. A similar sliding window is used by the receiver to keep track of which packets have been received, and it can use the sequence number to detect and discard duplicates.

Question 10.2   Assuming that 20 packets need to be sent with an average round-trip delay of 500 ms per packet, how much time is it possible to save by using a sliding window of 5 packets?

10.4 ☐ MULTICASTING

As mentioned above, an IP datagram can be broadcast to all machines on the local network by using the IP address 255.255.255.255 (the local broadcast address) as the destination address. However, there are many situations, particularly in connection with distributed systems, where it is desirable to communicate with several machines at once. For example, in a videoconferencing system, video updates need to be sent to all the participants in the videoconference, and these participants might be anywhere in the world. The local broadcast address allows datagrams to be sent to all machines on the local network, but it does not allow specific machines to be targeted, nor does it allow for the datagram to be routed onto any other network.

IP provides a solution for this known as **multicasting**. IP addresses beginning with 1110 (224.0.0.0 up to 239.255.255.255) are reserved as **multicast addresses**. The last 28 bits of the address identify the **multicast group**. Some multicast groups are reserved; for example, 224.0.0.0 cannot be used, and 224.0.0.1 is dedicated to the 'all hosts' group, which is used to reach all machines on the local network which belong to any multicast group. Multicast addresses can only be used as destination addresses; the source address will always be the normal IP address for the sender.

Each application that wishes to participate in a multicast group has to join the group before it can do anything else. Each multicast group belongs to a particular network, so the application must specify the network that the group belongs to as well as its multicast IP address. This allows the same multicast IP address to be used for different purposes on different networks. Only applications that have joined a particular multicast group are allowed to send datagrams to that group. The IP software on each machine has to remember which applications have joined which multicast groups so that it will accept datagrams sent to multicast groups which have participating applications on that machine, and so that if more than one application has joined the same multicast group, a copy of each incoming datagram will be sent to all of the participating applications, as shown in Figure 10.16. When applications leave the group, the IP software decrements the number of group members and stops receiving messages directed to the group once the last application has left it.

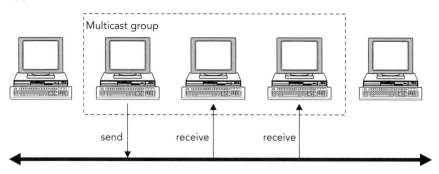

Figure 10.16 Multicasting.

A protocol called **IGMP** (Internet Group Management Protocol) is used to communicate group membership information. IGMP is actually part of the IP protocol suite and is only used internally by the IP software for the purposes of group management. Whenever a machine joins a new multicast group, it sends an IGMP datagram to the 'all host' multicast address 224.0.0.1 to declare its membership. A multicast router which receives such a datagram will propagate the group membership information to any other multicast routers that advertise membership of that group; that is, routers that are being used for multicast traffic to or from that particular group.

Multicast routers also use IGMP datagrams to find out which machines are still members of which groups. This happens once a minute at most. If no machines report membership of a particular group then after a few attempts the multicast router will stop advertising its membership of that group. Since only one machine needs to respond for the router to keep the group active, the machines will each send a response after a random delay of up to ten seconds and will not send a response at all if another machine responds first.

To avoid the Internet being swamped by multicast messages, the 'time-to-live' (TTL) value in a multicast datagram is used to control how far the datagram will be routed. Multicast routers will only route messages which have a TTL value which is above a particular threshold. In particular, a value of 0 means that the datagram will not be sent to any other machine, so this can be used for a multicast group which is restricted to a single machine. A value of 1 means that the datagram will not be forwarded by any router, so this can be used for a multicast group which is restricted to the local network.

10.4.1 A MULTICASTING EXAMPLE IN JAVA

Java provides a subclass of DatagramSocket called MulticastSocket which encapsulates most of the hard work involved in creating and connecting a multicast socket. The first step is to get an InetAddress object corresponding to the multicast address and create a MulticastSocket object which is bound to a specific port. You can then use the joinGroup method to join the MulticastSocket object to the multicast address specified by the InetAddress object, or the leaveGroup method to leave the multicast group.

Figure 10.17 gives the Java code for a simple multicast example. The idea is that each instance of the program sends a multicast message and then displays any multicast messages it receives after that. Line (1) creates an InetAddress for the multicast address 224.5.6.7, and line (2) creates a MulticastSocket which will be

```java
import java.net.*;
import java.io.*;
public class Multicaster {
    public static void main (String args[]) {
        try {
            InetAddress group =
                    InetAddress.getByName("224.5.6.7");   // (1)
            MulticastSocket s =
                    new MulticastSocket(2000);            // (2)
            s.joinGroup(group);
            String msg = "Hello from " + args[0];         // (3)
            s.send(new DatagramPacket(msg.getBytes(),
                                    msg.length(),
                                    group, 2000));
            s.setSoTimeout(60000);                        // (4)
            try {
                while (true) {                            // (5)
                    byte[] buf = new byte[100];
                    DatagramPacket r =
                            new DatagramPacket(buf, buf.length);
                    s.receive(r);                         // (6)
                    System.out.println(new String(r.getData()));
                }
            }
            catch (InterruptedIOException e) { }          // (7)
            s.leaveGroup(group);                          // (8)
        }
        catch (Exception e) {
            System.out.println("Exception: " + e.getMessage());
        }
    }
}
```

Figure 10.17 A Java multicast example.

bound to port 2000 and then joins the multicast group. The two statements beginning at (3) create a message using the first command line argument and send it as a
DatagramPacket to port 2000 of the multicast address. Line (4) then sets a timeout of
one minute (60,000 ms) before entering the main loop, which begins at line (5).

Line (6) waits to receive a DatagramPacket. This would block indefinitely if it
were not for the timeout set at line (4), so the loop will terminate with an
InterruptedIOException if nothing is received within one minute. If a datagram
is received the message it contains is displayed. Line (7) catches the
InterruptedIOException arising from a timeout, and the program then leaves the
multicast group at line (8) and then terminates.

If you run this program on a Unix system using a command like this:

```
java Multicaster John &
```

This will run the example as a background process which will display the message
'Hello from John'. If you run another copy of the program, both the new copy and
the one that is already running will display the message that the new copy sends. It
is clearer if you run each copy of the program in a separate window so that the
output produced by each copy is displayed separately. On Windows you can use
the command:

```
start java Multicaster John
```

which will run the program in a separate window.

Exercise 10.6   Try the program above and check that it works as advertised.

One of the details that I glossed over earlier is how machines identify themselves. If
you know the MAC address of another machine's Ethernet controller, you can send
a message to it, but until you know this, you can't. Similarly, you need to know the
IP address of any machine that you want to send an IP datagram to. All this needs to
be dealt with when the network device driver and the associated protocol stack are
loaded into memory. Until you know your own IP address you cannot use it as the
source of a datagram, and until you know the destination machine's IP address you
cannot specify the destination for your datagram, either of which will render you
effectively incommunicado. The problem is that IP addresses can be changed and
Ethernet cards can be replaced, so that you can't 'hard-wire' the local network
configuration into each of the machines on the network. Instead, yet another set of

network protocols needs to be used to handle network identification and configuration issues.

The main protocol involved is called ARP (Address Resolution Protocol). When a machine wants to translate the IP address of another machine into the corresponding Ethernet MAC address, it sends an ARP datagram which is packaged into an Ethernet frame in exactly the same way as an IP datagram would be packaged, and this is then broadcast to all machines on the local network. The ARP datagram includes the IP address to be translated as well as the source machine's IP address and the MAC address of its Ethernet controller. The machine whose IP address matches the one specified in the ARP packet sends a reply back which gives the MAC address of its Ethernet controller. Of course, since this is being broadcast to all machines on the local network, every machine sees the entire transaction, so each machine can keep its own tables up to date by storing the IP and MAC addresses of both the source machine and the destination machine.

This of course assumes that each machine knows its own IP address. It may well be that the IP address is preassigned and stored in a configuration file so that it is available when the operating system starts up, but in some circumstances this is not possible. For example, the machine may be a diskless workstation which relies entirely on a remote fileserver for all its storage requirements. Another situation arises when machines can connect to the network via temporary dial-up connections, in which case suitable IP addresses will need to be allocated dynamically. In such cases, there must be a way for machines to use the network to discover their own IP addresses.

RARP (Reverse Address Resolution Protocol) is a variant of ARP where the sender broadcasts its physical network address. One or more machines must be configured as RARP servers, and these reply to incoming RARP datagrams with an appropriate IP address. This works well with Ethernet, where the physical MAC address is always available, but other network technologies may use dynamically assigned physical addresses.

An alternative to RARP is BOOTP (Bootstrap Protocol), which involves broadcasting a UDP datagram to address 255.255.255.255 (the local broadcast address) with a source IP address of 0.0.0.0. This requires a BOOTP server which can respond to the datagram with an IP address. Since it has no other way to identify the machine which issued the request, the reply is also broadcast to 255.255.255.255. Since there may be several BOOTP requests outstanding at any given moment (especially if an entire network of workstations has just been started up), each request and reply needs to contain a transaction identification number. This can be randomly generated, as long as it serves to allow each requester to identify which reply corresponds to its original request. Some machine-specific value such as the MAC address can be used to ensure uniqueness.

The reply can also provide other information, such as the name of a remote disk image that diskless workstations can download to boot from; in this case, the initial protocol stack and related software will need to be held in ROM so that the whole process can take place before an operating system is loaded. An extension of BOOTP known as DHCP (Dynamic Host Control Protocol) allows IP addresses to be 'leased' from a pool of available addresses. Each lease has an associated time limit, and the client machine must renew its lease before the time limit expires or its IP address will no longer be valid. This is often used to assign IP addresses to transitory connections such as a dial-up connection over a modem.

10.6 ❑ SUMMARY

What network protocols do is to provide a way for one machine to communicate with another. The nature of this communication is application-specific, although a large numbers of standard protocols have been developed including HTTP, Telnet and so on. These can meet the needs of many applications, but application-specific protocols can also be developed for situations where there is no suitable standard protocol. Many protocols use TCP as a transport service since this provides a reliable stream-oriented communication system, so that it is as easy for an application to communicate with an application on another machine as it is to write to a file on a local disk.

Distributed systems often require a facility for one machine to communicate with several others, as for example in videoconferencing or multiplayer games. This requirement can also be accommodated by creating a multicast group and sending UDP datagrams to all the members of the group. An example of multicasting was presented earlier. Multicasting is often a more effective solution than point-to-point communication in distributed applications.

10.7 ❑ ADDITIONAL RESOURCES

Comer [2] is a very readable book which provides a more in-depth coverage of the material covered in this chapter. Ever more detailed coverage by the same author is given in [3], while [4] covers client and server programming using sockets. The Winsock specification [6] explains the differences between Windows sockets and standard (BSD) sockets. Ethernet is described in Metcalf and Boggs [7]. In addition, the formal specifications for the protocols described in this chapter are all available online as RFCs.

A series of three consecutive RFCs defines the TCP/IP protocol suite. RFC 791 [8] defines IP, RFC 792 [9] defines ICMP and RFC 793 [10] defines TCP. The standards for the application-level protocols mentioned in this chapter are also defined by RFCs: Telnet is defined in RFC 854 [11] and HTTP is defined in RFC 2068 [5]. URLs are defined by Berners-Lee *et al.* in RFC 1738 [1].

10.8 ❑ GLOSSARY

application protocol   a protocol used to enable two specific applications to communicate with each other across a network.

ARP (Address Resolution Protocol) a protocol included in the IP protocol suite which allows one machine to discover the MAC address of another machine on the same network using its IP address.

big-endian a byte ordering where the most significant byte appears first.

BOOTP a protocol used for booting diskless workstations across a network.

broadcast medium a communications medium like Ethernet where all messages are received by every machine on the network.

client a program which requests a service to be performed on its behalf by a separate server.

collision where two machines on a network attempt to transmit at the same time, so that each corrupts the other's message.

CSMA (Carrier Sense Multiple Access) a protocol where each machine checks that the line is idle before starting to transmit.

CSMA/CD (Carrier Sense Multiple Access with Collision Detect) the protocol used by Ethernet where each machine checks that the line is idle before starting to transmit, and stops and retries later if a collision occurs.

datagram a self-contained message transmitted as a single unit of data.

datalink layer the protocol layer responsible for transmitting frames across an underlying physical network connection.

directed broadcast address an address used to broadcast a message to all machines on a particular network.

DNS (Domain Name System) a mechanism for translating domain names into the corresponding IP addresses.

domain name a human-readable hierarchical name for a system on an internet.

frame the unit of data transmission used by Ethernet.

graceful degradation a gradual worsening of performance rather than an abrupt failure.

IANA (Internet Assigned Numbers Authority) the body responsible for assigning Internet-related numbers such as protocol port numbers and IP addresses.

IGMP (Internet Group Management Protocol) a protocol included in the IP protocol suite which is used to report membership of multicast groups to multicast routers.

Internet the globally connected internet.

internet any set of networks connected by routers, of which the Internet (with a capital 'I') is the largest example.

IP (Internet Protocol) the network protocol used on the Internet for packet transmission and routing.

IP address a unique address used to route IP packets across an internet.

IPv4 the most widespread version of IP which uses 32-bit IP addresses.

IPv6 a more recent but not yet widely used version of IP which uses 128-bit IP addresses.

iterative server a server which services requests sequentially.

limited broadcast address an address used to broadcast a message to all machines on the local network.

little-endian a byte ordering where the least significant byte appears first.

loopback address an address referring to the local machine which is never sent across a network.

MAC address (Media Access Control address) the hardware address of a network device such as an Ethernet controller.

mainframe a large centralised computer, now rarely seen.

multicast address an address which can be used to transmit a message to all members of a multicast group.

multicast group a logical group of applications to which a message can be broadcast as a single operation.

multithreaded server a server which can service multiple concurrent requests.

network byte ordering the standard byte ordering used for transmitting multi-byte values across a network.

network layer the protocol layer responsible for routing packets from one machine to another across a network. IP is a network layer protocol.

packet the unit of data sent across a network. A single message may be sent as a series of several packets which will be reassembled at the destination.

port the logical endpoint of a TCP or UDP connection.

private network address one of a set of IP addresses reserved for use by networks which are not connected to an internet.

protocol stack a set of layered protocols, where each protocol uses the facilities provided by the protocol below it in the stack.

RARP (Reverse Address Resolution Protocol) a protocol which maps MAC addresses to IP addresses, used by diskless workstations to discover their own IP addresses.

recursive resolution a method for resolving domain names by recursively searching a tree of domain name servers.

RFC (Request For Comments) one of a series of numbered Internet informational documents, some of which have been adopted as standards.

router a machine with connections to two or more networks, used to route messages between networks.

routing table a table used to decide the next machine to which an IP packet should be sent to route it to its ultimate destination.

server a program which provides a service in response to a request from a separate client program.

sliding window   a method for improving the efficiency of TCP, where a set number of additional packets can be sent before an acknowledgement is received for the first packet that was sent.

socket   the endpoint for a virtual connection between two processes on a network.

subnet mask   a bit mask used to identify which bits of an IP address represent the network address and which bits represent the machine address on that network.

TCP (Transmission Control Protocol)   the standard stream-oriented transport protocol used on the Internet. It is usually layered on top of IP, hence it is often referred to as TCP/IP.

thread pool   a set of threads on a multithreaded server which can be allocated to deal with new requests as they arrive.

token ring   a point-to-point datalink-layer communications protocol

transport layer   the protocol layer which provides virtual point-to-point connections between two ports across an internet. TCP and UDP are transport layer protocols

TTL (Time To Live)   a field which specifies how many routers an IP packet can pass through, used to prevent circular routing of IP packets or the dissemination of multicast packets beyond a certain point.

UDP (User Datagram Protocol)   a transport layer protocol used for the transmission of datagrams between endpoints, used instead of TCP where reliability and stream-oriented connections are an unnecessary overhead.

Winsock   an implementation of the standard sockets library for Windows.

10.9 ❑ REFERENCES

[1]   Berners-Lee, T., Masinter, L. and McCahill, M. *Uniform Resource Locators*. RFC 1738 (Dec 1994). Available online at http://www.rfc-editor.org/

[2]   Comer, D. E. *Computer Networks and Internets*. Prentice Hall (1997)

[3]   Comer, D. E. *Internetworking with TCP/IP Vol I: Principles, Protocols and Architecture*. Prentice Hall (1995)

[4]   Comer, D. E. *Internetworking with TCP/IP Vol III: Client–Server Programming and Applications*. Prentice Hall (1996)

[5]   Fielding, R., Gettys, J., Mogul, J., Frystyk, H. and Berners-Lee, T. *Hypertext Transfer Protocol: HTTP/1.1*. RFC 2068 (Jan 1997) Available online at http://www.rfc-editor.org/

[6]   Hall, M., Towfiq, M., Arnold, G., Treadwell, D. and Sanders, H. *Windows Sockets version 1.1* (Jan 1993). Available online at ftp://ftp.qdeck.com/pub/general/winsock.doc

[7]   Metcalf, R. M. and Boggs, D. R. Ethernet: distributed packet switching for local computer networks. *Communications of the ACM*, **19**(7) (Jul 1976), 395–403

[8]   Postel, J. *Internet Protocol*. RFC 791 (Sep 1981). Available online at http://www.rfc-editor.org/

[9]   Postel, J. *Internet Control Message Protocol*. RFC 792 (Sep 1981). Available online at http://www.rfc-editor.org/

[10] Postel, J. *Transmission Control Protocol*. RFC 793 (Sep 1981). Available online at http://www.rfc-editor.org/

[11] Postel, J. and Reynolds, J. K. *Telnet Protocol Specification*. RFC 854 (May 1983). Available online at http://www.rfc-editor.org/

11

DISTRIBUTED SYSTEMS

The previous two chapters have looked at several aspects of distributed system design. Chapter 9 looked at the overall architecture of multiprocessor and multicomputer systems and networked facilities such as distributed filesystems, remote procedure calls and middleware. Chapter 10 then looked at the basic networking infrastructure that can be used to implement distributed systems, including mechanisms for reliable stream-oriented communication (TCP) and limited message broadcast (multicast).

This chapter begins by examining some issues that need to be addressed when designing distributed systems: distributed notions of time, distributed mutual exclusion and deadlock detection, and fault tolerance and agreement protocols.

The facilities described in Chapter 9 provide mechanisms for individual machines to request services of different sorts from other machines. Rather than looking at a network of computers as a collection of separate machines which happen to be able to use remote services provided by other machines, it is possible to integrate a distributed system more tightly so that a network of computers can be made to look like a single more powerful computer to the outside world. This chapter looks at some examples of systems like this.

11.1 ☐ DISTRIBUTED SYSTEM ISSUES

We saw in Chapter 4 that multithreading provides new capabilities but also introduces new problems like deadlock. You will probably not be surprised to hear that distributed systems not only provide new opportunities but also a whole set of new problems as well.

One of the main problems in a distributed system is the lack of any sort of global state. There is no shared memory, so mutual exclusion using mutexes or semaphores

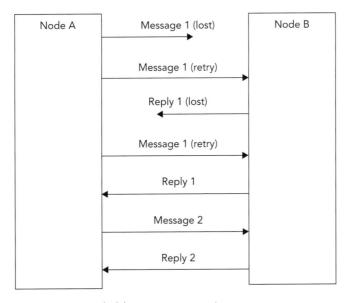

Figure 11.1 Reliable message passing.

is impossible. The only communication between the nodes of a distributed system is via the communications network that connects them. There is not even a global clock that can be used to generate a common timebase.

We can assume here that the communications network is reliable; that is, that any messages sent will eventually be received. This can be guaranteed by requiring a reply to every message; if a message is lost, the sender will not receive a reply and can retransmit the message after a suitable period. Of course, it may be the reply that has been lost, so it must be possible to identify and ignore duplicate messages when they are received. This can be done by including a sequence number in each message, as shown in Figure 11.1. We can also assume that each node sends messages in sequence, so that it will not send a message until a reply from each earlier message has been received. This is like TCP, but without the sliding window. Thus messages sent from one node to another will always arrive eventually and will arrive in sequence; this is, each message will have a higher sequence number than the previous message (or the same sequence number, in which case it is a duplicate message that can be ignored). The sequence numbers are not necessarily consecutive; a node might send message 1 to node A, message 2 to node B, and message 3 to node A, so that node A will just receive the messages with the sequence numbers 1 and 3.

However, if a node receives messages from two different nodes, it has no way of knowing which message was sent first. Even if both messages contain the current time (a **timestamp**) to say when they were sent, each timestamp will have been taken from the clock on the node where it originated, and there is no guarantee that the two clocks will agree with one another. The order in which the messages arrive doesn't tell you anything either, since the first message that was sent might have been delayed by network congestion, or it might have been lost *en route* and later retransmitted. Any distributed system implementation needs to be able to overcome these problems.

Question 11.1   Why can't clocks be kept synchronised accurately? Why can't a common clock server be used to provide a common timebase?

11.2 ☐ DISTRIBUTED GLOBAL TIME

On a local network such as Ethernet where all messages are received by all the nodes connected to it, a timestamp could be attached to each frame transmitted across the network. The driver for the Ethernet controller receives all messages and checks the MAC addresses that they contain to decide which ones it should deal with and which ones it should ignore. While it does this, it could also check the timestamp and compare it with the local clock, updating it if it is slow. In this way, the clock on every node can be adjusted to keep pace with the fastest-running clock on the local network with relatively little overhead. Unfortunately, with network technologies that do not send broadcast messages, or where more than one network is involved, this simple scheme breaks down. Also, the Ethernet frame format has no provision for including a timestamp.

In fact, for most purposes it is not important to know the absolute time at which some event occurred. All that is usually needed is to be able to determine the relative ordering of events. In other words, it is normally sufficient to be able to answer the question 'did event A occur before event B or after it?' A scheme devised by Lamport [6] allows us to use **logical clocks** to answer such questions, where the clocks measure the sequence of events rather than the absolute passage of time.

There are several situations where we can determine whether or not event A happened before event B. First, if events A and B both originated in the same node it is possible to say unambiguously whether A happened before B since a common clock is available to all threads running on that node. Second, if event A is a message being sent by one node and event B is that message being received by another node, we can definitely say that A happened before B. Finally, if we know that A happened before B and B happened before C, we also know that A happened before C. In the situations where we can determine the ordering of two events in this way, the events are **causally connected**. On the other hand, where there is no cause-and-effect relationship between A and B, there is no way to determine their relative ordering, and in this case A and B are said to be **concurrent** (that is, they might have happened in either order, or for that matter simultaneously).

A logical clock assigns a **timestamp** to all causally connected events so that the ordering can be determined by a comparison of their timestamps. The timestamp in this case can be as simple as the sequence number associated with each message, rather than a measure of actual elapsed time. The logical clock is therefore just a software service that generates successive message sequence numbers. Each event in a node causes its logical clock to be incremented, and the timestamp is simply the new value of the logical clock. This means that events within a single node are unambiguously ordered. Secondly, if a node receives a message with a timestamp T, it must if necessary update its own clock to a value which is greater than T, so that the timestamp for the act of receiving the message is greater than the timestamp showing when the message was sent. In this way the two nodes will have a consistent view of the order in which causally connected events have occurred.

Figure 11.2 shows the progress of threads on two different nodes, A and B. Initially the logical clock for node A is 5 and the logical clock for node B is 1. Time proceeds from left to right, with blobs indicating the times at which events occur. The arrows between the two horizontal lines represent messages being transmitted between the two nodes.

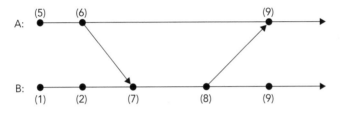

Figure 11.2 Two causally connected events.

A and B proceed concurrently; an event on node B increments its logical clock from 1 to 2, and at about the same time A sends a message to B, an event which increments its logical clock from 5 to 6. When B receives this message, it updates its logical clock (which would have been incremented from 2 to 3) so that it is greater than the timestamp of the received message, so that B's logical clock is now set to 7. Now B replies to A, giving the message a timestamp of 8. A then updates its clock (which would have been incremented from 6 to 7) so that it is greater than the timestamp of the received message; A's logical clock is now 9. Another event on node B increments its clock from 8 to 9 at about the same time.

We cannot tell whether the event at time 5 on A occurred before or after the event at time 1 on node B, because there is no causal link between these events. However, we can tell that event 5 on A occurred before event 6 on A, because both events occurred on the same node and were timestamped by the same clock. Similarly, we know that the event at time 6 on node A occurred before the event at time 7 on node B because B received a message sent at time 6 and updated its clock to show that it received the message after it was sent. We also know that the event at time 8 occurred after the event at time 7, since both happened on node B and the event at time 9 on node A occurred after the event at time 8 on node B, because A received a message sent at time 8 and updated its clock accordingly. We cannot tell which of the events with a timestamp of 9 occurred first, since there is no causal relationship between them.

The big problem here is that we cannot necessarily tell whether or not events are causally connected. Consider what happens if node A receives messages from node B and from node C. Which happened first? If the message from node C was the result of a message from node B (or vice versa) then the timestamps can be trusted as a way of determining the ordering of the messages, since B and C will have synchronised their logical clocks when they talked to each other. Figure 11.3 shows how A updates its clock to 10 when it receives B's message with a timestamp of 9. Similarly C updates its clock to 11 when it receives B's message with a timestamp of 10. C then sends a message with a timestamp of 12, and A updates its clock to 13 when it receives it. Because of the causal relationship between B and C, we can be sure that A's message from B happened before the message from C.

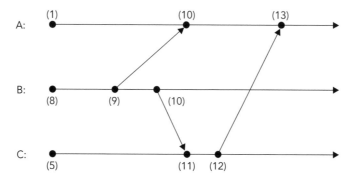

Figure 11.3 Three causally connected events.

If on the other hand nodes B and C sent messages independently, their clocks are not necessarily synchronised and so the timestamps in the messages cannot be meaningfully compared. Figure 11.4 shows what happens if there is no message from B to C in the previous example. A receives messages with timestamps 9 and 6 respectively. Was the message with timestamp 6 sent first but delayed, or was it sent after the message from node B with timestamp 9? There is no way for A to tell. Figure 11.4 also shows another way things could have happened with the same result for A, where the message from C was sent before the message from B but (due to network delays) arrived last: the real problem is that node A has no way of knowing whether or not the messages from the two nodes are causally connected, and so it has no way of knowing whether the timestamps in the messages it receives are at all meaningful.

A solution to this is to use a **vector timestamp**; that is, a vector containing the best-guess values for the timestamps in each of the nodes in the system. This is expensive, because each message must contain as many timestamps as there are nodes, but it does allow each node to distinguish causally connected events from concurrent events. The idea is that each node maintains its own vector containing the timestamps it knows about, and updates each of the timestamps from the vector of timestamps contained in the message. Figure 11.5 shows the situation where the messages from B and C are causally connected again, only this time showing a vector of three timestamps at each point.

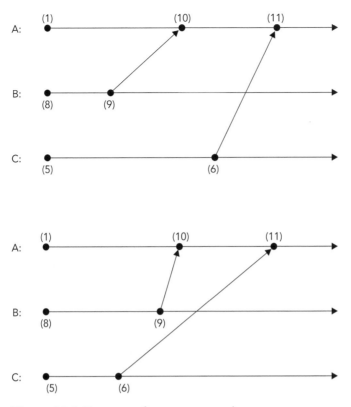

Figure 11.4 Two ways for unconnected events to occur.

Each node starts with a timestamp of 0 for the other two nodes, so that A has a timestamp of (1,0,0), which means 1 for node A and 0 for each of B and C. Similarly B has a timestamp of (0,8,0) which means 8 for node B and 0 for each of A and C. When B sends a message to A with a timestamp of (0,9,0), A updates its timestamp vector to the maximum of each of the three values and increments its own timestamp from 1 to 2, giving a result of (2,9,0). C's clock is similarly updated from (0,0,5) to (0,10,6) by the arrival of a message from B with a timestamp of (0,10,0). The message from C to A therefore has a timestamp of (0,10,7) and A updates its clock to (3,10,7) when it receives it.

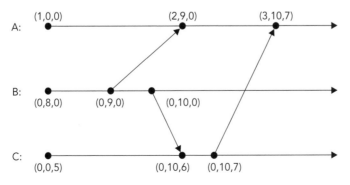

Figure 11.5 Connected events with vector timestamps.

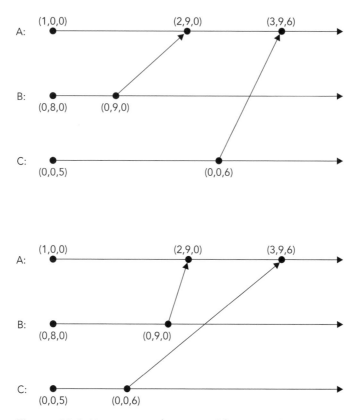

Figure 11.6 Unconnected events with vector timestamps.

Where there is no causal connection, the result looks like either of the situations depicted in Figure 11.6. From A's point of view, the two situations where there is no causal connection are the same, since the end result is a timestamp of (3,9,6) at A regardless of the ordering of events between B and C. The situation shown in Figure 11.5, where there is a causal connection, is quite different. Where there is a causal connection between two messages, the vectors will be different and all of the timestamps in the most recent message will be greater than or equal to the timestamps in the earlier message. The message from B has a timestamp of (0,9,0) while the message from C has a timestamp of (0,0,6); the message from B has a higher value for B (9 rather than 0) than the message from C does, but it also has a lower value for C (0 rather than 6). This shows that there is no causal connection between the two messages. Where there is a causal connection, as in Figure 11.5, the messages are timestamped (0,9,0) and (0,10,7); the two vectors are different, and each value in the latter message is greater than or equal to the corresponding value in the earlier message. We can therefore be sure that the messages are causally connected, and that they did in fact occur in this order.

Question 11.2   Why do vector timestamps work? What is the relevance of the condition that all of the timestamps in the most recent message will be greater than or equal to the timestamps in the earlier message? How does this guarantee that the messages are causally connected?

11.3 ☐ DISTRIBUTED MUTUAL EXCLUSION

The use of shared resources is as much a problem in a distributed system as it is in a single-computer system. A mechanism which guarantees mutual exclusion is still necessary. Single-computer systems can use mutexes for this, but this requires a shared memory to hold the mutexes so that they can be accessed by the threads that want to enter a critical section.

Where resources are controlled by a single node there is no problem. Any other node wishing to access the resource can do so by sending a message to the node that owns it, and this node can therefore handle mutual exclusion issues all by itself in the usual way before performing the requested operation. However, in systems where a resource is physically shared between two or more nodes, the problem of **distributed mutual exclusion** must be dealt with. For example, some systems share disks between two nodes for reliability purposes; if one node fails, the disk can still be accessed via the other node. There must be some way of guaranteeing that the two nodes do not simultaneously issue contradictory commands to the disk controller; for example one node moving the heads in the middle of a series of block writes by the other node, which would result in data being written to the wrong place on the disk.

A simple solution to the problem of distributed mutual exclusion would be to assign each mutex to a specific machine, and arrange for all other nodes to contact that machine to request that the mutex be locked or unlocked. After sending a request to lock a mutex, the requesting thread would wait for a reply. The node that is responsible for the mutex would put all lock requests in a queue and respond to them one by one as the mutex was unlocked. Unlock requests would result in the mutex being unlocked (assuming that the sender is the thread which currently holds a lock on the mutex), but the sender would still need to wait for a reply to ensure that the mutex had in fact been unlocked. If no reply were needed and an unlock request were lost, the sender would think that the mutex had been unlocked while the mutex owner would still think that it was locked, and this could lead to a deadlock.

Exercise 11.1   Explain in more detail how this would work. How could you deal with lost requests and replies?

There are several problems with this approach. First, there is a huge communications overhead, and it is all directed at the node which owns the mutex. This node is a single point of failure, and if it is swamped by the number of requests directed at it, other nodes will be blocked waiting for a response from it. All that this solution does is to make the node that owns the mutex solely responsible for the resource, which has much the same effect as connecting the resource to that node alone.

The objective of distributed mutual exclusion is to provide a mechanism that can be used to determine whether any other node is in a critical section which accesses a shared resource. Threads executing on an individual node can still use mutexes for mutual exclusion, so this mechanism is used for synchronizing access by nodes rather than by individual threads. The nodes must communicate by sending messages to each other, so each node that has access to a resource must know which other nodes it should notify.

One approach would be to broadcast a message to every node in the system, but this would be wasteful. A more efficient way of doing this is to use a **multicast group** associated with each resource. Nodes can register the fact that they might want to use a particular resource by joining a multicast group associated with that resource. Any messages sent to the multicast group will be sent to each of the group's members.

When any node wants to enter a critical section associated with a particular resource, it must notify the other interested nodes. This is so that the other nodes will know when the resource is in use. The node entering the critical section will also have been notified when any other node has entered it, so it should be able to work out whether or not it is in fact safe to enter. To keep things fair, access to the critical section should be allowed on a first come, first served basis, so that each request to enter a critical section is deal with in turn.

The first such algorithm was developed by Lamport, and is based on using the logical clocks that he developed. The idea is for each node to keep a queue of pending requests to enter a critical section (that is, to access a shared resource). When a node wants to enter the critical section, it uses its logical clock to create a timestamped request. It adds the request to its own queue and also sends a copy of the request to every other interested node. Each node sends a timestamped reply and adds the request to its own queue. This will mean that every node will have the same queue of requests as every other node.

The timestamps for the replies will necessarily be later than the timestamp for the original request. A node can enter the critical section safely if its request is the first request in its queue and also if a message has been received from every other node with a timestamp that is later than the one in the request. If two nodes both make a request to enter the critical section, one of the two must have an earlier timestamp than the other, and the one with the earlier timestamp will be dealt with first. The only other potential problem is if another node sent an even earlier request which, due to communication delays, has not yet arrived. Requiring that a message with a later timestamp has been received from every node guarantees that this is not the case; as discussed earlier, we can assume that messages always arrive in order from a particular node, so receiving a message guarantees that all earlier messages from that node have already arrived.

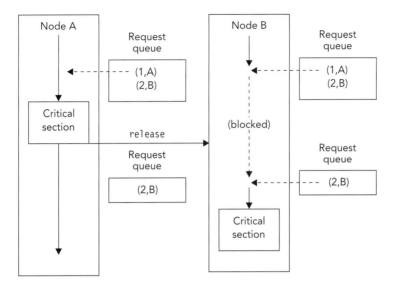

Figure 11.7 Distributed mutual exclusion.

After executing the critical section, the node sends a timestamped release message to every other interested node. When a release message is received, each node removes the corresponding request from its request queue. This will bring some other node's request to the front of the queue, in which case that node will be able to run a thread which enters the critical section. Figure 11.7 depicts the sequence of events where nodes A and B each have outstanding requests with timestamps 1 and 2. The first request (from node A) allows the thread running on node A to proceed into its critical section, but blocks the thread on node B. After executing the critical section, node A sends a release message to node B. Both nodes now remove the first request from their queues, and since node B's request is now at the front of the queue it is unblocked and allowed to enter its critical section.

Ricart and Agrawala [10] developed a modification of Lamport's algorithm which cuts down on the communications overhead by merging release messages with replies to requests. If node A sends a request to node B and node B either has a thread executing inside the critical section or is waiting to enter the critical section as the result of an earlier request than node A's, node B will not reply until the point where it would have sent a release message to node A. Node A will not be able to enter the critical section until it has had a reply from node B, so this is still safe. This means that in this case node B does not need to send node A a release message at all. Another modification by Carvalho and Roucairol [1] is based on the fact that once node A has had a reply to its request from node B, threads on node A can execute the critical section repeatedly until node B sends a request of its own, which cuts down on the number of messages needed still further.

Several other algorithms for distributed mutual exclusion exist, but there isn't space to describe them here. The algorithms described above show that the problem can be solved and they illustrate some specific ways in which this can be done.

Where nodes share resources, deadlocks can occur. As discussed in Chapter 4, deadlocks can be prevented by denying one or more of the necessary conditions for deadlock to occur; they can be avoided by using something like the Banker's Algorithm to identify potential deadlocks before they occur; or they can be allowed to happen and can then be detected and recovered from. Deadlock prevention and avoidance are difficult enough in non-distributed systems, but they are much more difficult in distributed systems. Deadlock prevention can be done by acquiring resources in a particular order, but this will significantly reduce the concurrency of the overall system, which is one of the primary motivations for building distributed systems. Deadlock avoidance involves keeping track of the global state of the whole system at every site to determine whether a resource request will lead to a potential deadlock. Determining the global state of a distributed system is very difficult to do. Deadlock detection is still the easiest way to handle deadlock.

Deadlock detection involves scanning the system looking for a cycle of threads which are waiting for resources held by other threads in the cycle. The big difference in a **distributed deadlock** is that it is much more difficult to get a snapshot of the current state of the whole system to detect whether a deadlock has occurred. One node might say it has resource X and is waiting for resource Y and another node might say that it has resource Y and is waiting for resource X. This is a classical deadlock cycle, but on a distributed system there is no guarantee that the reports from the two nodes relate to the situation at the same point in time. It is perfectly possible that one of the messages has been delayed and that as a result the nodes are reporting on conditions at two quite different points in time. One node might have acquired resource X and be waiting for resource Y at the time it sends the message, but it might then go on to acquire resource Y and release it before the other node acquires it and waits for resource X. In this case there is not really a deadlock.

A distributed deadlock algorithm must not report false deadlocks, but it must also detect all real deadlocks in a finite time. One such algorithm was developed by Ho and Ramamoorthy which uses one node to perform deadlock detection for the rest of the system. In this scheme, each node keeps track of which threads on which nodes are using or waiting for each of its resources, and also which resources in other nodes its own threads are using or waiting for. At regular intervals each node sends a copy of these two tables as a single message to the node that is responsible for deadlock detection. The fact that they are sent as a single message guarantees that they describe the situation at a single point in time.

The deadlock detector cross-references the tables sent by each node. If one node says that it has a thread waiting for some resource which is owned by another node, the appropriate table from the other node is checked to see whether the resource is in fact being requested by that thread. The information is only used where both tables agree; inconsistent information is simply ignored. This guarantees that false deadlocks will not be detected, and sooner or later any real deadlocks will show up.

Why does this guarantee that false deadlocks will not be detected?

The difficulty here is that a centralised deadlock detector is a single point of failure. If the node that is running the deadlock detector fails, deadlocks in the rest of the system will go undetected. In a distributed deadlock detection algorithm, no single node is responsible for detecting deadlocks. Instead, each node cooperates with the other nodes to detect deadlocks. Each node can initiate deadlock detection whenever a thread is forced to wait for a remote resource. There are several such algorithms, but for illustrative purposes I will only describe one of them, due to Chandy, Misra and Haas.

The idea is to determine dependencies between threads. Thread A is **dependent on** thread B if A is waiting for a resource held by B, or if there is a chain of threads starting with A and ending with B where each thread is blocked waiting for a resource held by the next one in the chain. A deadlock corresponds to the situation where a thread is dependent on itself; that is, there is a circular chain of threads where each thread is blocked waiting for a resource held by the next one in the chain. A **local dependency** is where all the threads in the chain are local to a single node.

A local dependency chain may end with a thread that is blocked waiting for a resource held by a thread executing on another node. Let's say that on node 1, thread A is about to be blocked. At this point all the local dependency chains starting from thread A are traced, as shown in Figure 11.8. These chains may end at a thread that is not blocked, in which case there is no deadlock along that particular chain, or back at thread A, in which case there is a local deadlock, or at some thread which is dependent on a thread which is being executed on another node. Let's say that thread A is locally dependent on thread B and that thread B depends on a thread C which is being executed on node 2. In this case, a **probe message**

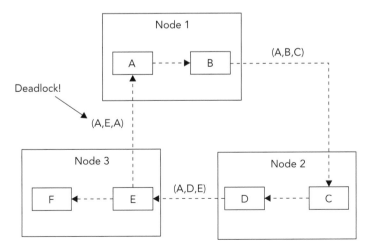

Figure 11.8 Distributed deadlock detection.

(*A,B,C*) is sent to node 2 when thread A becomes blocked. The probe message identifies the threads at the beginning and end of the local chain (A and B) and the remote thread C.

When node 2 receives the probe message (*A,B,C*), it checks whether thread C is blocked. If not, a reply can be sent back to confirm that this dependency chain is deadlock-free. If on the other hand thread C is blocked, all the local dependency chains starting from thread C are traced. If any of these chains terminate at a thread that is not blocked by another thread, there is no deadlock along that path. If after all of the chains have been checked none of them shows a deadlock, a reply can be sent to node 1 which confirms that the chain involving thread C is deadlock-free. However, if C is locally dependent on D and D is in turn dependent on a thread E executing on node 3, then a message (*A,D,E*) is sent to node 3, indicating a chain from A to D with a dependency between D and E. The same process is then carried out on that node. The probe messages therefore fan out along all the dependency chains starting from thread A.

This process will end in one of two ways. Either there will be no deadlock, in which case replies will be received from each of the probe messages that were sent out from A, or else thread A will eventually receive a probe message of the form (*A,X,A*). This indicates that a probe starting from thread A has been identified as dependent on thread X on some other node and that thread X is in turn dependent on thread A. When a probe message like this is received it confirms that there is a distributed deadlock. Figure 11.8 shows what happens if thread E is blocked by thread A; thread A receives the probe message (*A,E,A*). Note that thread E cannot be dependent on another thread in the cycle, such as thread B, since this situation would have been detected at the point where B became blocked by C.

Question 11.4   What guarantee is there that the system state will not change while a deadlock probe is being carried out so that either an undetected deadlock is created or a false deadlock is reported?

11.5 ☐ FAULT TOLERANCE

One of the most important differences between a distributed system and an individual machine, whether uniprocessor or multiprocessor, is the fact that in a distributed system the nodes that make up the system can fail independently of each other. The communications network can also fail. It is important to design distributed systems in such a way that a failure in one node cannot cause a failure in another node.

Failures in a communications link are relatively easy to detect. Either no replies will be received or messages will be corrupted. A garbled message can be detected by including a **checksum** in each message which is calculated from the contents of the message. If the checksum in the message doesn't match the checksum calculated by the receiver, the message has been corrupted. We can therefore assume that communication errors can be detected, and that the system can respond by resending any unacknowledged messages. Also, where there is more than one path connecting two nodes, an alternative path can be used to route messages between the nodes.

Node failures are more serious. A faulty node may continue to reply to messages and originate new messages based on faulty information. The faulty information can arise as the result of a program error. This is much harder to detect, and requires an **agreement protocol** that can be used to check whether each node agrees with each other node about the overall state of the system.

The **Byzantine Generals Problem** is a famous problem devised by Lamport *et al.* [7] which is often used to illustrate agreement protocols. Four generals in the Byzantine army have taken their troops to surround an enemy city ready for an attack, as shown in Figure 11.9. The generals need to coordinate their attack so that the city will be attacked on all sides at once, and they do this by sending messengers to run back and forth between each other's camps. The generals represent the processing nodes and the messengers represent the communications system.

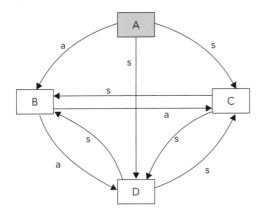

Figure 11.9 Byzantine generals with a traitorous supreme commander.

It can be assumed that the messengers are reliable; messages are encoded so that corrupt messages can be detected, and replacement messengers can be sent out if any messenger gets lost on the way there or on the way back. On the other hand, one of the generals is a traitor (a faulty node) who will try to betray the others. The problem is to coordinate the attack successfully despite the activities of the traitor.

In one version of the problem, one of the generals (A) is the supreme commander who makes all the decisions and communicates them to the other generals. However, he himself may be the traitor. If he is the traitor, he can say 'attack at dawn' (a) to one of the other generals and 'stay put' (s) to the others, in which case the one who was told to attack will attack with no reinforcement from the others. To prevent this happening, each general sends a copy of the order he has received from the supreme commander to all the others, as shown in Figure 11.9. Each general will end up with two orders saying 'stay put' and one saying 'attack at dawn', so they will each know that the 'attack' message is spurious and that the correct action is to stay put. Similarly, if one of the other generals is a traitor and the supreme commander orders an attack, the traitor will say 'attack at dawn' to one general and 'stay put' to the other. In this case, one general receives a 'stay put' order and two 'attack at dawn' orders, so again he can identify the correct course of action. This is shown in Figure 11.10, where the traitorous general C and sends a false message to D. General D receives two 'attack' orders and one 'stay put' order, so he knows that the correct action is to attack.

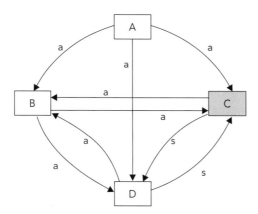

Figure 11.10 Byzantine generals with a loyal supreme commander.

Question 11.5   Is it possible to determine which general is the traitor? Explain your answer.

In another variation, there is no supreme commander. Each general observes the city and then sends a message to each of the other generals saying either 'attack at dawn' or 'stay put'. The majority view will be used to decide what each general does; a general who wants to stay put but is outvoted by the others will go along with the majority and attack. The loyal generals send the same message to every other general, but the traitor says 'attack at dawn' to some of the other generals and 'stay put' to the rest. How can we decide what the correct thing to do is, and how can we identify the traitor?

The solution is to have every general send copies of every message that he receives to every other general. Consider the situation of Figure 11.11. Here general A is the traitor, and sends a message saying 'attack' to general B and a message saying 'stay put' to each of generals C and D. Generals B and C both say 'attack' while general D says 'stay put'. After the initial exchange of messengers, A will have received two 'attack' messages from B and C and one 'stay put' message from D. B will have received 'attack' from A and C and 'stay put' from D. C will have received 'attack' from B and 'stay put' from A and D. D will have received 'attack' from B and

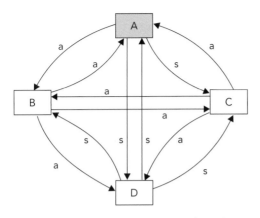

Figure 11.11 Byzantine generals with no supreme commander.

C and 'stay put' from A. If these messages were taken at their face value, A and B would attack (although A might not, since he is a traitor). C and D would be undecided because they would each have two decisions of each type (including their own decision).

However, the next step is for each general to exchange copies of the messages they have received, as shown in Figure 11.12. Each node sends a vector of four values (*a,b,c,d*) to each of the others. Ignoring general A, who as the traitor might send any value at all to each of the others, the values that each of the other nodes receives from each other are as follows:

- From B: (attack, attack, attack, stay)
- From C: (attack, attack, attack, stay)
- From D: (stay, attack, attack, stay)

Each node can see that A has sent inconsistent messages and so must be the traitor. The messages from A can therefore be ignored and a majority vote taken based on the values from B, C and D. This tells each of the loyal generals that they should attack.

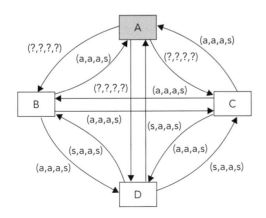

Figure 11.12 The second part of the Byzantine Generals message exchange.

The solutions presented here can detect n traitors out of a total of $3n+1$ generals, so one traitor out of four is the simplest case. In most cases it is reasonable to assume that the risk of any individual node failing is low. Inconsistent information from a particular node indicates a failure, so the node which has failed can be identified. In high-reliability situations, such as NASA's space shuttles, four primary processors are used to control the spacecraft so that a failure in one processor can be detected and a majority vote taken based on values from the remaining three. If another processor fails, there will only be two processors left, which will not be enough to provide a conclusive majority decision. At this point, control can be shifted to a separate backup processor. Since the first shuttle launch in 1981, there has never been a failure that has required the use of the backup processor.

11.6 ❑ CLUSTER SYSTEMS

The technologies described in Chapter 9 (RPC, RMI, CORBA, Jini, COM/DCOM and .Net) provide a set of mechanisms that can be used to build distributed systems. However, each of these presents a view of each machine as largely separate from the others with which it is networked. Applications are executed on the local machine, even though they may use services provided by remote systems. Even though you may not know where the remote services are located, the focus is still on the local machine. Your local machine's resources will not be used by other machines unless you explicitly advertise a service for others to use. In this section I am going to look at how cluster systems try to get away from these notions of locality.

A cluster system is a collection of networked machines that appears to the outside world as a single computer. In some ways this is going back to the idea of having a central powerful mainframe system, except that now the mainframe is a virtual mainframe composed from the combined processing power of the individual machines. As a result it is fault-tolerant; it avoids the possibility of a complete loss of service as the result of a failure of a single machine or single communication link. However, it allows unused processing power to be exploited by anyone who needs it, resulting in each user having access to a much more powerful system than any individual machine could provide, which can be scaled up easily if more power is needed.

11.6.1 BEOWULF

Beowulf is an early English epic poem about a hero who slew a dragon called Grendel. It is also the name of a distributed computing system assembled from standard PCs at NASA which gives supercomputer performance without the accompanying price tag. It is so cheap and easy to implement that many other organisations have built their own Beowulf systems from surplus PCs. Its success can be measured by the fact that many supercomputer manufacturers have since gone out of business.

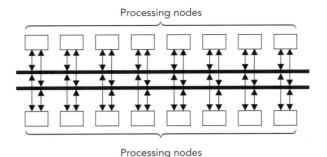

Figure 11.13 NASA Beowulf design.

The original NASA Beowulf system was built from a network of 16 nodes, each of which was a Linux-based PC connected to a pair of 10 Mbps Ethernet connections, as shown in Figure 11.13. Each node had two Ethernet controllers and could use either of the two networks to communicate directly with any other node. This gave a total aggregate bandwidth of 20 Mbps, which proved to be somewhat limiting. Alternative network topologies were also tried, exploiting the fact that each machine has two Ethernet controllers. Figure 11.14 shows a **routed mesh** topology, where each node is connected to three others in the same column by an Ethernet running north–south and to three others in the same row by another Ethernet running east–west. This means that each network only has to be able to cope with the traffic from four machines rather than from all 16, and each node can still contact six other nodes directly. The other nine nodes cannot be accessed directly; instead, messages to them must be routed through one of the other six nodes. Routing messages through intermediate nodes like this is normal practice in networks; each node just needs to act as a normal internet router. A standard Linux system already includes the software to handle this.

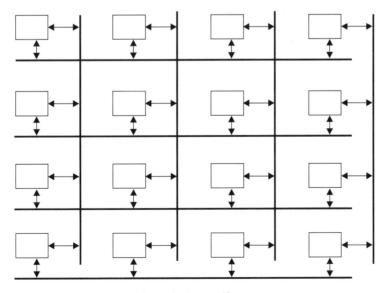

Figure 11.14 A routed mesh Beowulf system.

Switches

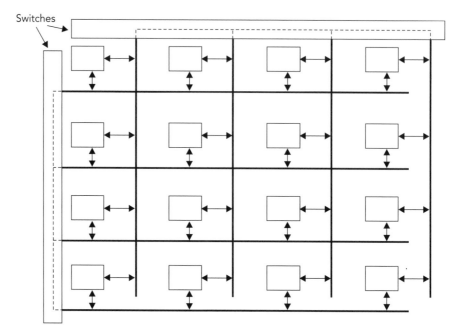

Figure 11.15 A routed mesh Beowulf system with switches.

Routing messages through intermediate nodes involves some overheads, however. Each routed message uses up bandwidth on two separate Ethernet segments, and there is an additional processing load for the node that performs the routing. An alternative is to use fast Ethernet switches to perform the routing, as shown in Figure 11.15. In this scheme, each switch can route messages from any column to any other column, or from any row to any other row. The disadvantage of this is the additional cost of the switches themselves.

Other network topologies have also been considered. For example, a system at Los Alamos used a **hypercube** configuration, where each node had four network controllers and each network segment connected two machines. This is a four-dimensional structure which can be implemented in three dimensions as two cubes with a node at each vertex and additional connections between the corresponding nodes in each cube, as illustrated in Figure 11.16. Hypercubes are not very scalable, as doubling the number of nodes will require an extra network controller in every node. As network speeds have increased from 10 Mbps to 100 Mbps, the extra bandwidth means that the routed mesh arrangement is fast enough to avoid network congestion even on much larger configurations than the original 16-node system. It is also an extremely cheap solution.

Exercise 11.2   Two important measures of an interconnection network are the diameter (the maximum number of hops between any pair of nodes) and the degree (the number of connections to each node). Compare the diameter and degree of routed meshes and hypercubes for the same number of nodes. How do these figures change as the number of nodes increases? Can you give a general formula for a network of *N* nodes?

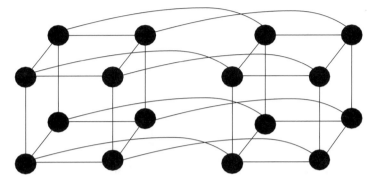

Figure 11.16 A hypercube.

The objective of Beowulf was to deal with computationally expensive tasks such as *N*-body simulations, where the interaction of anything from dozens to millions of separate bodies is simulated. For example, a wind tunnel simulation involves modelling how air molecules interact as they pass across a surface. Modelling the orbital dynamics of asteroids involves the simulation of the gravitational effects of other nearby asteroids. *N*-body problems are well suited to a distributed 'divide and conquer' approach, since the bulk of the interaction is between neighbouring bodies. This means that it is relatively easy to map neighbouring bodies onto neighbouring nodes. This sort of partitioning of the workload is known as a **crowd computation**, where the data to be processed is divided between the available nodes and then each node performs computations on its own data, exchanging intermediate results every so often.

Another approach is a **tree computation**, where the distribution of the workload fans out from one node and spreads through the system. For example, parallel sorting can be done by dividing the data into two halves and sending half the data to another node. Each of the two nodes then divides its half of the data in two and sends it to another node, so that there are now four nodes, each of which has a quarter of the data to deal with. When the data set reaches a certain size, or when there are no more nodes, each node sorts its own set of data and sends it back to its 'parent' node to be merged with the parent node's sorted data, repeatedly taking the smaller value from the beginning of each of the two sets of data as the next value of the merged sequence. This is illustrated in Figure 11.17, where four nodes (N1 to N4) are used to perform the processing.

Software for parallel processing is also freely available on Linux. PVM (Parallel Virtual Machine) is one such system. It is a message-passing system that enables a set of networked nodes to be used as a single distributed-memory parallel computer. In other words, the set of nodes operates as a single virtual machine that

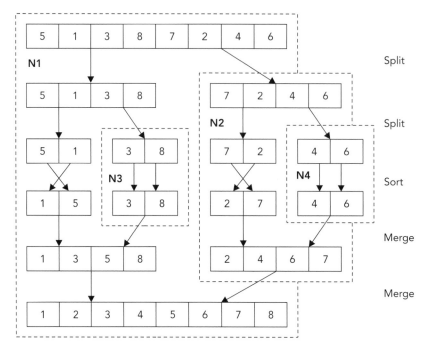

Figure 11.17 Parallel merge sorting using four nodes.

supports parallel execution. Each node must run a copy of pvmd, the PVM daemon which is responsible for handling inter-node communication. The user of a PVM system adds a set of nodes to the virtual machine and then typically runs a 'master' program which loads and executes a set of programs on the other nodes. Each program can add further nodes to the virtual machine if it wants to. More than one user can use PVM at the same time; a single physical node can belong to more than one virtual machine at a time. Nodes can also be deleted from the virtual machine, which is useful for dealing with faulty nodes or network connections.

Each program is run as a PVM **task**. A task corresponds to a Unix process, so each node can support more than one task. The relationship between nodes, tasks and virtual machines is illustrated in Figure 11.18. Tasks can spawn other tasks, just as Unix processes can spawn other processes. Each task has an identifier which is unique across the entire virtual machine, and the tasks can send messages to each other using PVM library functions. Messages can be sent to individual tasks or multicast to a group of tasks, so that each task in the group receives a copy of the same message. There are several operations provided for receiving messages:

- pvm_recv: a blocking operation which suspends the calling task until a message arrives.
- pvm_nrecv: a non-blocking operation which returns immediately with a result of zero if there is no message ready to be received.
- pvm_trcev: a blocking operation like pvm_recv but with a timeout. If no message is received within the specified timeout period then it returns a result of zero, just like pvm_nrecv.

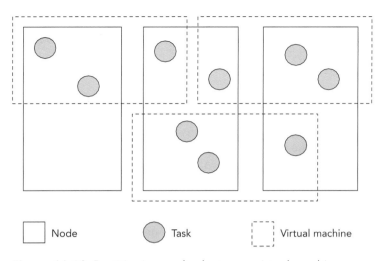

Node   Task   Virtual machine

Figure 11.18 Partitioning nodes between virtual machines.

Each message has a **message tag**, which is an integer identifier chosen by the user, and a task can choose to receive every message or just messages with a particular tag. It can also choose to receive messages from any task or just from one particular task. This provides the flexibility to support different models of communication, such as tree or crowd computation in different parallel algorithms.

11.6.2 WINDOWS CLUSTERS

Windows clustering (originally codenamed 'Wolfpack') is superficially similar to Beowulf systems. A Windows cluster is a distributed system consisting of a number of nodes which externally appears to users as a single machine. However, the motivation for Windows clustering is quite different from the goals of Beowulf. Beowulf is designed primarily to harness the parallelism of a group of machines for the efficient execution of computationally expensive parallel algorithms. In other words, its primary goal is supporting highly parallel distributed applications that would otherwise need a supercomputer system. Windows clustering is aimed more towards the goal of providing a fault-tolerant system which is scalable; if more processing power is needed, more nodes can be added. The individual applications that run on a cluster are not the sort of distributed algorithms that Beowulf is aimed at. Instead, clustering is intended for use in commercial application areas, such as high-volume fault-tolerant web or database servers which can cope with millions of requests and with failures in individual nodes. Rather than running a single application that is distributed across several nodes, a cluster is more likely to be used as a **server farm** consisting of nodes which are each running a separate copy of the same server software, where incoming requests are directed to individual nodes based on how heavily loaded each node is. If the load on each node is too great, additional nodes can be added to spread the load.

Question 11.6   If requests are sent to a domain name corresponding to a specific IP address, how can a server farm be organised so that the machine with that IP address does not become overloaded?

Nodes in a cluster can share physical resources such as disks, as shown in Figure 11.19. This means that if a node fails, the disk it uses will still be accessible via another node. Extra nodes can be added either as redundant elements to guard against failures or to provide additional processing power. This helps to meet the goals of reliability and scalability. Each node must have Microsoft Cluster Services (MSCS) installed, which incorporates a few relatively minor changes to the standard Windows kernel. These include modifications to the I/O subsystem to deal with the ability to share devices such as disks between nodes and modifications to the networking services to allow network names and addresses to be created and deleted dynamically.

Cluster management is performed by a Windows service (daemon process) called the Cluster Service (CS) which runs on each node. The CS is responsible for managing the resources of the system, which include not only physical resources such as disks and network cards but also logical resources such as filesystems, applications, TCP/IP addresses and databases. It consists of six tightly integrated components:

- The **node manager**, which handles cluster membership and monitors the health of other nodes in the system.

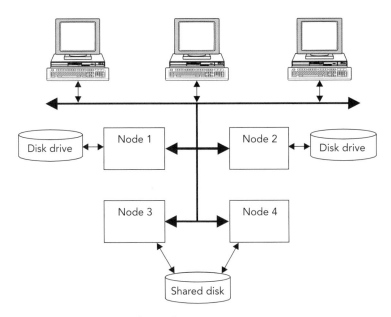

Figure 11.19 A Windows cluster.

- The **configuration database manager**, which maintains the cluster configuration database that holds information about the entities in the cluster: nodes, resource types, resources, groups and so on.
- The **resource/failover manager**, which is responsible for resource management decisions including starting and stopping resources and dealing with failures.
- The **event processor**, which manages cluster initialisation and propagation of event notifications to and from applications.
- The **communications manager**, which is responsible for managing the RPC mechanisms that are used for communication between nodes.
- The **global update manager**, which provides a global update notification service used by other components of the CS.

There are also two other essential components which are external to the CS itself:

- The **resource monitor** is a service which uses the CS to monitor the health of the resources managed by the cluster.
- The **time service** is a resource which provides nodes with a consistent timebase.

Resources are organised into **groups**. If one resource depends on another, both resources must be part of the same group. For example, a filesystem share might depend on a physical disk and a network name, and the network name might in turn depend upon an IP address, as shown in Figure 11.20. Each group resides on an individual node; that is, all the resources in a group must be available on the node where the group is located.

The resource manager component of the CS is responsible for allocating nodes to resource groups. When a group is created, the configuration database manager records the group membership information and the node that the group resides on, and uses the global update manager to notify the configuration database managers in the other nodes. If a node needs to be shut down for maintenance, the group can be moved to another node by stopping it and then restarting it on any node which has the necessary resources available. In the case of a node failure, the failover manager can move a group from the failed node to another suitable node by restarting the group's resources on the new node. Failures are detected by the node manager when a node stops sending **heartbeat** messages to show that it is still

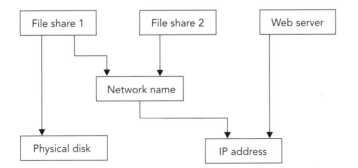

Figure 11.20 Resource dependencies in a resource group.

active. Also, the rate of heartbeat messages can be used to indicate how heavily loaded a node is, which allows the system to perform dynamic **load balancing**.

Resources are implemented by dynamic libraries (DLLs) whose interfaces are defined in the cluster system development kit. These are either loaded by the resource monitor or run as separate processes. Standard resource DLLs are provided for managing common resource types such as disks and volumes, filesystems, printers, applications, network names and IP addresses. For example, a database server application could be managed as a resource, and a resource group could include the application together with the database files it uses. Alternatively, a separate DLL could be written to implement a database resource. This would have the advantage that the resource would be a database rather than the server application that provides access to a database. As a particular resource can only be active on one node at a time, using the server application as a resource would mean that the cluster could only run one instance of the server at a time. Defining a database resource creates a new resource type, and any group can then include resources of this type.

11.7 ❑ DISTRIBUTED SHARED MEMORY

One of the big problems is designing efficient parallel algorithms for distributed systems like Beowulf that work by message-passing. The time it takes to interact with a remote machine is several orders of magnitude greater than it would take to access something on the local machine, and this implies that efficiency can only be achieved by partitioning the problem into a large number of components that compute intensively using local data and communicate infrequently with the other nodes. Not all problems can be partitioned like this. Matrix multiplication is an operation that can be partitioned fairly easily, but factoring into primes (or deciding whether a particular number is a prime or not) is a problem which cannot be dealt with using this sort of 'divide and conquer' approach.

Another problem is that programs that use message-passing for communication tend to be much more complex than programs that use shared memory. One solution is to use message-passing to implement a **distributed shared memory** that unites the memory in each node into a single virtual memory with a large virtual address space. Such systems are described as **NUMA** (Non-Uniform Memory Access) systems, since different regions of the address space may be much slower to access than others; in other words, the access times are not uniform across the whole address space.

In a distributed shared memory system, pages are spread among the various local memories, and a page fault is handled by copying the page from the node that currently holds it to the node that is trying to access it. Read-only pages are safe to copy, but writable pages are more of a problem. One approach is to delete the page from the original node after it has been copied; another approach is to use a scheme similar to directory-based cache coherence to notify nodes that have a copy of the page when any other node writes to the page. The big problem with distributed shared memory is achieving satisfactory levels of performance. Multiple nodes writing to the same page can generate a lot of network traffic. The Mirage system [4] tries to avoid excess traffic by defining a minimum time period before a node has to give up a page to another node.

However, if all these problems could be solved, distributed shared memory would combine the ease of use of SMP-style shared memory without the scalability limitations that SMP systems suffer from. There is a lot of work in this area as a result, and it will be interesting to see how it develops.

11.8 ❑ DISTRIBUTED OPERATING SYSTEMS

The major difference between a cluster and a collection of machines using a middleware layer to share resources is that a cluster operating system automatically makes the resources of each machine available to the others, including resources like processor time. Processes are not tied to particular nodes in the way that they are in a middleware-based system, and processes can migrate from one node to another when necessary. However, the operating systems used in distributed systems like Beowulf are just ordinary operating systems like Linux or Windows, possibly with a few relatively minor modifications. Each node in the system has its own separate copy of the operating system.

In a cluster, users still need to be aware of many issues such as the location of their files and other resources; for example, mounting a filesystem involves knowing about the volume that contains it. In contrast to this, the idea behind a distributed operating system is to make the use of a distributed system as transparent as possible. Ideally, all resources are equally accessible; there are no visible distinctions between local disks and remote disks, or processes executing on a local node or on a remote node. A directory entry for a file might be stored on a different disk than the file itself. The operating system itself is distributed across the various nodes in the system. From the point of view of a user logging in to a distributed operating system, all resources appear equally accessible.

The operating systems described in this section take us some way away from the Windows- and Unix-centric view of operating systems that I have adopted in the rest of this book, but this is necessary since neither Windows nor Unix has gone this far along the path of distributed processing yet.

11.8.1 AMOEBA

Amoeba was originally developed in 1980 by a research group headed by Andrew Tanenbaum at the Vrije Universiteit (Free University) in Amsterdam, and development has continued since then. An Amoeba system is composed of a number of workstations (usually diskless X-terminals) which users can use to log in to the system, a pool of processor nodes and a number of other nodes which act as specialised servers. It runs on a variety of platforms, including Pentium-based PCs, Sun SPARC workstations and Motorola 680x0 systems.

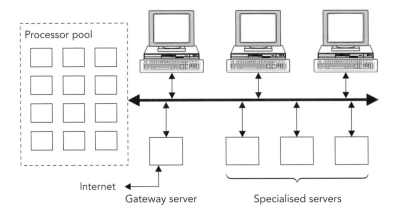

Figure 11.21 An Amoeba system.

When users log in, they are logging in to the system as a whole rather than to an individual node, so the view is very similar to a centralised time-sharing service as provided by a mainframe system of the 1960s or 1970s. There is no concept of a 'home' machine within the system; instead, there is a pool of **processor nodes**. When a user executes a process, it will be executed on any available processor node. There are also a number of specialised servers: file servers, database servers, and so on. One special server (the **process server**) monitors loading and performs automatic load-balancing, migrating processes to a different node if necessary. This is illustrated in Figure 11.21.

Because the system relies heavily on message passing between nodes, the performance of the system as a whole depends on the efficiency of the communication protocols used. A specially designed transport protocol is therefore used to minimise the protocol overheads that would otherwise be incurred, and special **gateway servers** are used to translate between the internal protocol used and an external TCP/IP network.

Amoeba is based around a microkernel architecture where the kernel itself is only responsible for the issues of process, memory and communication management, as well as handling the raw I/O devices within the system. The kernel is there basically to allocate processor power, memory and interprocess communication services to user processes, and everything else is handled by user processes with no special privileges. For example, every node has a **resource manager** process which controls the resources belonging to that node.

The basic communication mechanism is based on a form of remote procedure call. However, it also provides a reliable ordered multicast service which guarantees that a series of messages can be sent to a group of nodes and that each node will receive all of the messages in the same order in which they were sent.

Each service provides one or more **ports** specified by 48-bit values, and client processes use these ports to contact the service. A service may have several threads listening on the same port; the kernel chooses one of these threads at random to service an incoming request. Ordinary user processes can also provide services to other processes in the same way. Publicly available services such as file servers will have well-known port numbers, whereas user processes will generally not publicise their port numbers. Knowledge of a port number is sufficient to access a service, but since there are 256 trillion (2^{48}) possible ports, guessing port numbers is impractical. As an additional safeguard against users from listening on well-known ports to impersonate system services such as file servers, the actual port number is translated into a published port number, and it is impossible to work backwards from the published port number to find the corresponding actual port number. Requests sent to the published port number are automatically routed to the actual port number. This means that impersonators have no way to find out which actual port number to listen to in order to accept incoming requests.

Amoeba uses 128-bit values known as **capabilities** (like 'handles' or 'magic cookies') to identify objects uniquely within the system. These act as object names and also encapsulate object access permissions. They can be passed around freely between processes to allow other processes to access the same object. Capabilities are at the heart of the Amoeba design. Internally, they identify the server port and the object to be accessed. Each object contains a random number generated when the object was created, and this is used to check the validity of the capability. The capability contains a 56-bit value that the server translates to give a value which must match the object's random number, together with a set of access permission bits defining the types of access allowed by the capability. Figure 11.22 illustrates the process of validating a capability and accessing the relevant server.

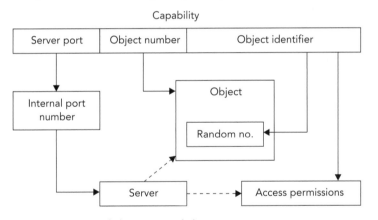

Figure 11.22 Validating capabilities.

Question 11.7   How does the use of a random number prevent someone from forging a capability or altering the access permissions of a capability?

The filesystem in Amoeba is an ordinary user process, in accordance with the microkernel design approach. The standard Amoeba filesystem is called Bullet, and this has several interesting features. For one thing, the filesystem is solely responsible for storing files. Files are identified by capabilities rather than by name; a separate **directory server** is used to associate file (or directory) names with capabilities. Finding a file is done by a similar process to NFS file lookups: a capability for the root directory is used to locate the name for the next part of the pathname, which gives yet another capability. This is turn is searched for the next part of the pathname to get a further capability, and this continues until the file itself is reached. Another interesting feature is that the filesystem is **immutable**. There is no operation to write to a file as such; if you want to modify a file you have to read it and then create a new file.

The memory model in Amoeba is based on the use of **segments** as described in Chapter 5 to provide memory protection. There is no paging as such in an Amoeba system; one of the consequences of this is that you cannot run programs which are bigger than the available physical memory. However, processes can still be swapped out of memory and reloaded later. When a process is created, a process descriptor is created which gives the size and address of each segment, as well as the contents of processor registers and any capabilities that the process owns. The process is identified by a capability which is passed back to its creator. The process descriptor is actually stored as part of the process image so that when a process is swapped out it can be reloaded as a whole by any available processor. This also makes it possible for the system to perform load-balancing by moving processes on heavily used nodes to nodes that are less heavily loaded.

A form of lottery scheduling is used, as described in Chapter 7; each process is given a number of tokens when it is created. The tokens are issued by a **bank server** and act as 'virtual money' which can be spent on acquiring resources. The priority of a process depends on the number of tokens it has, so a 'rich' process has a higher priority and a greater chance of being able to acquire the resources it needs.

Fault tolerance is managed by the **boot service**. Servers that wish to make use of this facility can register with the boot service at startup, and the boot service will ping each registered server at intervals. If the boot service does not receive a reply within a certain interval, the server is declared broken and a new copy is started. This is transparent to users, since the RPC mechanism times out any request for which it does not receive a reply within a certain time, and client programs can just resend any timed-out requests. To ensure that the boot service itself does not fail, several copies of the boot service are run so that they can check on each other's health as well as the health of other registered services.

11.8.2 CHORUS

Chorus is another microkernel system which was originally developed in 1979 at INRIA, the Institut National de Recherche en Informatique et Automatique in France. It has been redesigned and reimplemented several times since then. The microkernel manages **actors** (analogous to processes) and threads, interprocess communication and memory management. Other servers are layered on top of the kernel; in particular, the **network manager** handles communication with other nodes and the **mapper** which swaps pages in and out of memory. The kernel (referred to as the 'nucleus') in conjunction with a set of servers makes up a working operating system, but since the kernel treats all actors equally it is possible to run what are effectively completely different operating systems on top of a single kernel, where each operating system is comprised of a particular set of servers.

Actors are a central concept in Chorus. An actor is the unit to which resources are allocated. This includes memory, threads and communication ports. Actors are similar to processes in other systems. A **user actor** runs in user mode in a separate address space (together with a shared system address space), but **system actors** run in a shared kernel-mode address space. There are also **supervisor actors** which have the same address space organisation as user actors but which are able to call certain sensitive kernel operations. A standard set of actors (**boot actors**) are loaded when the system starts up, and additional actors can then be loaded dynamically. System actors can access kernel facilities via system calls, but this does not involve any mode changes since the servers are executing in kernel mode. Supervisor servers can also bind actor threads to particular exceptions (system traps) so that user actors on the same node can access the facilities they provide by what are effectively additional sets of system calls. In general, inter-actor communication is based on the use of **ports** which can be created and destroyed dynamically. Each port is bound to a particular actor, and there is normally a thread for each port within an actor which waits in an event loop for a message to arrive on that port.

Like Amoeba, Chorus uses 128-bit unique identifiers to identify objects such as actors, threads and ports in a system-wide way. Capabilities are used to identify other objects. These capabilities use the unique identifier of the server to which the objects belong, and they can be passed freely from one actor to another.

Chorus also provides a POSIX-compliant subsystem called Chorus/MiX which implements POSIX kernel features in terms of Chorus kernel operations together with a collection of independent servers to manage processes, filesystems, devices and sockets. Some additional features are provided; for example, the filesystem allows ports to be mounted, allowing an NFS-style distributed filesystem.

11.9 ☐ SUMMARY

Distributed systems are far more scalable than multiprocessor systems, but are also far more complex. The complexity arises from the fact that the nodes have no common view of the system state, as each node operates independently and communicates by sending messages to the other nodes across a communications network. Determining the sequence of events is difficult due to the absence of a common clock which all the nodes can access and the fact that the communications network can result in messages being delayed. Issues like mutual exclusion and deadlock detection are correspondingly more difficult. However, this chapter has described a selection of techniques that can be used to overcome these problems.

Nodes can also fail independently of each other, and where nodes need to cooperate to achieve a common goal it is necessary to be able to detect failures. Techniques have also been described to overcome this which will work as long as less than a third of the nodes are likely to fail at any given moment.

Distributed systems are evolving beyond the point where a system is composed of individual machines which share resources and provide services. The next step along the path is the development of clusters and systems built around distributed operating systems, where the individual machines providing the services are no longer visible as separate entities. Such systems are relatively rare at present, but the ease with which they can provide supercomputer processing power, high reliability and great scalability will mean that such systems will become more widespread. Ultimately this will probably spread in the same way that the Internet has spread, except that the end result will be a single distributed computer system spanning the entire planet, so that when you run a program, you have no idea where in the world your files are stored or which machines are providing you with the memory and processor power that you're accessing. At this point, having a pocket-sized computer with a wireless network link will give you exactly the same computational power and connectivity as someone with direct access to a vast supercomputer (although they might have a slightly better response time than you do).

However, Waldo *et al.* [21] inject a note of caution into this utopian vision. They argue that distributed computation is inherently different from local computation because of latency issues (the time it takes to access remote data) and partial failures (where one node or link fails while the rest of the system keeps working). As a result, attempting to 'paper over the cracks' by making the two look identical to the programmer can result in the worst of both worlds. This either produces unnecessary overheads for local objects by making them behave like remote objects, or it makes remote objects look local, thus losing the facilities for fine control over responses to partial failures. In their view, local and remote objects are quite different and any attempts to make them look the same are misguided (and possibly dangerous).

The extreme accessibility of distributed systems is also potentially dangerous in itself. Allowing other people to execute programs on your machine leaves you open to the possibility that errors or malicious intent in the programs that they run might compromise your system and might lose or corrupt vital data. The next chapter looks at a range of security and safety issues that need to be addressed in any system, but particularly in the case of networked systems.

11.10 ☐ ADDITIONAL RESOURCES

Logical clocks were defined by Lamport [7] and extended to vector clocks by Fidge [3]. The distributed mutual exclusion problem was also dealt with by Lamport [7] and refined by Ricart and Agrawala [14], and refined further by Carvalho and Roucairol [1]. Ho and Ramamoorthy [5] described distributed deadlock detection using a central system, while Chandry *et al.* [2] explained the algorithm described in this chapter for distributed deadlock detection. The Byzantine Generals problem was described by Lamport *et al.* [8]. All these issues are covered in detail by Singhal and Shivaratri [16], which also describes many other techniques that can be used to deal with them.

Kronenberg *et al.* [6] is an early paper on clusters for VAX systems. The Beowulf HOWTO [13] provides a good introduction to Beowulf systems and includes some useful links to further information. Beowulf was originally described by Sterling *et al.* [17], and Sterling has also written a book on the subject [18]. Windows clusters are less well documented, although a white paper from Microsoft [10] gives a good outline, while Lee [9] goes into the detail of setting up and managing a Windows cluster.

A general introduction to distributed operating systems is presented in a survey by Tanenbaum and van Renesse [19], and Tanenbaum and van Steen [21] is an excellent book covering the entire spectrum of distributed systems. Protić *et al.* [12] give a wide-ranging survey of distributed shared memory; the Mirage system mentioned earlier is described by Fleisch and Popek [4]. Waldo *et al.* [22] provide a cautionary note. Amoeba is described by Tanenbaum and van Renesse in [20], and more details are given by Mullender and Tanenbaum [11]. The structure of Chorus is explained by Rozier *et al.* [15].

11.11 ☐ GLOSSARY

actor the unit of resource allocation in Chorus.

agreement protocol a protocol used by the nodes of a distributed system to reach an agreement about the overall state of the system.

Byzantine Generals problem a problem used to illustrate agreement protocols in the presence of failures.

capability an unforgeable token giving a specific type of access to a specific object

causal connection a cause-and-effect relationship between two events which allows the events to be ordered according to the time of their occurrence.

cluster a distributed system which behaves like a single fault-tolerant high-performance machine to the outside world.

concurrent activities two activities without a causal connection which cannot be ordered according to the time of their occurrence.

crowd computation a parallel computation where the workload is partitioned between nodes at the start of the computation and each node then processes its own set of data.

dependency a relationship between two threads where one thread is waiting for a resource held by another.

dependency chain a linked series of dependency relationships between threads.

distributed deadlock a deadlock situation which exists between threads located on different nodes of a distributed system.

distributed mutual exclusion mutual exclusion between threads located on different nodes of a distributed system.

distributed shared memory the simulation of a single memory shared by all the nodes in a distributed system from the separate memory associated with each node.

heartbeat message a message sent at regular intervals to confirm that a system is still operational.

load balancing keeping nodes evenly loaded by migrating processes from heavily loaded nodes to lighter-loaded ones.

local dependency a dependency between threads located on a single node of a multiprocessor system.

logical clock a simulated clock used to assign an ordering to events in a distributed system, but with no necessary relationship to the elapsed time between events.

PVM (Parallel Virtual Machine) a software system which allows a network of machines to be used as a single distributed parallel processor.

server farm a cluster of servers which acts as a single server, allowing high levels of demand to be catered for.

timestamp a value used to indicate the time at which a message was sent.

tree computation a parallel computation where the workload fans out across a number of nodes as the computation proceeds.

vector timestamp a list of timestamps from different nodes in a distributed system which can be used to determine whether events are causally connected.

11.12 ☐ REFERENCES

[1] Carvalho, O. S. F. and Roucairol, G. On mutual exclusion in computer networks. *Communications of the ACM*, **26**(2) (Feb 1983), 146–148

[2] Chandry, K. M., Misra, J. and Haas, L. M. Distributed deadlock detection. *ACM Transactions on Computer Systems*, **1**(2) (May 1983), 144–156

[3] Fidge, J. Partial orders for parallel debugging. *Proceedings of the ACM SIGPLAN/SIGOPS Workshop on Parallel and Distributed Debugging* (1989), pp. 183–194

[4] Fleisch, B. D. and Popek, G. J. Mirage: a coherent distributed shared memory design. *Proceedings of the 12th ACM Symposium on Operating System Principles* (Dec 1989), 211–233

[5] Ho, G. S. and Ramamoorthy, C. V. Protocols for deadlock detection in distributed database systems. *IEEE Transactions on Software Engineering*, **SE-8**(6) (Nov 1982), 554–557

[6] Kronenberg, N., Levy, H. and Strecker, W. D. VAX clusters: a closely-coupled distributed system. *ACM Transactions on Computer Systems*, **4**(2) (May 1986), 130–146

[7] Lamport, L. Time, clocks, and the ordering of events in a distributed system. *Communications of the ACM*, **21**(7) (Jul 1978), 558–565

[8] Lamport, L., Shostak R. and Pease, M. The Byzantine Generals problem. *ACM Transactions on Programming Languages and Systems*, **4**(3) (Jul 1982), 382–401

[9] Lee, R. R. *Windows NT: Microsoft Cluster Server*. McGraw-Hill (2001)

[10] Microsoft Corporation. *Windows 2000 Clustering Technologies: Cluster Service Architecture* (2000). Available online at http://www.microsoft.com/

[11] Mullender, S. J. and Tanenbaum A. S. The design of a capability-based operating system. *Computer Journal*, **29**(4) (Aug 1986), 289–299

[12] Protić, J, Tomašević, M. and Milutinović, V. Distributed shared memory: concepts and systems. *IEEE Parallel and Distributed Technology*, **4**(2) (Summer 1996), 63–79

[13] Radajewski, J. and Eadline, D. *Beowulf HOWTO* (Nov 1988). Available online at http://www.tldp.org/HOWTO/Beowulf-HOWTO.html

[14] Ricart, G. and Agrawala, A. K. An optimal algorithm for mutual exclusion in computer networks. *Communications of the ACM*, **24**(1) (Jan 1981), 9–17

[15] Rozier, M., Abrossimov, V., Armand, F., Boule, I., Gien, M., Guillemont, M., Herrmann, F., Kaiser, C., Langlois, S., Léonard, P. and Neuhauser, W. Overview of the CHORUS distributed operating systems. *Proceedings of USENIX Workshop on Microkernels and Other Kernel Architectures* (Apr 1992), pp. 39 – 69. Available online at http://guir.cs.berkeley.edu/projects/osprelims/papers/chorus.ps.gz

[16] Singhal, M. and Shivaratri, N. G. *Advanced Concepts in Operating Systems*. McGraw-Hill (1994)

[17] Sterling, T., Savarese, D., Becker, D. J., Dorband, J. R., Ranawake, U. A. and Packer, C. V. Beowulf: a parallel workstation for scientific computation. *Proceedings of the 24th International Conference on Parallel Processing*, Vol. I (1995), pp. 11–14

[18] Sterling, T. *Beowulf Cluster Computing with Linux*. MIT Press (2001)

[19] Tanenbaum, A. S. and van Renesse, R. Distributed operating systems. *ACM Computing Surveys*, **17**(4) (Dec 1985), 419–470

[20] Tanenbaum, A. S. and van Renesse, R. Experiences with the Amoeba distributed operating system. *Communications of the ACM*, **33**(12) (Dec 1990), 46–63

[21] Tanenbaum, A. S. and van Steen, M. *Distributed Systems: Principles and Paradigms*. Prentice Hall (2002)

[22] Waldo, J., Wyant, G., Wollrath, A. and Kendall, S. A note on distributed computing. *Sun Microsystems Technical Report TR-94-29* (Nov 1994). Available online at http://research.sun.com/techrep/1994/

SAFETY AND SECURITY

As computer systems become more widely used, the damage that can be caused by failures becomes more and more expensive. We depend on computers to function reliably, but the more complex they are the more potential points of failure there are. Chapter 11 looked at how distributed systems can be designed to guard against failures in individual nodes; this chapter describes techniques for both distributed systems and single computer systems to mitigate the losses that can be caused by failures of this kind.

Thanks to the Internet, one of the greatest problems at present is not the risk of hardware failure but rather attacks by outsiders. These attacks can exploit security loopholes to cause systems to fail or to access confidential information, particularly financial information. If Internet access is not to be avoided altogether, some precautions need to be taken to prevent such attacks. In this chapter we look at the ways in which attacks can be mounted and some approaches to defending systems against them.

12.1 ☐ SECURITY ISSUES

Computers have become an indispensable part of modern life, and we depend upon them to behave reliably. We expect that our bank will keep accurate records of our accounts, our utility companies will calculate our bills accurately, our doctors and dentists will have accurate information about our medical history, and the airliners we use will fly us safely around the world. Computer failures of any sort, whether they occur as the result of accident or malicious intent, are the stuff of which disaster movies are made.

Problems may arise from simple hardware failures; a disk sector might be corrupted, a network packet might not be delivered. They may arise from interference between two processes which update shared data in an unsafe way and thereby corrupt the data. They may arise from a programming error which crashes the system and thus loses data.

However, there is also the risk of attacks on a system by malicious users. Being able to alter one's account details in a bank would be a very effective way to rob a bank, and much less risky than the conventional way. This could also be done by someone on the other side of the world. Industrial espionage would be another possible motive for wanting to breach a system's security. The ability to corrupt data belonging to a business rival (or a foreign government) would be a very effective method of waging a bloodless war. If terrorists could compromise embedded systems such as aircraft autopilots, they could use this ability to kill innocent people by the planeload.

At the most fundamental level, the hardware has to provide the necessary mechanisms which can be used to enforce security. These include a separate user mode and kernel mode, so that programs run by ordinary users have limited powers; a memory protection mechanism such as virtual memory, which can be used to prevent one process from corrupting memory belonging to another (or from snooping in the memory of another process for confidential information). However, it is up to the operating system to use these hardware mechanisms correctly in order to construct effective security measures.

12.2 ☐ PASSWORD PROTECTION

Security depends to a large extent on **user authentication** to prevent unauthorised access to a system. Most systems require users to **log in** before they can do anything else. Users identify themselves using a **username** issued to them by the system administrator, but for the sake of security they must also confirm their identity in order to be able to log in successfully. This is normally done using a **password** which only the user knows, and keeping this password secret is a major part of ensuring security. Not even the system administrator knows a user's password, although if the user forgets the password it is possible for the system administrator to change it. The same technique is used in many other situations where authentication is required; for example, Figure 12.1 shows an example of a login dialog

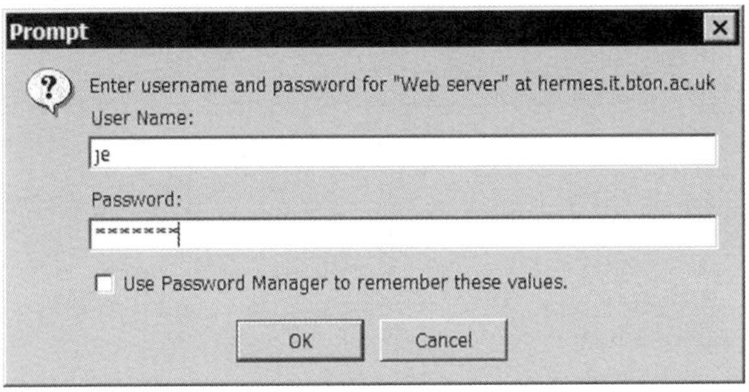

Figure 12.1 A login prompt.

which is presented by a web browser to allow users to gain access to a protected website. The authentication may use the same database as is used for normal system logins, in which case only users who have a login account on the machine that is running the web server will be able to access the website.

Each user is granted specific privileges when they log in (for example, the ability to access a user-specific **home directory**), and anyone who knows the user's password can masquerade as that user, with the power to do anything that the user is allowed to do (for example, deleting all the files in the user's home directory). The most important password of all is the system administrator's password (also know as the **root** or **superuser** password). The system administrator (called 'administrator' on Windows systems and 'root' on Unix systems) necessarily has complete control over the system, including the ability to access any file, change any password, and shut the system down completely. Most attacks on system security involve finding a way to masquerade as the system administrator, so the first level of defence is always to ensure that the administrator password is kept secret. An additional level of security can be provided by requiring the system administrator to log in from a specific terminal device, so that physical access to the system is required in addition to knowledge of the password.

Forgetting or losing the administrator's password is disastrous. To guard against the system administrator being run over by a bus, the administrator password is usually written down and stored in a safe somewhere, or parts of the password are given to trusted senior individuals for safekeeping. For example, a 12-character password could be divided into four groups of three characters each and given to four individuals for safekeeping (again, making sure that there are copies stored in a safe place in case all four people are killed in a plane crash), as shown in Figure 12.2. In this way no single person can masquerade as the system administrator. How far you take such precautions depends on how much you value the data stored on your system.

There are of course several alternatives to the use of passwords as a way of authenticating a user's identity, although they tend to be less common. One possibility is the use of a physical device such as a key or a swipe card, in which case security can be maintained by keeping the device physically secure. Cash dispensers maintain security by requiring the use of a bank card in combination with a four-digit password. As with passwords, security can be improved by requiring physical access to

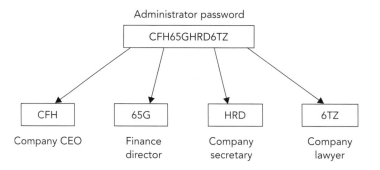

Figure 12.2 Keeping a secure copy of an administrator password.

the machine. Many PCs used to use a key which could be used to lock the system against use by disabling the keyboard, but modern machines rarely have this feature. Physical security like this is only practical if you are never going to want to access the system from a remote site, which may be true in the case of military systems but is rarely true for other systems.

Another possibility is to use biometric data such as a fingerprint, voiceprint or retinal pattern as a unique way of identifying the user. Systems like this are still rare, mainly because with current technology it is hard to recognise features such as fingerprints reliably; you have to ensure that the authorised user will always be recognised but that imposters will not be. The system must be sufficiently discriminating that it will always recognise the authorised user as well as always rejecting imposters, and this is very difficult to do. A hand injury might prevent a fingerprint from being recognised; contact lenses might affect a retinal scan; and a heavy cold might cause voice recognition to fail. If the matching were to be done more loosely, the possibility of successful impersonation would also increase. There are also problems involved in preventing the system from being fooled into accepting a photocopy of the authorised user's fingerprint or retina, or a recording of the user's voice. However, progress is being made in this field all the time.

The other general category of techniques involves recognising actions which are difficult to duplicate, such as the pattern of movements involved in writing a signature. One method which has been suggested is to time the pattern of keystrokes when typing a password. Different users typing the same password have recognisably different patterns of timing between keystrokes, but using this as a means of authentication might be problematic. A hand injury could prevent a user from logging in. Tiredness or intoxication might also vary the timing enough to make the system reject the password, although it could be argued that tired or intoxicated users should probably give up trying to log in and go to bed instead!

12.2.1 KEEPING PASSWORDS SECURE

Password security relies on never letting anyone see a password. On some systems, passwords are not echoed as they are typed in; on others, whatever you type is displayed as a series of asterisks or some other character, as shown in Figure 12.1. This is marginally less secure than not echoing the input at all, as it reveals the number of characters in the password to anyone watching, but it is more user-friendly as users can see that their input is being accepted.

Question 12.1   Why is revealing the length of the password a security risk?

Other precautions involve the use of **encryption**. Encryption involves scrambling a **plaintext** input into an unrecognisable **ciphertext** which can only be turned back (**decrypted**) into the original plaintext if you know the correct **encryption key**. Any confidential information transmitted over a communications link should be encrypted, as otherwise it is fairly easy to listen in on the communications link in a similar way to tapping a phone line.

One useful feature of passwords is that you never need to know anything except whether a submitted password is correct, so it is never necessary to decrypt a password. All you have to have is a copy of the correct password after it has been encrypted, and you can check whether the submitted password encrypts to give the same result. This means that a **one-way encryption algorithm** can be used. Such algorithms are not (easily) reversible. For example, multiplying two large prime numbers together is easy; factoring the product back into its constituent primes is not. Provided that different inputs give different encrypted results (at least most of the time), encrypted passwords which match indicate with (almost) complete certainty that what was entered was the correct password.

One well-known one-way algorithm which is widely used is known as **MD5** (the Message Digest algorithm, version 5). This takes text of any length and pads it to 64 bits less than a multiple of 512 bits. It then appends a 64-bit message length so that the result is a multiple of 512 bits in length, and then transforms it into a single 128-bit (16 byte) value. It begins with a 128-bit constant; each 512-bit block in turn is divided into 16 blocks of 32 bits each. Each of these blocks is permuted in four steps using the previous 128-bit value, as shown in Figure 12.3. This algorithm has the property that any two different messages have a vanishingly small chance of being transformed into the same result, and there is no way to reconstruct the original message from the digest.

Many systems will prevent you from choosing a password that would be easy to guess. For example, passwords which are too short would be possible to try exhaustively until the correct one is found. The usual requirement is a password that is at least six characters in length consisting of a mixture of letters and digits. There are about 436 million different possible six-character passwords containing

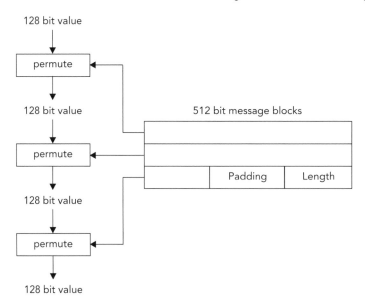

Figure 12.3 The MD5 algorithm.

at least one letter and one digit. The requirement that the password consists of a mixture of letters and digits is to prevent choosing an easily remembered word that might be found in a dictionary; it would be much easier to search a dictionary of about 50,000 words rather than working through 436 million possibilities. However, if you could write a program to make rapid login attempts, you could work through 436 million possibilities quite quickly. If you could make 1000 attempts per second, it would only take about five days to try all the possibilities, and less than a minute to try every word in a 50,000-word dictionary. At a million attempts per second, you could work through 436 million possibilities in less than eight minutes. As computers get faster all the time, this is a distinct possibility, so the login process usually incorporates a delay of a second or so when validating a password. Working through 436 million possibilities at one attempt per second would take nearly 14 years!

Of course, if an attacker has access to your encryption algorithm (which is certainly true of systems like Linux, where the source code is available), the algorithm can be run at full speed on another machine. This relies on having a copy of the encrypted password available, so it is necessary to protect the file containing the encrypted passwords to prevent copies being made for offline cracking purposes. On Linux systems the password file /etc/passwd contains other useful information as well as a list of usernames and passwords, so a **shadow file** is used to protect it. The real password file is the file /etc/shadow, which is only accessible to the system administrator, and /etc/passwd is a copy of the real thing from which all the encrypted passwords have been removed. A set of library functions is provided for the system administrator to use to manipulate the contents of the shadow password file.

For additional security, many systems have mechanisms to force users to change their passwords at regular intervals, and to prevent the same password being reused again later. Another approach is to issue randomly generated passwords, rather than allowing users to choose their own passwords. Both of these approaches have their problems, however. If passwords are changed too often, users will either resort to writing them down or using simple sequences like 'password1', 'password2', 'password3', and so on. Neither of these possibilities enhances system security. Similarly, randomly generated passwords tend to be unmemorable, so users are likely to need to write them down.

Question 12.2   Is it better to allow users to choose their own passwords and to leave them unchanged indefinitely?

12.3 ☐ ENCRYPTION TECHNIQUES

Data encryption is used to prevent sensitive information from unauthorised access. Encryption techniques have been in use for thousands of years; the Greeks and Romans both used simple encryption techniques to send messages in times of war. Encryption is now routinely used as a way of preserving security for private information.

12.3.1 SYMMETRIC CRYPTOSYSTEMS

Historically, most encryption techniques have relied on knowledge of an **encryption key** which was used for both encryption and decryption. The key is used to scramble the plaintext using a reversible algorithm to produce a ciphertext, and the process is reversed using the same key to regenerate the plaintext from the ciphertext. Because the processes of encryption and decryption are symmetric, these are known as **symmetric cryptosystems.** A simple example of a symmetric cryptosystem is a **substitution cipher** which involves replacing each character (or byte of data) with another character which is N positions further on; for example, with $N = 2$, A would be replaced by C, B would be replaced by D, and so on. At the end of the alphabet the values 'wrap around', so Y would be replaced by A and Z by B. Reversing this is easy; you just replace each character with the character which is N positions earlier. The key here is the value of N, which tells you how many positions to move each character.

This is a very simple (and easily broken) cipher, and the modern equivalents naturally use much more sophisticated algorithms than this. It still has a place, though; **ROT-13** is a version of the cipher above where only letters of the alphabet are encrypted, using $N = 13$ as the encryption key. This has the pleasing property that encryption and decryption are identical, since two consecutive rounds of encryption will have shifted each letter 26 places forward in the alphabet, equivalent to no shift at all. This is illustrated in Figure 12.4. ROT-13 is often used on Usenet newsgroups to conceal 'spoilers' such as descriptions of the endings of movies that readers might not have seen. Most newsreader software incorporates a 'ROT-13 transform' command (or messages can be piped through the Unix command 'tr A-Za-z N-ZA-Mn-za-m' to perform the transformation). Anyone who wants to read the message can do so easily, but anyone who doesn't want to know how a movie ends can remain blissfully ignorant.

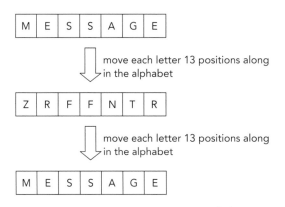

Figure 12.4 ROT-13 encryption and decryption.

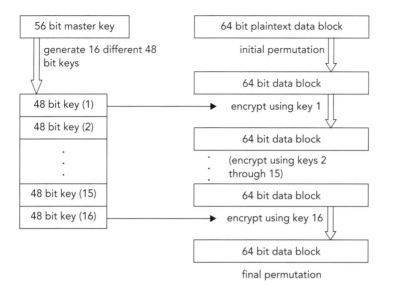

Figure 12.5 DES encryption.

In the early 1970s, the US National Bureau of Standards developed a standard symmetric cryptographic algorithm known as the **Data Encryption Standard (DES)** which used a 56-bit key to encrypt blocks of 64 bits at a time. The 56-bit master key is used to generate a set of 16 keys of 48 bits each, and the data is then encrypted using 16 separate permutations involving each of the 16 keys, as shown in Figure 12.5. The permutations are computationally quite simple, so this is a very easy and efficient algorithm to implement. The number of possible keys is so large that cracking the cipher is very difficult, although it was rumoured that the key length was restricted to 56 bits to allow US government agencies with access to powerful supercomputers to crack DES-encrypted messages. However, as computers have become more powerful, such ciphers have become relatively easy to crack unless much longer keys are used. The algorithm can be modified for use with longer keys; financial institutions normally use at least 128-bit keys to guarantee security against any present-day decryption systems.

Question 12.3   Why are encryption algorithms such as DES made public, rather than trying to increase security by keeping the algorithms themselves a secret?

12.3.2   PUBLIC KEY ENCRYPTION

The big problem with symmetric encryption techniques like the ones described above is that the key must be kept secret. Someone wanting to send an encrypted message must somehow notify the intended recipient of the key to be used, and this must be done securely. Before a private message can be sent, another private message is needed to pass the key to the recipient. This is known as the **key distribution problem**. Typically this chicken-and-egg situation used to be resolved using private couriers to physically carry keys between the parties involved, but with the advent of electronic mail it is unacceptable to wait for a courier to deliver a key before you can read your mail.

Exercise 12.1   One solution to key distribution works like this: Alice sends Bob a key inside a box locked with a padlock that Bob doesn't have to key to. Bob adds his own padlock which Alice doesn't have the key to and sends the box back to Alice. Alice removes her padlock and sends the box back to Bob. Bob can now remove his own padlock and open the box. Explain why this is a safe way to distribute keys. Can you devise an equivalent software technique for key distribution?

Diffie and Hellman developed a solution to this problem known as a **public key cryptosystem**, and this was further developed by Rivest, Shamir and Adleman to produce a practical technique now known as **RSA encryption**, after their initials. The idea of public key cryptosystems is that they use two keys rather than one. The recipient publishes one key (the **public key**) for use by anyone who wants to send a message, and keeps the other key (the **private key**) secret. The public key is a pair of integers (e,n) and the private key is a pair of integers (d,n). The value n is the product of two large prime numbers, and e is calculated from d and n, but even knowing e and n the only way to compute the value of d is to factorise n, which is very difficult to do.

The RSA algorithm can also be used to generate **digital signatures** which guarantee the authenticity of any message. This is because the algorithm has the property that a message encrypted using the private key can be decrypted using the public key; the encryption and decryption process are permutations which are each other's inverse. The idea is that the sender encrypts the message using his or her private key to produce the signature, and then encrypts both the message and the signature using the recipient's public key. The recipient uses his or her private key to decrypt the message and the signature, and then verifies the signature by using the sender's *public* key to decrypt the signature and then comparing the decrypted signature with the message. If the decrypted signature matches the message, then it guarantees that the message is genuine (since it matches the decrypted signature) and that it originated from the sender (since only the sender could have encrypted it with the private key so that it could be decrypted using the sender's public key). Alternatively the sender could encrypt a message digest created using a one-way algorithm like MD5, and the receiver could verify the signature by creating an MD5 digest of the original message and then comparing it with the decrypted signature, as shown in Figure 12.6.

Because the overhead of encrypting messages using the RSA algorithm is much higher than it is for private key cryptosystems such as DES, a combined approach is

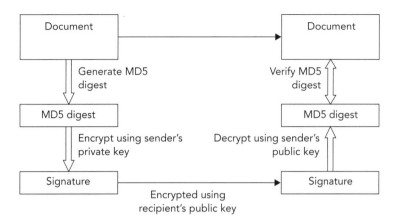

Figure 12.6 Digital signatures.

often used. RSA is used as a secure way to transmit a DES private key, thus solving the key distribution problem. The private key is then used to communicate using DES-encrypted messages.

There is a popular implementation of the RSA algorithm for most platforms, developed by Phil Zimmermann, called PGP ('Pretty Good Privacy'). The US government tried to prosecute Zimmermann for releasing PGP on the Internet, claiming that this constituted 'exporting' encryption software (which was illegal under US law), but later dropped the case. A Norwegian Internet site has continued publishing new versions of PGP together with the source code, using a loophole in the law that enables it to import printed copies of the source code (which is not 'software' in the legal sense of the word) and then scan it in and compile it. This is good news for people who want to be able to communicate securely, but bad news for government and law enforcement agencies who want to be able to eavesdrop.

12.3.3 STEGANOGRAPHY

In Britain, the government is so worried about the potential of secure encryption for use by criminals and terrorist organisations that they have passed laws which enable them to demand encryption keys or plaintext versions of encrypted messages from anyone they suspect of illegality. A similar situation exists in the USA. However, this relies on knowing whether the parties involved are exchanging encrypted messages. Another technique that can be used to communicate surreptitiously is known as **steganography** (from the Greek for 'hidden writing'). This is a technique for concealing data inside other messages such as image files.

An image file is essentially a two-dimensional grid of pixels, each one of which is a multi-bit value (typically 24 bits) which represents the colour to be displayed at a particular point in the grid. By using the least significant bits of each pixel to store a message, the pixel colours will change slightly but in a way that is not apparent to the human eye. Also, only some of the pixels might be used to encode the message.

It is therefore impossible to tell just by looking at an image whether it contains a hidden message; you would have to know that it did, and which bits of which pixels to look at, in order to extract the message. As a result, it would appear that government attempts to control the use of encryption technologies is doomed to failure. However, there are other more legitimate uses for steganography. It can be used to embed invisible 'watermarks' into copyright material such as movies or music. If a watermarked file is copied and distributed illegally, the presence of the watermark can be used to prove an infringement of copyright.

12.3.4 SSL

Since Internet traffic is usually processed by a number of different routers as it makes it way from source to destination, there is nothing to protect Internet traffic against eavesdropping. This is a particular concern when sensitive information is being transferred, such as credit card details and site passwords when shopping on the Internet (Figure 12.7).

The Secure Sockets Layer (SSL) provides a solution to this problem. SSL fits between an application protocol such as HTTP and the underlying transport protocol, typically TCP. HTTP requests and responses are encrypted before being transferred by TCP and decrypted by the receiver. It uses a mixture of the techniques described above: public key cryptosystems, symmetric cryptosystems and digest algorithms. I will assume here that RSA, DES and MD5 are used, although any equivalent algorithms could be used instead. SSL can use a number of different algorithms, and the first thing that is done when setting up a secure link using SSL is to agree on the encryption algorithms to be used.

Suppose I want to establish a secure link to an online store. First, we have to agree on the encryption algorithms we want to use (RSA, DES and MD5 in this case). I also need to generate a brand new, arbitrarily chosen DES key that we can use for

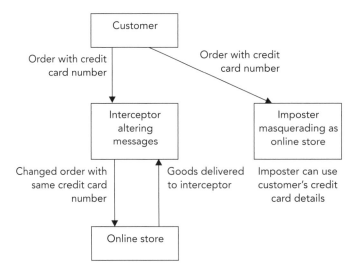

Figure 12.7 Some potential risks of using credit cards online.

the bulk of the session. I can then use the store's public key to encrypt my DES key and send it to the store. The store can use its private key to decrypt this.

There is a risk here that an intruder could garble messages in transit so that I end up ordering a load of stuff I don't really want instead of the stuff I do want. To make sure that messages aren't garbled *en route*, we can each append a digital signature to every message as described earlier and use the other party's public key to verify the signature. It is practically impossible for a message to be garbled in such a way that the signature is still correct.

Now, how do I know that I am really talking to the store and not some imposter who is intercepting my messages? The imposter could have substituted their own public key for the store's when I picked it up from the store, in which case the imposter can decrypt all my messages and use my credit card number to order goods from the store. The answer is to use a third party as a **certification authority**. There are a number of well-known certification authorities in place (e.g. VeriSign, Thawte and RSA Security) whose public keys are well known and easily verified.

What I do is to request a certificate which will verify that I really am talking to the store. The certificate which is sent back in response to my request will have been encrypted by the certification authority and will include the store's name, public key and an expiry date. It will also be digitally signed by the certification authority. I can use the certification authority's well-known public key (which I already know) to decrypt the certificate. By checking the signature (using the certification authority's well-known public key once again) I can verify that the certificate is valid and that the information it contains has not been tampered with.

What happens if the certificate is issued by a certification authority for which I don't already have a public key? I then have to obtain a certificate for the certification authority and validate it. I may have to go through a chain of several certification authorities until I reach a **root authority** whose public key I already have. It is also possible to ask root authorities to certify each other. It should always be possible to trace the chain of certification back to an authority which I already have a certificate for. Web browsers that support SSL will have built-in certificates for a range of well-known root authorities.

In a situation where the server needs to confirm my identity (for example, when dealing with my bank), the server can also ask me to supply it with a certificate. Similarly, online stores need to supply a valid certificate when dealing with a certification authority. When I open an online bank account, the bank itself can act as a certification authority to issue me with a certificate for use in future transactions and will be able to validate my certificate using its own key. In this way we will both be able to confirm that we are dealing with who we think we are dealing with.

The actual sequence of events in establishing an SSL session to a secure server is illustrated in Figure 12.8. In more detail, the sequence is as follows:

- The client contacts the server with a list of possible encryption protocols and the server replies specifying which ones it will use. The client and server also send each other a 224-bit random number.

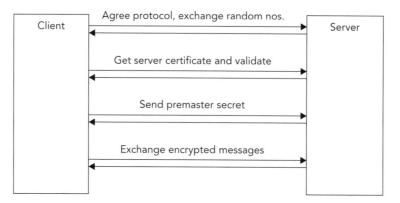

Figure 12.8 Basic structure of an SSL session.

- The server sends a certificate to the client and optionally requests a certificate from the client.

- The client validates the certificate using the certification authority's public key and records the server's public key. Public keys for a number of certification authorities are built in to most web browsers. If necessary the client sends a certificate to the server, which will validate it in the same way.

- The client sends a randomly generated 48-byte value known as the **premaster secret** to the server using the server's public key to encrypt it.

- The client and server use the plaintext value of the premaster secret together with the two random numbers exchanged earlier to generate a 48-byte **master secret**. The master secret is used to generate keys for the various cryptographic algorithms being used.

- The client and server can now exchange messages using the symmetric crypto-system, using an encrypted MD5 digest in each message to guard against messages being corrupted.

The above discussion is somewhat simplified; it ignores many other issues such as message compression and the possibility of switching to a different cryptosystems during a session.

12.4 ❑ SYSTEM ATTACKS

Many of the most serious risks to modern systems involve attacks by outsiders which exploit security loopholes to gain access to the system. Once access has been established, an intruder can steal copies of files, including private encryption keys, or corrupt files in order to damage the system or further compromise its security. These attacks come in several forms, generally classified as Trojans, viruses and worms, although some attacks involve hybrids of these general classifications.

12.4.1 TROJANS

According to legend, the Trojan war was won because the Greeks built a huge wooden horse filled with Greek soldiers, which intrigued the Trojans so much that they brought it into the city to examine it. At night, the hidden soldiers slipped out and opened the city gates, and let the rest of the Greek army in.

The truth is undoubtedly much more complex than this simplistic account, but the concept is a powerful one. A 'Trojan horse program' (or just **Trojan** for short) is one that does something unexpected (and generally hostile) when it is executed in order to breach your security. This could either be planted as the result of an initial security breach, or you might be persuaded to install it under false pretences. An example of this is the increasing amount of 'spyware' which sends information about your machine to a remote system elsewhere on the Internet. Keeping an eye on network traffic makes this fairly easy to spot, but it means that you have to have installed something to monitor network traffic; and of course, this too might be compromised. It might show all the network traffic except what the Trojan generates. You have to have something that you know you can trust before you can decide whether anything else is trustworthy.

Trojans that run in kernel mode are the most dangerous, naturally. In kernel mode, they have complete control over your system. This means that device drivers, screen savers, and anything else that your operating system runs in kernel mode is a potential source of threats. Also, server processes which are started when the system is first booted are often run from the system administrator's account, which again gives them an alarming amount of control over your system. Modern versions of Windows use digital signatures to verify that the drivers have been validated by Microsoft, but many third-party device drivers still don't incorporate a signature. Windows will warn you when you try to install an unsigned driver, but leaves it up to you to decide whether you trust the supplier and want to install the driver anyway.

Many Trojans are concerned with password cracking. A simple Trojan approach to password gathering involves writing a program that mimics the system login dialog, which can be run from any user's account. When an unsuspecting user enters a password, the Trojan records it, displays a copy of the system's 'invalid password' error message, and then logs out so that the real login dialog will be displayed. Windows NT and later versions prevent this by requiring the user to type the 'three-fingered salute' (Ctrl-Alt-Del) to bring up the login dialog. Ordinary programs cannot trap this key combination, and it will bring up the system security manager dialog if someone is already logged in.

Question 12.4 Do other operating systems with which you are familiar have any way of preventing this sort of attack, and if so how do they do it?

A subtler approach is to replace the system login program with a doctored copy, either one which records all the usernames and passwords that are entered, or one which always accepts a hard-coded 'backdoor' password as correct. This requires the attacker to break into the system in order to replace the program, but once this has happened, changing all the passwords won't help keep the attacker out in future. Of course, checking the size of the program file will show that it has been changed, and the original version can be restored from a backup. A clever attacker will of course have changed the system time and date temporarily so that the new file is given the same creation date as the original.

Trojans don't have to concentrate on password cracking. Another possibility is a compromised encryption utility which records any encryption keys that are used. For this reason, the documentation for the PGP encryption utility described earlier encourages users to compile the source code themselves to ensure that they don't end up installing a version which includes a Trojan.

Dennis Thompson, one of the creators of Unix, described an even more subtle approach in his Turing Award lecture [14]. Rather than modifying the login program, he suggests modifying the C compiler so that whenever a particular source code fragment is seen, the compiler generates object code containing the Trojan. The compiler would insert the Trojan code whenever the login program was recompiled, and there would be no need to modify the source code of the login program to do it. To carry it one stage further, modify the compiler so that it also recognises a particular sequence of source code in the compiler itself and generates Trojan code in response. Now recompiling the compiler would generate a binary version of the compiler which would insert Trojan code whenever the compiler or the login program was recompiled, as shown in Figure 12.9. Restore the original source code of the compiler and recompile it, and hey presto, the binary version of the compiler will still contain the Trojan code, even though there is nothing anywhere in any of the source code to reveal its presence!

Question 12.5   How could you defend yourself against an attack like this?

12.4.2   VIRUSES

A **virus** is a program which 'infects' other programs by inserting self-replicating code into them. This code can copy itself when an infected program is executed, and might also act as a Trojan. Executing any infected program can infect other files on the machine it is executed on. One method by which files can be infected is to copy the viral code to the end of the executable file, as shown in Figure 12.10, and modify the program's start address so that the viral code is executed first. Any executable files transferred from the infected machine are a further possible source of infection. However, the only way a virus can spread is by executing some

Modified version of compiler source code

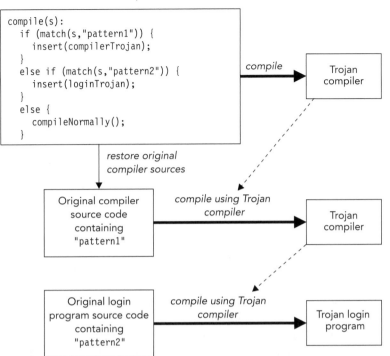

```
compile(s):
   if (match(s,"pattern1")) {
      insert(compilerTrojan);
   }
   else if (match(s,"pattern2")) {
      insert(loginTrojan);
   }
   else {
      compileNormally();
   }
```

compile → Trojan compiler

restore original compiler sources

Original compiler source code containing "pattern1"

compile using Trojan compiler → Trojan compiler

Original login program source code containing "pattern2"

compile using Trojan compiler → Trojan login program

Figure 12.9 A self-perpetuating Trojan.

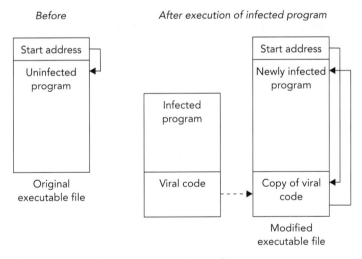

Before

After execution of infected program

Start address
Uninfected program

Original executable file

Infected program

Viral code

Start address
Newly infected program

Copy of viral code

Modified executable file

Figure 12.10 Viral code infecting a file.

infected code, so just looking at a file with a text editor is harmless. The problem is that 'infected code' can hide in all sorts of unexpected places.

Some word processors, notably Microsoft Word, incorporate a 'macro language' which can be used to create new commands. In the case of Microsoft Word, the macro language is a version of Visual Basic which has all sorts of powerful capabilities. It can read and write external files, create network connections to other machines, read and write the system registry, execute other programs, and do just about anything else you can think of. It is certainly a powerful enough language to write viruses in. You can also incorporate an 'autoexec' macro in a document which is automatically executed when the document is opened, so that just opening an infected Word document can transmit the infection to your machine.

One of the most popular email clients for Windows is a program called Outlook, another Microsoft product, which lets you see a preview of incoming mail messages. If a message contains a Word document, Word will be used to open the document and generate a preview of its contents, so just opening your mailbox with Outlook can be enough to infect your system if someone has sent you an infected file. It is possible to disable all these 'features', but in many versions of Windows they are enabled by default (although it appears that Microsoft is starting to learn their lesson in more recent versions of their products). Many users leave these features enabled, either because they don't know how to disable them, or because they don't realise how much danger they're in. Thanks to Microsoft's market dominance, the majority of computer users use Windows, Word and Outlook on their systems, and virus writers tend to target these systems. Any monoculture is susceptible to epidemics, and a software monoculture is no different. One of the simplest ways to defend yourself against many of the viruses in circulation is just to avoid using products which have a dominant market position.

Another source of infection is booting from an infected floppy disk. Many people don't realise that the message that gets displayed when you boot a system from a non-system disk is actually displayed by a program in the boot sector of the floppy disk. If this program is infected, you can infect your machine just by forgetting to remove a floppy disk when you turn the machine on. Modern machines allow you to set up a choice of boot devices using the system BIOS, and it is always advisable to set your system up to boot from hard disk only. If you ever want to boot from a floppy disk, you can just change the setting (but don't forget to change it back again afterwards!).

Some viruses are relatively harmless; others are intended as practical jokes. The effects vary: some appear to do nothing (except infect other machines, given the opportunity); others display messages, perhaps only once a year to commemorate some anniversary or other. More malicious viruses may attempt to delete files or format disks, or they may be more subtle and cause occasional random damage to files over a long period of time. Even non-destructive viruses cause damage by wasting disk space, memory, and processor power, not to mention the time and expense wasted in cleaning up infected systems.

Virus scanners are the first line of defence against viruses. A virus scanner looks for particular characteristic binary patterns within infected files. Since new viruses appear all the time, it is important to keep virus scanners up-to-date by downloading new 'signature files' as they appear. The signature files contain the patterns that the virus scanner will look for. Inevitably, there is an 'arms race' between virus writers and scanner writers. For example, **polymorphic viruses** were developed to be undetectable by early versions of scanning software. When a polymorphic virus copies itself, it makes some changes in the copy which make it harder to detect a characteristic signature. This in turn led to the development of a new generation of scanners which could detect polymorphic viruses despite the constant mutation. And so it goes on.

Once a file has been infected, you need to replace it with a clean copy. This might involve installing a complete new copy of a software package, or even the operating system itself. For this, you need to have prepared an uninfected floppy disk earlier that you can use to restart the system without activating the virus and then delete any infected files before you restore them. Otherwise, the virus might have infected operating system components, and it might for example transfer the infection to another file when you delete any infected file.

12.4.3   WORMS

A **worm** is a program that autonomously copies itself from machine to machine, but doesn't necessarily infect any files (although worms can be used to propagate a virus or to replace existing files with Trojan versions). It usually spreads across network connections, exploiting operating system loopholes to establish itself on new machines. The name was adopted from the 'tapeworms' described in John Brunner's novel *The Shockwave Rider*, which was published in 1975, before worms became feasible. Alas, it didn't take long for fact to catch up with fiction.

The most famous worm was the Internet worm of November 1988, which brought the Internet to a grinding halt for about three days. When you consider that the Internet was designed to able to withstand a nuclear strike, this was no mean feat. It was eventually traced back to Robert Morris Jr, a graduate student at Cornell University. The worm had a few bugs in it that made it detectable; it isn't clear whether it was supposed to be detectable, or whether it was released accidentally while it was still under development.

Exercise 12.2   Find out what happened to Robert Morris Jr as a result.

The worm spread by exploiting security loopholes to transfer a small 'grappling hook' program from one machine to another, as illustrated in Figure 12.11. If this program could be transferred and executed successfully it would then establish a connection back to the original machine and download the 'payload' of the worm. This was a program that tried to crack user passwords and to transmit copies of the worm to neighbouring machines.

If a password were successfully cracked, the worm could try to establish a remote shell connection to another machine via the Unix rsh command. If this failed, two other methods were tried to get a copy of the worm up and running on another machine. The first approach was to exploit a bug present in many of the Unix finger daemons. The finger program allows you to access information about a user

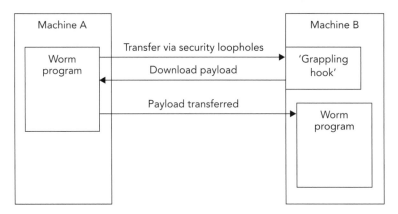

Figure 12.11 The Internet worm.

on a remote machine, such as whether the user is currently logged in, the user's full name, and other contact details. The attack relied on a **buffer overrun** bug in the fingerd daemon that serviced finger requests from other machines. It was expected that the username would never exceed 512 characters, but no check was made that this was actually the case. A username longer than 512 characters would overflow the buffer space that had been set aside to hold the username. The worm sent a 536-character 'username' that overwrote the return address on the stack. When the function that was reading the username terminated, it returned to an address that was actually inside the 512-byte username buffer. This is illustrated in Figure 12.12.

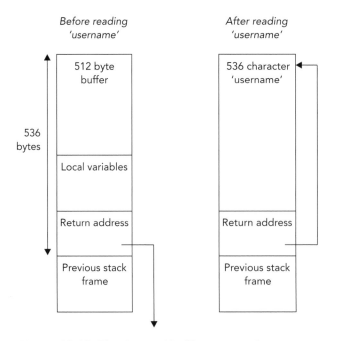

Figure 12.12 The fingerd buffer overrun bug.

The sequence of bytes making up the 'username' was actually a short program which would start a shell running in place of the `fingerd` daemon.

The other approach relied on a 'feature' of the `sendmail` SMTP daemon. For ease of debugging remote mail systems, `sendmail` provided a 'debug' command which allowed a mail message to be piped into a command for processing, rather than being sent to another user in the normal way. Although this could be disabled, it rarely was, and the worm used this as another way to establish a shell running on the remote machine.

If any of these methods of gaining access succeeded, the 'grappling hook' would then transfer a copy of the main body of the worm and start it running. This would then trawl through various system files looking for the names of nearby machines to infect. It would also try cracking user passwords using a variety of simple tricks: no password, the username as the password, two copies of the username, the user's first and last names, and the username reversed. This was successful in an amazingly high number of cases, but if it failed then each word in a dictionary of a few hundred words was tried in turn.

To avoid detection, the worm regularly used the Unix `fork` system call to create a new copy of itself, and then the original copy would terminate. This avoided having a single long-running process which would show up in the system logs. Instead, it appeared as several short-running processes which would attract little notice. It also checked to see whether the machine being attacked was already running a copy of the worm, and would give up if so. There were some bugs in the worm which prevented these measures working correctly, and as a result machines gradually filled up with multiple copies of the worm and ran slower and slower as the load increased. This is what made people notice that something was wrong.

Rebooting infected machines did no good. It would kill any existing copies of the worm, but as soon as the machine's network connections were restored, it would be attacked by all the neighbouring machines and reinfected. It took about three days of continuous hard work at a number of institutions to capture a copy of the worm, understand how it worked, and institute an effective countermeasure.

The buffer overrun attack used to take over the `finger` daemon exploits one of the commonest security weaknesses in most operating systems. For many years, the languages of choice for writing operating systems have been C and its successor, C++. Unfortunately, the standard libraries of these languages include a number of string-handling functions which do not check whether the destination buffer is big enough to hold the result. Since these functions are enshrined in the ANSI standards for C and C++, all implementations must provide them despite their glaring potential for disaster. As long as C and C++ are still used, security hazards like this will remain, and the only protection is to avoid using unsafe functions.

Question 12.6   Why are C and C++ still the most popular languages for writing operating systems and system utilities?

Recently, a number of worms have been detected which attack security loopholes in particular versions of Windows. Since Windows is in such widespread use, this has had devastating consequences for many sites. The worm spreads to any vulnerable machine connected to a network and installs a viral payload. Treating the virus is no cure, as the treated machines will immediately be reinfected by neighbouring machines as soon as they are reconnected to the network. Microsoft produced a set of security fixes for the affected versions of Windows which blocked the worm's access points, so the problem could be solved by downloading and installing the latest security fixes (which are of course digitally signed) and then repairing the changes made by the viral payload. However, doing this only makes your system safe until the bad guys find another security loophole.

12.4.4 DENIAL OF SERVICE ATTACKS

A popular way of attacking another system is to mount a **denial of service** (DoS) attack, which attempts to overload the machine being attacked so that it can't respond to any legitimate requests. For example, **mail bombing** consists of bombarding the machine under attack with a continual stream of email messages which will keep genuine email from getting through and will also put a heavy load on the machine so that overall throughput will drop substantially. **Spam** (junk email) can also be seen as a kind of DoS attack, as users will find that they receive so much mail that finding messages of interest becomes like looking for a needle in a haystack. The mail server can also end up being overloaded by the sheer volume of incoming mail.

Simple DoS attacks from a single source are easy to repulse; simply configuring the relevant servers to ignore any incoming messages from the attacker will take care of the problem. However, a more sophisticated form of attack is a **distributed denial of service** (DDoS) attack, where the attack comes from several (preferably several thousand) different machines at the same time, as illustrated in Figure 12.13. The attack software could be distributed to several thousand machines by a virus, for example. This type of attack is much harder to block, as each new machine that joins the attack will need to be added to the list of systems to be

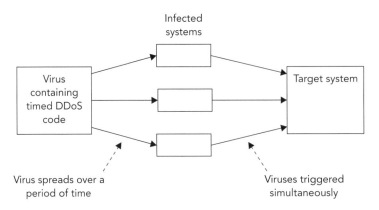

Figure 12.13 A distributed denial of service attack.

ignored, and ultimately the machine under attack will end up ignoring practically everyone, which in itself constitutes a denial of service.

Other ways to mount DoS attacks are to use client-side scripting systems such as JavaScript and Java applets embedded in web pages. Although elaborate precautions have been taken to make Java and JavaScript as safe as possible, it is still possible to use them to mount simple but effective denial-of-service attacks. For example, in Java it is possible to create new windows which, when created, start up as the active window. Creating large numbers of new windows will obscure the screen, making use of the mouse difficult, and also the keyboard focus will be diverted to each new window as it appears, making use of the keyboard difficult as well. If the windows created are a million pixels wide and a million pixels high and are located beyond the top left corner of the screen, each new window will obscure the entire screen. The applet can spawn a new thread to create each new window, and each thread can detect when it is being terminated and can spawn one or more new threads to replace itself before this happens. Modern browsers can usually be configured to prevent such 'pop-up' windows from being displayed to prevent this sort of DoS attack.

12.5 ❑ SANDBOXES

One approach to preventing attacks is to use a **sandbox** to encapsulate any untrusted code. A sandbox provides a controlled execution environment which restricts the action that a program is allowed to perform. The emulators illustrated in Chapter 1 are one example of a sandbox. An emulator provides a complete simulation of a computer system, and as a result any attack by a hostile program will only affect the system being modelled by the emulator rather than the underlying machine. Emulators provide a great way to isolate and study viruses, since only the emulation gets infected and it can be stopped and restarted. Emulators can also provide debugging facilities to allow you to spy on the actions performed by the programs being executed. The effect is the same as running untrusted programs on an entirely separate machine which can be restored to its original state after use.

Linux systems provide a variety of ways to restrict what programs can do. The effective user and group can be changed by calling setuid and setgid, so that programs can be run as if by an unprivileged user. Resource limits for memory, processor time, network access and file output can be set using setrlimit, and the effective root of the filesystem can be changed using chroot so that only a subtree of the filesystem is accessible to the program. Windows has fewer facilities of this sort, although there is a runas command which can be used to run programs as an unprivileged user, and the normal filesystem access restrictions can be used to limit access to files.

12.5.1 JAVA SECURITY MANAGEMENT

Where an interpreter is involved, as in the Java Virtual Machine (JVM), it is possible to enforce much greater security. One of the intended uses of Java is to allow

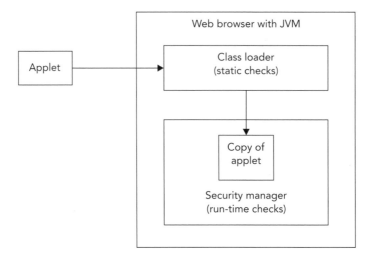

Figure 12.14 Loading an applet.

applets (mobile applications) to be embedded in web pages to allow some processing to take place on a client system. When a web page containing an applet is loaded by a Java-aware web browser, the compiled bytecodes for the applet class are loaded into the browser's JVM. The JVM acts as a sandbox which checks the validity of each operation to prevent unsafe operations. For the sake of efficiency, as many checks as possible are carried out statically when classes are loaded. This process is illustrated in Figure 12.14.

The JVM class loader incorporates a **bytecode verifier** which checks the integrity of each class as it is loaded. This includes checks on the version of each class to ensure that the class is not derived from a base class which has since been modified, as well as checks on the code of each class method. For instance, checks are made to ensure that branch instructions do not lead to addresses outside the method that they belong to, and that any instruction which stores a value in a variable uses a value of the correct type. This means that many potential errors can be detected statically when a class is loaded.

Applets also run under the control of a **security manager** which vets potentially unsafe operations that cannot be checked statically. For example, applets should not be allowed to access files or to run native-code programs on the client system. They may be allowed to create sockets to perform data transfers across the network, but they should only be allowed to connect to the machine from which the applet was loaded. These restrictions are enforced by a security manager object which is loaded into the JVM before an applet is executed. In the case of a web browser, the security manager is normally loaded as soon as the JVM starts up. Once a security manager has been loaded it cannot be disabled short of restarting the virtual machine.

Exercise 12.3   Find out what restrictions applets are subject to, and explain why each restriction is necessary.

Potentially dangerous operations in the standard Java API check for the presence of a security manager by calling System.getSecurityManager(), and if the result is not null (i.e. if there is a security manager installed) they can then use the security manager's operations like checkRead and checkWrite to test whether a particular operation is allowed. If an operation is not allowed by the security manager, a SecurityException will be reported.

Digital signatures can also be used to identify 'trusted' classes, and the security manager can relax selected aspects of its security policy for trusted classes. Java 2 includes a class java.security.Permission which is the base class for objects representing permissions to access resources. Several classes are derived from this in the standard API, such as the class java.io.FilePermission, which controls whether or not access to particular files will be allowed. The checkPermission method of the class AccessController will check whether or not the permission is valid for the current execution context. This involves a mechanism known as **stack inspection**.

Each method call adds a **stack frame** to the stack containing the return address, local variables and so on. The standard stack frame is augmented with additional information identifying the **principal** for each method call, which in the simplest case is either 'system' (trusted) or 'untrusted', and the permissions that have been granted. An untrusted method is unable to obtain any permissions, while a 'system' method can only obtain additional permissions if it has been called (directly or indirectly) from a system method which already has the required permission. System methods can also explicitly ask for a permission to be disabled, to prevent methods that it calls from obtaining that permission.

What stack inspection does is to trace backwards through the current thread's stack looking for a system frame with the required permission (which means that the permission will be granted) or either an untrusted frame or a system frame with the permission explicitly disabled (which means that permission will be denied). If the bottom of the stack is reached, this means that all the frames on the stack were system frames without the required permission. In this case permission is normally granted, although the implementation used by Netscape Navigator will refuse permission in this situation. Once permission has been granted, it is recorded in the current stack frame and will automatically be revoked at the end of the method when the stack frame is removed from the stack.

Figure 12.15 illustrates this mechanism, and shows a sequence of method calls (methodA calls methodB, which calls methodC, which calls methodB). methodD can obtain the privilege it requires because it is a system method and methodC (which is also a system method) already has the required privilege. If methodC did not have the required privilege then the stack inspection would reach the frame for the untrusted method methodB and be rejected. Alternatively, methodC could have explicitly disabled the requested privilege, which would again lead to rejection.

Requested
permission

	Principal	Method called
?	System	methodD
Y	System	methodC
–	Untrusted	methodB
–	System	methodA

(Bottom of stack)

Figure 12.15 Stack inspection.

The security that Java provides is only as good as the implementation of the security management system in a particular JVM, although to be fair it is worth noting that no Java viruses have ever been identified. Implementations are sometimes inconsistent (as noted above for stack inspection with Netscape Navigator) and are sometimes buggy. Each web browser will have its own JVM implementation, and a number of security loopholes have been discovered in all major Java-aware web browsers including Netscape Navigator, Microsoft's Internet Explorer and Sun's own HotJava browser. This means that keeping web browsers up-to-date can be as important as downloading the latest operating system security patches.

Even without security loopholes, some attacks are still possible using Java applets. Java applets can be used to conduct denial-of-service attacks as mentioned earlier; they can also just be used as annoyances, such as an applet that plays a sound repeatedly in a separate thread so that the sound keeps playing even after you've left the web page containing the applet. However, it has been said that the time it takes to perform security checks on complex applets is in itself a form of denial-of-service attack, as the web browser will generally stop responding while the applet is being checked. Java-heavy pages can sometimes take several minutes to load with current web browsers, although this is somewhat extreme.

More seriously, Java applets can be used to send email by connecting to the server's SMTP port. Any mail sent will appear to come from the client system. By using techniques like this, a Java applet can be used to mount a distributed denial-of-service attack from any machine that loads the malicious applet. One obvious solution is not to put an SMTP server on the same machine as a web server; another is to use a firewall as described below to block access to the SMTP port.

Another possibility is the 'business assassin' attack, in which an applet monitors other threads in the JVM. If an applet is loaded from a particular location, the 'business assassin' applet can kill any threads it creates, making it impossible to run any applets loaded from a particular site. Since applets are often used on Internet commerce sites, this can prevent anyone from buying goods from the site being attacked, and this could seriously damage the profits of the company whose site it is. Java and JavaScript security systems are continuing to evolve as possibilities such as this are discovered. Recent versions of security managers prevent applets from accessing resources which were loaded from a different site, for example.

12.6 ☐ FIREWALLS AND PROXIES

A common approach to preventing network attacks is to use a **firewall** to handle all Internet traffic. The general idea of a firewall is to block packets or allow them through according to a set of rules devised by the systems administrator. Packets might be blocked if they use particular protocols or are directed at particular ports on particular machines, for example.

The firewall might run on an individual machine, or it might be on a separate dedicated server. For example, an organisation might use one or more firewall systems which are the only machines with direct connections to the outside world. This establishes a security perimeter for the other machines, as illustrated in Figure 12.16. The machines inside can still communicate freely with each other, but all communication with sites outside the organisation must go through the firewall.

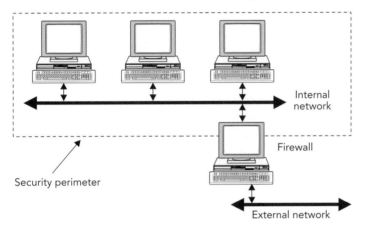

Figure 12.16 A firewall.

When a packet arrives from outside which is directed at a machine inside the firewall, the firewall will either route it to its destination or discard it according to its set of rules. Access could therefore be restricted to port 80 (the normal HTTP port) on machines which are known to be running web servers, and any packets directed to any other port on those machines would be discarded. Other machines not acting as servers could have all their ports blocked.

One problem with setting up a firewall that just blocks access to all but a few well-known ports is that it will be impossible for clients to connect to servers outside the firewall. Remember that when a client establishes a connection with a server, it allocates a port for the purpose which is not one of the well-known ports and which is not otherwise being used. It then uses this port to connect to the well-known port on the server. When the server replies, the reply will be directed at the client's port and will therefore be blocked by the firewall. The firewall therefore has to keep track of outgoing connections so that it can distinguish between incoming replies and other incoming messages. Acknowledgement packets can be allowed through, since these are identified by a specific bit in the TCP packet header, but the firewall also needs to allow delivery of packets originating from the server which are directed to the client's port. Since a TCP connection is defined by its two endpoints (the port number on the server and the port number on the client) the firewall has to keep track of active connections using both endpoints for each connection and to use this information to allow packets to be transferred between the endpoints of any active connection.

A related idea is to use a **proxy server** to control outgoing connections, as shown in Figure 12.17. A proxy server is a secure machine that is configured so that it is allowed to connect directly to machines outside the firewall. For example, a proxy server could be used to handle HTTP traffic. To request a web page from outside the organisation, a request is sent to the proxy server which includes the URL to be accessed. The proxy server then carries out the request on behalf of the originator of the request and sends back the reply it receives. It can also cache frequently accessed web pages to minimise the use of network bandwidth. Another effect is that all HTTP traffic appears to originate from the proxy server, and the names and IP addresses of the machines inside the security perimeter are never revealed to the outside world. The same approach can be applied to other application protocols.

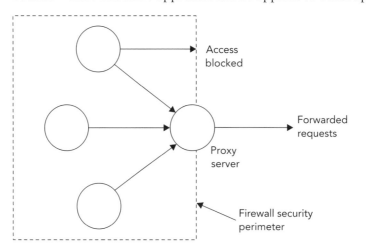

Figure 12.17 A proxy server and firewall.

Firewalls can also be used as **application-level gateways** rather than just as packet filters. Rather than just inspecting packet headers, this kind of firewall inspects packet contents as well. This can be used to provide virus checking and spam filtering on incoming mail, or it can be used to control access to a digital library by limiting access to abstracts only unless a payment has been made.

12.7 ☐ SUMMARY

Ultimately, there is no such thing as perfect security. The best you can manage is to make the cost of breaching the system's security measures higher than the benefit that would be gained from breaching it. High-risk military systems are protected by keeping them isolated from any networks, so that you have to gain physical access to be able to do anything. Banking systems need to be networked, but all network traffic is heavily encrypted to guard against eavesdroppers and fake messages. Yes, you could break the encryption, but it would take so long that the information you gained would be ancient history by the time you succeeded.

At the same time, some elementary precautions are easy to justify:

- Use a reputable virus scanner to scan any new software you download, and make sure you keep the scanner up-to-date.
- Use a firewall to block unwanted Internet access.
- Keep backup copies of important files so that you can recover if anything nasty happens.
- Avoid downloading software from untrusted sources.
- Keep your operating system up to date by applying the latest security fixes from the system vendor.
- Compile critical applications like encryption tools from source if you want to be really safe.

A lot of attacks exploit bugs in operating system code or programs with superuser privileges. One of the commonest bugs is to allow buffer overruns to occur by using unsafe functions provided in languages like C and C++. Using a language that enforces bounds checking (e.g. Ada) can prevent this, but even so it is always possible to write unsafe code in any language which is sufficiently powerful to be used for writing an operating system. Vigilant scrutiny of all programs which have special access privileges is the only true solution.

12.8 ❑ ADDITIONAL RESOURCES

There are several good books on computer security. Cohen [1], who is credited with have coined the term 'computer virus', gives a very readable anecdotal account of the history of viruses and the theory behind them. Denning [2] is a wide-ranging collection of articles on many aspects of computer security, including the ethical and legal dimensions as well as the technical. Thompson's Turing Award lecture [14] describes techniques for concealing Trojans and concludes that ultimately you can really only trust code that you have written yourself.

The encryption standards described in this chapter are mostly available online. DES is defined in [6], MD5 in [9] and SSL in [7]. Diffie and Hellman's original paper on public key encryption [3] was extended to give the RSA algorithm in [10]. Source code and precompiled binaries for PGP are available from PGP International (http://www.pgpi.com/).

The Internet worm must be the most heavily documented network attack ever recorded. RFC 1135 [8] describes how the attack was dealt with, and a special issue of *Communications of the ACM* (June 1989) was devoted to the subject; Spafford [13] gives a blow-by-blow account of the infection, and Rochlis and Eichin [11] describe the inner workings of the worm, while Seeley [12] deals with password security. In a later issue of the same magazine, Joyce and Gupta [4] describe using keystroke timing as a mechanism for authenticating users.

With the spread of mobile code, Java security is a prime concern. McGraw and Felten [5] is a very readable description of potential Java security problems and how they are handled. Stack inspection is one of the more recent security mechanisms used in Java, and its safety is demonstrated by Wallach and Felten in [15].

12.9 ❑ GLOSSARY

applet a Java program which can be loaded and executed as an attachment to a web page.

application-level gateway a firewall that filters packets based on their content

authentication the process of verifying a user's identity

buffer overrun an error where data is accepted which is larger than the buffer provided to hold it, thereby overwriting other values held in memory

bytecode verifier the part of a Java class loader which performs static checks on the code being loaded.

certification authority an entity (usually a trusted company) which issues digital certificates to allow other entities to prove their identity.

ciphertext the encrypted form of a message.

decryption the process of reconstituting the original plaintext of a message from a ciphertext.

denial of service attack an attack on a server which overloads it to prevent it from responding to legitimate processing requests.

DES (Digital Encryption Standard) a standard algorithm for performing secure symmetric encryption.

digital signature an encrypted message which can be decrypted using the sender's public key, proving that it was sent by someone who knows the sender's private key.

distributed denial of service attack a denial of service attack mounted from several sources at the same time.

encryption the conversion of a plaintext message into a ciphertext which cannot be read without a corresponding decryption key

firewall a gateway machine which acts to protect access to a local network from other networks.

key a value required to encrypt or decrypt a message.

key exchange in symmetric cryptosystems, the act of communicating the key used to encrypt and decrypt messages.

log in to connect to an authenticated system as a known user so that subsequent actions can be recorded in a system log.

mail bombing   attempting to overload a mail server by bombarding it with massive amounts of messages.

MD5 (Message Digest 5)   a one-way hashing function used to produce an unforgeable check on the contents of a file.

one-way function   a function which is easy to compute but whose inverse is extremely difficult to compute.

password   a secret value used for authentication purposes.

plaintext   the original form of a message prior to encryption.

polymorphic virus   a virus which, when executed, generates an altered but functionally identical copy of itself to make it harder to detect by looking for a particular 'signature' value.

proxy   a system which acts as an intermediary by performing requests on behalf of other systems.

public key encryption   an asymmetric cryptosystem which uses two different but related keys for encryption and for decryption.

root password   the password for the system administrator, whose username is 'root' on Unix systems.

ROT-13   a simple substitution cipher often used in Usenet newsgroups to conceal information which users might not wish to know, such as endings of books or movies or solutions to puzzles.

RSA (Rivest–Shamir–Adleman)   a public key cryptosystem named after the initials of its three authors.

sandbox   a protected environment within which untrusted programs can be executed without risking damage to the rest of the system.

security manager   in Java, a mechanism used to check that untrusted objects loaded from remote sites can be granted permission to perform potentially unsafe operations.

shadow file   on Unix systems, a copy of the system password file from which copies of encrypted passwords have been removed.

spam   electronic junk mail, named after a song from the television series *Monty Python's Flying Circus*.

SSL (Secure Sockets Layer)   a protocol devised by Netscape Communications Corporation which provides secure encrypted communication facilities.

stack inspection   a technique used in Java virtual machines to verify whether permission to perform potentially insecure operations should be granted.

steganography   a technique for transmitting secret messages by hiding them in images or other digital representations of analogue information.

substitution cipher   an encryption technique which involves replacing characters in a plaintext message by other characters according to some regular scheme.

symmetric cryptosystem   a cryptosystem where the encryption key is the same as the key used for decryption.

Trojan   a malicious program which is used to breach a system's security but which is disguised as something benign and innocuous.

username   an identifier used to identify the user of a system.

virus   a self-replicating program that infects other programs by embedding a copy of itself within them. The infected programs will often act as Trojans to breach system security in some way.

worm   a program which propagates across a network by copying itself from one machine to another. Worms are often used as a mechanism for transmitting viruses or Trojans.

12.10 ❑ REFERENCES

[1]   Cohen, F. B. *A Short Course on Computer Viruses*. John Wiley & Sons (1994)

[2]   Denning, P. J. *Computers Under Attack: Intruders, Worms and Viruses*. Addison-Wesley (1990)

[3]   Diffie, W. and Hellman, M. New directions in cryptography. *IEEE Transactions on Information Theory*, **22**(6) (Nov 1976), 644–654

[4]   Joyce, R. and Gupta, G. User authorization based on keystroke latencies. *Communications of the ACM*, **33**(2) (Feb 1990), 168–176

[5]   McGraw, G. and Felten, E. *Securing Java*. John Wiley & Sons (1999) Available online at http://www.securingjava.com/

[6]   National Institute of Standards and Technology, *Data Encryption Standard (DES)*. Federal Information Processing Standards publication 46-2 (Jan 1988). Available online at http://www.itl.nist.gov/fipspubs/fips46-2.htm

[7]   Netscape Communications Corporation. *SSL 3.0 Specification*. Available online at http://wp.netscape.com/eng/ssl3/

[8]   Reynolds, J. K. *The Helminthiasis of the Internet*. RFC 1135 (Dec 1989). Available online at http://www.rfc-editor.org/

[9]   Rivest, R. L. *The MD5 Message Digest Algorithm*. RFC 1321 (Apr 1992). Available online at http://www.rfc-editor.org/

[10] Rivest, R. L., Shamir, A. and Adleman, L. A method for obtaining digital signatures and public-key cryptosystems. *Communications of the ACM*, **21**(2) (Feb 1978), 120–126

[11] Rochlis, J. A. and Eichin, M. W. With microscope and tweezers: the worm from MIT's perspective. *Communications of the ACM*, **32**(6) (Jun 1989), 689–699

[12] Seeley, D. Password cracking: a game of wits. *Communications of the ACM*, **32**(6) (Jun 1989), 700–705

[13] Spafford, E. H. The Internet worm: crisis and aftermath. *Communications of the ACM*, **32**(6) (Jun 1989), 678–688

[14] Thompson, K. Reflections on trusting trust. *Communications of the ACM*, **27**(8) (Aug 1984), 761–763

[15] Wallach, D. S. and Felten, E. W. 'Understanding Java stack inspection. *Proceedings of the IEEE Symposium on Security and Privacy* (May 1998), pp. 52–63. Available online at http://www.cs.princeton.edu/sip/pub/oakland98.html

GLOSSARY

absolute pathname   a pathname identifying a file which starts from the root directory.

access control list   a list of users or groups of users and the permissions they have each been granted for accessing a file

active window   in a graphical user interface, the window which is currently in active use and which will respond to the mouse and keyboard.

actor   the unit of resource allocation in Chorus.

address bus   a set of electrical connections used to transmit addresses from one hardware device to another.

address space   the range of addresses that can be referenced by a process.

address translation   the translation of the virtual addresses used by a process into the corresponding physical addresses used by the underlying physical memory.

agreement protocol   a protocol used by the nodes of a distributed system to reach an agreement about the overall state of the system.

APC (Asynchronous Procedure Call)   in Windows, a procedure that must be executed in the context of a particular process in order to complete servicing an interrupt.

API (Application Program Interface)   the interface by which an application program accesses services provided by the operating system and others.

applet   a Java program which can be loaded and executed as an attachment to a web page.

application-level gateway   a firewall that filters packets based on their content

application protocol   a protocol used to enable two specific applications to communicate with each other across a network.

ARP (Address Resolution Protocol)   a protocol included in the IP protocol suite which allows one machine to discover the MAC address of another machine on the same network using its IP address.

associative memory   a form of memory whose contents are accessed by matching a value against the contents of each cell, rather than by specifying a positional address.

asynchronous operation an operation which, once started, proceeds independently of its initiator.

at-most-once operation an operation which must be performed once or not at all, which will produce an erroneous situation if executed more than once.

atomic action an action which is performed as a single, noninterruptible operation.

atomic transaction in database systems, a set of updates and other operations which is treated as a single operation which either succeeds or fails completely.

authentication the process of verifying a user's identity

bad block a disk block which is physically faulty and which should not be used by the filesystem.

Banker's Algorithm an algorithm for predicting potential deadlocks.

base and limit registers a simple system of virtual memory where the base register specifies an offset used to calculate a physical address and the limit register defines an upper bound for the address space of the process.

batch file the name used for shell scripts on Windows systems.

big-endian a byte ordering where the most significant byte appears first.

block the smallest unit of storage which can be allocated by the filesystem.

block device an I/O device such as a disk which transfers data a block at a time.

blocking operation an operation which prevents a process from continuing until the operation is complete.

BOOTP a protocol used for booting diskless workstations across a network.

bootstrap the program loaded from a disk which is then responsible for loading the operating system into memory.

bottom half in Linux, a routine which is queued for later execution in order to complete the servicing of an interrupt.

broadcast medium a communications medium like Ethernet where all messages are received by every machine on the network.

buddy blocks a memory allocation system which uses blocks whose sizes are a power of two. Blocks can be split into two halves if a smaller block is needed, and are recombined into larger blocks when they are freed.

buffer a storage area used to marshal blocks of data being read or written to an I/O device.

buffer cache in Linux, a cache of recently accessed disk blocks. Other systems provide an equivalent facility.

buffer overrun an error where data is accepted which is larger than the buffer provided to hold it, thereby overwriting other values held in memory

bus a set of related electrical connections.

bus snooping in a multiprocessor machine, a mechanism for ensuring cache coherence by monitoring activity on the address and data buses generated by other processors.

busy waiting   waiting for a resource by continually checking the state of the resource in a loop, thereby keeping the processor busy while the thread is waiting.

bytecode verifier   the part of a Java class loader which performs static checks on the code being loaded.

Byzantine Generals problem   a problem used to illustrate agreement protocols in the presence of failures.

cache   a fast memory used to keep copies of data which has recently been accessed from a slower memory to avoid the delay in accessing the slower memory if the data is needed again.

cache coherence   in multiprocessor machines, the problem of ensuring that the data held in each processor's cache is consistent with the data held in the caches of the other processors.

call instruction   an instruction used to call subroutines, which stores the return address before jumping to the beginning of the subroutine.

callback function   a function provided by the user which will be called when a specified event occurs, used by the X Window System to notify clients programs when user interface events occur.

capability   an unforgeable token giving a specific type of access to a specific object

causal connection   a cause-and-effect relationship between two events which allows the events to be ordered according to the time of their occurrence.

certification authority   an entity (usually a trusted company) which issues digital certificates to allow other entities to prove their identity.

CGI script (Common Gateway Interface script)   a program executed by a web server to produce dynamic content.

character device   an I/O device such as a modem which transfers data a single character at a time.

checkpoint   a record of the state of a filesystem or database which can be used to restore it if an error occurs.

child process   a process which inherits characteristics of its execution environment (including environment variables and opened files) from the parent process which created it.

CIFS (Common Internet File System)   an Internet-based filesystem derived from Microsoft's earlier SMB protocol.

ciphertext   the encrypted form of a message.

CISC (Complex Instruction Set Computer)   a processor which provides a set of instructions which can combine several low-level operations such as accessing memory and performing arithmetic operations.

client   a program which requests a service to be performed on its behalf by a separate server.

client–server system   a system arranged as one or more client programs which request services provided by one or more server programs.

clipboard a metaphorical storage device used to transfer information between applications in a GUI system.

clock policy a policy used to choose pages to swap out where pages are considered in a cyclical order.

clock tick the interval between updates of a hardware timer.

closest block first a disk scheduling algorithm which services the request closest to the current head position.

cluster a distributed system which behaves like a single fault-tolerant high-performance machine to the outside world.

collision where two machines on a network attempt to transmit at the same time, so that each corrupts the other's message.

COM (Component Object Model) a mechanism developed by Microsoft and DEC which is used extensively on Windows systems to allow communication between objects which may be located in separate processes.

command line argument a string passed to a program as part of the command line used to start the program, often used to supply the names of files to be processed by a program.

commit in database systems, completing a transaction and finalising any database updates.

committed page a page to which some physical memory has been allocated.

communications stub in RPC, the part of a stub which is responsible for communicating a request across the network.

concurrent activities two activities without a causal connection which cannot be ordered according to the time of their occurrence.

connection-oriented protocol a protocol involving a sequence of requests and responses.

connectionless protocol a protocol where each message is treated as a separate transaction from any other requests.

console application the name used on Windows systems for non-graphical (text-based) programs.

context switch a switch from the execution of one thread to another, where the context (state) of the old thread is saved and replaced by the saved context of the new one.

cookie a token identifying a transaction which allows later transactions to be related back to it.

copy-on-write a mechanism for minimising the duplication of pages, where pages are shared and only copied when they are written to.

CORBA (Common Object Request Broker Architecture) a protocol which defines a standard interface mechanism for accessing objects in a distributed system.

critical section a section of code which can only be executed safely by a single thread at a time.

crowd computation a parallel computation where the workload is partitioned between nodes at the start of the computation and each node then processes its own set of data.

CSMA (Carrier Sense Multiple Access) a protocol where each machine checks that the line is idle before starting to transmit.

CSMA/CD (Carrier Sense Multiple Access with Collision Detect) the protocol used by Ethernet where each machine checks that the line is idle before starting to transmit, and stops and retries later if a collision occurs.

current directory the directory currently in use, which relative pathnames are taken to be relative to.

cylinder a set of corresponding tracks on different disk surfaces on a multi-platter hard disk.

daemon a program which is usually started when the system first starts, runs invisibly and lies dormant waiting for some event to happen.

data bus a set of electrical connections used to transmit data from one hardware device to another.

datagram a self-contained message transmitted as a single unit of data.

datalink layer the protocol layer responsible for transmitting frames across an underlying physical network connection.

DCOM (Component Object Model) an extension of COM developed by Microsoft to deal with objects which are potentially distributed across the nodes in a distributed system.

deadlock a situation where two or more threads block each other so that neither can proceed.

decryption the process of reconstituting the original plaintext of a message from a ciphertext.

defragmenting rearranging the layout of files on a disk to increase the efficiency of accessing them.

demand paging a mechanism whereby reserved pages are only committed (loaded into memory) when they are referenced.

denial of service attack an attack on a server which overloads it to prevent it from responding to legitimate processing requests.

dependency a relationship between two threads where one thread is waiting for a resource held by another.

dependency chain a linked series of dependency relationships between threads.

DES (Digital Encryption Standard) a standard algorithm for performing secure symmetric encryption.

desktop the background of a graphical user interface, which models a set of documents arranged on the surface of a desk.

device driver   a program associated with the operating system which manages a particular type of hardware device ; a module (executed in kernel mode on both Linux and Windows) which controls a specific type of hardware device.

device object   in Windows, a data structure representing a particular type of device.

digital signature   an encrypted message which can be decrypted using the sender's public key, proving that it was sent by someone who knows the sender's private key.

Dining Philosophers Problem   a famous problem used to illustrate deadlock and related problems.

direct access device   a storage device which allows any stored item of information to be accessed in essentially the same amount of time as any other.

direct access file   a file where any position within it can be accessed equally easily.

directed broadcast address   an address used to broadcast a message to all machines on a particular network.

directory   a special type of file which holds information identifying a set of files and directories that it contains.

directory-based protocol   in multiprocessor systems, a mechanism for achieving cache coherence by using a directory to keep track of which processors have cached copies of which memory locations.

dirty page   a page which has been written to and for which there is no corresponding copy on disk.

discovery protocol   in Jini, the protocol by which clients discover the range of services available.

dispatch routine   an I/O function such as read or write in the device driver associated with the device being accessed, which is called via a table of pointers held by the driver object associated with the driver.

distributed deadlock   a deadlock situation which exists between threads located on different nodes of a distributed system.

distributed denial of service attack   a denial of service attack mounted from several sources at the same time.

distributed mutual exclusion   mutual exclusion between threads located on different nodes of a distributed system.

distributed shared memory   the simulation of a single memory shared by all the nodes in a distributed system from the separate memory associated with each node.

DLL (Dynamic Link Library)   the name used for a shared library on Windows systems.

DNS (Domain Name System)   a mechanism for translating domain names into the corresponding IP addresses.

domain name   a human-readable hierarchical name for a system on an internet.

double buffering   the use of two buffers to allow one buffer to be filled while the other is being emptied.

DPC (Deferred Procedure Call) in Windows, a routine which is queued for later execution in order to complete the servicing of an interrupt.

driver object in Windows, a data structure describing a device driver which contains pointers to the functions provided by the driver and a list of the individual devices managed by the driver.

dynamic memory a form of memory whose contents need to be refreshed at intervals to prevent the data from being lost.

elevator algorithm a disk scheduling algorithm which services the request closest to the current head position in the current direction of head travel. The direction of head travel is reversed when there are no more requests for blocks in the current direction.

emulator a program which mimics the operation of a hardware system.

encryption the conversion of a plaintext message into a ciphertext which cannot be read without a corresponding decryption key

environment variable a value accessible to a program which provides information about the environment in which it is executing (for example, the name of the user who is executing the program).

event-driven system a program which responds to events (such as mouse clicks and key presses) in whatever order they may occur.

event loop in a graphical program, the main loop within the program which waits for a user interface event to occur and then processes it.

exception handler a part of a program to which control will be transferred when an exception occurs.

exception vector a value specifying the address to which control should be transferred when a particular exception occurs.

exception a condition which unexpectedly changes the flow of control in a program, often as the result of an error.

exception an indication of an error or other exceptional event which changes the normal flow of program execution.

exponential backoff a technique for breaking a livelock by retrying an operation at ever-increasing intervals.

ext2fs the Second Extended File system, a standard filesystem on Linux systems

extension a suffix for a filename generally used to identify the type of the corresponding file.

fat proxy a proxy which performs a substantial amount of local processing before passing a request to the remote object.

FAT (File Allocation Table) a simple but universally understood filesystem introduced by MS-DOS which is still used on some Windows systems. It is also a standard format for floppy disks.

FCFS (first come first served) a disk scheduling algorithm which services requests in order of their arrival.

federation of services in Jini, a set of distributed objects which collaborate to provide a particular set of services.

file handle a value used to identify a file which has been opened.

file object a data structure representing the state (current position etc.) of an open file, referenced via a file handle.

filesystem a system for organising the layout of files and directories on a storage device.

firewall a gateway machine which acts to protect access to a local network from other networks.

folder a near-synonym for 'directory' used on GUI systems (although some folders on Windows systems are not directories).

frame the unit of data transmission used by Ethernet.

garbage collection the reclamation of resources that can no longer be referenced.

graceful degradation a gradual worsening of performance rather than an abrupt failure.

guard condition in Ada, a condition used to block or allow access to an entry in a protected record.

GUI (graphical user interface) a method of communicating with a computer using a pointing device to interact with graphical objects such as windows and icons.

HAL (Hardware Abstraction Layer) in Windows, a layer of software between the kernel and the hardware which encapsulates the machine-dependent portions of the kernel code.

heartbeat message a message sent at regular intervals to confirm that a system is still operational.

heuristic a rule of thumb which will produce a reasonable answer most of the time. Heuristics are generally used in situations where there is no algorithm that will always produce the 'correct' answer.

HFS the Hierarchical File System, a filesystem standard used on Apple Macintosh systems.

hibernation an alternative to shutting down a computer, where the contents of memory and other relevant state information is saved to disk so that the machine can be restarted later in exactly the same state.

hierarchical filesystem a filesystem organised as a hierarchical tree of directories.

hit rate the proportion of accesses to a cache which successfully retrieve the data being sought.

home directory on a multi-user system, the directory allocated as the base directory for the files owned by an individual user.

hot-swappable disk a disk unit which can be removed and replaced while the machine is running.

HTTP (Hyper-Text Transfer Protocol) a standard Internet protocol used to transfer web pages and related items between machines.

IANA (Internet Assigned Numbers Authority) the body responsible for assigning Internet-related numbers such as protocol port numbers and IP addresses.

icon a small picture representing an object such as a file or program in a graphical user interface.

ICPP (Immediate Ceiling Priority Protocol) a deadlock-free technique used to avoid priority inversions.

idempotent operation an operation that can safely be performed several times, which leaves the state of the system unchanged when performed a second time.

IDL (Interface Definition Language) a language used to specify the interface between objects for use in a distributed object system such as CORBA.

idle process a process (or thread) which is executed only when there are no other processes ready to run, which is used to ensure that there is always at least one process (or thread) which is ready to run.

IGMP (Internet Group Management Protocol) a protocol included in the IP protocol suite which is used to report membership of multicast groups to multicast routers.

incremental backup a backup system which only copies files which have been modified since the previous backup.

indexed file a file where items stored in a file are located using a corresponding key rather than an absolute position within the file.

inode a data structure which encapsulates information about a file on Unix systems.

interface a specification of the services provided by an object which does not define how those services are implemented.

interface stub in RPC, the part of a stub which is responsible for parameter marshalling.

internet any set of networks connected by routers, of which the Internet (with a capital 'I') is the largest example.

Internet the globally connected internet.

interprocessor interrupt in a multiprocessor system, an interrupt sent from one processor to another.

interrupt a signal to the processor from an external hardware device indicating that something important has happened; an exception generated by an external hardware device.

interrupt dispatcher a mechanism which calls each interrupt handler associated with a particular interrupt in turn.

interrupt handler the part of a device driver which handles interrupts originated by a particular device.

interrupt service routine the part of a device driver that responds to an interrupt from the hardware device it is responsible for.

invalidation marking a cache entry as being out-of-date (invalid).

inverted page table   a technique used on systems with large address spaces to minimise page table size, mapping page frames to pages rather than pages to frames.

I/O-bound job   a job which spends most of its time waiting for input and output.

I/O manager   in Windows, the part of the kernel that routes I/O requests to the appropriate device driver.

I/O stream   a sequential stream of characters which is consumed by or produced by a program.

IP (Internet Protocol)   the network protocol used on the Internet for packet transmission and routing.

IP address   a unique address used to route IP packets across an internet.

IPv4   the most widespread version of IP which uses 32-bit IP addresses.

IPv6   a more recent but not yet widely used version of IP which uses 128-bit IP addresses.

IRP (I/O request packet)   in Windows, a data structure describing an I/O operation which is passed by the I/O manager to the appropriate device driver.

ISR (interrupt service routine)   a routine which is responsible for dealing with interrupts generated by a particular type of device.

iterative server   a server which services requests sequentially.

Jini   a Java-specific distributed object management system.

job control language   the language interpreted by a shell which is used to control a sequence of execution of programs being executed as a single job.

join protocol   in Jini, the protocol by which a proxy is loaded to access a remote service.

jump instruction   an instruction which transfers control to a different part of the program, breaking the normal flow of control from one instruction to the next.

kernel mode   an execution mode where any instruction, including privileged instructions, can be executed, and which also allows access to protected regions of the address space.

kernel modules   software modules (such as device drivers) which are loaded by the kernel and which execute in kernel mode.

kernel swap daemon   on Linux systems, a daemon process which maintains a minimum number of free memory pages. Other systems have a corresponding process or thread.

kernel   the core of an operating system.

key exchange   in symmetric cryptosystems, the act of communicating the key used to encrypt and decrypt messages.

key   a value required to encrypt or decrypt a message.

latency   the delay due to disk rotation before data can be read from or written to a disk.

lazy writing   performing write operations by writing to a buffer which is only written to the device when it is convenient to do so.

level 1 cache   a small cache built in to the processor chip which caches values from the level 2 cache.

level 2 cache   a larger cache external to the processor which caches values from main memory.

limited broadcast address   an address used to broadcast a message to all machines on the local network.

line   the unit of data transfer to or from a cache.

link   on Unix systems, one of several directory entries which refers to a single file via its inode.

little-endian   a byte ordering where the least significant byte appears first.

livelock   a situation similar to deadlock in that two or more threads prevent each other from performing any useful work, although the individual threads are not blocked and can continue executing.

load balancing   keeping nodes evenly loaded by migrating processes from heavily loaded nodes to lighter-loaded ones.

local dependency   a dependency between threads located on a single node of a multiprocessor system.

locked page   a page which must remain resident in memory and must not be swapped out to disk.

log in   to connect to an authenticated system as a known user so that subsequent actions can be recorded in a system log.

logical clock   a simulated clock used to assign an ordering to events in a distributed system, but with no necessary relationship to the elapsed time between events.

lookup service   a means of discovering available objects which implement a particular interface.

loopback address   an address referring to the local machine which is never sent across a network.

lottery scheduling   a scheduling mechanism involving issuing each process or thread with a set of 'lottery tickets', one of which is chosen at random to select the next process or thread to run.

MAC address (Media Access Control address)   the hardware address of a network device such as an Ethernet controller.

magic cookie   a cookie whose value is encoded in a way that is meaningless to its recipient.

mail bombing   attempting to overload a mail server by bombarding it with massive amounts of messages.

mainframe   a large centralised computer, now rarely seen.

major device number   in Unix, a number identifying a particular type of device (and hence a particular device driver).

marshalling   organising parameters for a remote procedure call into a form that can be transmitted across a network.

MD5 (Message Digest 5)   a one-way hashing function used to produce an unforgeable check on the contents of a file.

memory management unit   the hardware unit responsible for address translation.

memory-mapped I/O   input/output devices whose addresses are located in the same address space as memory.

mickey   the unit in which mouse movement is measured.

mickey-to-pixel ratio   the ration defining the relationship between the distance a mouse moves and the distance the mouse cursor moves on the screen.

microkernel   a kernel which provides a minimal set of facilities, all other aspects of the operating system being provided by server processes with no special privileges.

microkernel system   an operating system with a minimal kernel.

middleware   a layer of software which acts as an intermediary between an application and a network.

minor device number   in Unix, a number identifying a single device out of a group of devices of this type, used by the device driver to identify the particular device being used.

MMU (memory management unit)   a hardware device responsible for performing address translation and checking access permissions.

monitor   a structured mechanism for mutual exclusion.

mounting   on Unix systems, overlaying a directory in one filesystem with a reference to the root directory of a filesystem on a separate volume, so that the two filesystems are united as a single tree.

mount point   on Unix systems, a directory which is overlaid with the root directory of another filesystem which is being mounted.

mount protocol   the protocol used by NFS for mounting remote filesystems.

multi-user system   a system which can be used by several users at the same time.

multicast address   an address which can be used to transmit a message to all members of a multicast group.

multicast group   a logical group of applications to which a message can be broadcast as a single operation.

multithreaded server   a server which can service multiple concurrent requests.

mutex   a simple binary mechanism for ensuring mutual exclusion.

mutual exclusion   where one thread excludes other threads from executing the same critical section.

name resolution   the process of finding the object that a name refers to.

namespace   a set of unique names.

naming service   a service providing a mechanism for name resolution in a distributed system.

NBNS (NetBIOS Naming Service)   a mechanism used in SMB and CIFS for name resolution.

.Net   Microsoft's cross-platform successor to COM and DCOM.

NetBEUI (NetBIOS Extended User Interface)   a transport protocol used to transfer NetBIOS requests and replies across a network.

NetBIOS   an API providing a set of commands for transmitting data between nodes on a network.

network byte ordering   the standard byte ordering used for transmitting multi-byte values across a network.

network device   an I/O device which is accessed via a network connection.

network layer   the protocol layer responsible for routing packets from one machine to another across a network. IP is a network layer protocol.

NFS (Network File System)   a stateless connectionless distributed filesystem developed by Sun Microsystems.

node   an individual machine in a distributed system.

non-maskable interrupt   an interrupt which is always enabled, used to report system-critical events such as power failures that should never be ignored.

NTFS   the NT File System, introduced by Windows NT and now a standard filesystem on later versions of Windows.

null pointer   a memory address which refers to an address which is guaranteed to be invalid (usually zero).

one-way function   a function which is easy to compute but whose inverse is extremely difficult to compute.

operating system   a program which controls the resources of a computer system.

opportunistic lock   in CIFS, a file lock granted to allow increased efficiency when there are no other users of a file.

ORB (Object Request Broker)   in CORBA, the mechanism used to connect applications to the services they require.

packet   the unit of data sent across a network. A single message may be sent as a series of several packets which will be reassembled at the destination.

page fault   an exception generated by the MMU in a virtual memory system when a page is accessed which is not present in memory.

page frame   a physical block of memory allocated to hold a page.

page frame database   in Windows, a mechanism for keeping track of the status of each physical page frame. Other systems have an equivalent facility.

page table   an operating system table which maps page numbers to page frames for each process.

page   a fixed-size block of addresses within the address space of a process.

parent directory   the directory that contains another directory, which can usually be referred to as '..'.

partition a part of a disk which is treated as a separate volume.

password a secret value used for authentication purposes.

pathname a sequence of directory names providing a route through a hierarchical directory tree to a particular file.

path separator the character used to separate the elements of a pathname, typically '/' or '\'.

persistent object an object which can be saved in a file or database and restored later.

physical address an address in physical memory.

physical program counter a cached copy of the physical address corresponding to the virtual address held in the program counter register.

pipe a double-ended I/O stream used to connect an output stream generated by one program to an input stream being consumed by another.

plaintext the original form of a message prior to encryption.

polymorphic virus a virus which, when executed, generates an altered but functionally identical copy of itself to make it harder to detect by looking for a particular 'signature' value.

port the logical endpoint of a TCP or UDP connection.

port mapper in RPC, a service to enable clients to discover the port to use for a particular remote procedure call.

port-based I/O input/output devices whose addresses are in a separate address space from memory, which are accessed using special 'in' and 'out' instructions.

principle of locality the principle that, if an address is referenced, it (or a nearby address) is likely to be referenced again in the near future.

print spooling a technique for allowing several users to share a printer by storing the documents to be printed on a disk.

priority inversion a situation where a low-priority thread blocks the execution of a higher-priority thread.

private network address one of a set of IP addresses reserved for use by networks which are not connected to an internet.

privileged instruction a machine instruction intended for use by the operating system which cannot be executed directly by a normal process.

privileged instruction a machine instruction which cannot be executed directly by a normal process.

privileged instruction an instruction intended for use by the operating system only, which will generate an exception if an unprivileged user program attempts to execute it.

/proc filesystem in Unix systems, a directory of pseudo-files associated with kernel modules which dynamically generate the data being read or consume the data being written. This is used to provide a simple mechanism for user processes to communicate with kernel modules.

process the environment for the execution of a program provided by an operating system, which behaves like a completely independent computer.

process descriptor a data structure describing the state of a process, including the saved context, which can be held in any of several system queues depending on the process status.

processor-bound job a job which uses the processor intensively.

program counter the processor register which is used to hold the address of the next instruction to be fetched from memory.

program status word a processor register containing a variety of status information, usually including condition codes set by the previous instruction, the processor mode and interrupt mask bits.

prompt a message displayed by a text-based shell or other program to indicate that it is ready to accept some input.

protected record a mechanism used in Ada 95 for mutual exclusion.

protocol stack a set of layered protocols, where each protocol uses the facilities provided by the protocol below it in the stack.

protocol a formal set of rules describing the format of data being transferred between software modules; an agreed standard which allows one system to communicate meaningfully with another.

proxy a system which acts as an intermediary by performing requests on behalf of other systems.

public key encryption an asymmetric cryptosystem which uses two different but related keys for encryption and for decryption.

PVM (Parallel Virtual Machine) a software system which allows a network of machines to be used as a single distributed parallel processor.

quantum the period of time that a thread will be allowed to run before a context switch will be forced.

race condition an anomalous situation whose outcome depends crucially on the timing of events, and which can have different results at different times.

RAID (Redundant Array of Inexpensive/Independent Disks) a set of disks used as a single volume arranged to provide data redundancy in case of the failure of any single disk.

RARP (Reverse Address Resolution Protocol) a protocol which maps MAC addresses to IP addresses, used by diskless workstations to discover their own IP addresses.

recursive resolution a method for resolving domain names by recursively searching a tree of domain name servers.

redirection changing the source of an input stream or the destination of an output stream.

reentrant code   code which can be safely executed by more than one thread at a time without the actions performed by any thread having any effect on the behaviour of any of the other threads.

register   one of a small number of high-speed storage locations within a processor which are used to hold status information and temporary values.

registry   in Windows, a central repository holding system configuration information.

registry server   in RMI, a name resolution service which allows objects to be located on a network.

relative pathname   a pathname which is relative to the current directory (that is, a path from the current directory to a particular file).

request queue   a queue of data structures describing pending disk transfers.

reserved page   a page which has been allocated within the address space of a process but which has not yet been allocated a corresponding page frame in physical memory.

return address   the address to which control should return at the end of a subroutine.

return instruction   an instruction used at the end of a subroutine to transfer control to the return address.

RFC (Request For Comments)   one of a series of numbered Internet informational documents, some of which have been adopted as standards.

RISC (Reduced Instruction Set Computer)   a processor which provides a set of simple instructions which, because of their simplicity, can be executed extremely quickly.

RMI (Remote Method Invocation)   the Java-specific equivalent of RPC, allowing methods of remote objects to be called.

rollback   in database systems, restoring a database to an earlier checkpointed state after a failure.

root directory   the primary directory of a filesystem, which is not contained within any other directory.

root password   the password for the system administrator, whose username is 'root' on Unix systems.

ROT-13   a simple substitution cipher often used in Usenet news groups to conceal information which users might not wish to know, such as endings of books or movies or solutions to puzzles.

round-robin scheduling   a scheduling policy where each process in turn is allowed to run.

router   a machine with connections to two or more networks, used to route messages between networks.

routing table   a table used to decide the next machine to which an IP packet should be sent to route it to its ultimate destination.

RPC (Remote Procedure Call)   a mechanism for invoking a computation on a remote node of a distributed system.

RSA (Rivest-Shamir-Adleman)   a public key cryptosystem named after the initials of its three authors.

sandbox   a protected environment within which untrusted programs can be executed without risking damage to the rest of the system.

scheduler   the part of the kernel which manages the switching of control betweenn different threads and processes.

scheduler queue   in Linux, a queue of calls to bottom-half routines which should be executed before a new process is resumed.

scheduling policy   the policy by which the operating system chooses which process it should allocate processor time to.

sector   the smallest accessible unit of physical storage on a disk.

security manager   in Java, a mechanism used to check that untrusted objects loaded from remote sites can be granted permission to perform potentially unsafe operations.

seek time   the time taken to move the heads to the correct track or cylinder on a disk.

segmentation   a rarely used memory management technique which involves providing a process with multiple logically separate address spaces, each of which can be a different size.

semaphore   a mechanism for mutual exclusion and synchronization based on a non-negative counter.

sequential device   a storage device which only allows information to be accessed sequentially.

sequential file   a file whose contents can only be read or written sequentially.

server farm   a cluster of servers which acts as a single server, allowing high levels of demand to be catered for.

server   a program which provides a service in response to a request from a separate client program.

service protocol   in Jini, a set of RMI interfaces defining a service.

service   the name used on Windows systems for a daemon process.

set associative cache   a cache consisting of a number of sets of lines, where a particular line in each set can be matched associatively in a single operation against the address being sought.

shadow file   on Unix systems, a copy of the system password file from which copies of encrypted passwords have been removed.

shareable device   a device which can be shared by several users rather than having to be dedicated to use by a single user.

shared library a module containing library functions which is loaded into memory once by the first process which requests its use, and is shared by any other processes that request it subsequently.

shell a program which is executed when a user first logs in, used to allow the user to run other programs; the program which allows a user to interact with a computer system.

shell script a sequence of commands stored in a file which can be executed by a shell as if it were a single command.

shortcut on Windows, a file similar to a Unix soft link which refers to another file elsewhere.

sliding window a method for improving the efficiency of TCP, where a set number of additional packets can be sent before an acknowledgement is received for the first packet that was sent.

SMB (Server Message Block) a protocol to enable file and printer sharing on a network, or a command defined by this protocol.

SMP (Symmetric Multi-Processor) a multiprocessor system where there is no special processor acting as a 'master' processor which is responsible for executing operating system code, where all processors are equally able to execute operating system code.

socket the endpoint for a virtual connection between two processes on a network.

soft link on Unix systems, a file which contains a reference to another file (which may or may not exist). Accesses to a soft link are automatically redirected to the corresponding file.

spam electronic junk mail, named after a song from Monty Python's Flying Circus.

spin lock in multiprocessor systems, a mechanism for ensuring mutual exclusion between different processors.

SSL (Secure Sockets Layer) a protocol devised by Netscape Communications Corporation which provides secure encrypted communication facilities.

stack a region of memory used for temporary storage, including local variables and return addresses within subroutines.

stack inspection a technique used in Java virtual machines to verify whether permission to perform potentially insecure operations should be granted.

stack pointer the processor register which identifies the top (most recently used location) on the stack.

standard error stream an output stream provided for writing error messages to, normally connected to the display screen.

standard input stream the primary input stream for a program, normally connected to the keyboard.

standard library a set of functions provided as a standard part of the implementation of a high-level language.

standard output stream the primary output stream for a program, normally connected to the display screen.

standby a processor mode which reduces power consumption by switching off all the hardware except that needed to keep dynamic memory refreshed.

starvation a situation where a thread is prevented from proceeding by the combined actions of two or more threads.

stateless protocol a protocol which treats each request as an independent transaction unrelated to any previous transactions.

static memory a form of memory which does not need to be refreshed regularly, unlike dynamic memory.

steganography a technique for transmitting secret messages by hiding them in images or other digital representations of analogue information.

stripe a segment of a block of data, so that each segment of the block can be written to a separate disk in a RAID system.

stub a proxy used in RPC and RMI to invoke a remote procedure or method.

subnet mask a bit mask used to identify which bits of an IP address represent the network address and which bits represent the machine address on that network.

subroutine an independent section of a program which can be called from many different places within the same program, usually referred to as a 'procedure' or a 'function' in most high-level languages.

substitution cipher an encryption technique which involves replacing characters in a plaintext message by other characters according to some regular scheme.

superblock on Unix systems, the block at the start of a volume which defines the layout of the rest of the volume.

swapping copying pages between memory and disk.

symmetric cryptosystem a cryptosystem where the encryption key is the same as the key used for decryption.

synchronized method a mechanism used in Java for mutual exclusion.

synchronous operation an operation which must complete before the caller can continue executing.

system call the mechanism by which a process requests the operating system to perform a service on its behalf.

tag the part of the address used to verify that a cache line contains the data being sought.

task queue in Linux, a queue of calls to bottom-half routines.

TCP (Transmission Control Protocol) the standard stream-oriented transport protocol used on the Internet. It is usually layered on top of IP, hence it is often referred to as TCP/IP.

TCP/IP TCP over IP, the stream-oriented reliable protocol suite used on the Internet comprising TCP as the transport protocol supported by IP as the network protocol.

Telnet   the standard application protocol used for remote logins and terminal emulation on the Internet..

test-and-set instruction   a machine instruction which tests the value of a variable and sets it to a specific value as a single atomic action.

thin proxy   a proxy which performs little or no local processing before passing the request to the remote object.

thrashing   a condition arising from excessive swapping, where page faults are happening faster than the system can load the corresponding pages.

thread   a component of a process which executes independently of other threads, analogous to an emulation of a processor within a computer system.

thread context   the information needed to resume execution of a suspended thread, notably the contents of the processor registers.

thread descriptor   a data structure describing the state of a thread, including the saved context, which can be held in any of several system queues depending on the thread status.

thread pool   a set of threads on a multithreaded server which can be allocated to deal with new requests as they arrive.

timer queue   a queue of processes or threads which have asked to be suspended until a specified time, or (in Linux), a queue of bottom-half routines to be executed after the next timer interrupt (and also, confusingly, the name of a queue of processes which have suspended themselves until a particular time).

timeslice   the amount of processor time allocated to an individual process before the use of the processor will be transferred to another process.

timestamp   a value used to indicate the time at which a message was sent.

TLB (Translation Lookaside Buffer)   a cache within the MMU which is used to hold recently accessed page table entries.

token ring   a point-to-point datalink-layer communications protocol

top half   in Linux, the part of an interrupt service routine which is executed immediately to service the interrupt.

track   one of a set of concentric circular sets of sectors on a disk.

transport layer   the protocol layer which provides virtual point-to-point connections between two ports across an internet. TCP and UDP are transport layer protocols.

tree computation   a parallel computation where the workload fans out across a number of nodes as the computation proceeds.

Trojan   a malicious program which is used to breach a system's security but which is disguised as something benign and innocuous.

TTL (Time To Live)   a field which specifies how many routers an IP packet can pass through, used to prevent circular routing of IP packets or the dissemination of multicast packets beyond a certain point.

UDP (User Datagram Protocol) a transport layer protocol used for the transmission of datagrams between endpoints, used instead of TCP where reliability and stream-oriented connections are an unnecessary overhead.

UNC (Uniform Naming Convention) a Windows naming convention that can be used to identify a file on a remote file server.

uniprocessor a computer system with a single processor.

UPS (Uninterruptible Power Supply) a power supply which can maintain the power to a system for a certain amount of time in the event of a failure in the mains supply,

user mode an execution mode which restricts the actions that can be performed. Attempting to execute privileged instructions or access restricted regions of the address space result in an exception.

username an identifier used to identify the user of a system.

vector timestamp a list of timestamps from different nodes in a distributed system which can be used to determine whether events are causally connected.

VFS (Virtual File System) on Linux systems, a filesystem which provides unified access to files which may be stored on different devices or different machines.

virtual address descriptor a data structure describing a block of virtual memory allocated to a process.

virtual address an address within the address space of a process, which can correspond to different physical addresses at different times as pages are swapped in and out of memory.

virtual machine an abstraction of a computer system implemented in software.

virtual memory a technique for managing memory using fixed-size pages which are independently mapped to page frames in physical memory.

virus a self-replicating program that infects other programs by embedding a copy of itself within them. The infected programs will often act as Trojans to breach system security in some way.

vnode on Linux systems, the VFS equivalent of an inode specifying a server identifier and an inode number on that server.

volatile memory memory whose contents are lost in the absence of a power supply.

volume a logical unit which behaves as a single storage device, but which can span several physical disks or can be just part of a physical disk.

WDM (Windows Driver Model) in Windows, a standard for the way that device drivers are organised..

wildcard character a special character which is interpreted by the shell as standing for any character or sequence of characters in a filename.

window an area of the display screen used to display the output of an individual program.

window manager in the X Window System, the program which defines the 'look and feel' of the graphical user interface presented to the user.

WINS (Windows Naming Service) Microsoft's implementation of NBNS, a name which is now used commonly as a synonym for NBNS.

Winsock an implementation of the standard sockets library for Windows..

working set the set of pages that a process needs to be resident in memory in order to avoid excessive numbers of page faults.

worm a program which propagates across a network by copying itself from one machine to another. Worms are often used as a mechanism for transmitting viruses or Trojans.

write-back cache a cache where information is written back to memory lazily, when it is necessary to do so.

write-though cache a cache where updates are written to memory immediately.

X Window System the standard graphical user interface used on Unix systems.

XDR (External Data Representation) in RPC, a data representation which is portable between different machine architectures.

BIBLIOGRAPHY

Accetta, M., Baron, B., Golub, D., Rashid, R., Tevanian, A. and Young, M. Mach: a new kernel foundation for UNIX development. *Proc. Summer '86 USENIX Conference* (1986), pp. 93–112

Aivazian, T. *Linux Kernel 2.4 Internals.* The Linux Documentation Project (Mar 1996). Available online at `http://www.tldp.org/LDP/lki/`

Apple Corporation, *Inside Macintosh: Files.* Addison-Wesley (1992) Available online at `http://developer.apple.com/documentation/mac/Files/Files-2.html`

Arnold, K., Gosling, J. and Holmes, D. *The Java Programming Language.* Addison-Wesley (2000)

Arnold, K., O'Sullivan, B., Scheifler, R. W., Waldo, J. and Wollrath, A. *The Jini Specification.* Addison-Wesley (1999)

Asche, R. R. *The Little Device Driver Writer* (1994). Available online at `http://msdn.microsoft.com/developer/`

Baker, A. and Lozano, J. *The Windows 2000 Device Driver Book: A Guide for Programmers.* Prentice Hall (2000)

Barnes, J. G. P. *Programming in Ada 95.* Addison Wesley (1998)

Berners-Lee, T., Masinter, L. and McCahill, M. *Uniform Resource Locators.* RFC 1738 (Dec 1994). Available online at `http://www.rfc-editor.org/`

Bovet, D. P. and Cesati, M. *Understanding the Linux Kernel.* O'Reilly & Associates (2002)

Brinch Hansen, P. The programming language Concurrent Pascal. *IEEE Transactions on Software Engineering,* **SE-1** (Jun 1975), 199–207

Burkett, B. S., Goldt, S., Harper, J. D., van der Meer, S. and Welsh, M. *The Linux Programmer's Guide.* The Linux Documentation Project (Mar 1996). Available online at `http://www.tldp.org/LDP/lpg/`

Burns, A. and Wellings, A. *Concurrency in Ada.* Cambridge University Press (1998)

Burns, A. and Wellings, A. *Real Time Systems and Programming Languages.* Addison-Wesley (2001)

Card, R., Ts'o, T. and Tweedie, S. Design and implementation of the Second Extended File system. *Proceedings of the First Dutch International Symposium on Linux* (1995). Available online at `http://www.mit.edu/~tytso/linux./ext2intro.html`

Carvalho, O. S. F. and Roucairol, G. On mutual exclusion in computer networks. *Communications of the ACM,* **26**(2) (Feb 1983), 146–148

Chandry, K. M., Misra, J. and Haas, L. M. Distributed deadlock detection. *ACM Transactions on Computer Systems,* **1**(2) (May 1983), 144–156

Chen, P. M., Lee, E. K., Gibson, G. A., Katz, R. H. and Patterson, D. A. RAID: high-performance, reliable secondary storage. *ACM Computing Surveys,* **26**(2) (Jun 1994), 145–185

Clements, A. *Microprocessor Systems Design: 68000 Hardware, Software and Interfacing.* Wadworth Publishing (1987)

Coffman, E. G., Elphick, M. J. and Shoshani, A. System deadlocks. *ACM Computing Surveys*, **3**(2) (Jun 1971), 67–78

Cohen, F. B. *A Short Course on Computer Viruses*. John Wiley & Sons (1994)

Comer, D. E. *Computer Networks and Internets*. Prentice Hall (1997)

Comer, D. E. *Internetworking with TCP/IP Vol I: Principles, Protocols and Architecture*. Prentice Hall (1995)

Comer, D. E. *Internetworking with TCP/IP Vol III: Client–Server Programming and Applications*. Prentice Hall (1996)

Conti, C. J., Gibson, D. H. and Pitkowsky, S. H. Structural aspects of the System/360 Model 85, Part 1: General Organization. *IBM System Journal*, **7**(1) (1968), 2–14

Cooper, M. *Advanced Bash-Scripting Guide*. The Linux Documentation Project (Dec 1996). Available online at http://www.tldp.org/LDP/abs/

Cornes, P. *The Linux A–Z*. Prentice Hall (1997)

Cragon, H. G. *Memory Systems and Pipelined Processors*. Jones and Bartlett (1996)

Creasy, R. J. The origin of the VM/370 time-sharing system. *IBM Journal of Research and Development*, **25**(5) (Sep 1981), 483–490

Denning, P. J. The working set model for program behaviour. *Communications of the ACM*, **11**(5) (May 1968), 323–333

Denning, P. J. Virtual memory. *ACM Computing Surveys*, **2**(3) (Sep 1970), 153–189

Denning, P. J. *Computers Under Attack: Intruders, Worms and Viruses*. Addison-Wesley (1990)

Diffie, W. and Hellman, M. New directions in cryptography. *IEEE Transactions on Information Theory*, **22**(6) (Nov 1976), 644–654

Dijkstra, E. W. Cooperating sequential processes, In Genuys, F. (ed.) *Programming Languages*. Academic Press (1965). Available online at http://www.cs.utexas.edu/users/EWD/ewd01xx/EWD123.PDF

Dijkstra, E. W. Hierarchical ordering of sequential processes. *Acta Informatica*, **1**(2) (1971), 115–138. Available online at http://www.cs.utexas.edu/users/EWD/ewd01xx/EWD310.PDF

Dubois, M. and Thakkar, S. Cache architectures in tightly coupled multiprocessors. *IEEE Computer*, **23**(6) (Jun 1990), 9–11

Edwards, W. K. *Core Jini*. Prentice Hall (2000)

Engler, D. R., Kasshoek, M. F. and O'Toole J. Exokernel: an operating system architecture for application-level resource management. *Proceedings of the 15th ACM Symposium on Operating Systems Principles* (Dec 95), pp. 251–266. Available online at http://www.pdos.lcs.mit.edu/papers/exokernel-sosp95.ps

Feng, T. A survey of interconnection networks. *IEEE Computer*, **14**(12) (Dec 1981), 12–27

Fidge, J. Partial orders for parallel debugging. *Proceedings of the ACM SIGPLAN/SIGOPS Workshop on Parallel and Distributed Debugging* (1989), pp. 183–194

Fielding, R., Gettys, J., Mogul, J., Frystyk, H. and Berners-Lee, T. *Hypertext Transfer Protocol: HTTP/1.1*. RFC 2068 (Jan 1997) Available online at http://www.rfc-editor.org/

Fleisch, B. D. and Popek, G. J. Mirage: a coherent distributed shared memory design. *Proceedings of the 12th ACM Symposium on Operating System Principles* (Dec 1989), 211–233

Fotheringham, J. Dynamic storage allocation in the Atlas computer, including an automatic use of a backing store. *Communications of the ACM*, **4**(10) (Oct 1963), 435–436

Frampton, S. *Linux System Administration Made Easy*. The Linux Documentation Project (Nov 1999). Available online at http://www.tldp.org/LDP/lame/LAME/linux-admin-made-easy/

Goldstein, A. C. *VMS file system (ODS2) Files-11 On-Disk Structure Specification* (Jan 1985) Available online at http://vms.tuwien.ac.at/freeware/ODS2/

Greenfield, L. *The Linux User's Guide*. The Linux Documentation Project (Dec 1996). Available online at http://www.ibiblio.org/pub/Linux/docs/linux-doc-project/users-guide/

Hall, M., Towfiq, M., Arnold, G., Treadwell, D. and Sanders, H. *Windows Sockets version 1.1* (Jan 1993). Available online at ftp://ftp.qdeck.com/pub/general/winsock.doc

Hertel, C. *Implementing CIFS, the Common Internet File System*. Prentice Hall (2003)

Hill, T. *Windows NT Shell Scripting*. Que (1998)

Ho, G. S. and Ramamoorthy, C. V. Protocols for deadlock detection in distributed database systems. *IEEE Transactions on Software Engineering*, **SE-8**(6) (Nov 1982), 554–557

Hoare, C. A. R. Monitors: an operating system structuring concept. *Communications of the ACM*. **17**(10) (Oct 1974), 549–547

Hyde, R. *The Art of Assembly Language*. No Starch Press (2003). Available online at http://webster.cs.ucr.edu/

IEEE. *Standard 1003.1-2001: POSIX* (2001). Available online at http://www.opengroup.org/onlinepubs/007904975/toc.htm

Intel Corporation. *82093A I/O Advanced Programmable Interrupt Controller*. Document no. 290566-001 (May 1996). Available online at http://www.intel.com/

Intel Corporation. *IA-32 Intel Architecture Software Development Manual vol. 1: Basic Architecture*. Order no. 245470-012 (2003). Available online at ftp://download.intel.com/design/Pentium4/manuals/24547012.pdf

Intel Corporation. *IA-32 Intel Architecture Software Development Manual vol. 2: Instruction Set Reference*. Order no. 245471-012 (2003). Available online at ftp://download.intel.com/design/Pentium4/manuals/24547012.pdf

Intel Corporation. *IA-32 Intel Architecture Software Development Manual vol. 3: System Programming Guide*. Order no. 245472-012 (2003). Available online at ftp://download.intel.com/design/Pentium4/manuals/24547012.pdf

Intel Corporation. *Multiprocessor Specification*. Document no. 242016-006 (May 1997). Available online at http://www.intel.com/

International Organization for Standardization. *Reference Manual for the Ada Programming Language*. ISO/8652-1995 (1995)

Jacob, B. and Mudge, T. Virtual memory in contemporary microprocessors. *IEEE Micro*, **18**(5) (Jul/Aug 1998), 61–75

Jacob, B. and Mudge, T. Virtual memory: issues of implementation. *IEEE Computer*, **31**(6) (Jun 1998), 33–43

Joy, B., Steele, G., Gosling, J. and Bracha, G. *The Java Language Specification*. Addison-Wesley (2000)

Joyce, R. and Gupta, G. User authorization based on keystroke latencies. *Communications of the ACM*, **33**(2) (Feb 1990), 168–176

Kernighan, B. W. and Pike, R. *The UNIX Programming Environment*. Prentice Hall (1984)

Kilburn, T., Edwards, D. B. G., Lanigan, M. J. and Sumner, F. H. One-level storage system. *IRE Transactions*, **EC-11**(2) (Apr 1962), 223–235

Knuth, D. E. *The Art of Computer Programming vol. 1: Fundamental Algorithms*. Addison-Wesley (1997)

Kochan, S. and Wood, P. *Unix Shell Programming*. Sams Publishing (2003)

Kronenberg, N., Levy, H. and Strecker, W. D. VAX clusters: a closely-coupled distributed system. *ACM Transactions on Computer Systems*, **4**(2) (May 1986), 130–146

Lamport, L. Time, clocks, and the ordering of events in a distributed system. *Communications of the ACM*, **21**(7) (Jul 1978), 558–565

Lamport, L., Shostak R. and Pease, M. The Byzantine Generals problem. *ACM Transactions on Programming Languages and Systems*, **4**(3) (Jul 1982), 382–401

Lee, R. R. *Windows NT: Microsoft Cluster Server*. McGraw-Hill (2001)

Love, R. *Linux Kernel Development*. Sams (2003)

McGraw, G. and Felten, E. *Securing Java*. John Wiley & Sons (1999) Available online at http://www.securingjava.com/

McKusick, M. K., Joy, W. N., Leffler, S. J. and Fabry, R. S. A fast file system for Unix. *ACM Transactions on Computer Systems*, **2**(3) (Aug 1984), 181–197

Metcalf, R. M. and Boggs, D. R. Ethernet: distributed packet switching for local computer networks. *Communications of the ACM*, **19**(7) (Jul 1976), 395–403

Microsoft Corporation. *FAT32 File System Specification* (Dec 2000). Available online at
    http://www.microsoft.com/whdc/hwdev/hardware/fatgen.mspx

Microsoft Corporation. *Open Source Software: A (New?) Development Methodology.* (Nov 98).
    Available online at http://www.opensource.org/halloween/

Microsoft Corporation. *Windows 2000 Clustering Technologies: Cluster Service Architecture*
    (2000). Available online at http://www.microsoft.com/

Motorola Corporation. *68000 Family Programmer's Reference Manual.* Document M68000PM/
    AD (1992) Available online at
    http://e-www.motorola.com/files/archives/doc/ref_manual/M68000PRM.pdf

Mudge, T. N., Hayes, J. P. and Winsor, D. C. Multiple bus architectures. *IEEE Computer*, **20**(6)
    (Jun 1987), 42–48

Mullender, S. J. and Tanenbaum A. S. The design of a capability-based operating system.
    Computer Journal, **29**(4) (Aug 1986), 289–299

National Institute of Standards and Technology, *Data Encryption Standard (DES).* Federal Infor-
    mation Processing Standards publication 46-2 (Jan 1988). Available online at
    http://www.itl.nist.gov/fipspubs/fips46-2.htm

Nebbett, G. *Windows NT/2000 Native API Reference.* Que (2000)

NetBIOS Working Group. *Protocol Standard for a NetBIOS Service on a TCP/UDP Transport:
    Concepts and Methods.* RFC 1001 (Mar 1987). Available online at
    http://www.rfc-editor.org/

NetBIOS Working Group. *Protocol Standard for a NetBIOS Service on a TCP/UDP Transport:
    Detailed Specifications.* RFC 1002 (Mar 1987). Available online at
    http://www.rfc-editor.org/

Netscape Communications Corporation. *SSL 3.0 Specification.* Available online at
    http://wp.netscape.com/eng/ssl3/

Nye, A. *Xlib Programming Manual.* O'Reilly & Associates (1992)

Object Management Group. *The Common Object Request Broker Architecture: Core Specifica-
    tion.* OMG document formal/02-12-02 (2002). Available online at
    http://www.omg.org/docs/formal/02-12-02.pdf

Oney, W. *Programming the Microsoft Windows Driver Model.* Microsoft Press (2002)

Parmake, R. P., Peterson, T. I., Tillman, C. C. and Hatfield, D. J. Virtual storage and virtual
    machine concepts. *IBM Systems Journal*, **11** (1972), 99–130

Patterson, D. A. and Séquin, C. H. RISC 1: a reduced instruction set VLSI computer. *Proceed-
    ings of the 8th International Symposium on Computer Architecture*, ACM Press (May
    1981), pp. 443–457

Patterson, D. A., Gibson, G. A. and Katz, R. H. A case for redundant arrays of inexpensive disks
    (RAID). *Proceedings of the ACM International Conference on Management of Data*, ACM
    Press (1988), pp. 109–116

Petzold, C. *Programming Windows.* Microsoft Press (1998)

Postel, J. *Internet Protocol.* RFC 791 (Sep 1981). Available online at
    http://www.rfc-editor.org/

Postel, J. *Internet Control Message Protocol.* RFC 792 (Sep 1981). Available online at
    http://www.rfc-editor.org/

Postel, J. *Transmission Control Protocol.* RFC 793 (Sep 1981). Available online at
    http://www.rfc-editor.org/

Postel, J. and Reynolds, J. K. *Telnet Protocol Specification.* RFC 854 (May 1983). Available
    online at http://www.rfc-editor.org/

Prosise, J. *Programming Microsoft .NET.* Microsoft Press (2002)

Protić, J, Tomašević, M. and Milutinović, V. Distributed shared memory: concepts and systems.
    IEEE Parallel and Distributed Technology, **4**(2) (Summer 1996), 63–79

Radajewski, J. and Eadline, D. *Beowulf HOWTO* (Nov 1988). Available online at
    http://www.tldp.org/HOWTO/Beowulf-HOWTO.html

Raymond, E. S. *The Cathedral and the Bazaar* (1998). Available online at
    `http://www.openresources.com/documents/cathedral-bazaar/`

Raymond, E. S. *The Cathedral and the Bazaar*. O'Reilly & Associates (2001)

Reynolds, J. K. *The Helminthiasis of the Internet*. RFC 1135 (Dec 1989). Available online at
    `http://www.rfc-editor.org/`

Ricart, G. and Agrawala, A. K. An optimal algorithm for mutual exclusion in computer networks.
    Communications of the ACM, **24**(1) (Jan 1981), 9–17

Richter, J. *Applied Microsoft .NET Framework Programming*. Microsoft Press (2002)

Ritchie, D. M. and Thompson, K. The Unix timesharing system. *Communications of the ACM*,
    17(7) (Jul 1974), 365–375

Rivest, R. L. *The MD5 Message Digest Algorithm*. RFC 1321 (Apr 1992). Available online at
    `http://www.rfc-editor.org/`

Rivest, R. L., Shamir, A. and Adleman, L. A method for obtaining digital signatures and public-
    key cryptosystems. *Communications of the ACM*, **21**(2) (Feb 1978), 120–126

Rochlis, J. A. and Eichin, M. W. With microscope and tweezers: the worm from MIT's perspec-
    tive. *Communications of the ACM*, **32**(6) (Jun 1989), 689–699

Rogerson, D. *Inside COM*. Microsoft Press (1997)

Rozier, M., Abrossimov, V., Armand, F., Boule, I., Gien, M., Guillemont, M., Herrmann, F.,
    Kaiser, C., Langlois, S., Léonard, P. and Neuhauser, W. Overview of the CHORUS distrib-
    uted operating systems. *Proceedings of USENIX Workshop on Microkernels and Other
    Kernel Architectures* (Apr 1992), pp. 39 – 69. Available online at
    `http://guir.cs.berkeley.edu/projects/osprelims/papers/chorus.ps.gz`

Rubini, A. and Corbet, J. *Linux Device Drivers*. O'Reilly & Associates (2001)

Rusling, D. A. *The Linux Kernel*. The Linux Documentation Project (Jan 1998). Available online
    at `http://www.tldp.org/LDP/tlk/`

Salzman, P. J. and Pomerantz, O. *The Linux Kernel Module Programming Guide*. Linux Docu-
    mentation Project (Apr 2003). Available online at `http://www.tldp.org/LDP/lkmpg/`

Sawchuk, A. A., Jenkins, B. K. and Raghavendra, C. S. Optical crossbar networks. *IEEE
    Computer*, **20**(6) (Jun 1987), 50–60

Schreiber, S. B. *Undocumented Windows 2000 Secrets: A Programmer's Cookbook*. Addison-
    Wesley (2001)

Seeley, D. Password cracking: a game of wits. *Communications of the ACM*, **32**(6) (Jun 1989),
    700–705

Siegel, J. CORBA and the OMA in enterprise computing. *Communications of the ACM*, **41**(10)
    (Oct 1998), 37–43

Siegel, J. (ed.) *CORBA 3 Fundamentals and Programming*. John Wiley & Sons (2000)

Singhal, M. and Shivaratri, N. G. *Advanced Concepts in Operating Systems*. McGraw-Hill (1994)

Solomon, D. A. and Russinovich M. E. *Inside Microsoft Windows 2000*. Microsoft Press (2000)

Spafford, E. H. The Internet worm: crisis and aftermath. *Communications of the ACM*, **32**(6)
    (Jun 1989), 678–688

Sterling, T. *Beowulf Cluster Computing with Linux*. MIT Press (2001)

Sterling, T., Savarese, D., Becker, D. J., Dorband, J. R., Ranawake, U. A. and Packer, C. V.
    Beowulf: a parallel workstation for scientific computation. *Proceedings of the 24th Interna-
    tional Conference on Parallel Processing*, Vol. I (1995), pp. 11–14

Sun Microsystems. *NFS: Network File System Protocol Specification*. RFC 1094 (Mar 1989).
    Available online at `http://www.rfc-editor.org/`

Sun Microsystems. *RPC: Remote Procedure Call Protocol Specification: Version 2*. RFC 1057
    (Jun 1988). Available online at `http://www.rfc-editor.org/`

Sun Microsystems. *XDR: External Data Representation Standard*. RFC 1014 (Jun 1987). Avail-
    able online at `http://www.rfc-editor.org/`

Tanenbaum, A. S. *Structured Computer Organization*. Prentice Hall (1999)

Tanenbaum, A. S. and van Renesse, R. Distributed operating systems. *ACM Computing Surveys*, **17**(4) (Dec 1985), 419–470

Tanenbaum, A. S. and van Renesse, R. Experiences with the Amoeba distributed operating system. *Communications of the ACM*, **33**(12) (Dec 1990), 46–63

Tanenbaum, A. S. and van Steen, M. *Distributed Systems: Principles and Paradigms*. Prentice Hall (2002)

Thai, L. T. and Oram, A. *Learning DCOM*. O'Reilly & Associates (1999)

Thompson, K. Reflections on trusting trust. *Communications of the ACM*, **27**(8) (Aug 1984), 761–763

Uhlig, R., Nagle, D., Stanley, T., Mudge, T., Secrest, T. and Brown, R. Design Tradeoffs for Software-Managed TLBs. *ACM Transactions on Computer Systems*, **12**(2) (Aug 1994), 175–205

Waldo, J. The Jini architecture for network-centric computing. *Communications of the ACM*, **42**(7) (Jul 1999), 76–82

Waldo, J., Wyant, G., Wollrath, A. and Kendall, S. A note on distributed computing. *Sun Microsystems Technical Report TR-94-29* (Nov 1994). Available online at http://research.sun.com/techrep/1994/

Wallach, D. S. and Felten, E. W. 'Understanding Java stack inspection. *Proceedings of the IEEE Symposium on Security and Privacy* (May 1998), pp. 52–63. Available online at http://www.cs.princeton.edu/sip/pub/oakland98.html

Watkins, D., Hammond, M. and Abrams, B. *Programming in the .NET Environment*. Addison-Wesley (2002)

Welsh, M., Hughes, P., Bandel, D., Beletsky, B., Dreilinger, S., Kiesling, R., Liebovitch, E. and Pierce, H. *Linux Installation and Getting Started Guide*. The Linux Documentation Project (Mar 1998). Available online at http://www.tldp.org/LDP/gs/

Wollrath, A. and Waldo, J. RMI. In Campione, M. (ed.), *The Java Tutorial Continued: The Rest of the JDK*. Addison-Wesley (1999). Available online at http://java.sun.com/docs/books/tutorial/rmi/

INDEX